NEGIMA!

34

Ken Akamatsu

TRANSLATED AND ADAPTED BY
Alethea Nibley and Athena Nibley

LETTERING AND RETOUCH BY
Scott O. Brown

KC
KODANSHA
COMICS

A word from the author

I JUST LOVE THIS KIND OF THING. EVEN WITH MY MANGA MANUSCRIPTS, THE CLOSER I GET TO A DEADLINE, THE MORE PUMPED I GET. (NOT REALLY.)

THE WORSE THE SITUATION, THE MORE VALUE THERE IS IN FINDING A STRATEGY. THIS VOLUME PUTS THE CLASSMATES IN THE WORST PINCH THEY'VE SEEN YET, AND THEY HAVE TO FIND THE BEST WAY OUT OF IT WITH THEIR LIMITED RESOURCES.

Presenting a personal favorite of mine, **volume 34!**

...And I have a big announcement! The *Negima!* movie has become a collaborative project with *Hayate the Combat Butler!* (published by Viz). And it will be the final installment of the *Negima!* anime...most likely!

What will really happen!? Keep your eyes peeled!

Ken Akamatsu's home page address*
http://www.ailove.net/

*Please note the webpage is in Japanese.

NEGIMA!

MAGISTER NEGI MAGI

34

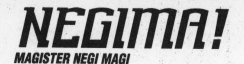

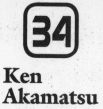

Ken Akamatsu

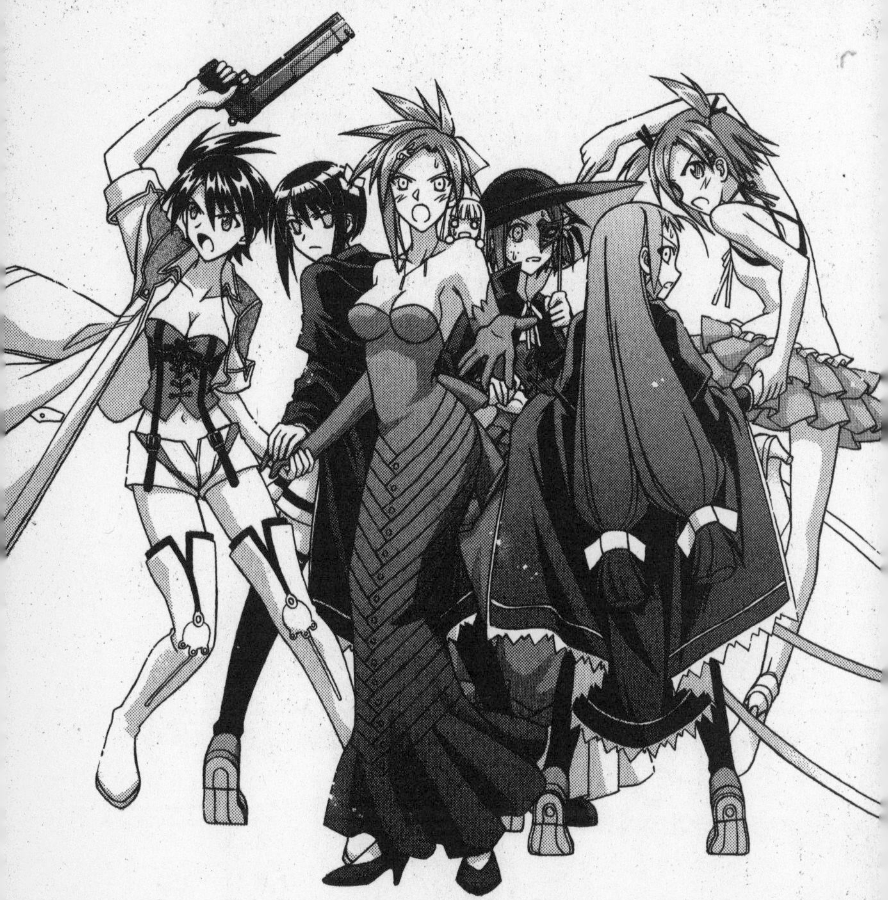

CONTENTS

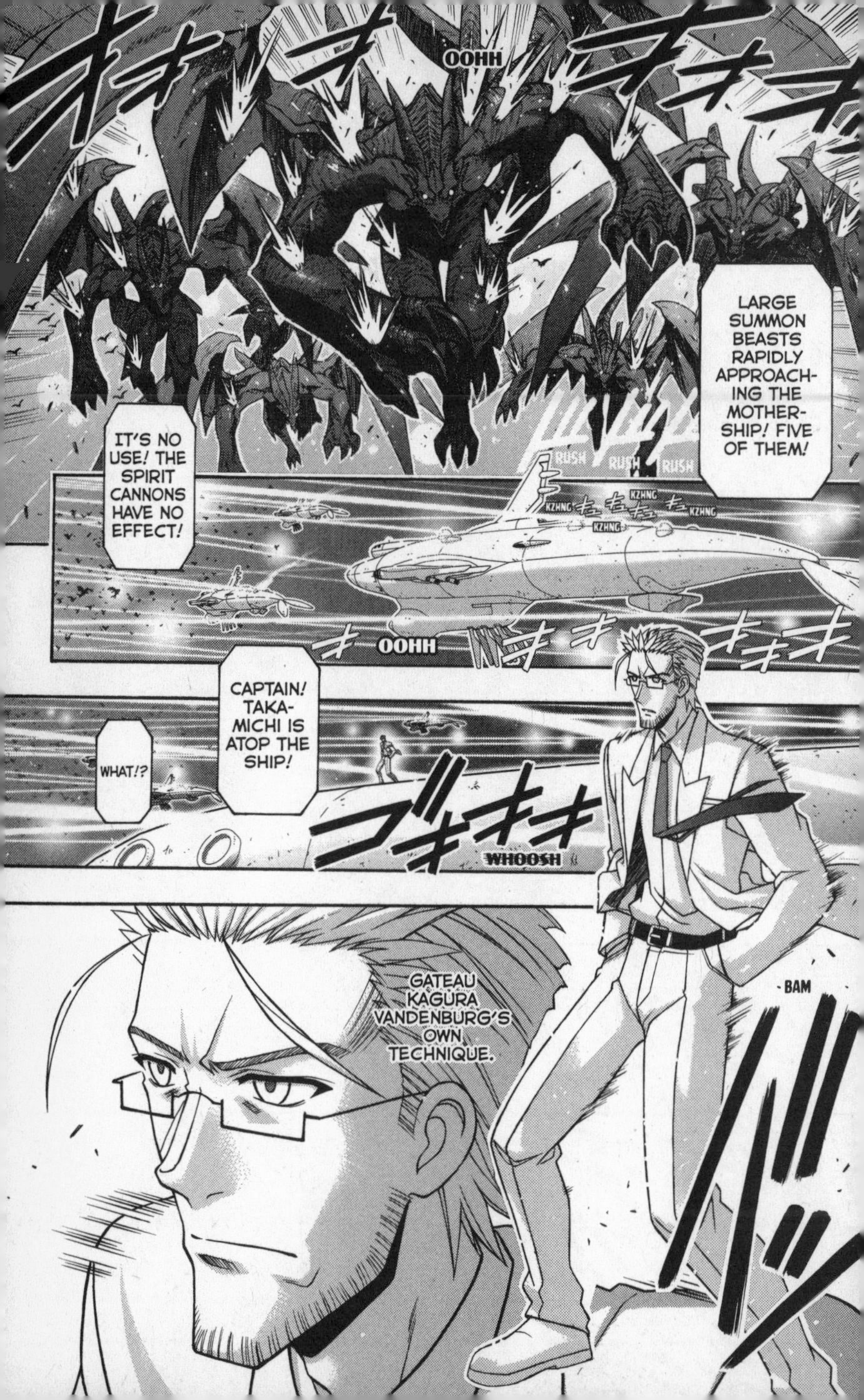
OOHH
LARGE SUMMON BEASTS RAPIDLY APPROACHING THE MOTHERSHIP! FIVE OF THEM!
RUSH RUSH RUSH
IT'S NO USE! THE SPIRIT CANNONS HAVE NO EFFECT!
KZHNG KZHNG KZHNG KZHNG
OOHH
CAPTAIN! TAKAMICHI IS ATOP THE SHIP!
WHAT!?
WHOOSH
GATEAU KAGURA VANDENBURG'S OWN TECHNIQUE.
BAM

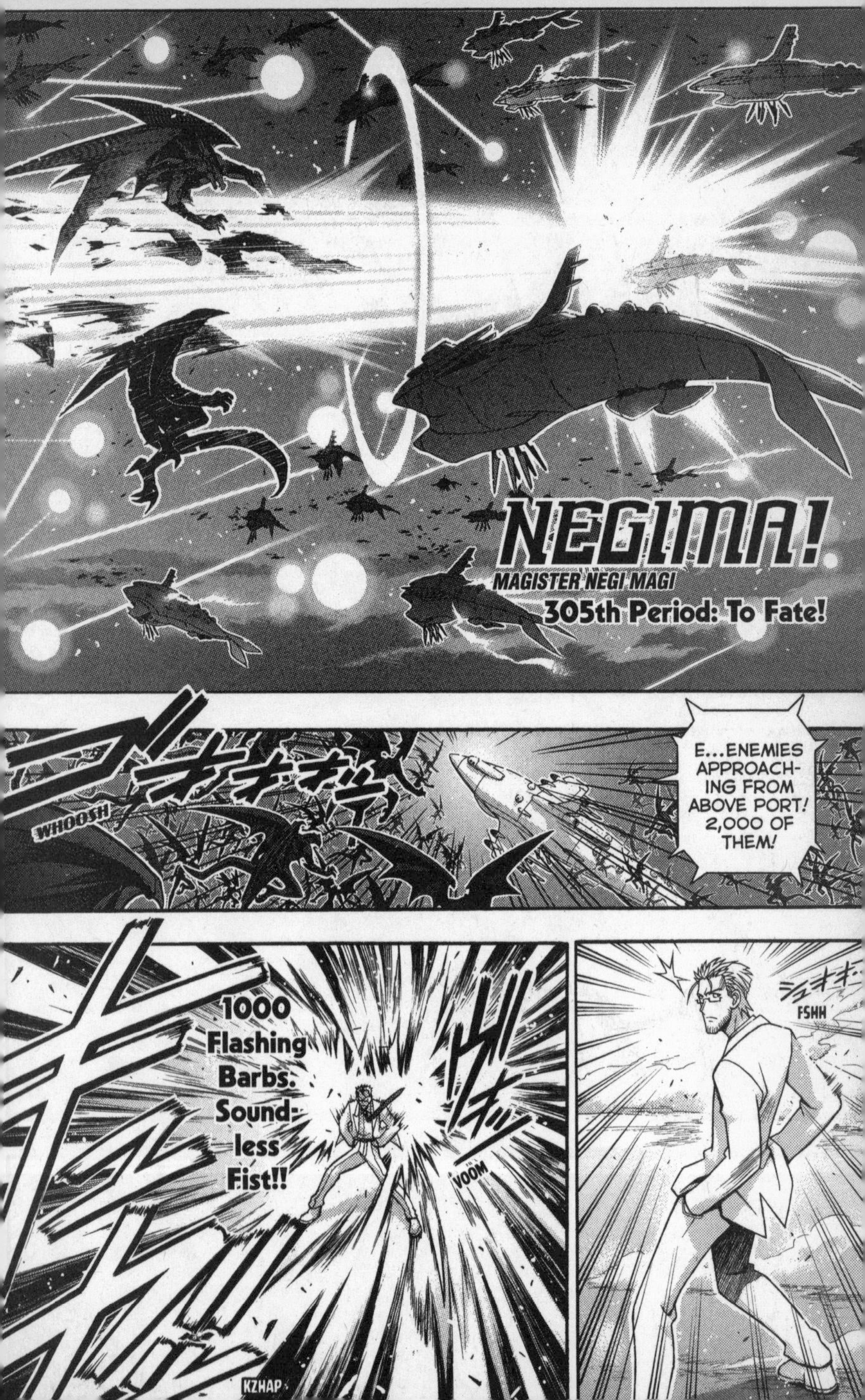
NEGIMA!
MAGISTER NEGI MAGI
305th Period: To Fate!
E...ENEMIES APPROACHING FROM ABOVE PORT! 2,000 OF THEM!
WHOOSH
FSHH
1000 Flashing Barbs. Soundless Fist!!
VOOM
KZHAP

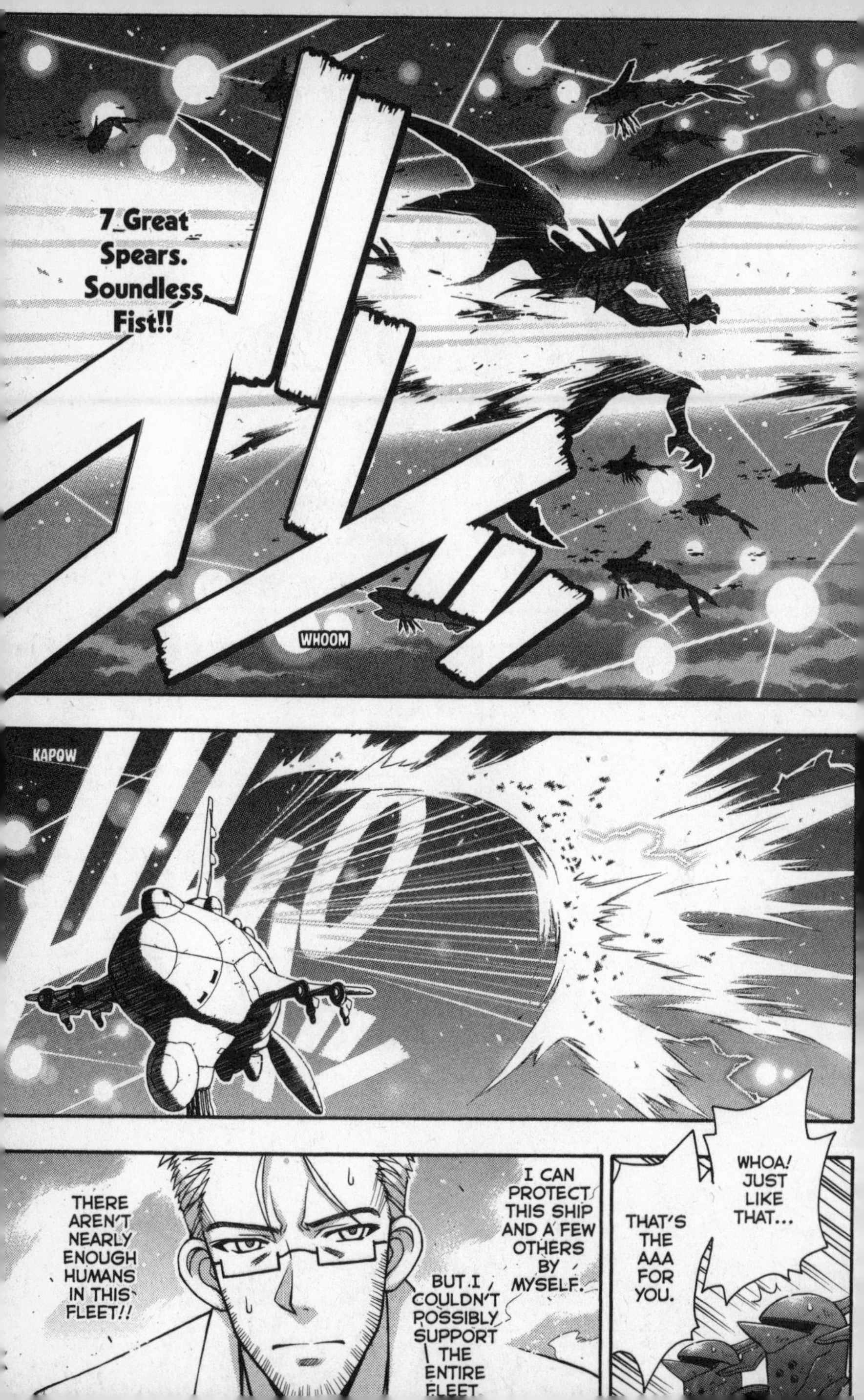
7_Great Spears. Soundless Fist!!
WHOOM
KAPOW
WHOA! JUST LIKE THAT...
THAT'S THE AAA FOR YOU.
I CAN PROTECT THIS SHIP AND A FEW OTHERS BY MYSELF.
BUT I COULDN'T POSSIBLY SUPPORT THE ENTIRE FLEET.
THERE AREN'T NEARLY ENOUGH HUMANS IN THIS FLEET!!

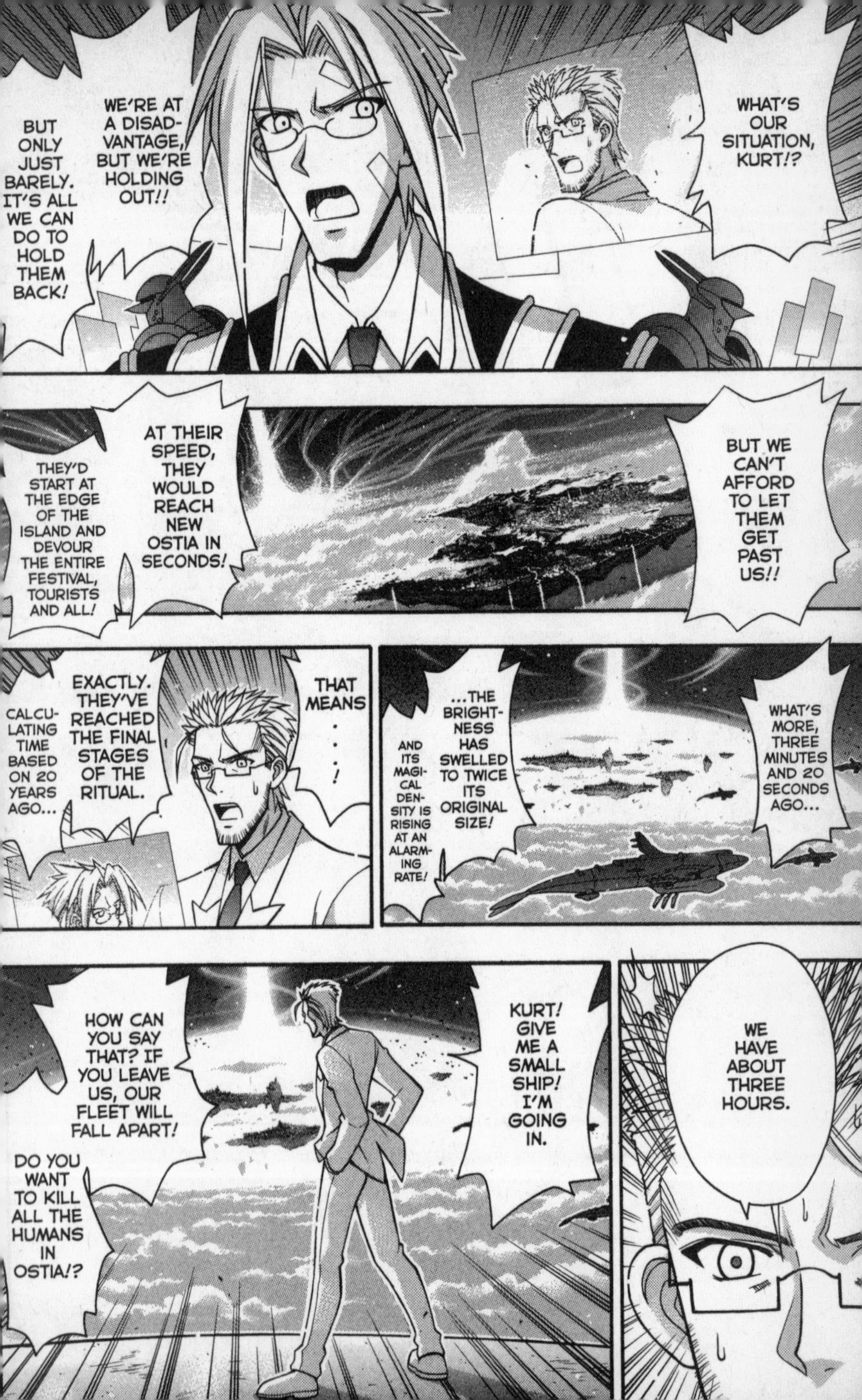
WHAT'S OUR SITUATION, KURT!?
WE'RE AT A DISADVANTAGE, BUT WE'RE HOLDING OUT!!
BUT ONLY JUST BARELY. IT'S ALL WE CAN DO TO HOLD THEM BACK!
BUT WE CAN'T AFFORD TO LET THEM GET PAST US!!
AT THEIR SPEED, THEY WOULD REACH NEW OSTIA IN SECONDS!
THEY'D START AT THE EDGE OF THE ISLAND AND DEVOUR THE ENTIRE FESTIVAL, TOURISTS AND ALL!
WHAT'S MORE, THREE MINUTES AND 20 SECONDS AGO...
...THE BRIGHTNESS HAS SWELLED TO TWICE ITS ORIGINAL SIZE!
AND ITS MAGICAL DENSITY IS RISING AT AN ALARMING RATE!
THAT MEANS...!
EXACTLY. THEY'VE REACHED THE FINAL STAGES OF THE RITUAL.
CALCULATING TIME BASED ON 20 YEARS AGO...
WE HAVE ABOUT THREE HOURS.
KURT! GIVE ME A SMALL SHIP! I'M GOING IN.
HOW CAN YOU SAY THAT? IF YOU LEAVE US, OUR FLEET WILL FALL APART!
DO YOU WANT TO KILL ALL THE HUMANS IN OSTIA!?

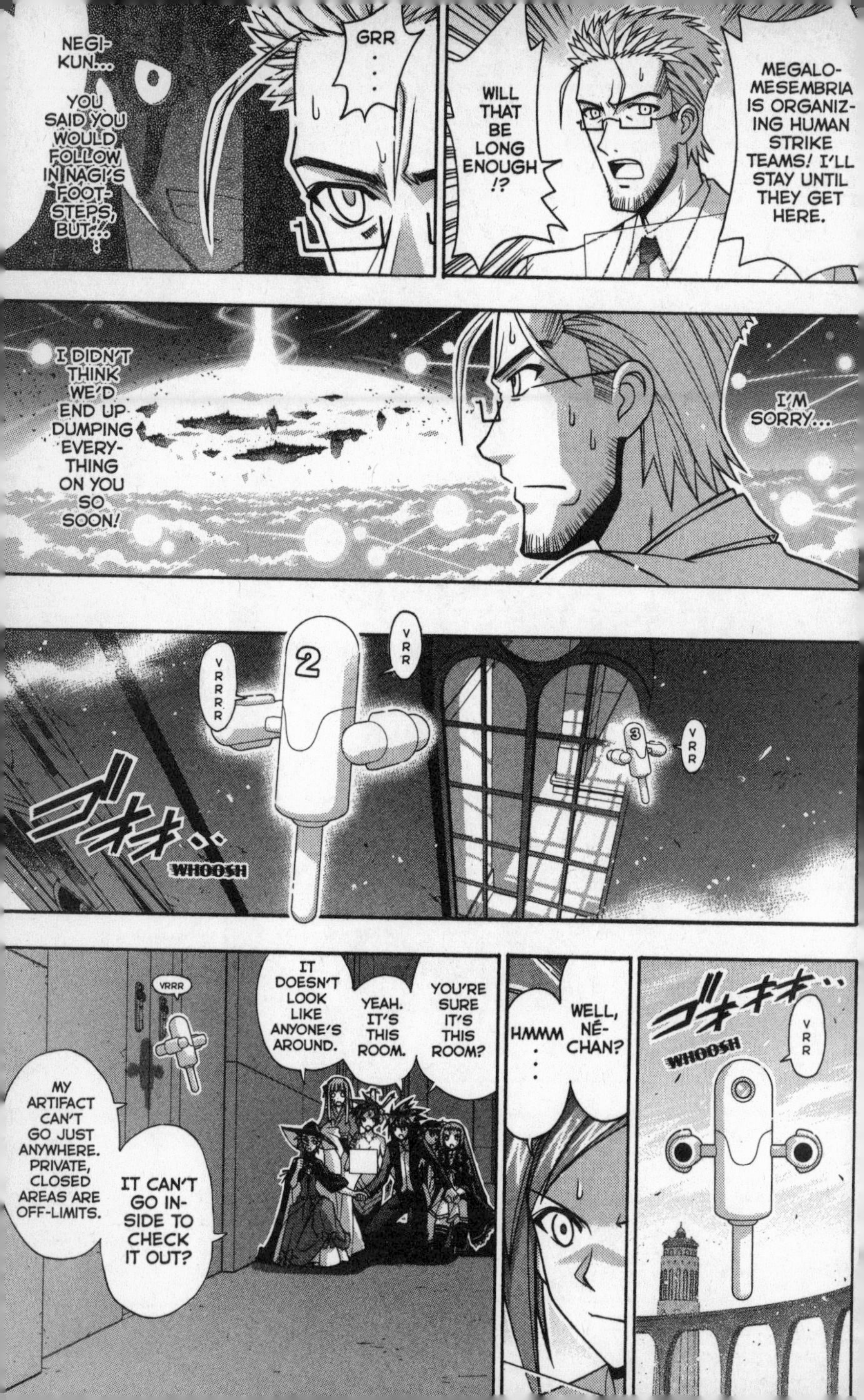
MEGALO-MESEMBRIA IS ORGANIZING HUMAN STRIKE TEAMS! I'LL STAY UNTIL THEY GET HERE.
WILL THAT BE LONG ENOUGH!?
GRR...
NEGI-KUN...
YOU SAID YOU WOULD FOLLOW IN NAGI'S FOOTSTEPS, BUT...!
I'M SORRY...
I DIDN'T THINK WE'D END UP DUMPING EVERYTHING ON YOU SO SOON!
VRR
VRR
VRRRR
WHOOSH
VRR
WHOOSH
WELL, NÉ-CHAN?
HMMM...
YOU'RE SURE IT'S THIS ROOM?
YEAH. IT'S THIS ROOM.
IT DOESN'T LOOK LIKE ANYONE'S AROUND.
VRRR
IT CAN'T GO INSIDE TO CHECK IT OUT?
MY ARTIFACT CAN'T GO JUST ANYWHERE. PRIVATE, CLOSED AREAS ARE OFF-LIMITS.

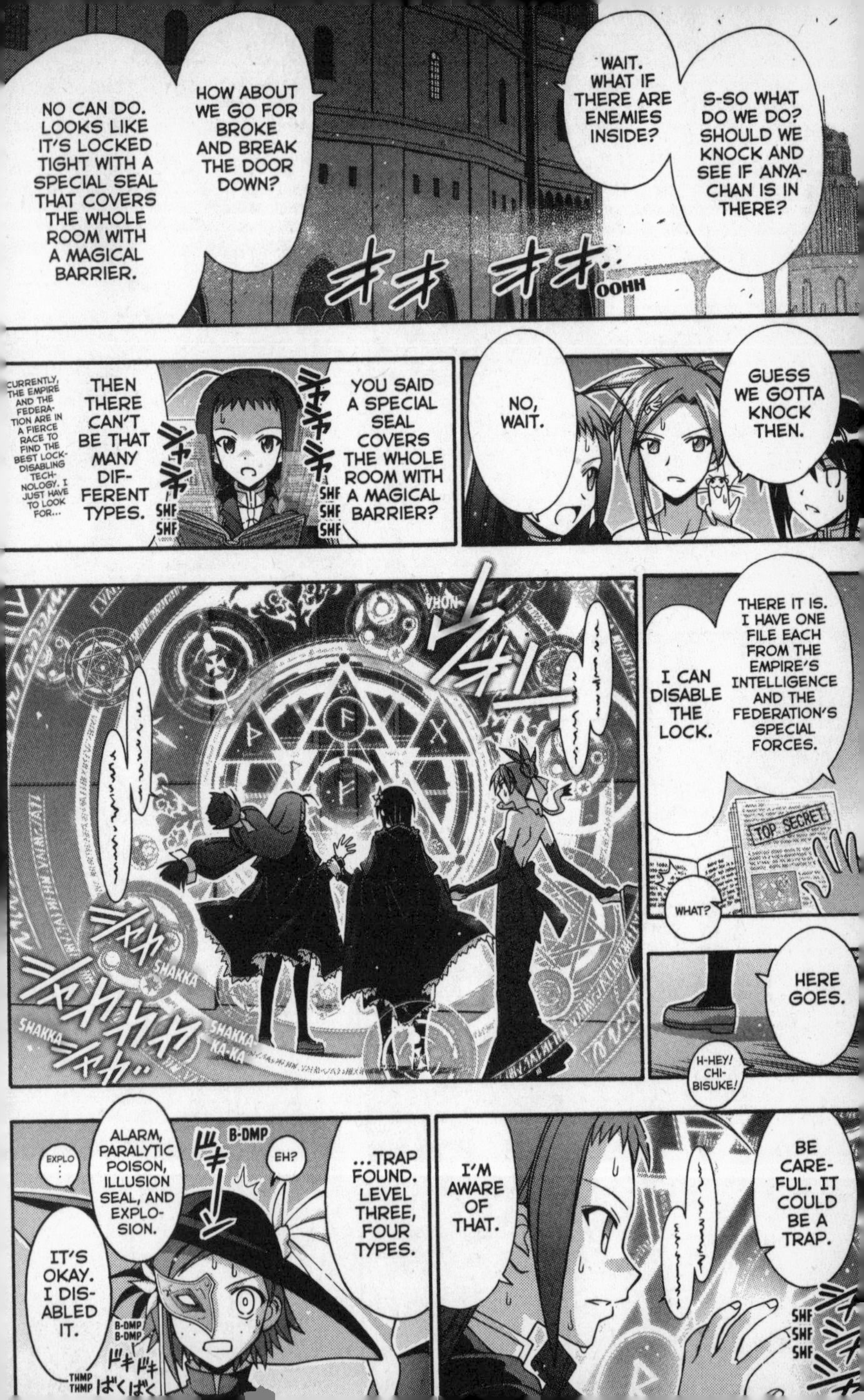
S-SO WHAT DO WE DO? SHOULD WE KNOCK AND SEE IF ANYA-CHAN IS IN THERE?
WAIT. WHAT IF THERE ARE ENEMIES INSIDE?
HOW ABOUT WE GO FOR BROKE AND BREAK THE DOOR DOWN?
NO CAN DO. LOOKS LIKE IT'S LOCKED TIGHT WITH A SPECIAL SEAL THAT COVERS THE WHOLE ROOM WITH A MAGICAL BARRIER.
OOHH
GUESS WE GOTTA KNOCK THEN.
NO, WAIT.
YOU SAID A SPECIAL SEAL COVERS THE WHOLE ROOM WITH A MAGICAL BARRIER?
SHF SHF SHF
THEN THERE CAN'T BE THAT MANY DIF-FERENT TYPES.
SHF SHF
CURRENTLY, THE EMPIRE AND THE FEDERA-TION ARE IN A FIERCE RACE TO FIND THE BEST LOCK-DISABLING TECH-NOLOGY. I JUST HAVE TO LOOK FOR...
THERE IT IS. I HAVE ONE FILE EACH FROM THE EMPIRE'S INTELLIGENCE AND THE FEDERATION'S SPECIAL FORCES.
I CAN DISABLE THE LOCK.
TOP SECRET
WHAT?
HERE GOES.
H-HEY! CHI-BISUKE!
VHON
SHAKKA
SHAKKA-KA-KA
SHAKKA
BE CARE-FUL. IT COULD BE A TRAP.
SHF SHF SHF
I'M AWARE OF THAT.
...TRAP FOUND. LEVEL THREE, FOUR TYPES.
EH?
B-DMP
ALARM, PARALYTIC POISON, ILLUSION SEAL, AND EXPLO-SION.
EXPLO...
IT'S OKAY. I DIS-ABLED IT.
B-DMP B-DMP
THMP THMP

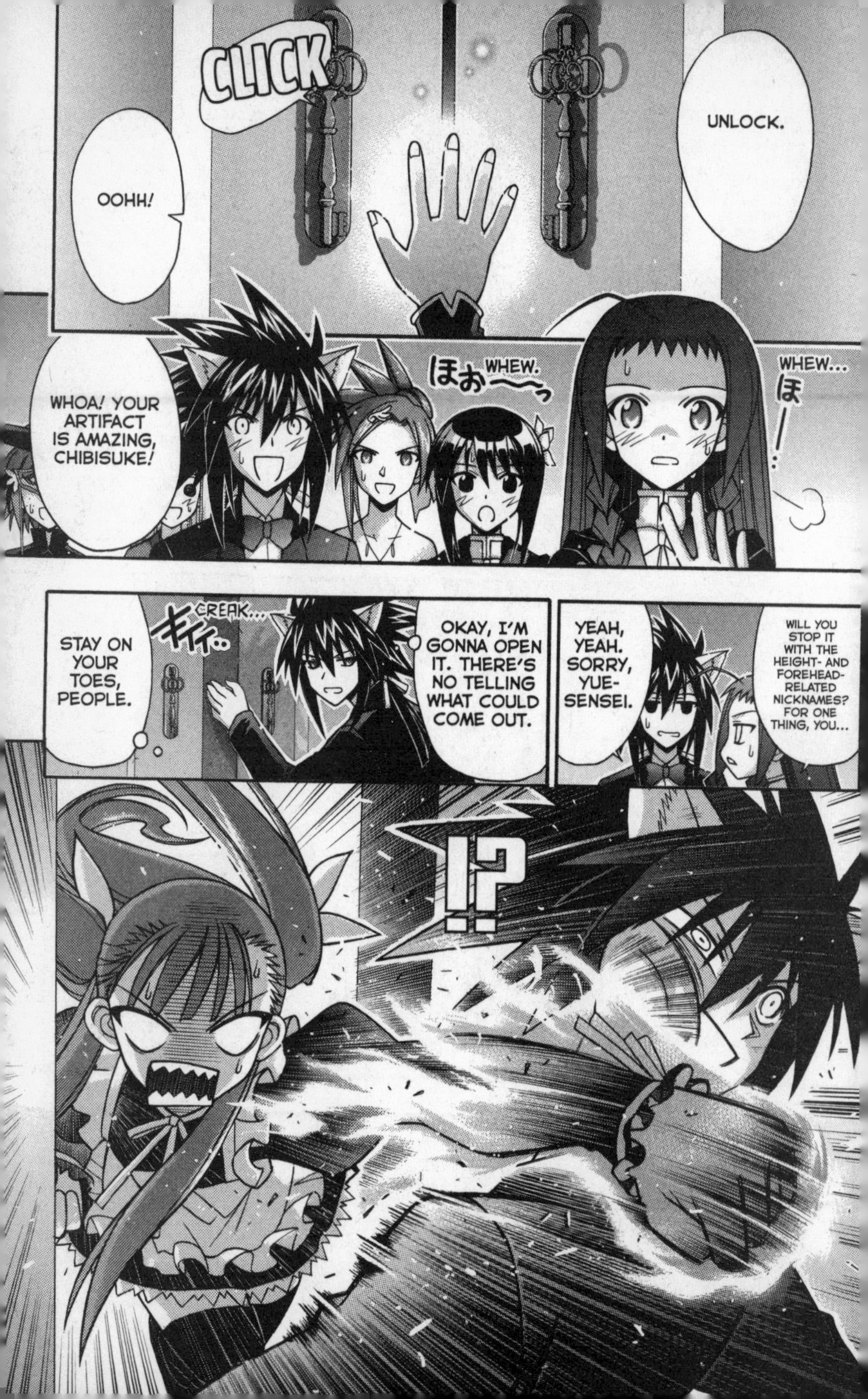
UNLOCK.
CLICK
OOHH!
WHEW...
ほー
ほぉ〜〜っ
WHEW.
WHOA! YOUR ARTIFACT IS AMAZING, CHIBISUKE!
WILL YOU STOP IT WITH THE HEIGHT- AND FOREHEAD-RELATED NICKNAMES? FOR ONE THING, YOU...
YEAH, YEAH. SORRY, YUE-SENSEI.
OKAY, I'M GONNA OPEN IT. THERE'S NO TELLING WHAT COULD COME OUT.
CREAK...
キィィ..
STAY ON YOUR TOES, PEOPLE.
!?

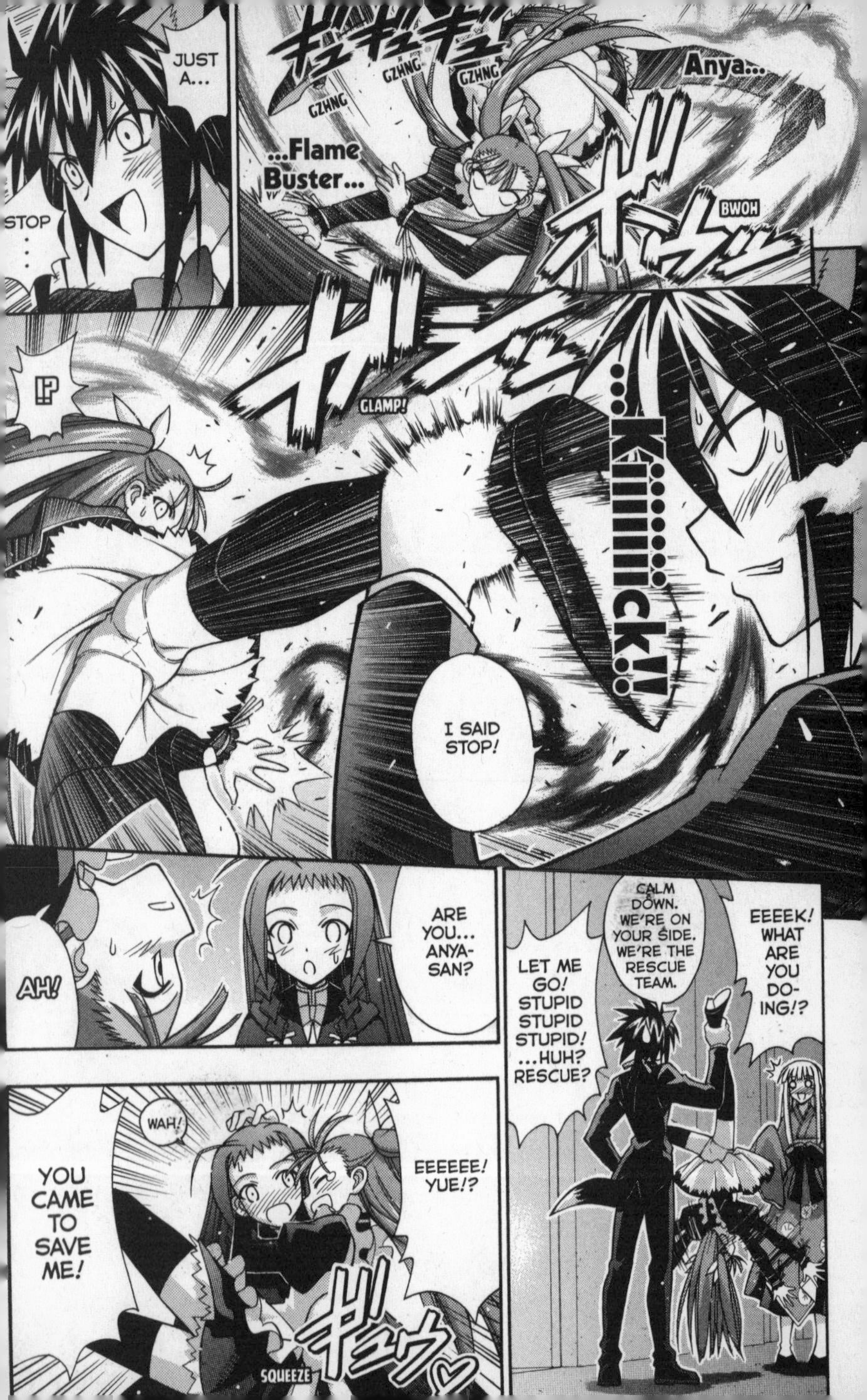

GZHNG
GZHNG
GZHNG
Anya...
...Flame Buster...
BWOH
JUST A...
STOP...
GLAMP!
...Kiiiiiiiick!!
!?
I SAID STOP!
EEEEK! WHAT ARE YOU DO-ING!?
CALM DOWN. WE'RE ON YOUR SIDE. WE'RE THE RESCUE TEAM.
LET ME GO! STUPID STUPID STUPID! ...HUH? RESCUE?
ARE YOU... ANYA-SAN?
AH!
WAH!
EEEEEE! YUE!?
YOU CAME TO SAVE ME!
SQUEEZE

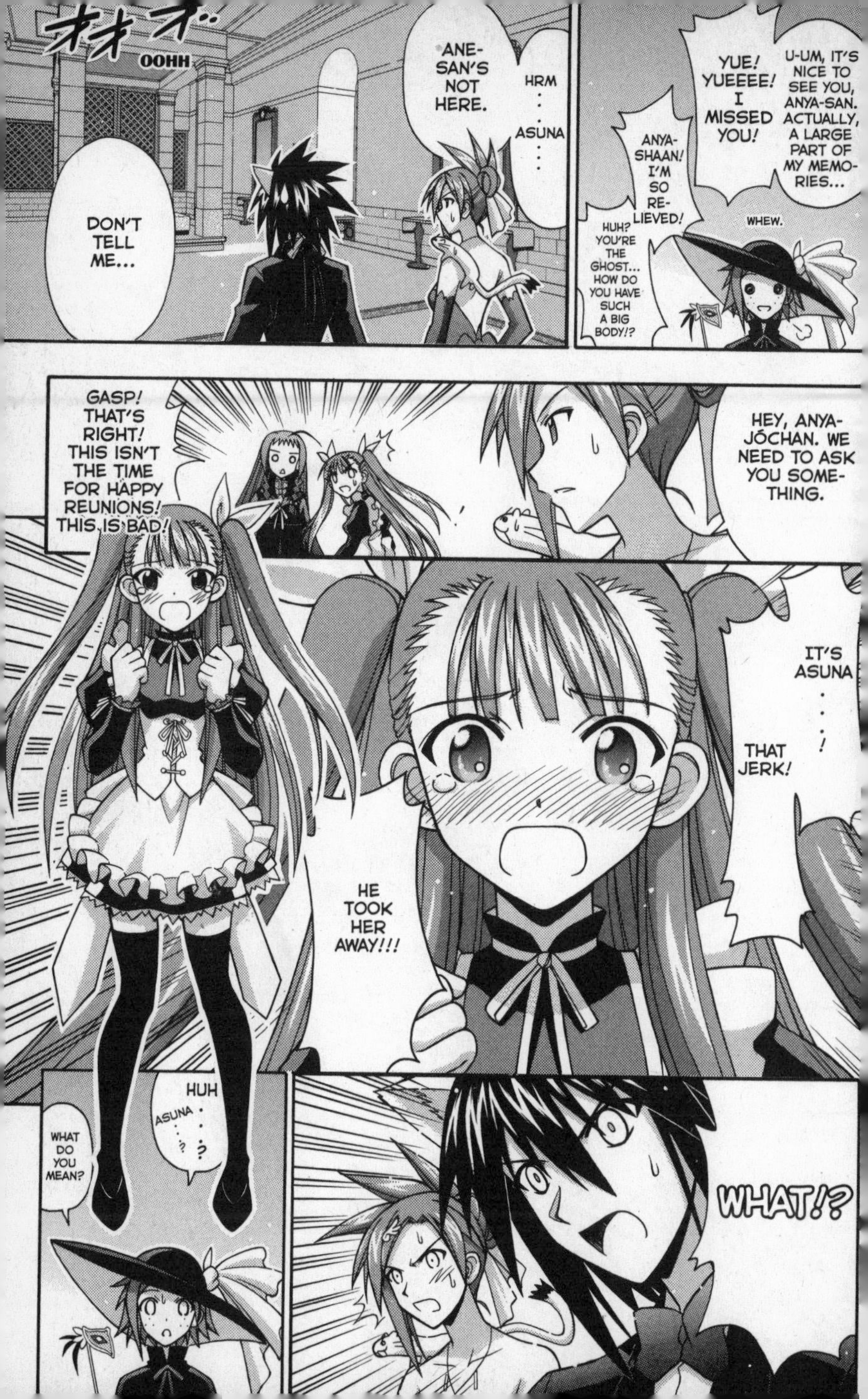

U-UM, IT'S NICE TO SEE YOU, ANYA-SAN. ACTUALLY, A LARGE PART OF MY MEMORIES...
YUE! YUEEEE! I MISSED YOU!
ANYA-SHAAN! I'M SO RELIEVED!
WHEW.
HUH? YOU'RE THE GHOST... HOW DO YOU HAVE SUCH A BIG BODY!?
ANE-SAN'S NOT HERE.
HRM... ASUNA...
オオオ
OOHH
DON'T TELL ME...
HEY, ANYA-JÓCHAN. WE NEED TO ASK YOU SOMETHING.
GASP! THAT'S RIGHT! THIS ISN'T THE TIME FOR HAPPY REUNIONS! THIS IS BAD!
IT'S ASUNA...!
THAT JERK!
HE TOOK HER AWAY!!!
WHAT!?
HUH ASUNA...?
WHAT DO YOU MEAN?

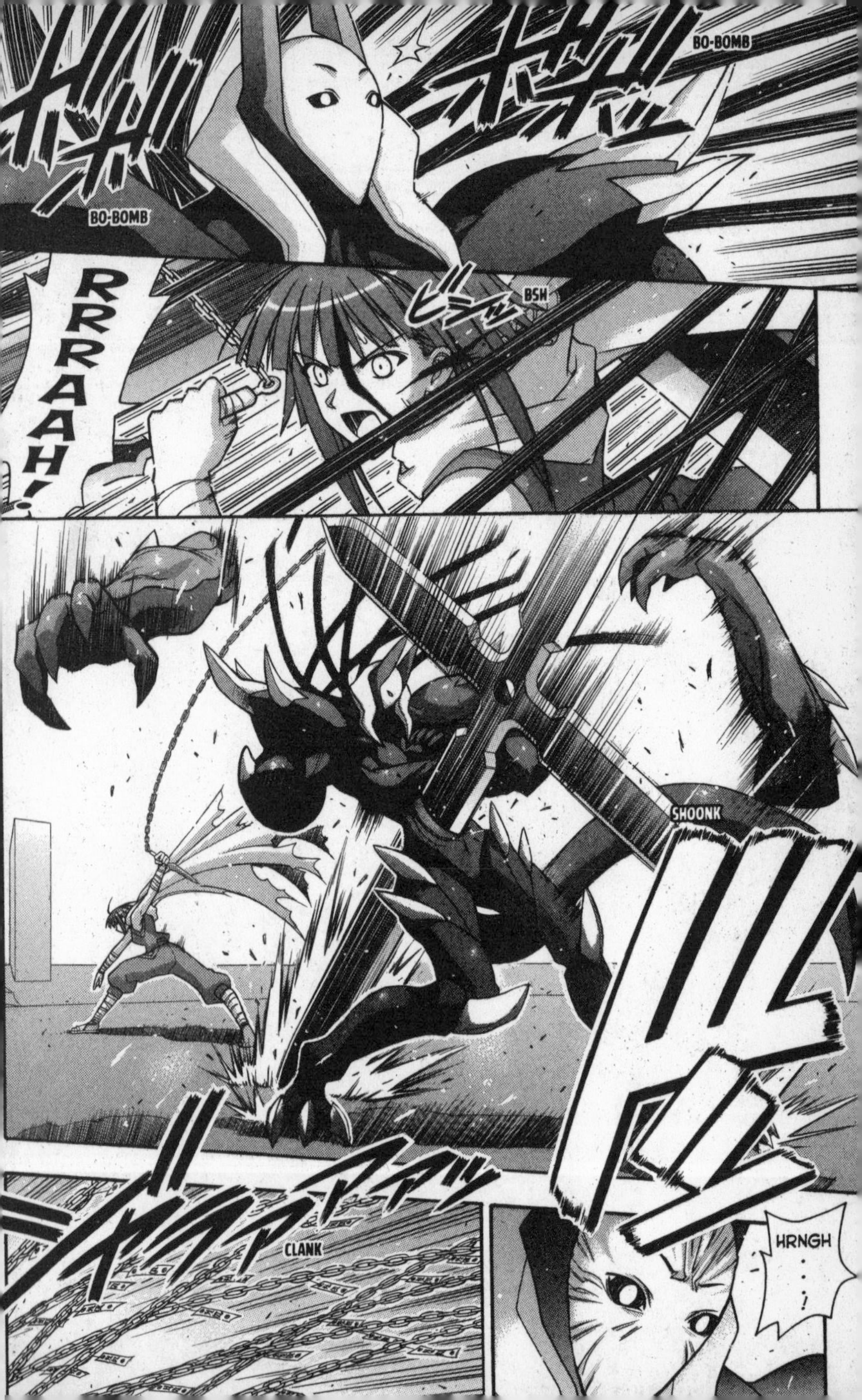
BO-BOMB
BO-BOMB
BSH
RRRAAH!!
SHOONK
HRNGH ...!
CLANK

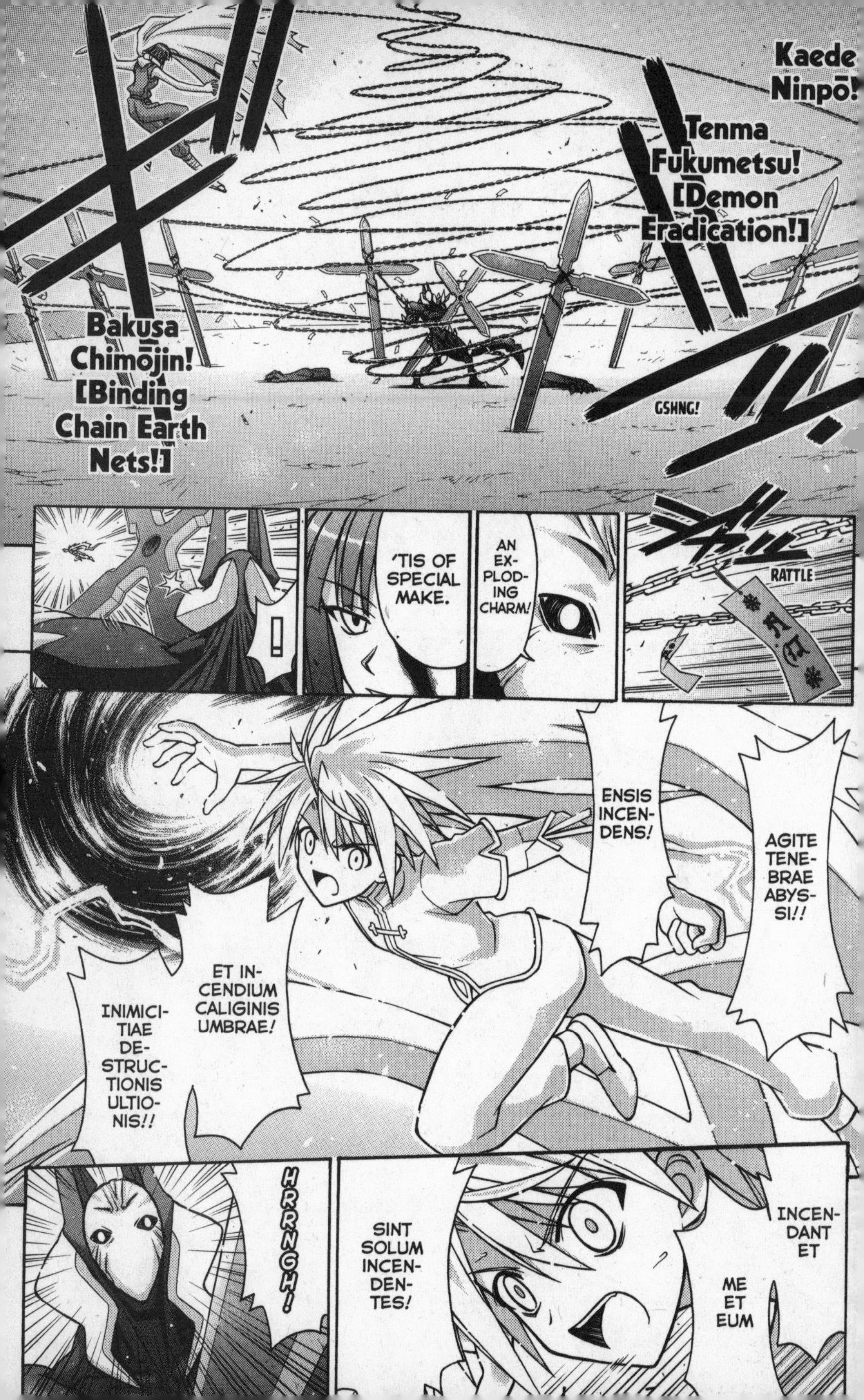
Kaede Ninpō!
Tenma Fukumetsu! [Demon Eradication!]
Bakusa Chimōjin! [Binding Chain Earth Nets!]
GSHNG!
RATTLE
AN EXPLODING CHARM!
'TIS OF SPECIAL MAKE.
!
AGITE TENEBRAE ABYSSI!!
ENSIS INCENDENS!
ET INCENDIUM CALIGINIS UMBRAE!
INIMICITIAE DESTRUCTIONIS ULTIONIS!!
INCENDANT ET
ME ET EUM
SINT SOLUM INCENDENTES!
HRRNGH!

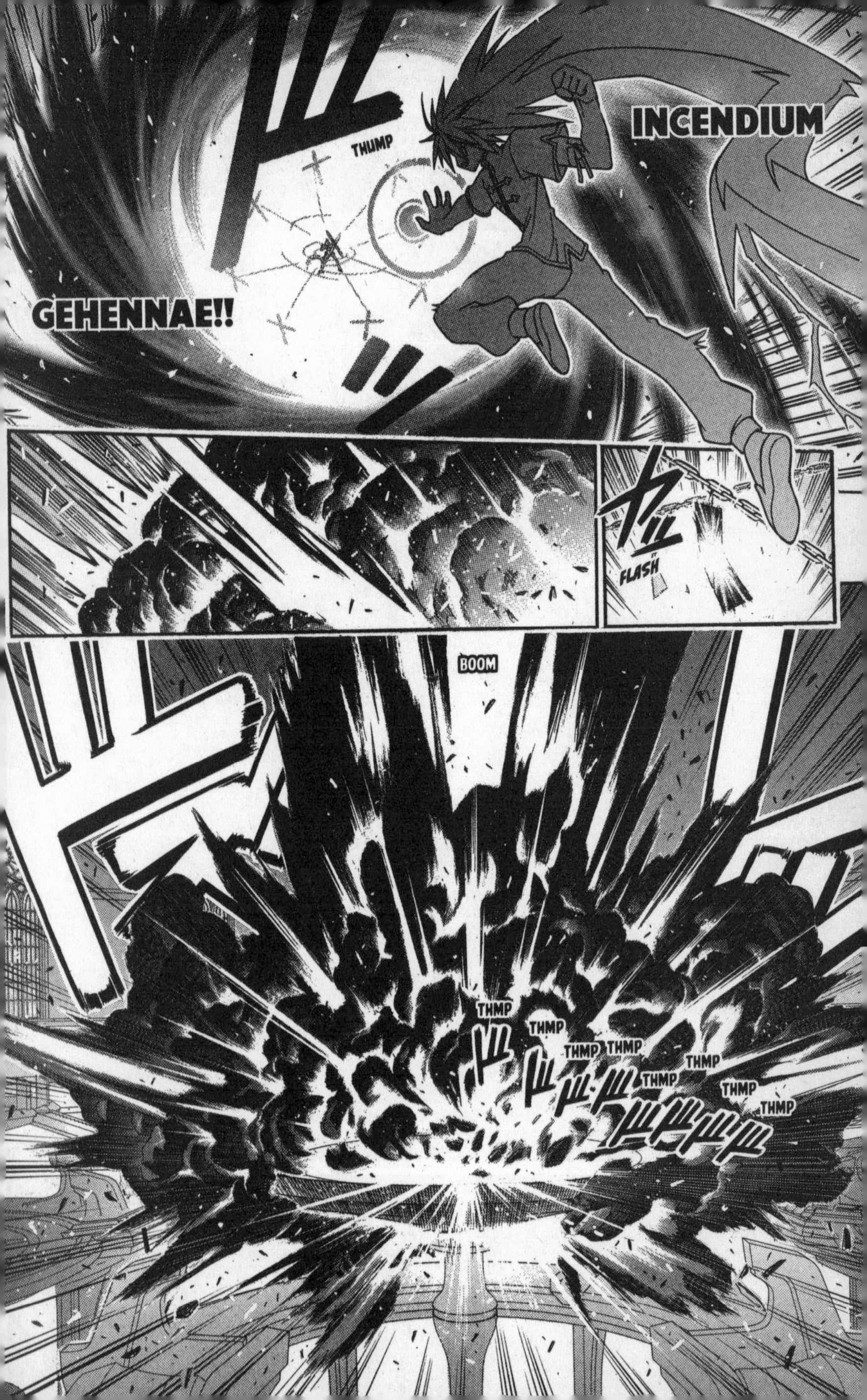
INCENDIUM
THUMP
GEHENNAE!!
FLASH
BOOM
THMP
THMP
THMP
THMP
THMP
THMP
THMP
THMP

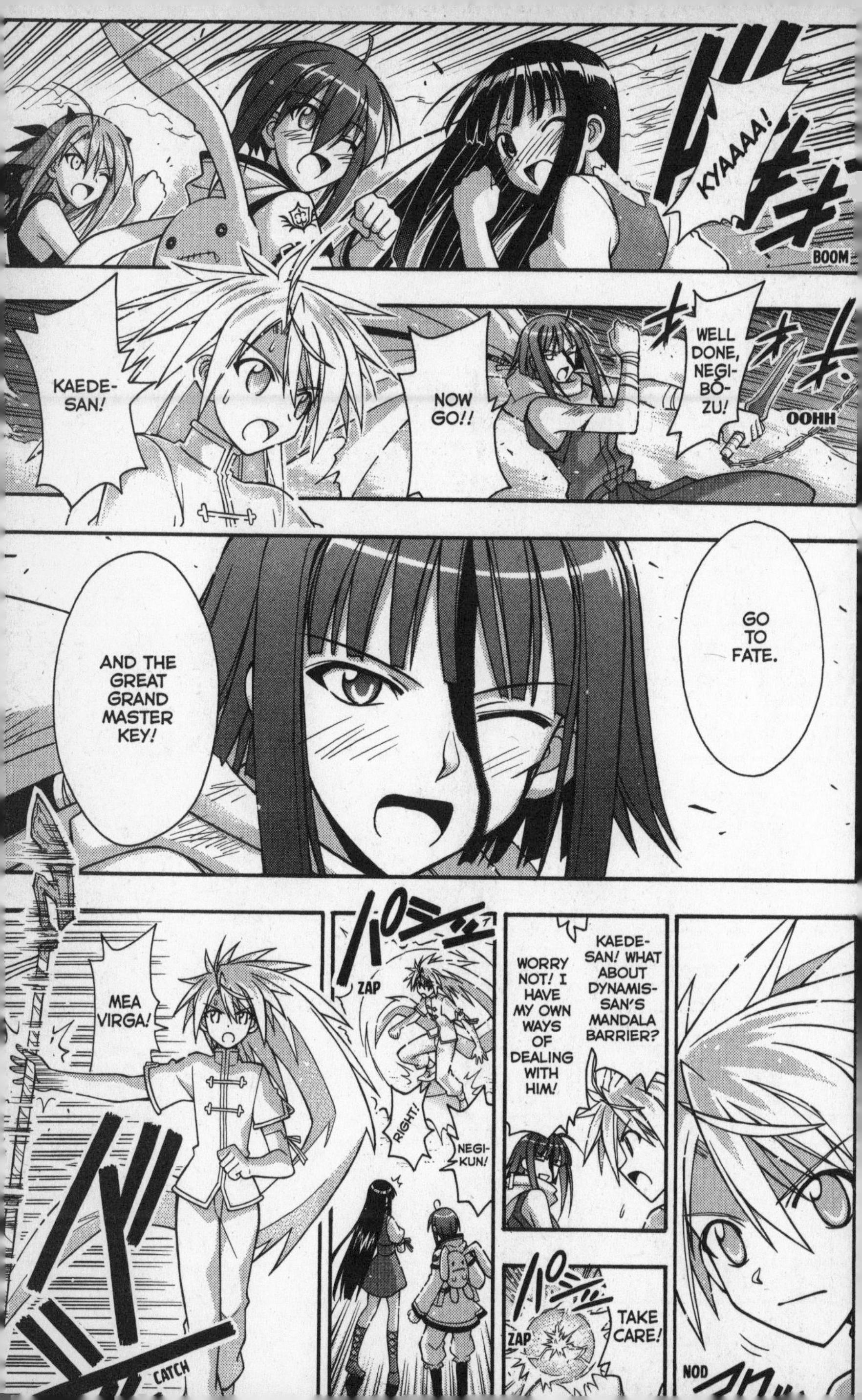
KYAAAA!
BOOM
WELL DONE, NEGI-BŌ-ZU!
OOHH
NOW GO!!
KAEDE-SAN!
GO TO FATE.
AND THE GREAT GRAND MASTER KEY!
NOD
KAEDE-SAN! WHAT ABOUT DYNAMIS-SAN'S MANDALA BARRIER?
WORRY NOT! I HAVE MY OWN WAYS OF DEALING WITH HIM!
TAKE CARE!
ZAP
ZAP
RIGHT!
NEGI-KUN!
MEA VIRGA!
CATCH

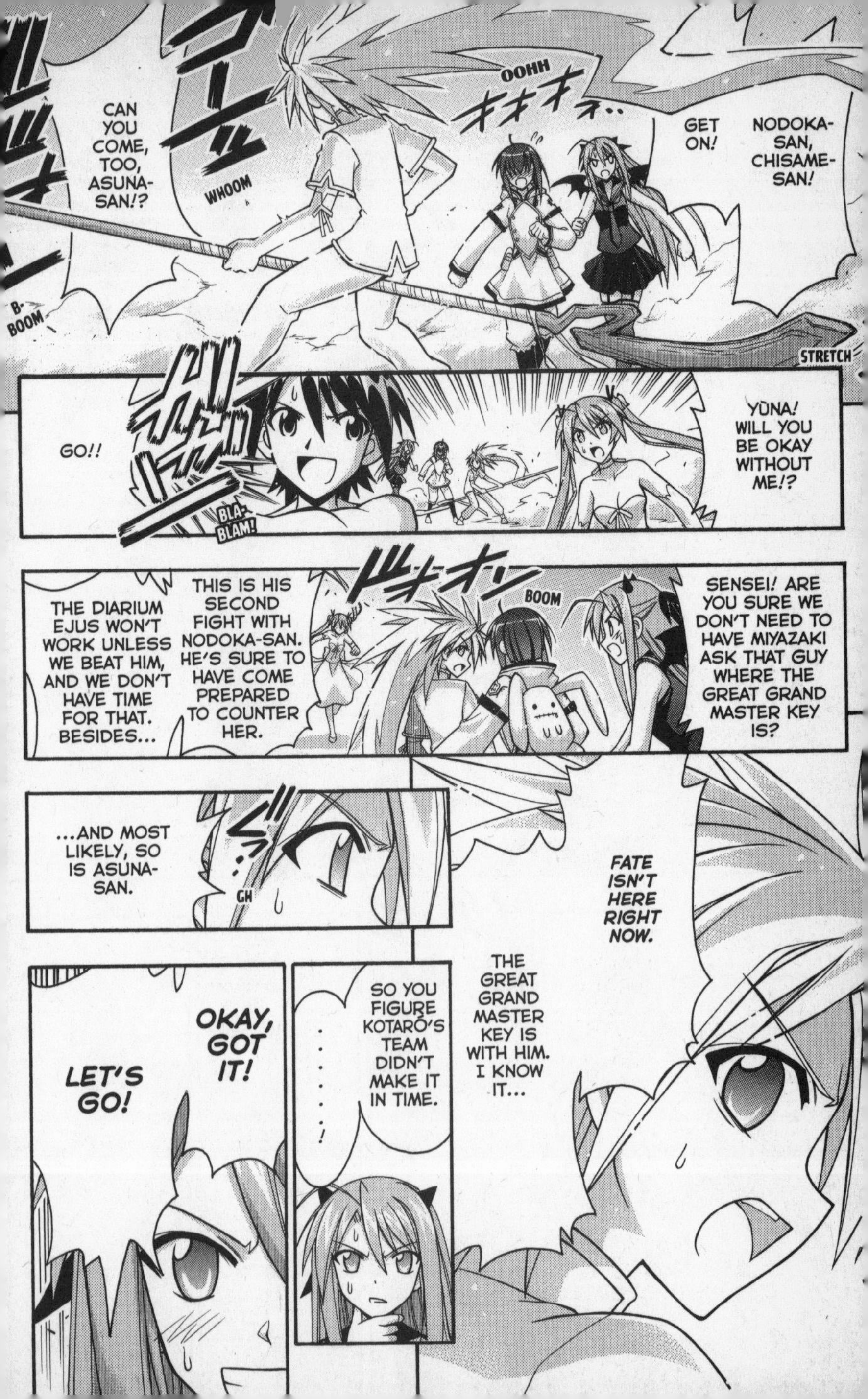
NODOKA-SAN, CHISAME-SAN!
GET ON!
OOHH
STRETCH
WHOOM
CAN YOU COME, TOO, ASUNA-SAN!?
B-BOOM
YŪNA! WILL YOU BE OKAY WITHOUT ME!?
GO!!
BLA-BLAM!
SENSEI! ARE YOU SURE WE DON'T NEED TO HAVE MIYAZAKI ASK THAT GUY WHERE THE GREAT GRAND MASTER KEY IS?
BOOM
THIS IS HIS SECOND FIGHT WITH NODOKA-SAN. HE'S SURE TO HAVE COME PREPARED TO COUNTER HER.
THE DIARIUM EJUS WON'T WORK UNLESS WE BEAT HIM, AND WE DON'T HAVE TIME FOR THAT. BESIDES...
FATE ISN'T HERE RIGHT NOW.
THE GREAT GRAND MASTER KEY IS WITH HIM. I KNOW IT...
...AND MOST LIKELY, SO IS ASUNA-SAN.
GH
SO YOU FIGURE KOTARŌ'S TEAM DIDN'T MAKE IT IN TIME.
. . . . . . !
OKAY, GOT IT!
LET'S GO!

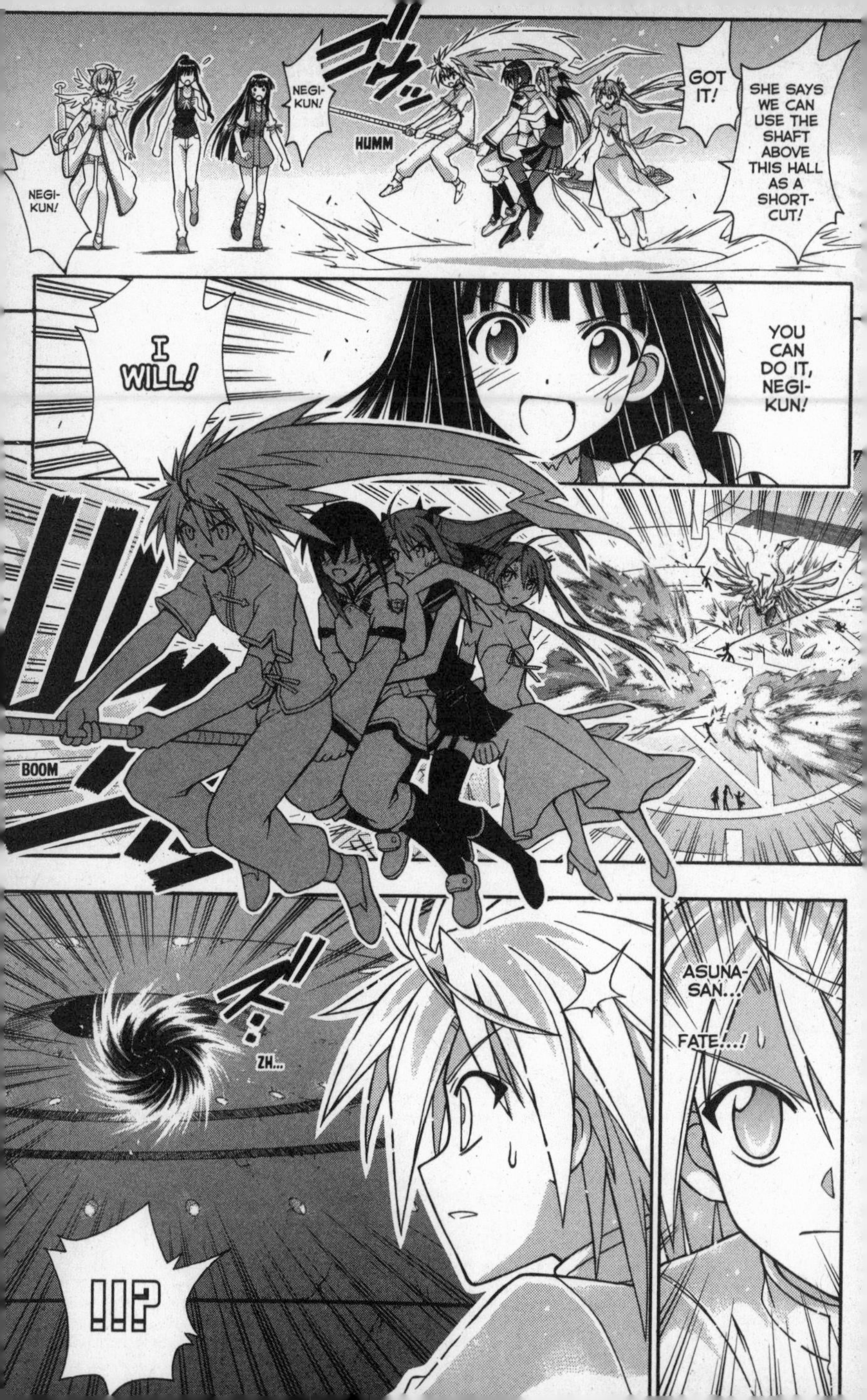
SHE SAYS WE CAN USE THE SHAFT ABOVE THIS HALL AS A SHORT-CUT!
GOT IT!
NEGI-KUN!
HUMM
NEGI-KUN!
YOU CAN DO IT, NEGI-KUN!
I WILL!
BOOM
ASUNA-SAN...!
FATE...!
ZH...
!!?

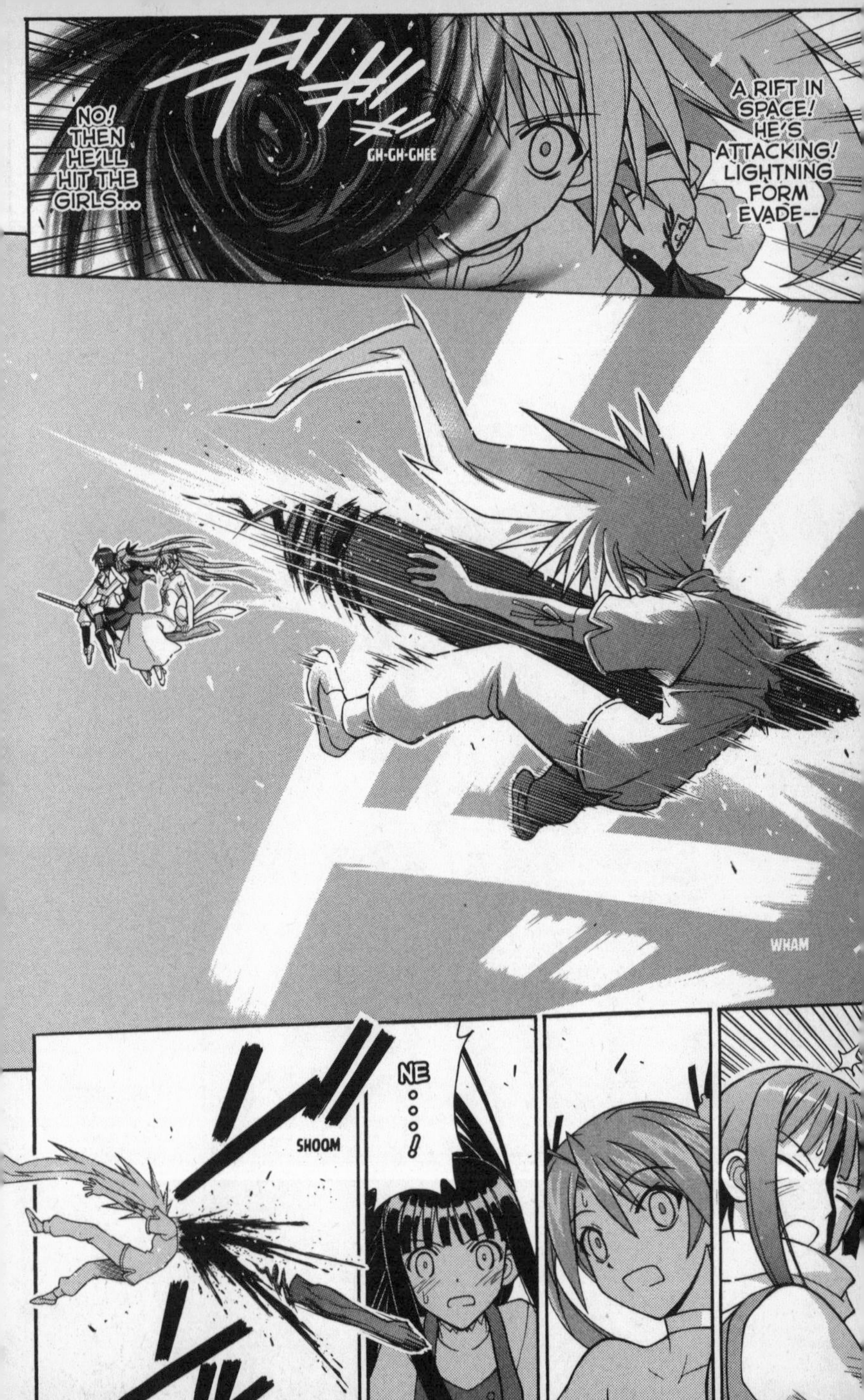
A RIFT IN SPACE! HE'S ATTACKING! LIGHTNING FORM EVADE--
GH-GH-GHEE
NO! THEN HE'LL HIT THE GIRLS...
WHAM
NEoooo!
SHOOM

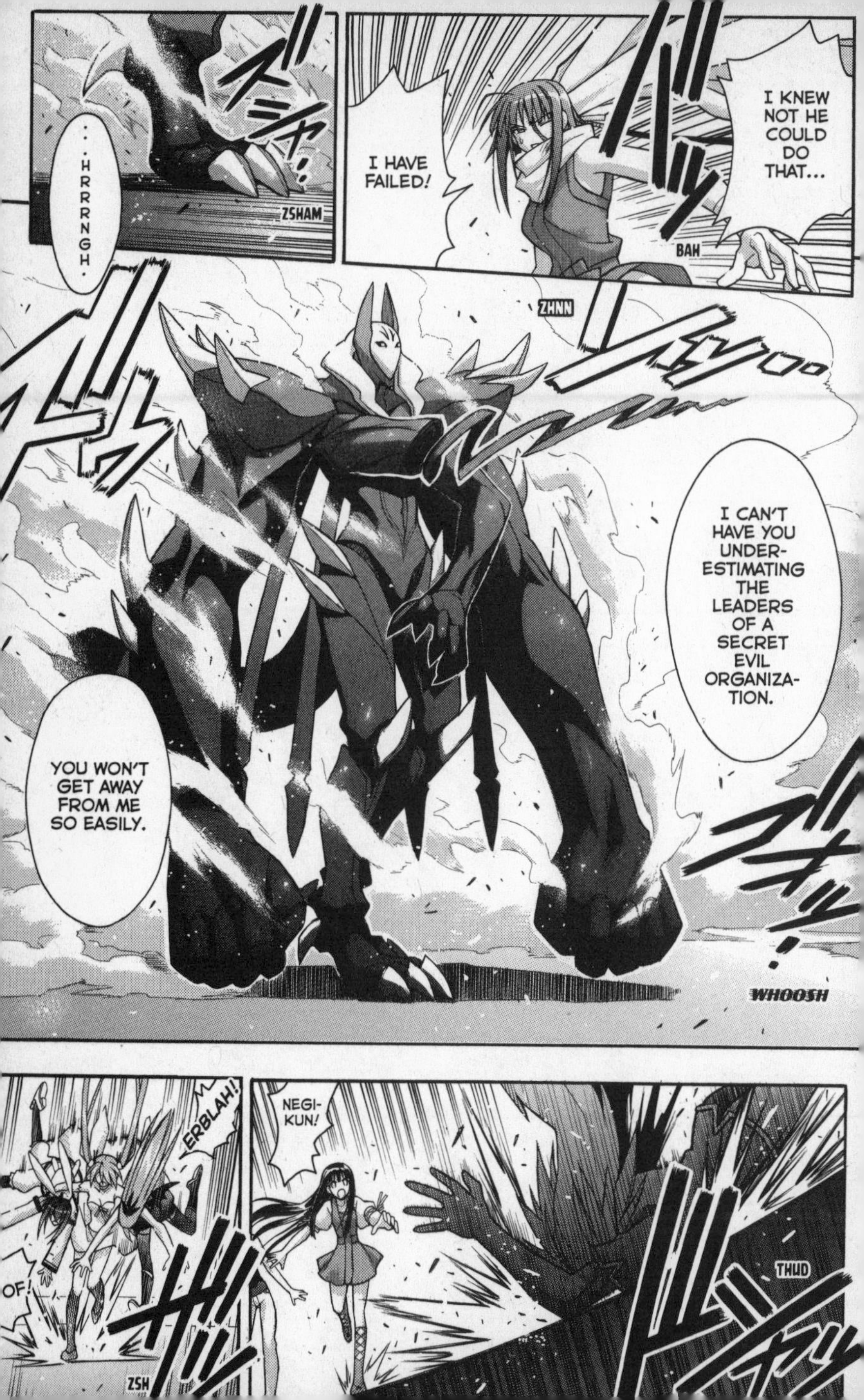
I KNEW NOT HE COULD DO THAT...
I HAVE FAILED!
BAH
ZSHAM
...HRRRNGH...
ZHNN
I CAN'T HAVE YOU UNDER-ESTIMATING THE LEADERS OF A SECRET EVIL ORGANIZA-TION.
YOU WON'T GET AWAY FROM ME SO EASILY.
WHOOSH
NEGI-KUN!
THUD
ERBLAH!
OF!
ZSH

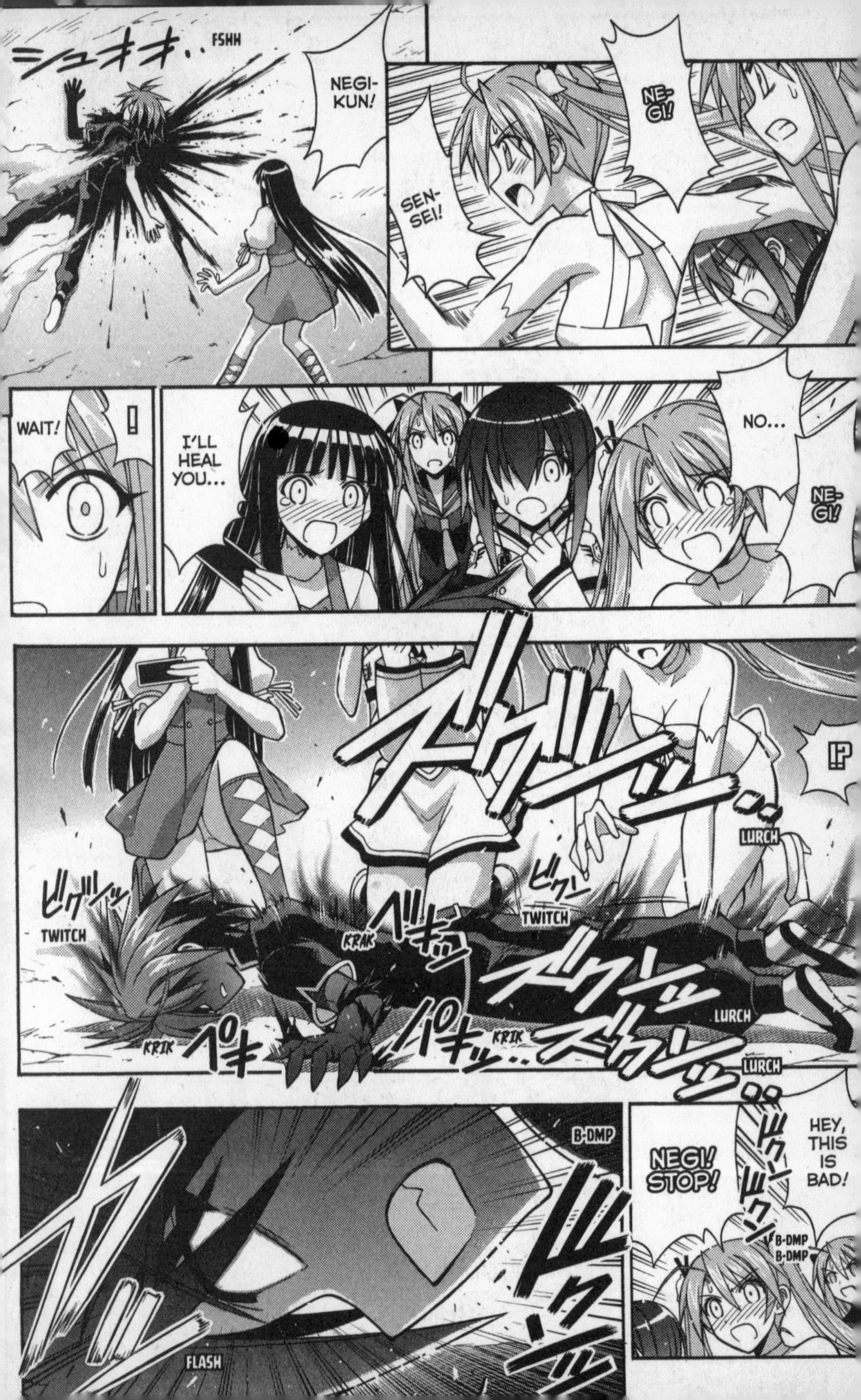

NE-GI!
SEN-SEI!
NEGI-KUN!
シュオオ..
FSHH
NO...
NE-GI!
I'LL HEAL YOU...
!
WAIT!
!?
LURCH
TWITCH
KRAK
TWITCH
LURCH
KRIK
KRIK
LURCH
HEY, THIS IS BAD!
NEGI! STOP!
B-DMP
B-DMP
B-DMP
FLASH

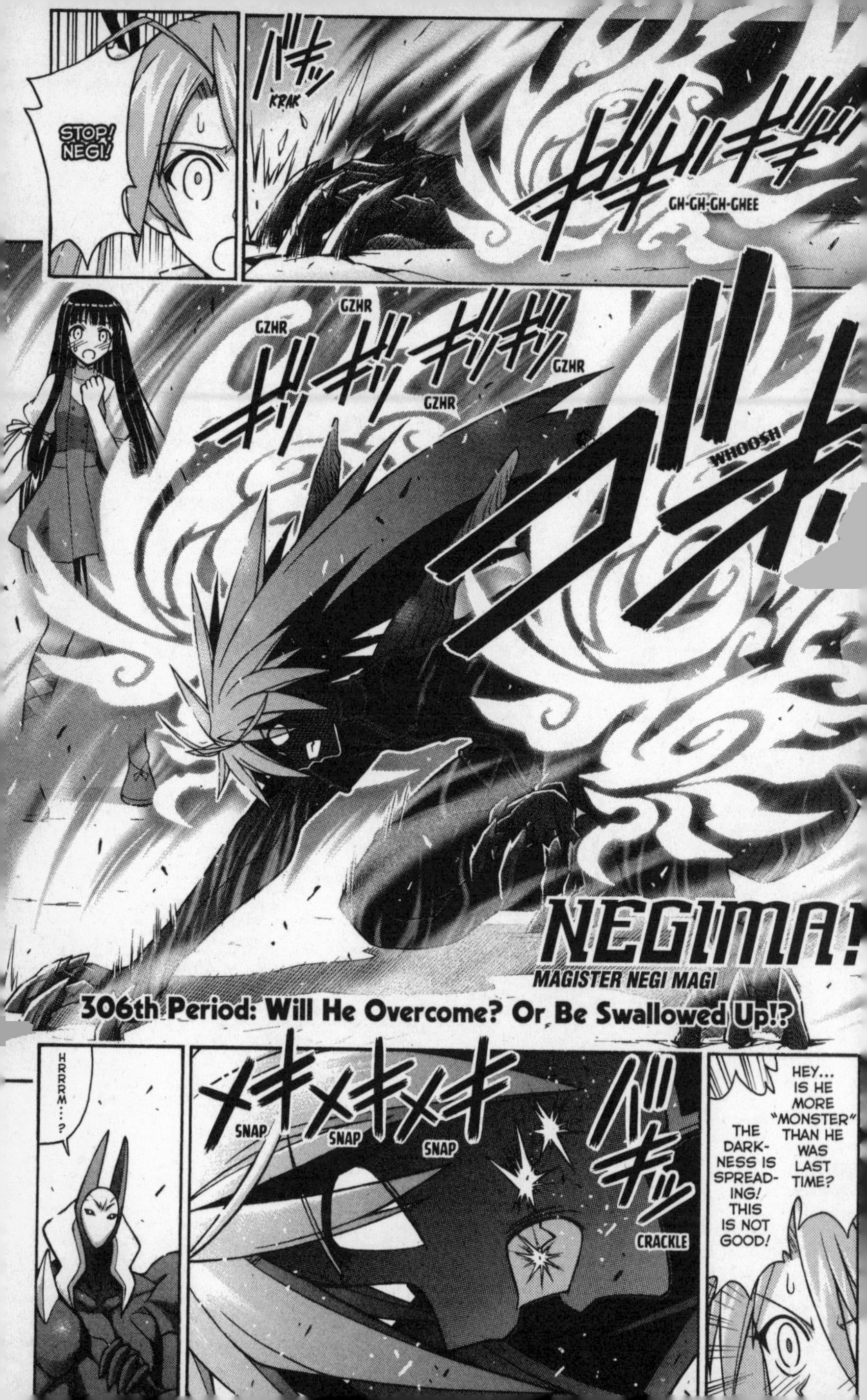
KRAK
GH-GH-GH-GHEE
STOP! NEGI!
GZHR
GZHR
GZHR
GZHR
WHOOSH
NEGIMA!
MAGISTER NEGI MAGI
306th Period: Will He Overcome? Or Be Swallowed Up!?
HEY... IS HE MORE "MONSTER" THAN HE WAS LAST TIME?
THE DARKNESS IS SPREADING! THIS IS NOT GOOD!
SNAP
SNAP
SNAP
CRACKLE
HRRRM...?

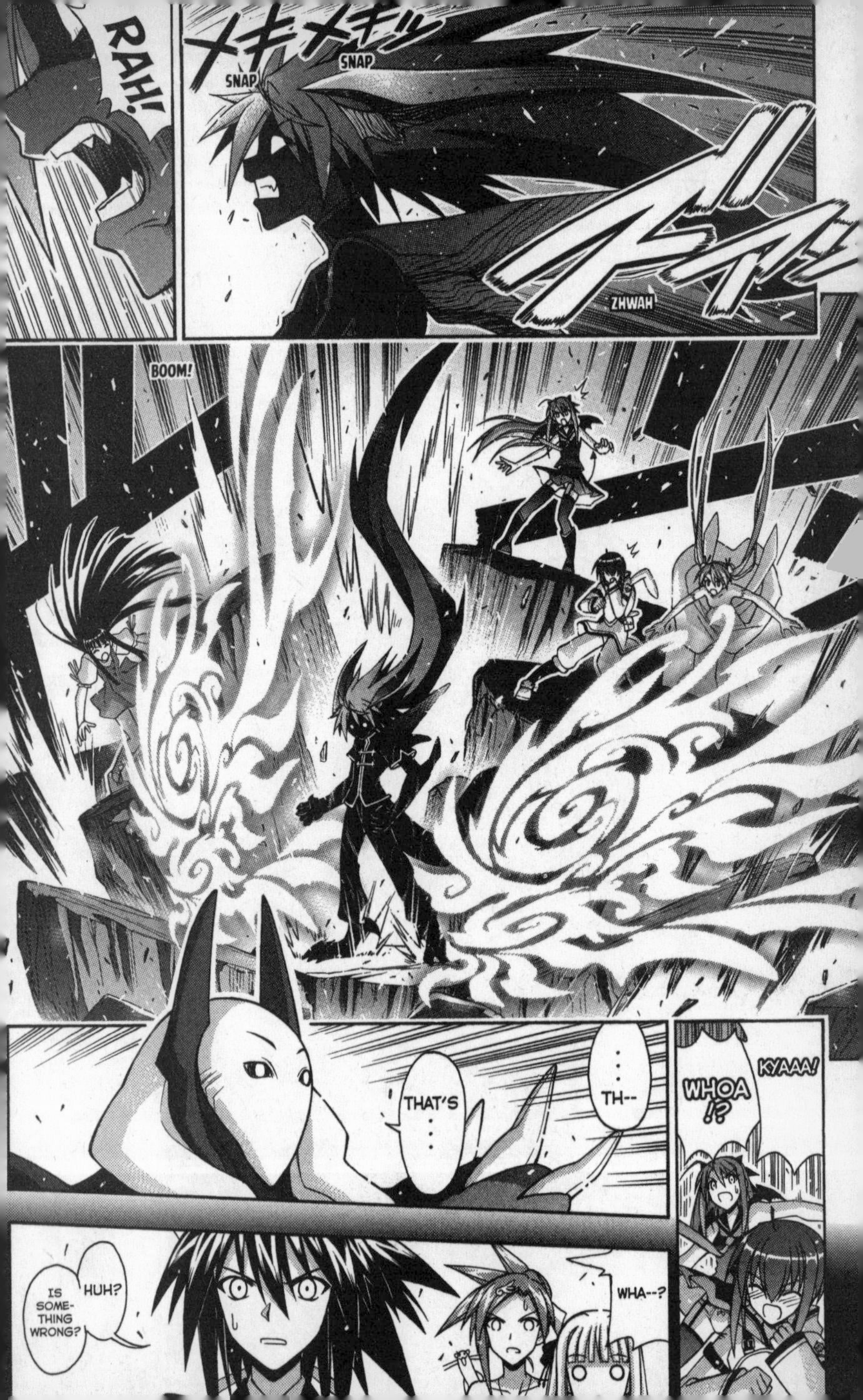

メキメキッ
SNAP
SNAP
ZHWAH
RAH!
BOOM!
KYAAA!
WHOA !?
...TH--
THAT'S...
WHA--?
HUH?
IS SOMETHING WRONG?

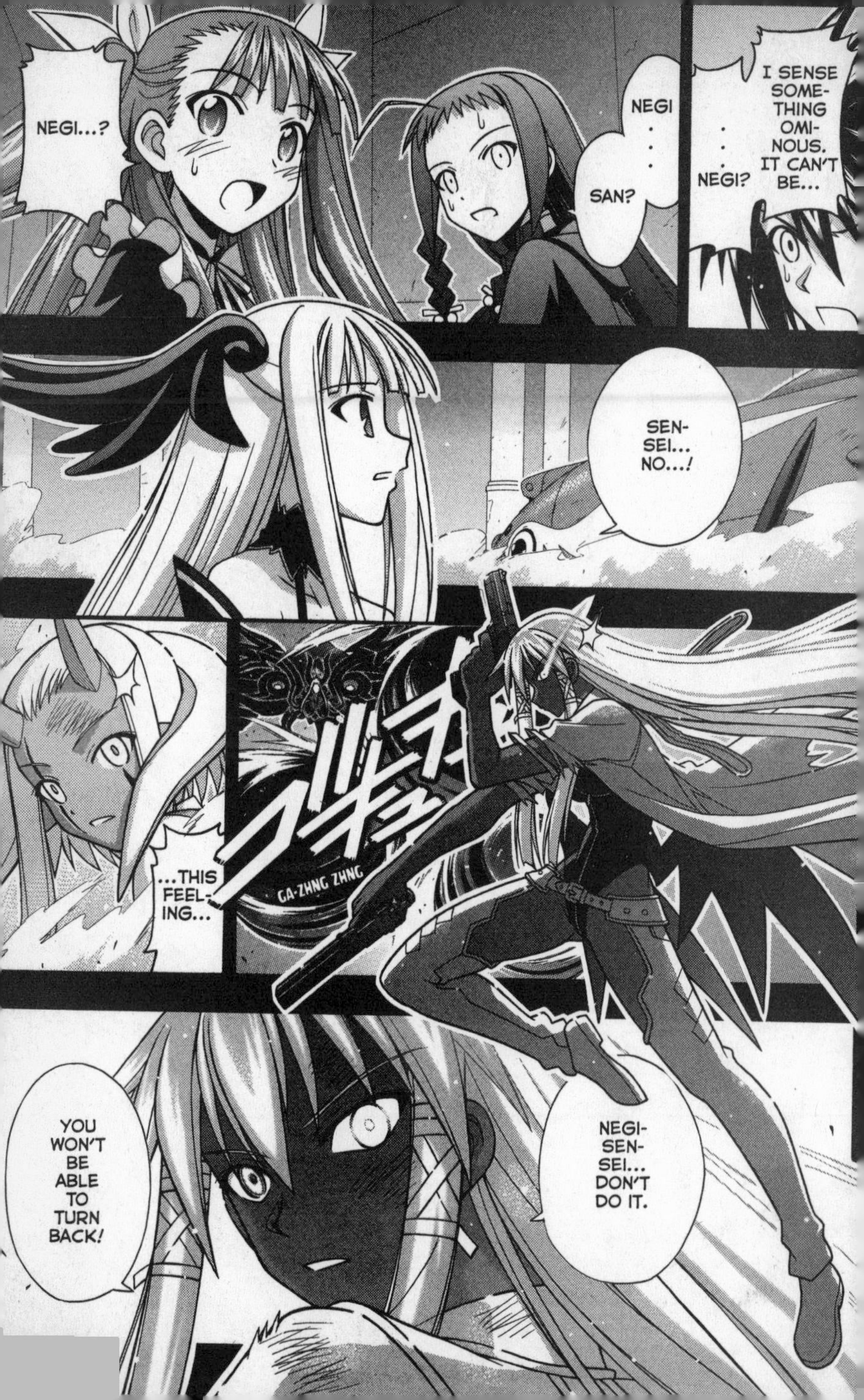
I SENSE SOMETHING OMINOUS. IT CAN'T BE...
. . . NEGI?
NEGI . . . SAN?
NEGI...?
SENSEI... NO...!
GA-ZHNG ZHNG
...THIS FEELING...
NEGI-SENSEI... DON'T DO IT.
YOU WON'T BE ABLE TO TURN BACK!

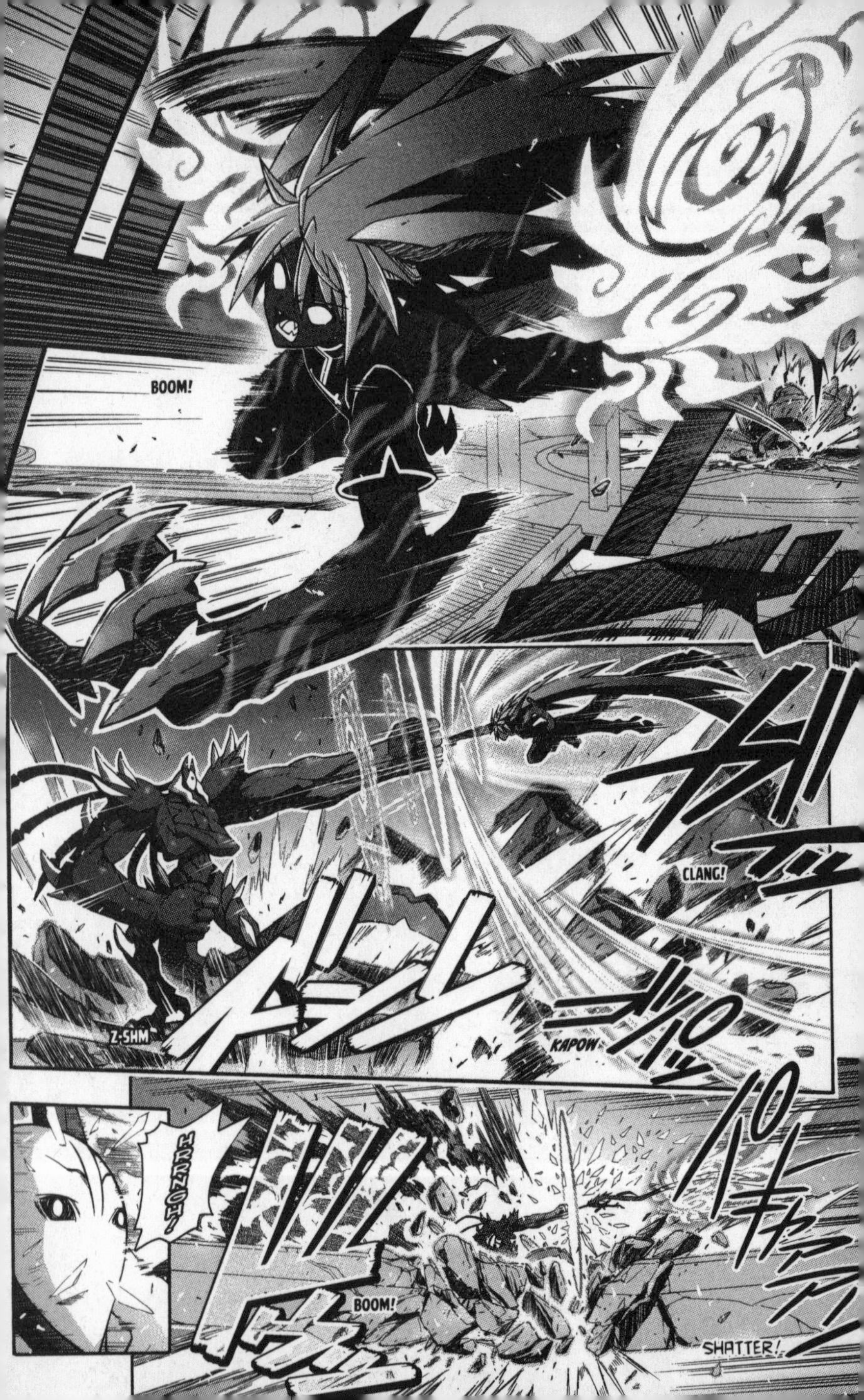
BOOM!
CLANG!
KAPOW
Z-SHM
SHATTER!
BOOM!
HRNNGH!

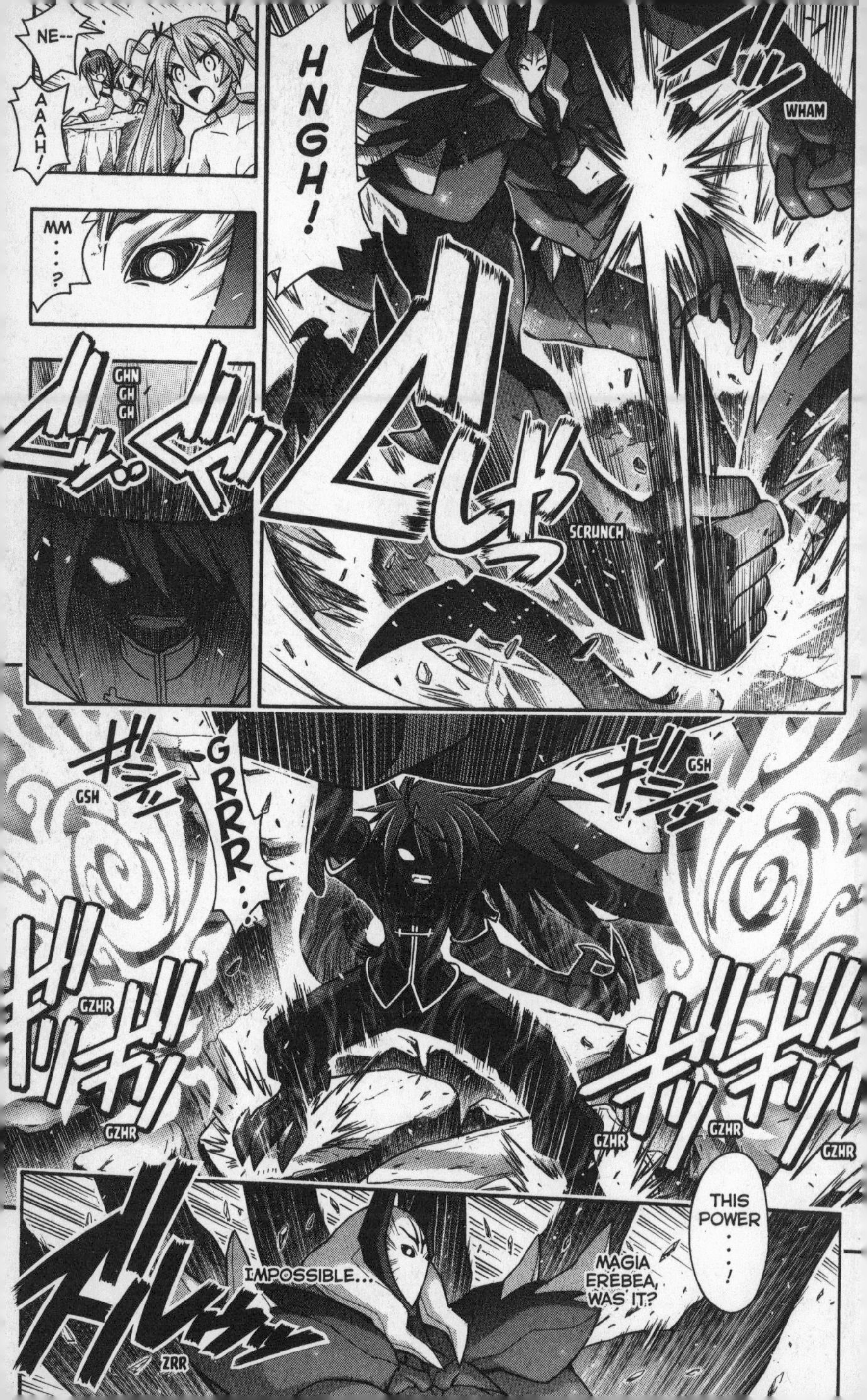
WHAM
HNGH!
SCRUNCH
NE--
AAAH!
MM...?
GHN GH GH
GSH
GRRR...
GSH
GZHR
GZHR
GZHR
GZHR
GZHR
THIS POWER...!
MAGIA EREBEA, WAS IT?
IMPOSSIBLE...
ZRR

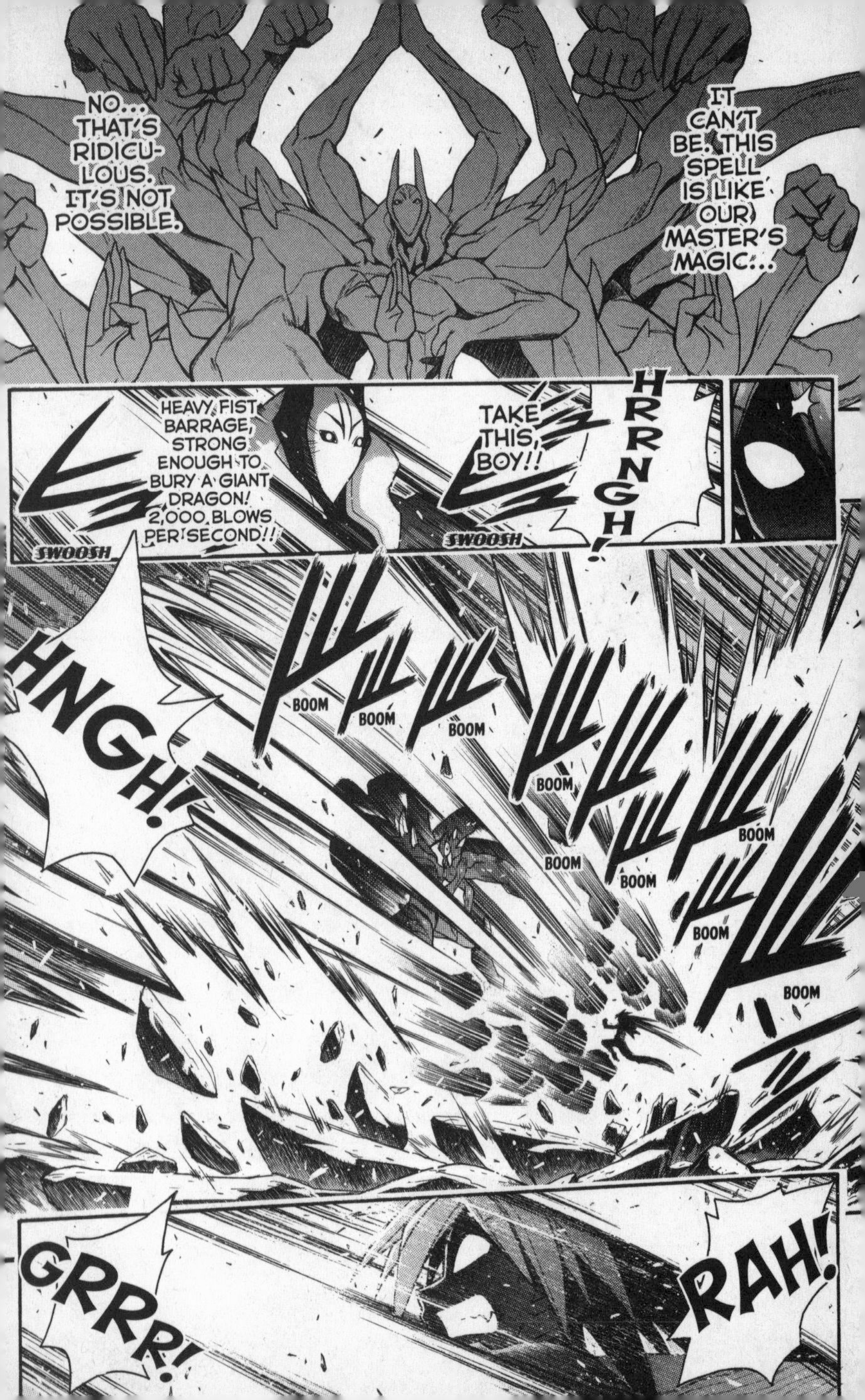
IT CAN'T BE. THIS SPELL IS LIKE OUR MASTER'S MAGIC...
NO... THAT'S RIDICU-LOUS. IT'S NOT POSSIBLE.
HRRNGH!
TAKE THIS, BOY!!
SWOOSH
HEAVY FIST BARRAGE, STRONG ENOUGH TO BURY A GIANT DRAGON! 2,000 BLOWS PER SECOND!!
SWOOSH
BOOM
BOOM
BOOM
BOOM
BOOM
BOOM
BOOM
BOOM
BOOM
HNGH!
RAH!
GRRR!

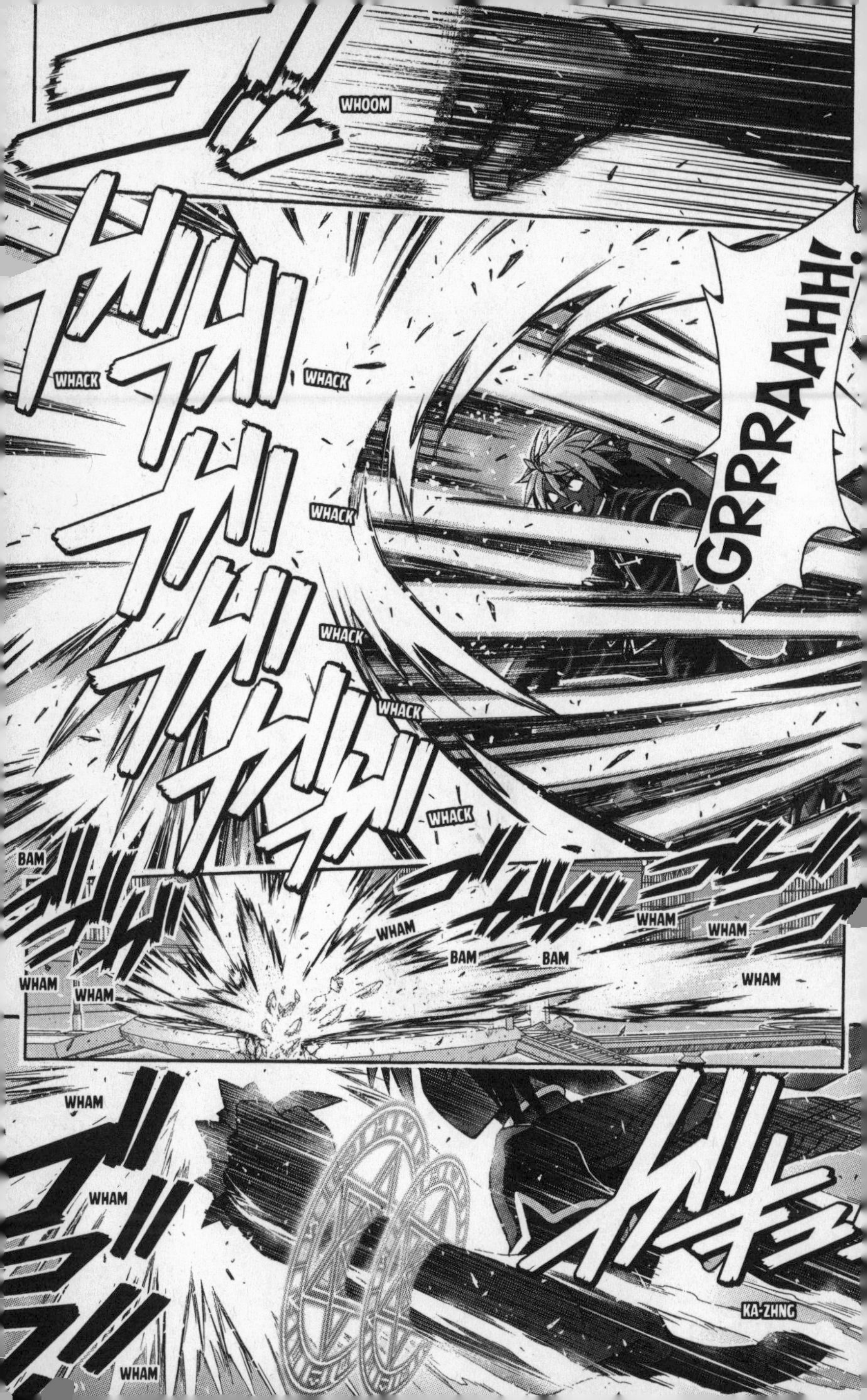

WHOOM
GRRRAAHH!
WHACK
WHACK
WHACK
WHACK
WHACK
WHACK
WHAM
WHAM
BAM
BAM
WHAM
WHAM
BAM
WHAM
WHAM
KA-ZHNG
WHAM
WHAM
WHAM

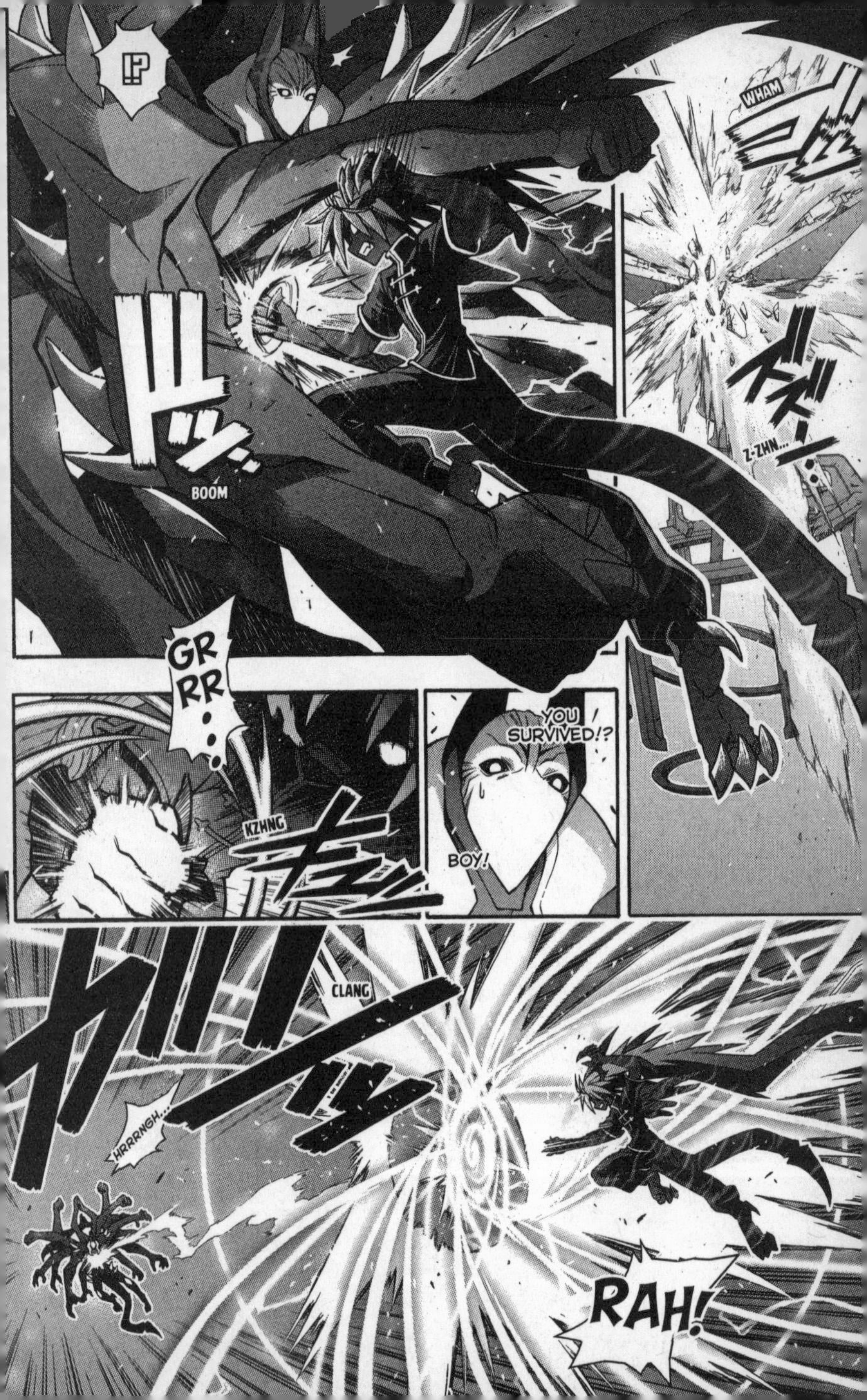
WHAM
Z-ZHN...
!?
BOOM
YOU SURVIVED!?
BOY!
GR RR...
KZHNG
CLANG
HRRRNGH...
RAH!

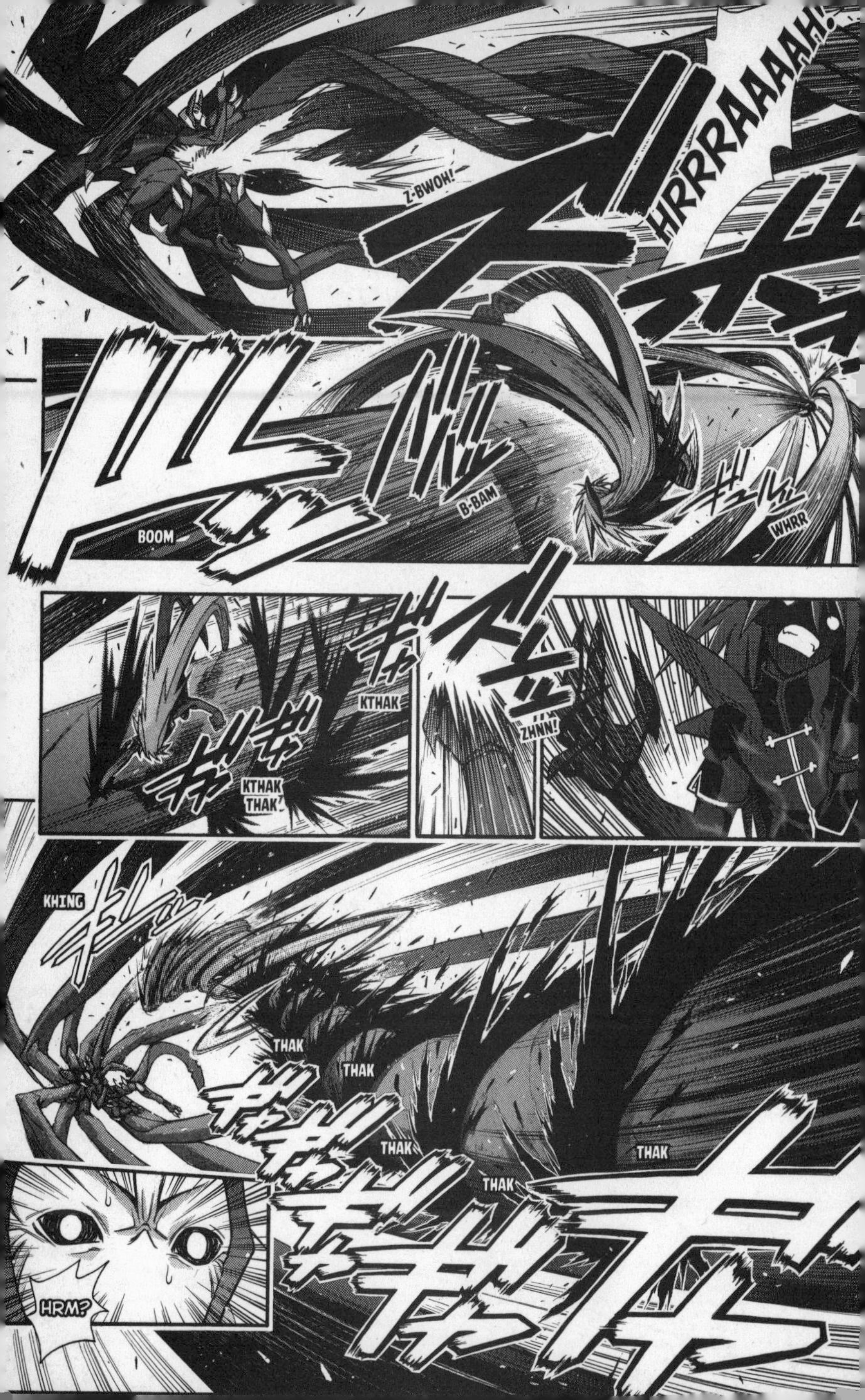
HRRAAAAH!
Z-BWOH!
WHRR
B-BAM
BOOM
ZHNN!
KTHAK
KTHAK
THAK
THAK
THAK
THAK
THAK
THAK
KHING
HRM?

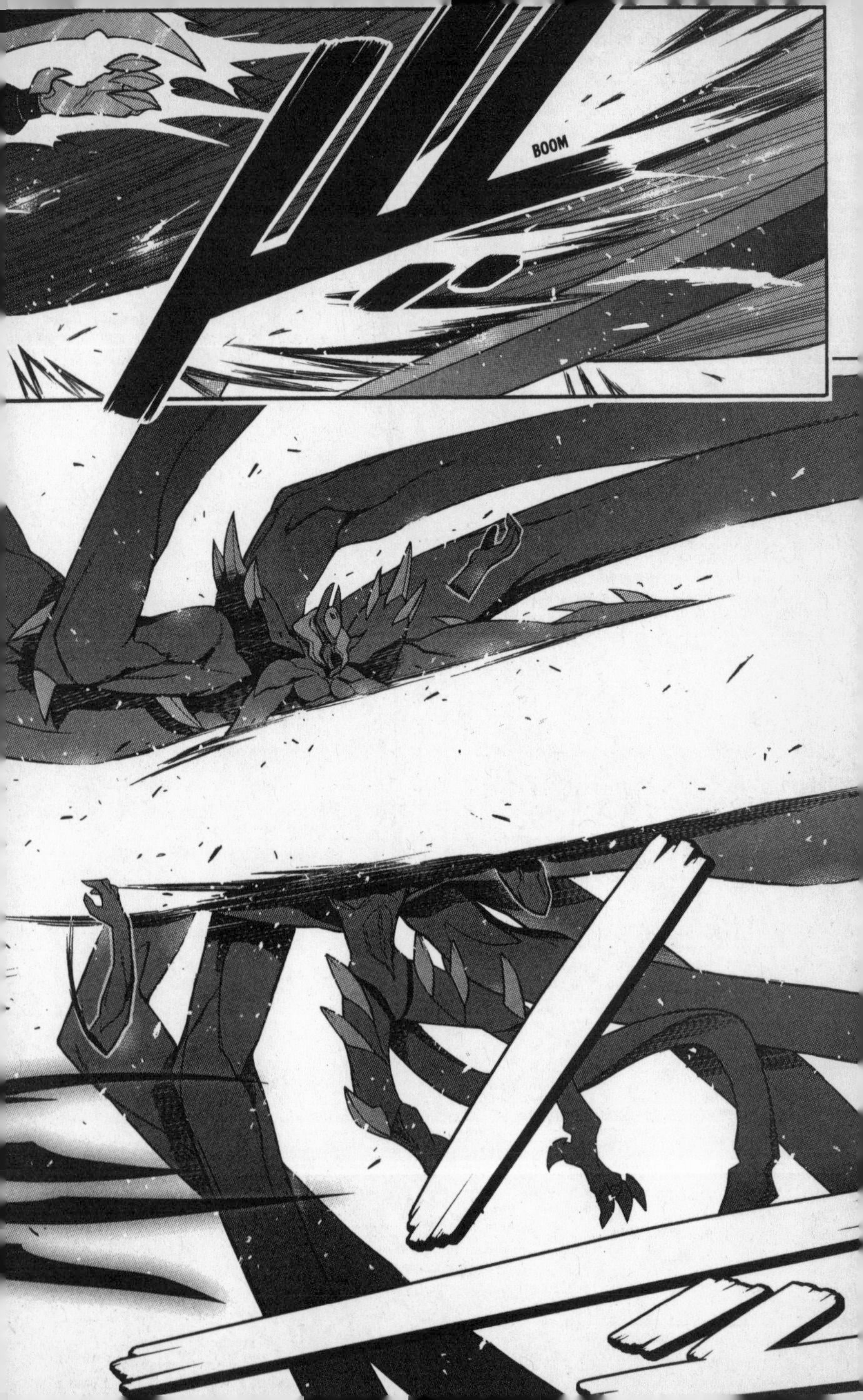
BOOM

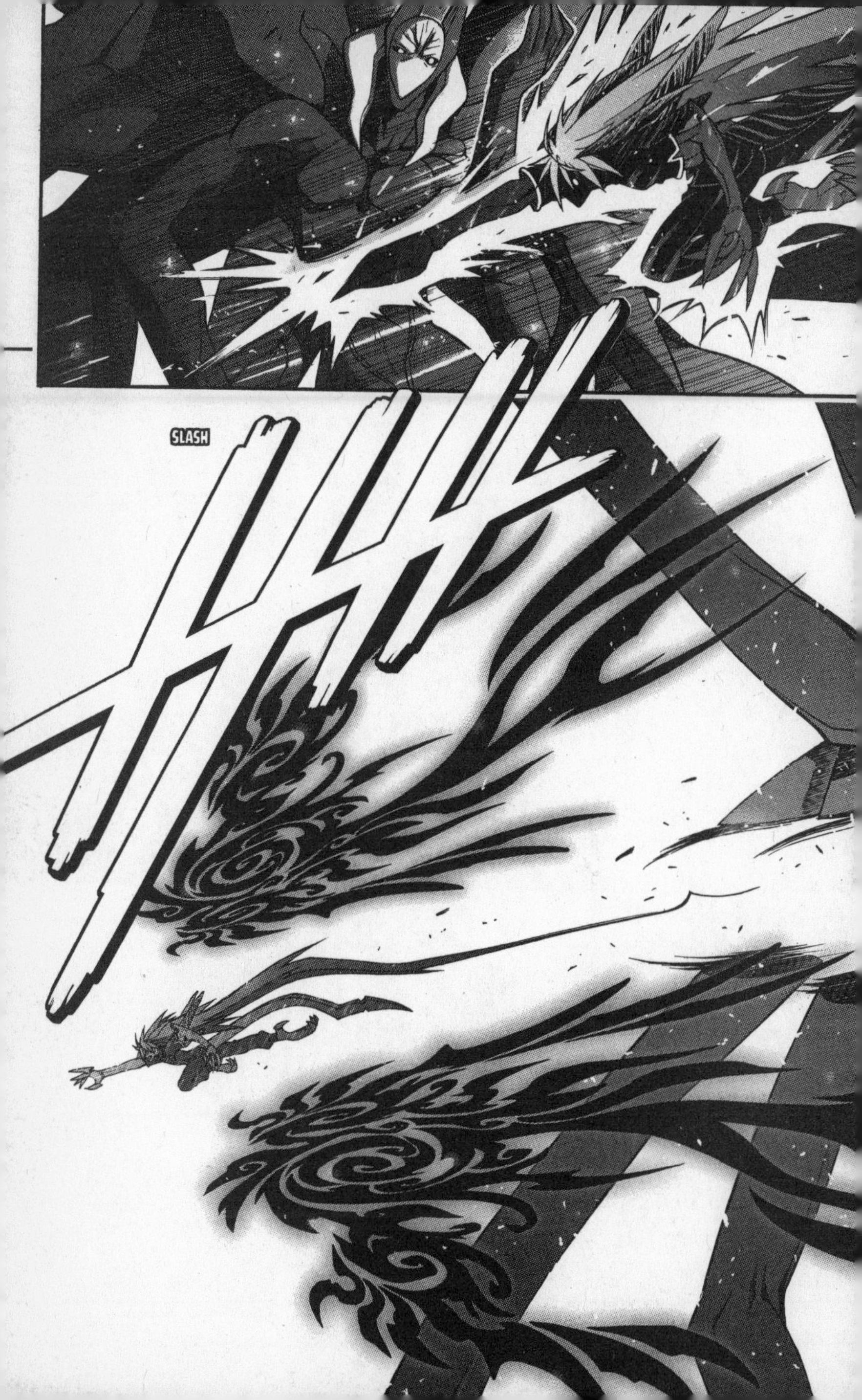
SLASH

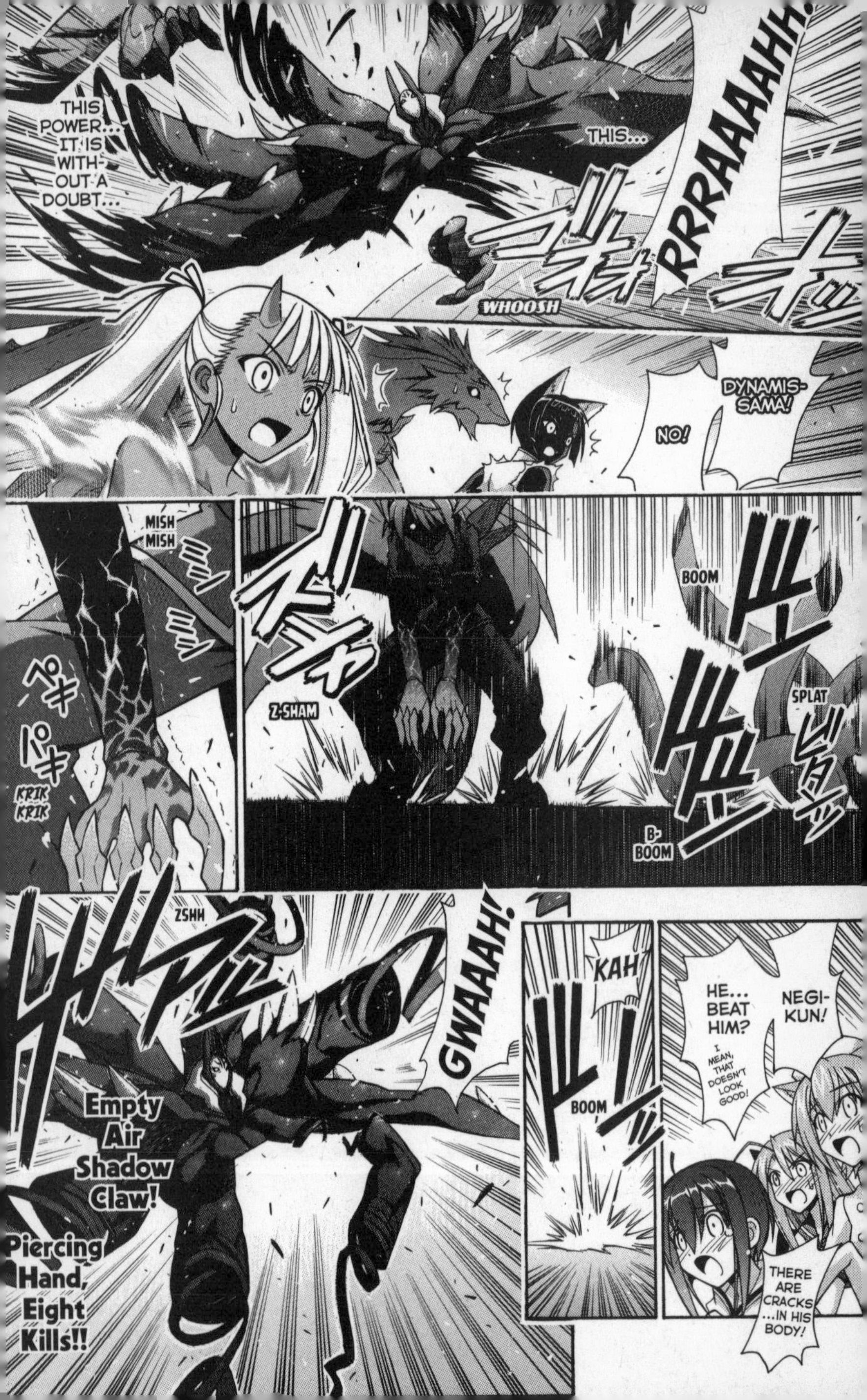
RRRAAAAHH!
THIS...
THIS POWER... IT IS WITH-OUT A DOUBT...
WHOOSH
DYNAMIS-SAMA!
NO!
BOOM
SPLAT
B-BOOM
Z-SHAM
MISH MISH
ペキ
パキ
KRIK KRIK
NEGI-KUN!
HE... BEAT HIM?
I MEAN, THAT DOESN'T LOOK GOOD!
THERE ARE CRACKS ...IN HIS BODY!
KAH
BOOM
GWAAAH!
ZSHH
Empty Air Shadow Claw!
Piercing Hand, Eight Kills!!

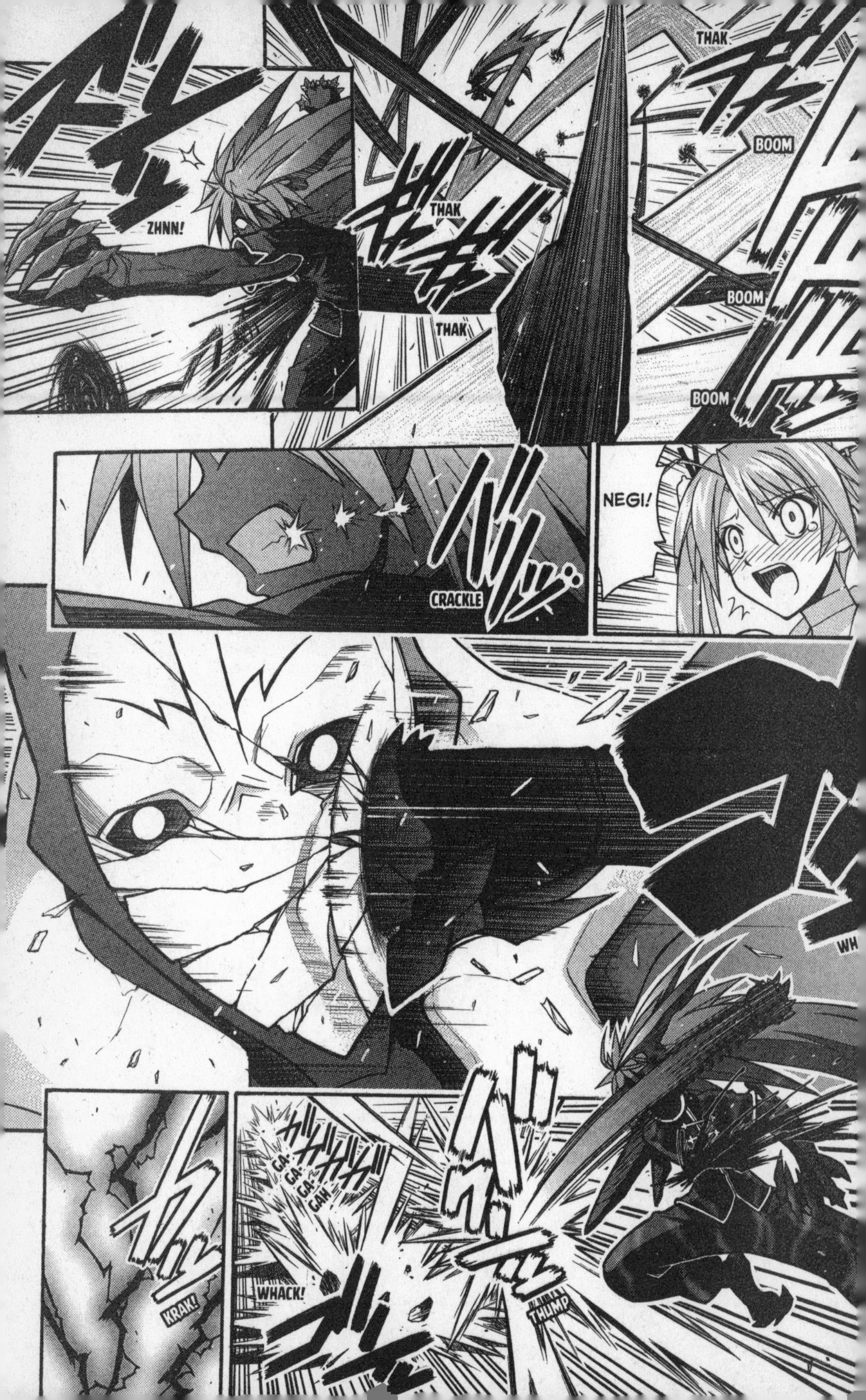

THAK
BOOM
BOOM
BOOM
THAK
THAK
ZHNN!
NEGI!
CRACKLE
WH
THUMP
GA-
GA-
GA-
GAH
WHACK!
KRAK!

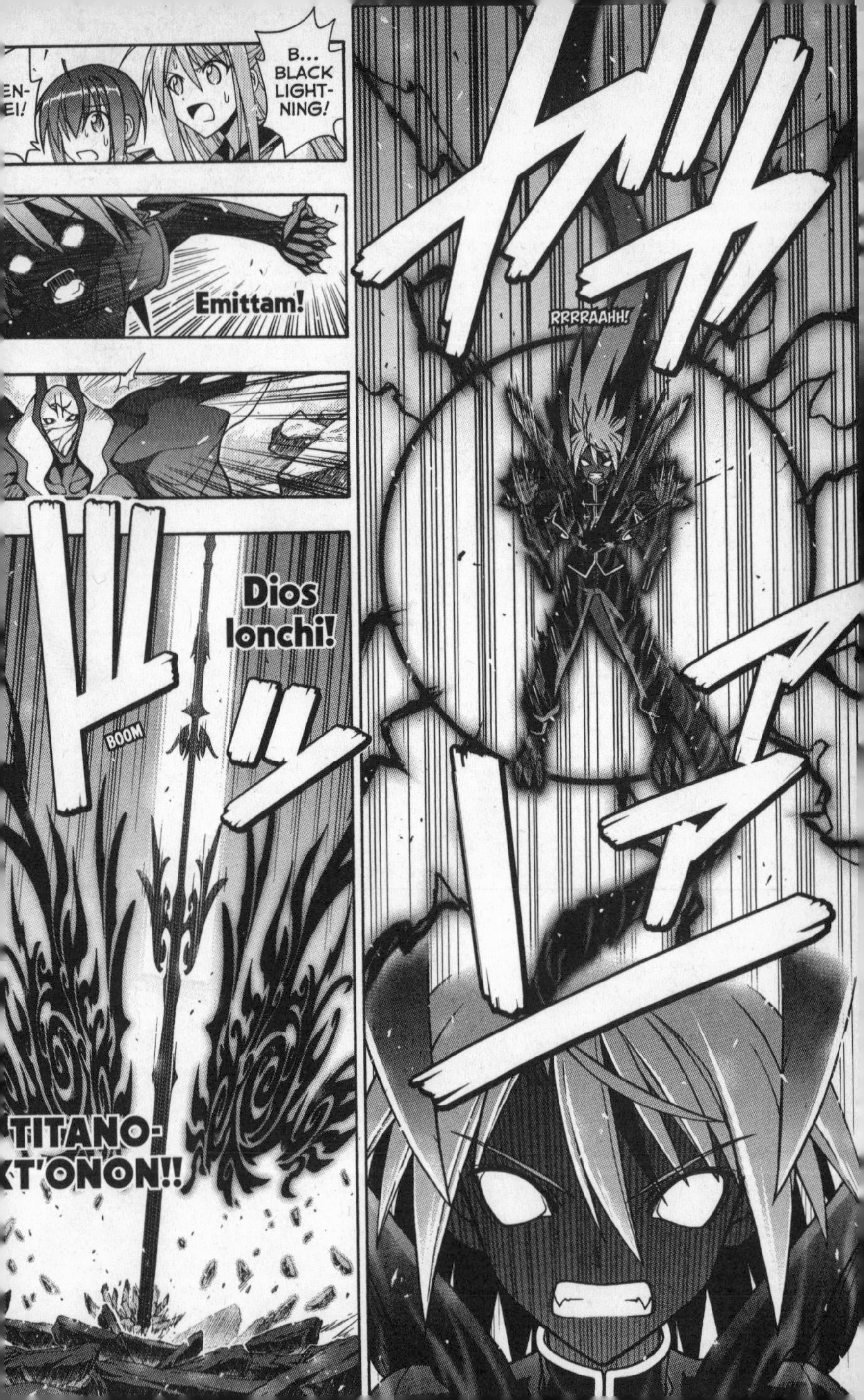
RRRRAAHH!
B... BLACK LIGHT-NING!
EN-EI!
Emittam!
Dios lonchi!
BOOM
TITANO-T'ONON!!

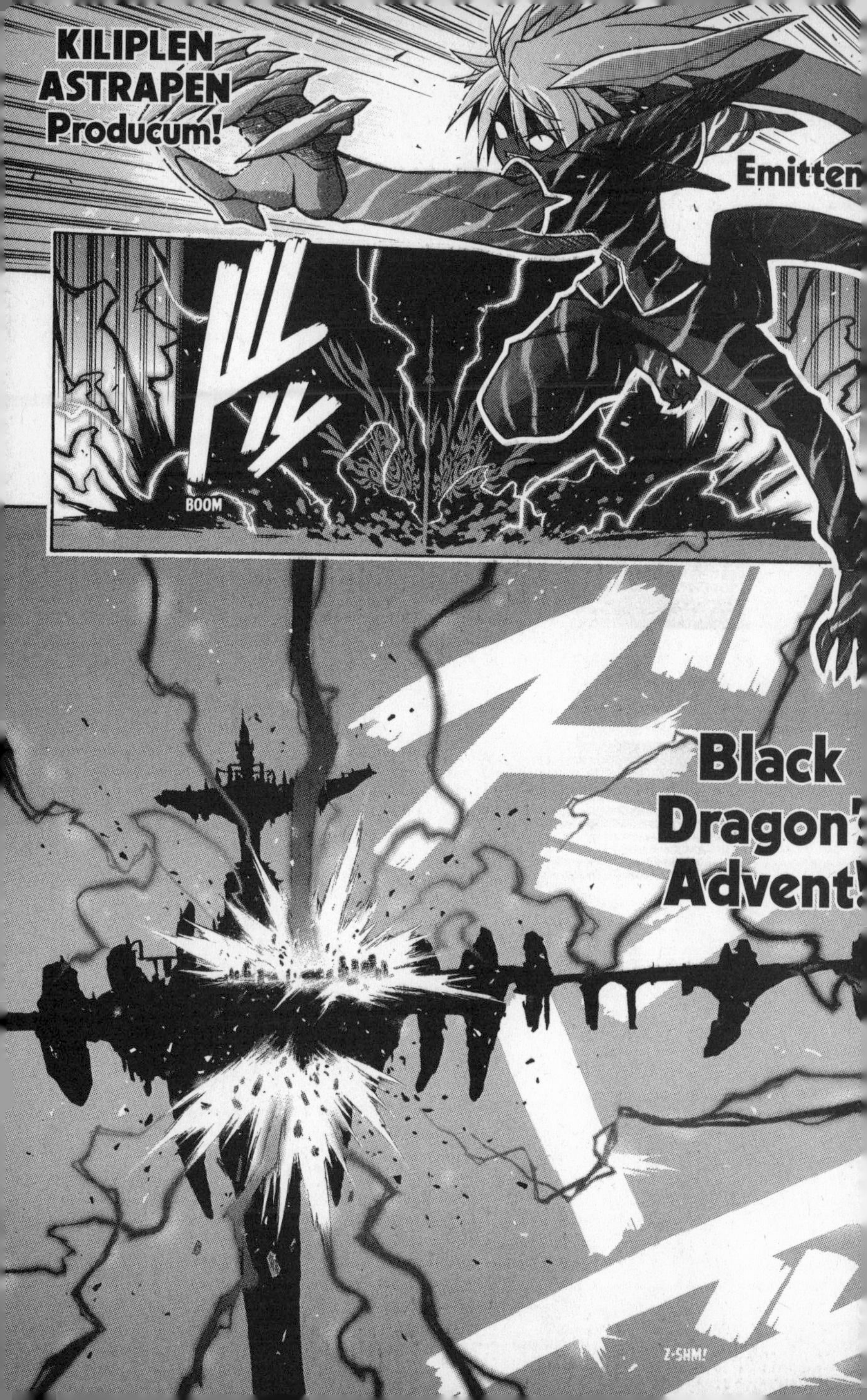
KILIPLEN ASTRAPEN Producum!
Emitten
BOOM
Black Dragon' Advent!
Z-SHM!

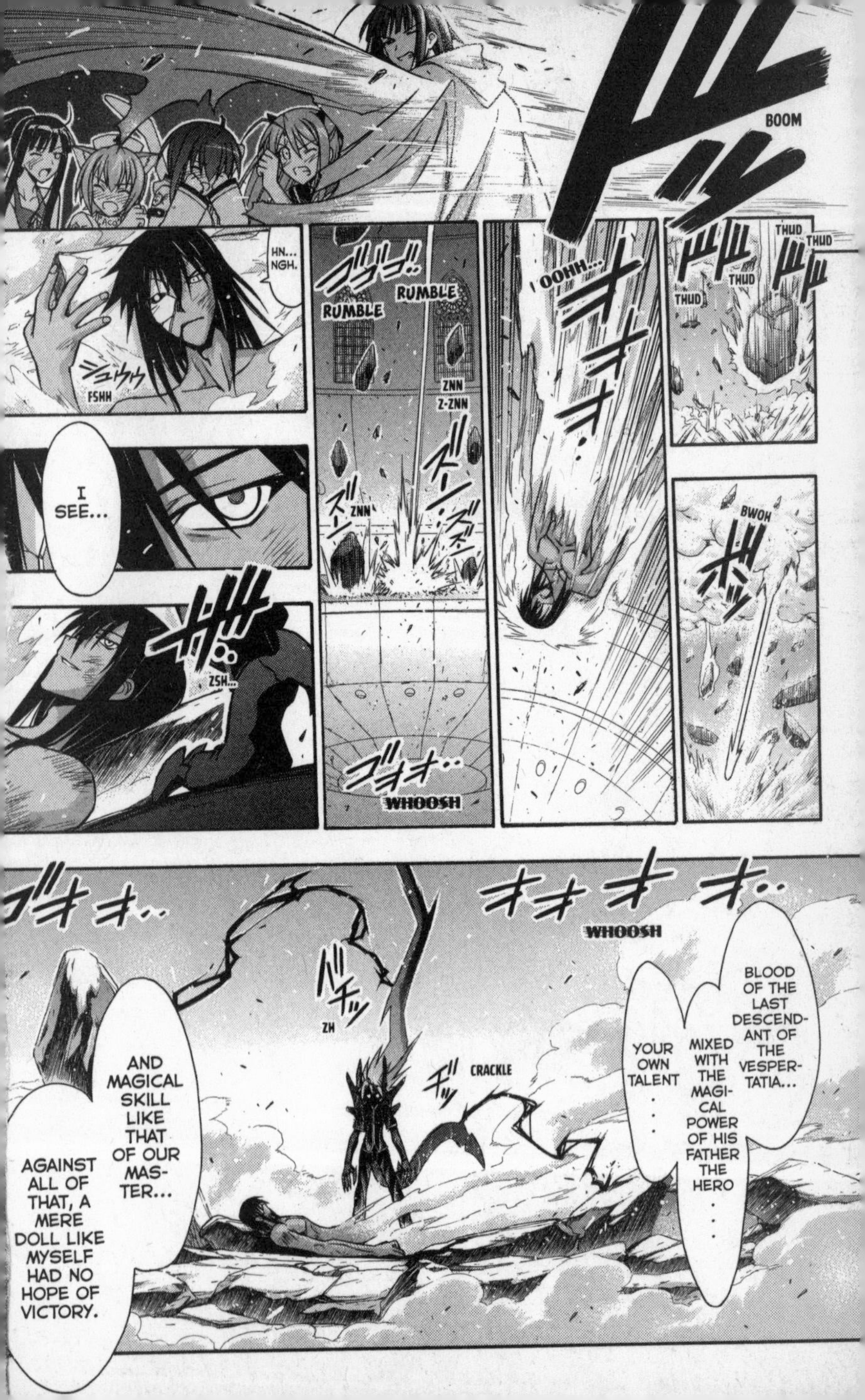
BOOM
THUD THUD
THUD THUD
BWOH
OOHH...
RUMBLE
RUMBLE
ZNN
Z-ZNN
ZNN
WHOOSH
HN... NGH.
FSHH
I SEE...
ZSH...
WHOOSH
BLOOD OF THE LAST DESCENDANT OF THE VESPERTATIA...
MIXED WITH THE MAGICAL POWER OF HIS FATHER THE HERO...
YOUR OWN TALENT...
CRACKLE
ZH
AND MAGICAL SKILL LIKE THAT OF OUR MASTER...
AGAINST ALL OF THAT, A MERE DOLL LIKE MYSELF HAD NO HOPE OF VICTORY.

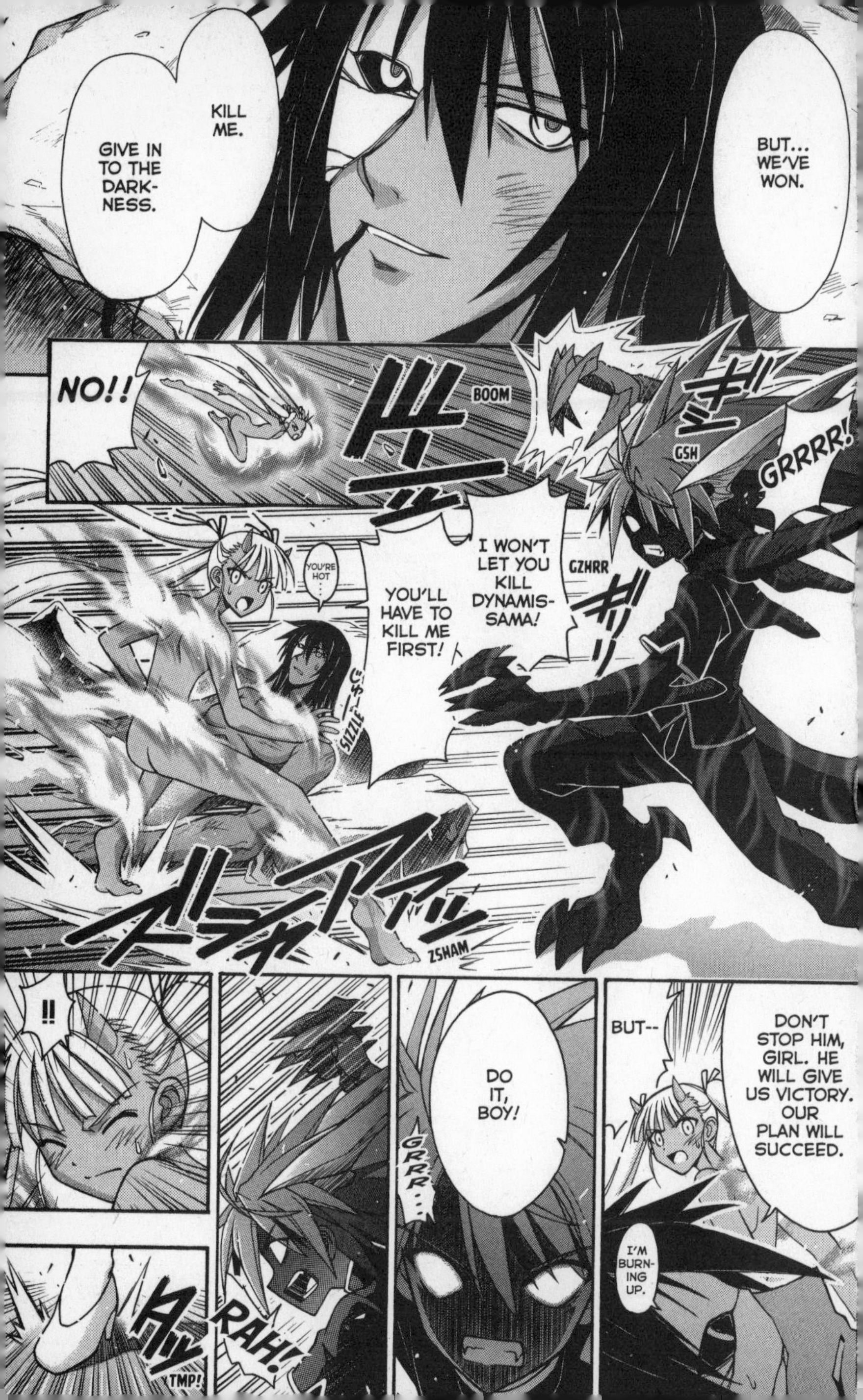
BUT... WE'VE WON.
KILL ME.
GIVE IN TO THE DARKNESS.
GRRRR!
GSH
BOOM
NO!!
I WON'T LET YOU KILL DYNAMIS-SAMA!
GZHRR
YOU'LL HAVE TO KILL ME FIRST!
YOU'RE HOT...
SIZZLE
ZSHAM
DON'T STOP HIM, GIRL. HE WILL GIVE US VICTORY. OUR PLAN WILL SUCCEED.
BUT--
I'M BURNING UP.
DO IT, BOY!
GRRR...
RAH!
!!
TMP!

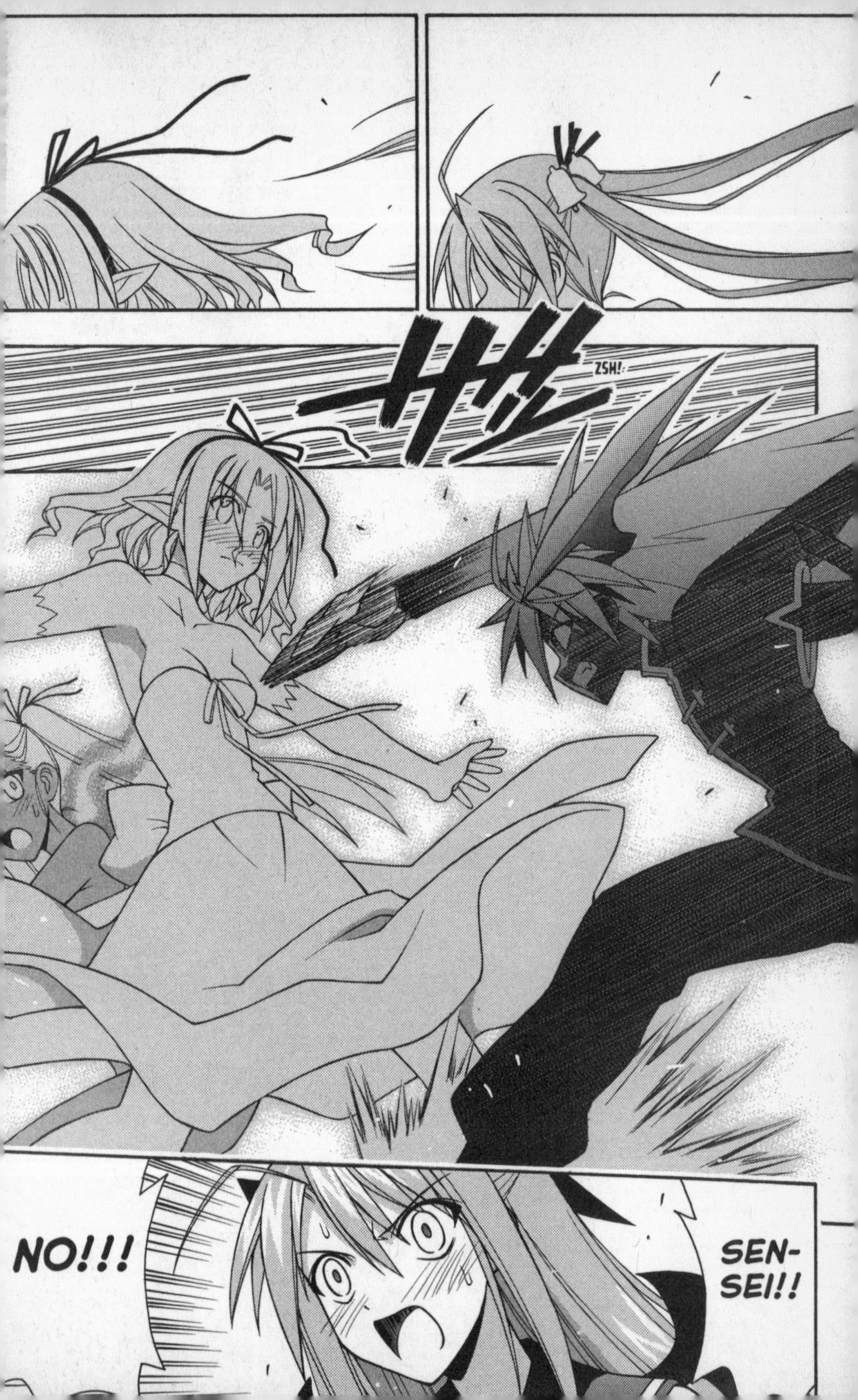
ZSH!
SEN-
SEI!!
NO!!!

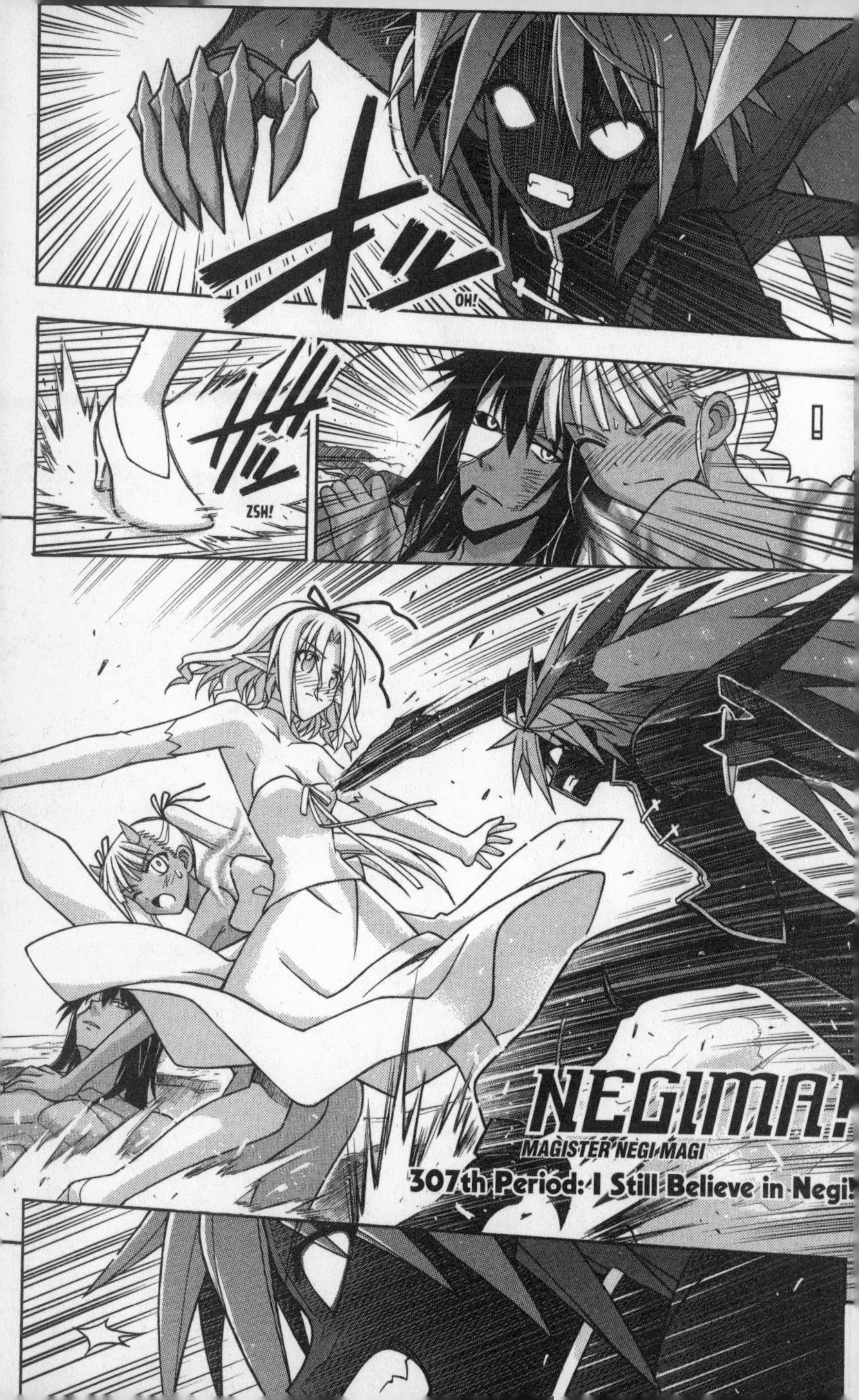
OH!
!
ZSH!
NEGIMA!
MAGISTER NEGI MAGI
307th Period: I Still Believe in Negi!

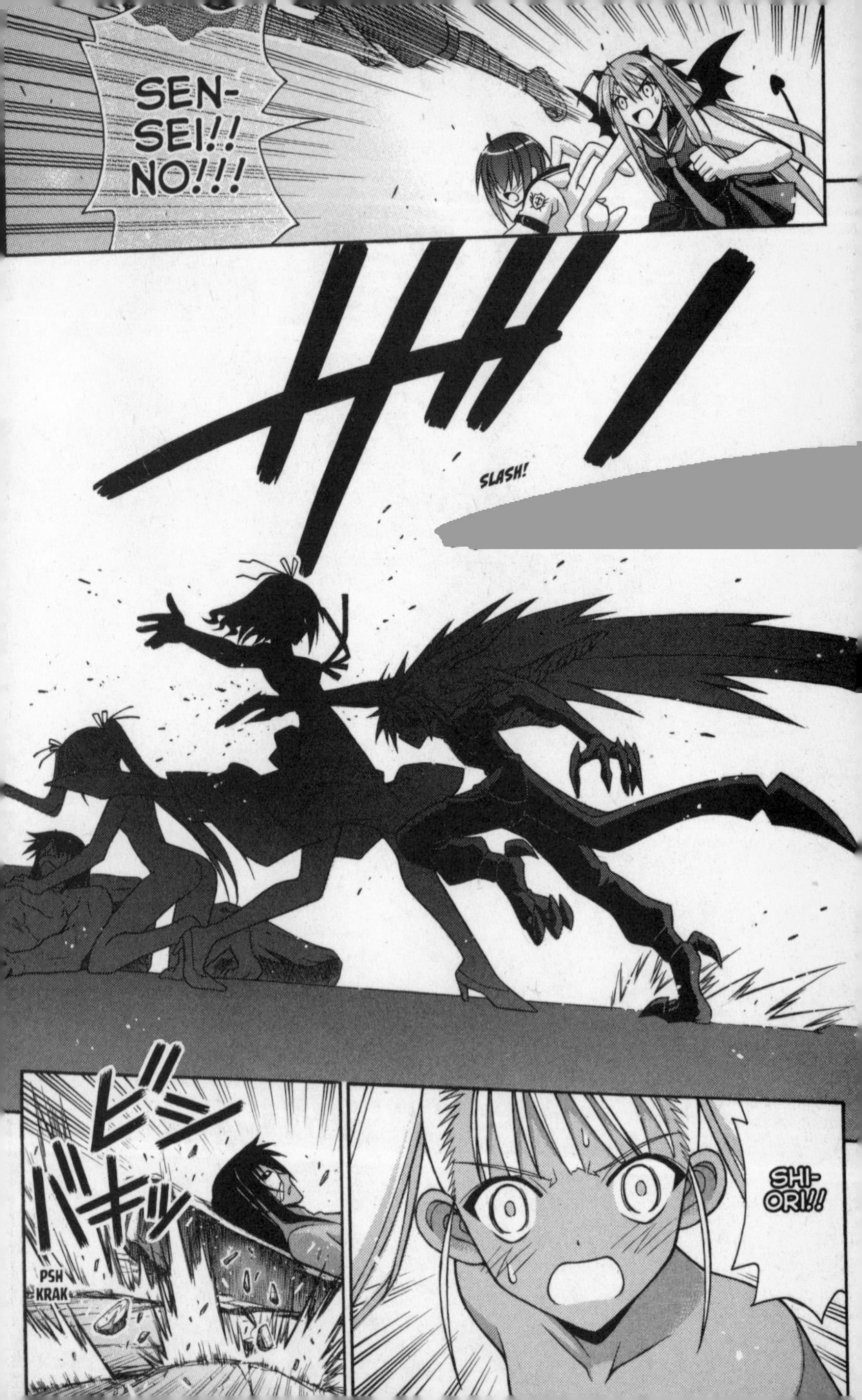
SEN-SEI!! NO!!!
SLASH!
SHI-ORI!!
PSH KRAK

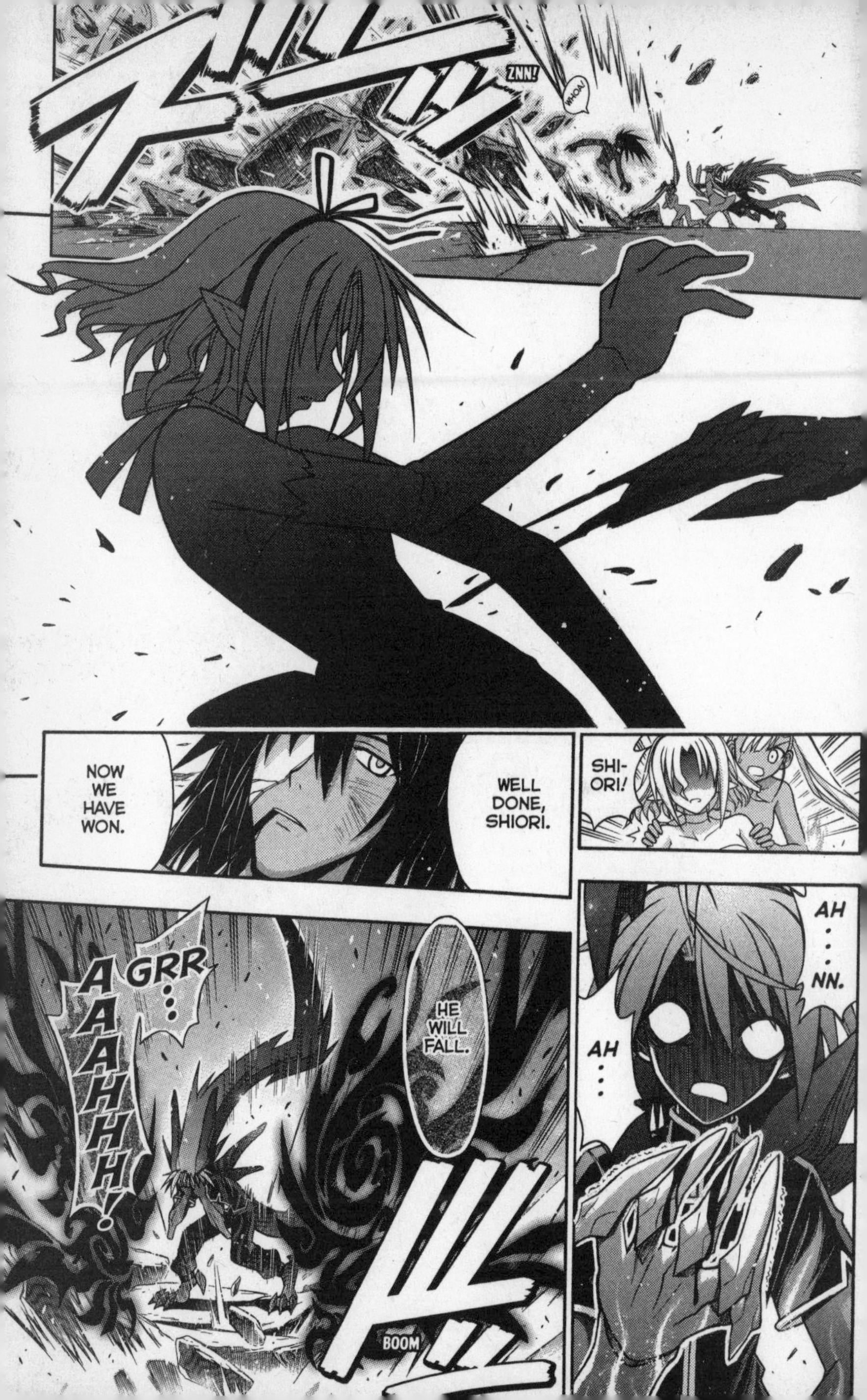
ZNN!
WHOA!
SHI-ORI!
WELL DONE, SHIORI.
NOW WE HAVE WON.
AH... NN.
AH...
HE WILL FALL.
GRR...
AAAAHHHH!
BOOM

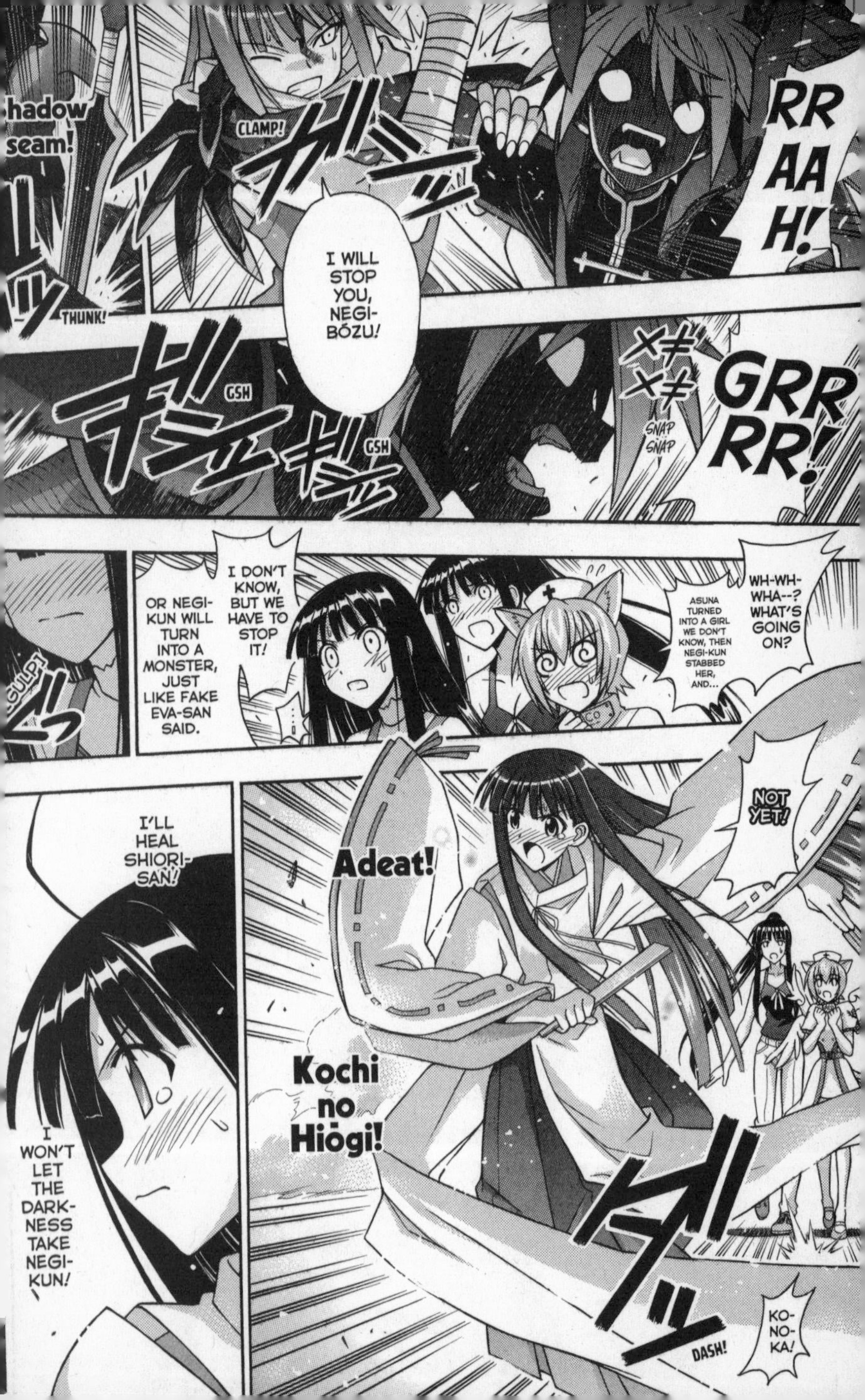
RRAAH!
CLAMP!
hadow seam!
THUNK!
I WILL STOP YOU, NEGI-BŌZU!
GRRRR!
SNAP SNAP
GSH
GSH
WH-WH-WHA--? WHAT'S GOING ON?
ASUNA TURNED INTO A GIRL WE DON'T KNOW, THEN NEGI-KUN STABBED HER, AND...
I DON'T KNOW, BUT WE HAVE TO STOP IT!
OR NEGI-KUN WILL TURN INTO A MONSTER, JUST LIKE FAKE EVA-SAN SAID.
GULP!
NOT YET!
Adeat!
Kochi no Hiōgi!
KO-NO-KA!
DASH!
I'LL HEAL SHIORI-SAN!
I WON'T LET THE DARKNESS TAKE NEGI-KUN!

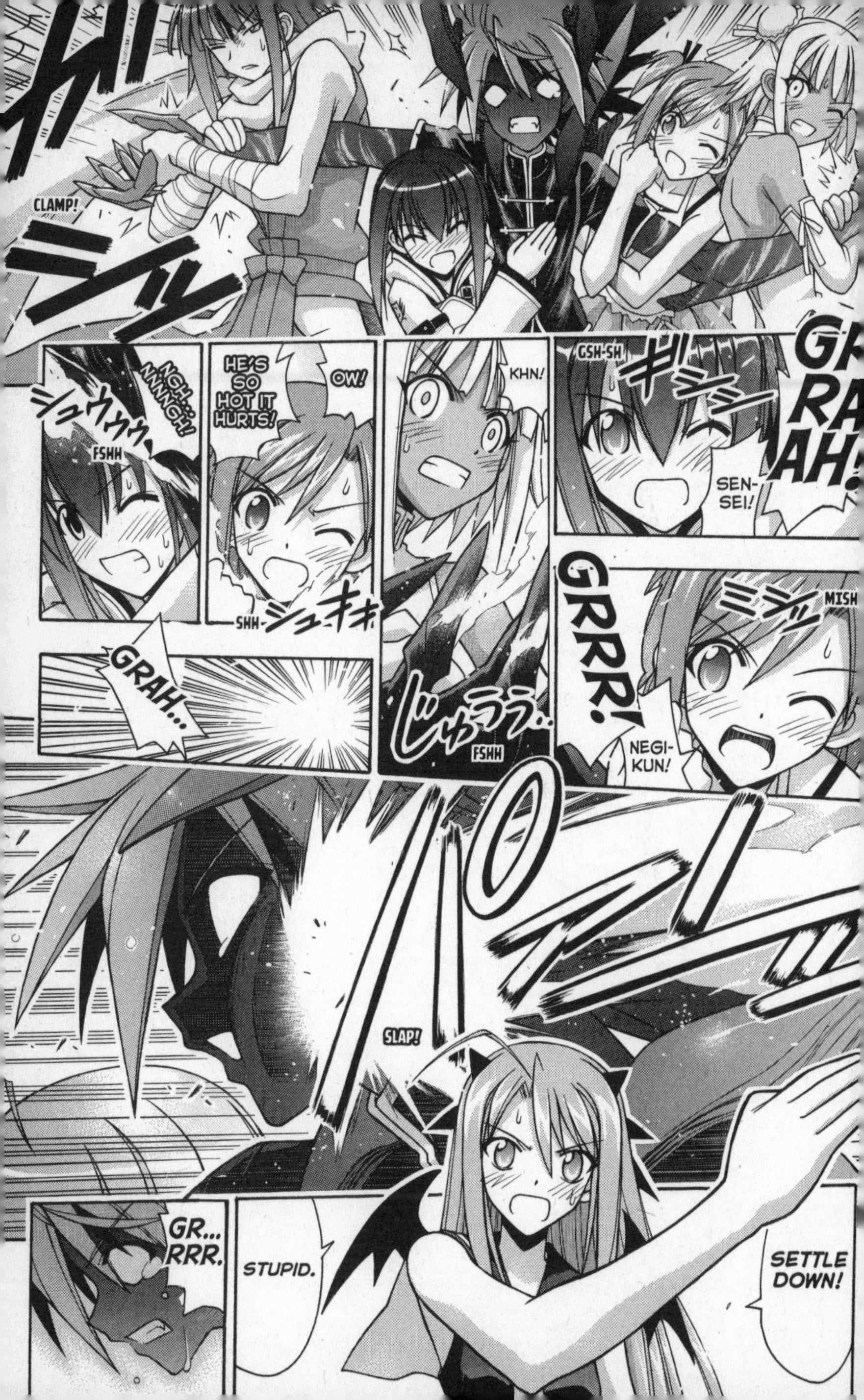
CLAMP!
GR RA AH!
SEN-SEI!
GSH-SH
KHN!
OW!
HE'S SO HOT IT HURTS!
SHH-
NGH... NNNNGH!
FSHH
MISH
GRRR!
NEGI-KUN!
FSHH
GRAH...
SLAP!
SETTLE DOWN!
STUPID.
GR... RRR.

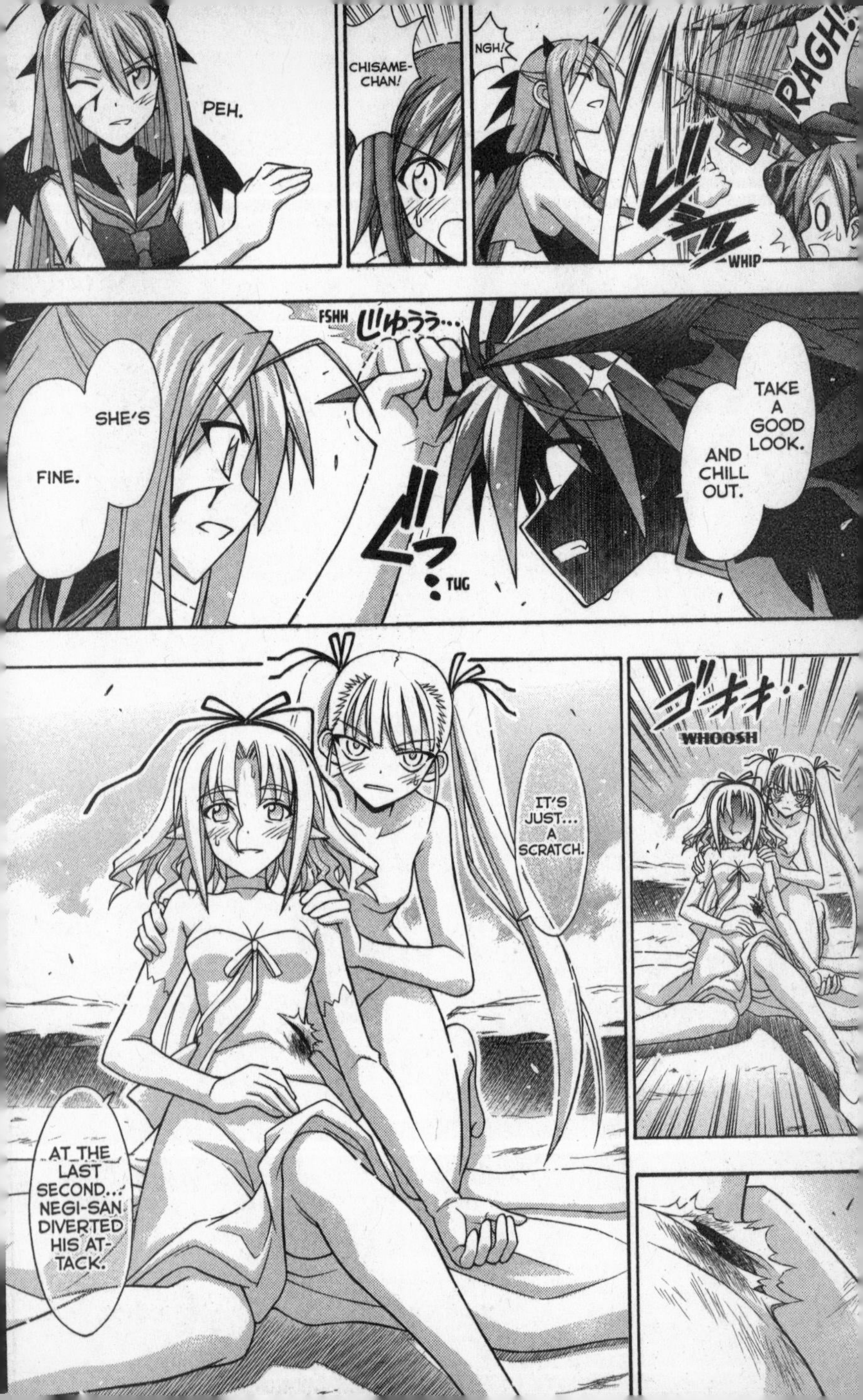
RAGH!
WHIP
NGH!
CHISAME-CHAN!
PEH.
TAKE A GOOD LOOK.
AND CHILL OUT.
FSHH
TUG
SHE'S FINE.
WHOOSH
IT'S JUST... A SCRATCH.
AT THE LAST SECOND... NEGI-SAN DIVERTED HIS AT-TACK.

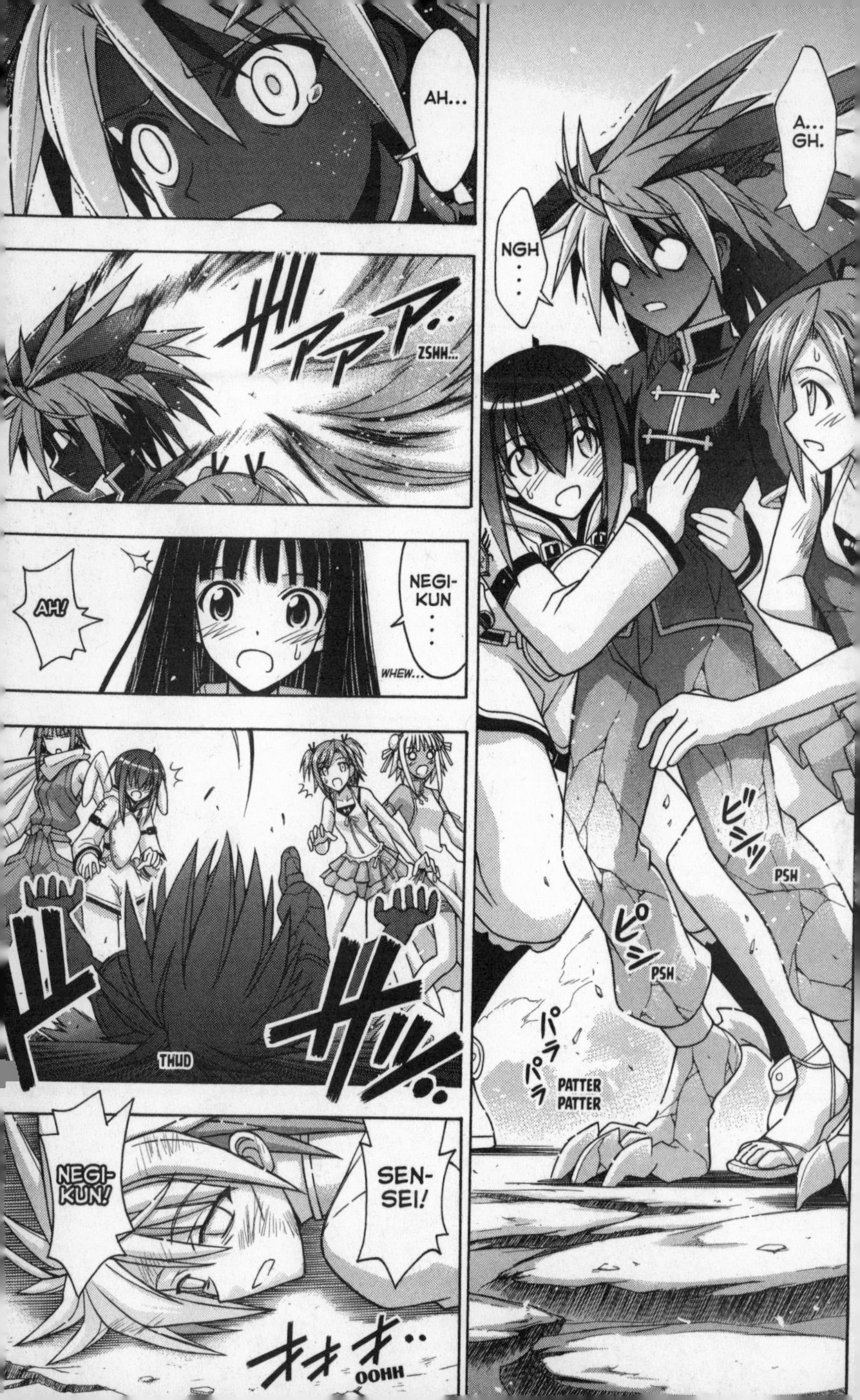
A... GH.
NGH ...
ビシッ
PSH
ピシッ
PSH
パラパラ
PATTER PATTER
AH...
ザァァァ..
ZSHH...
NEGI-KUN ...
AH!
WHEW...
ドサッ
THUD
SEN-SEI!
NEGI-KUN!
オォォ..
OOHH

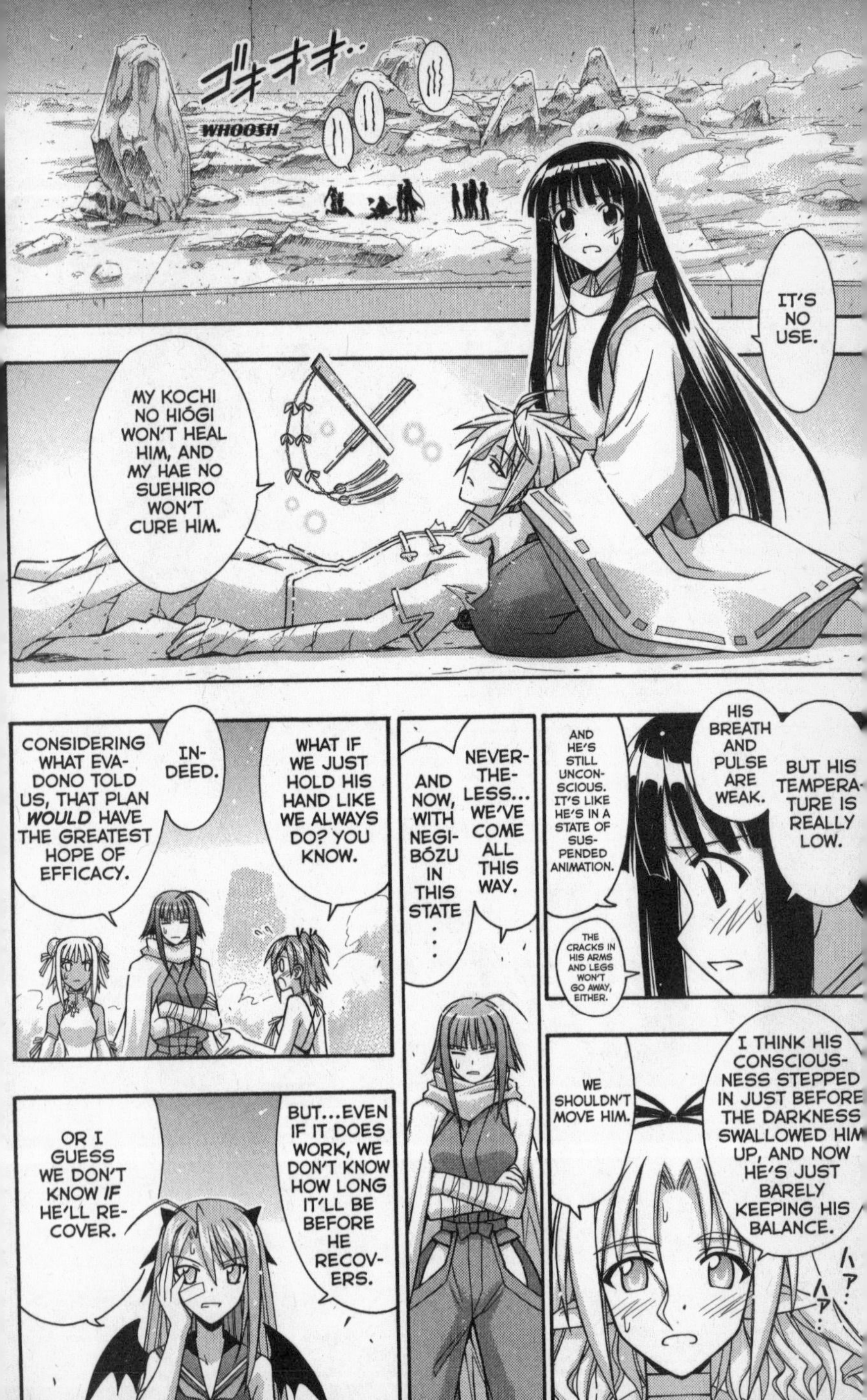
ゴォオオ…
WHOOSH
IT'S NO USE.
MY KOCHI NO HIÓGI WON'T HEAL HIM, AND MY HAE NO SUEHIRO WON'T CURE HIM.
HIS BREATH AND PULSE ARE WEAK.
BUT HIS TEMPERATURE IS REALLY LOW.
AND HE'S STILL UNCONSCIOUS. IT'S LIKE HE'S IN A STATE OF SUSPENDED ANIMATION.
THE CRACKS IN HIS ARMS AND LEGS WON'T GO AWAY, EITHER.
NEVERTHELESS... WE'VE COME ALL THIS WAY.
AND NOW, WITH NEGI-BÓZU IN THIS STATE...
WHAT IF WE JUST HOLD HIS HAND LIKE WE ALWAYS DO? YOU KNOW.
INDEED.
CONSIDERING WHAT EVA-DONO TOLD US, THAT PLAN *WOULD* HAVE THE GREATEST HOPE OF EFFICACY.
I THINK HIS CONSCIOUSNESS STEPPED IN JUST BEFORE THE DARKNESS SWALLOWED HIM UP, AND NOW HE'S JUST BARELY KEEPING HIS BALANCE.
ハァ… ハァ…
WE SHOULDN'T MOVE HIM.
BUT...EVEN IF IT DOES WORK, WE DON'T KNOW HOW LONG IT'LL BE BEFORE HE RECOVERS.
OR I GUESS WE DON'T KNOW *IF* HE'LL RECOVER.

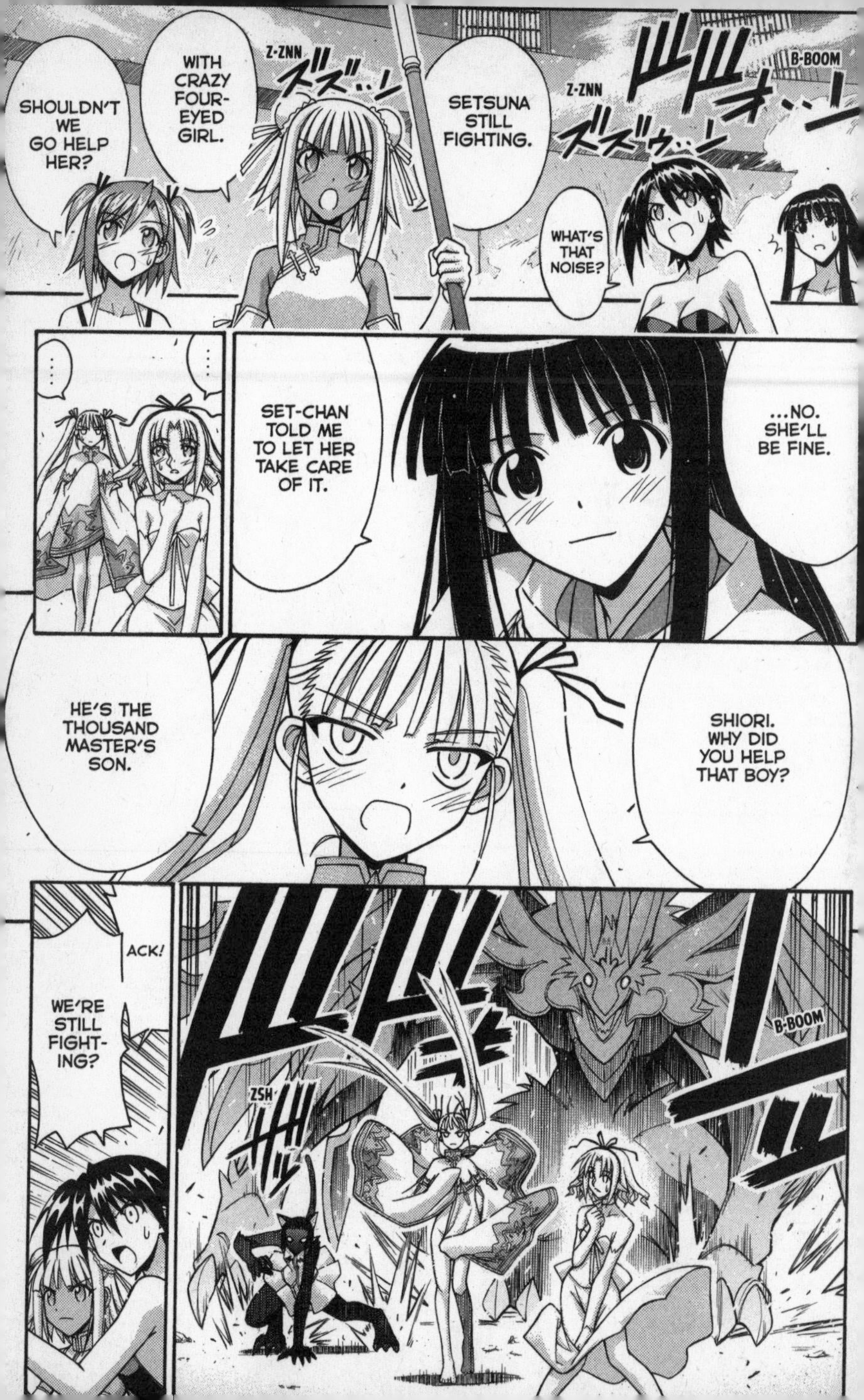
B-BOOM
Z-ZNN
SETSUNA STILL FIGHTING.
Z-ZNN
WITH CRAZY FOUR-EYED GIRL.
SHOULDN'T WE GO HELP HER?
WHAT'S THAT NOISE?
...NO. SHE'LL BE FINE.
SET-CHAN TOLD ME TO LET HER TAKE CARE OF IT.
...
...
SHIORI. WHY DID YOU HELP THAT BOY?
HE'S THE THOUSAND MASTER'S SON.
B-BOOM
ZSH
ACK!
WE'RE STILL FIGHT-ING?

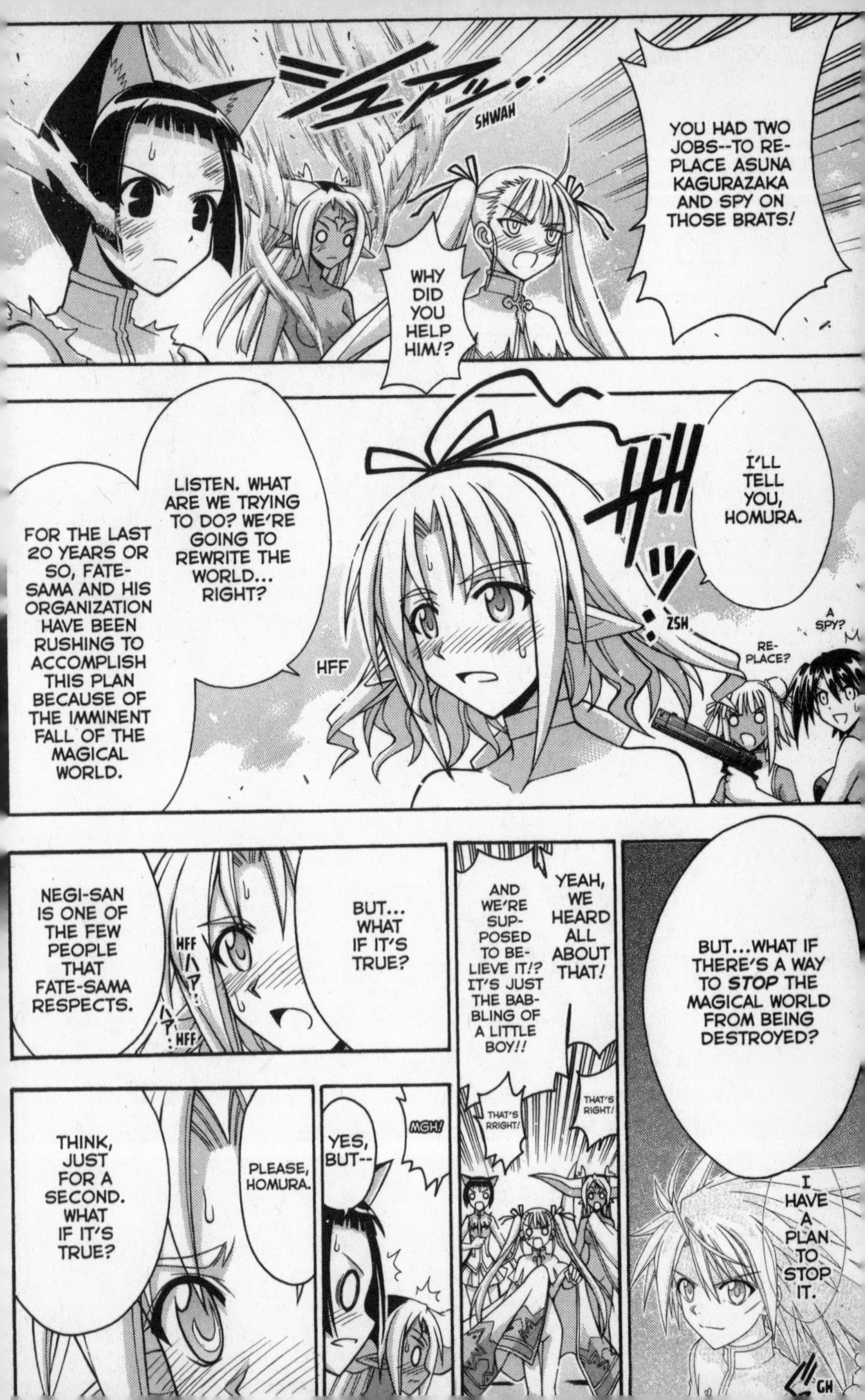
YOU HAD TWO JOBS--TO RE-PLACE ASUNA KAGURAZAKA AND SPY ON THOSE BRATS!
SHWAH
WHY DID YOU HELP HIM!?
I'LL TELL YOU, HOMURA.
ZSH
A SPY?
RE-PLACE?
LISTEN. WHAT ARE WE TRYING TO DO? WE'RE GOING TO REWRITE THE WORLD... RIGHT?
HFF
FOR THE LAST 20 YEARS OR SO, FATE-SAMA AND HIS ORGANIZATION HAVE BEEN RUSHING TO ACCOMPLISH THIS PLAN BECAUSE OF THE IMMINENT FALL OF THE MAGICAL WORLD.
BUT...WHAT IF THERE'S A WAY TO STOP THE MAGICAL WORLD FROM BEING DESTROYED?
I HAVE A PLAN TO STOP IT.
GH
YEAH, WE HEARD ALL ABOUT THAT!
AND WE'RE SUP-POSED TO BE-LIEVE IT!? IT'S JUST THE BAB-BLING OF A LITTLE BOY!!
THAT'S RIGHT!
THAT'S RRIGHT!
BUT... WHAT IF IT'S TRUE?
HFF
HFF
NEGI-SAN IS ONE OF THE FEW PEOPLE THAT FATE-SAMA RESPECTS.
MGH!
YES, BUT--
PLEASE, HOMURA.
THINK, JUST FOR A SECOND. WHAT IF IT'S TRUE?

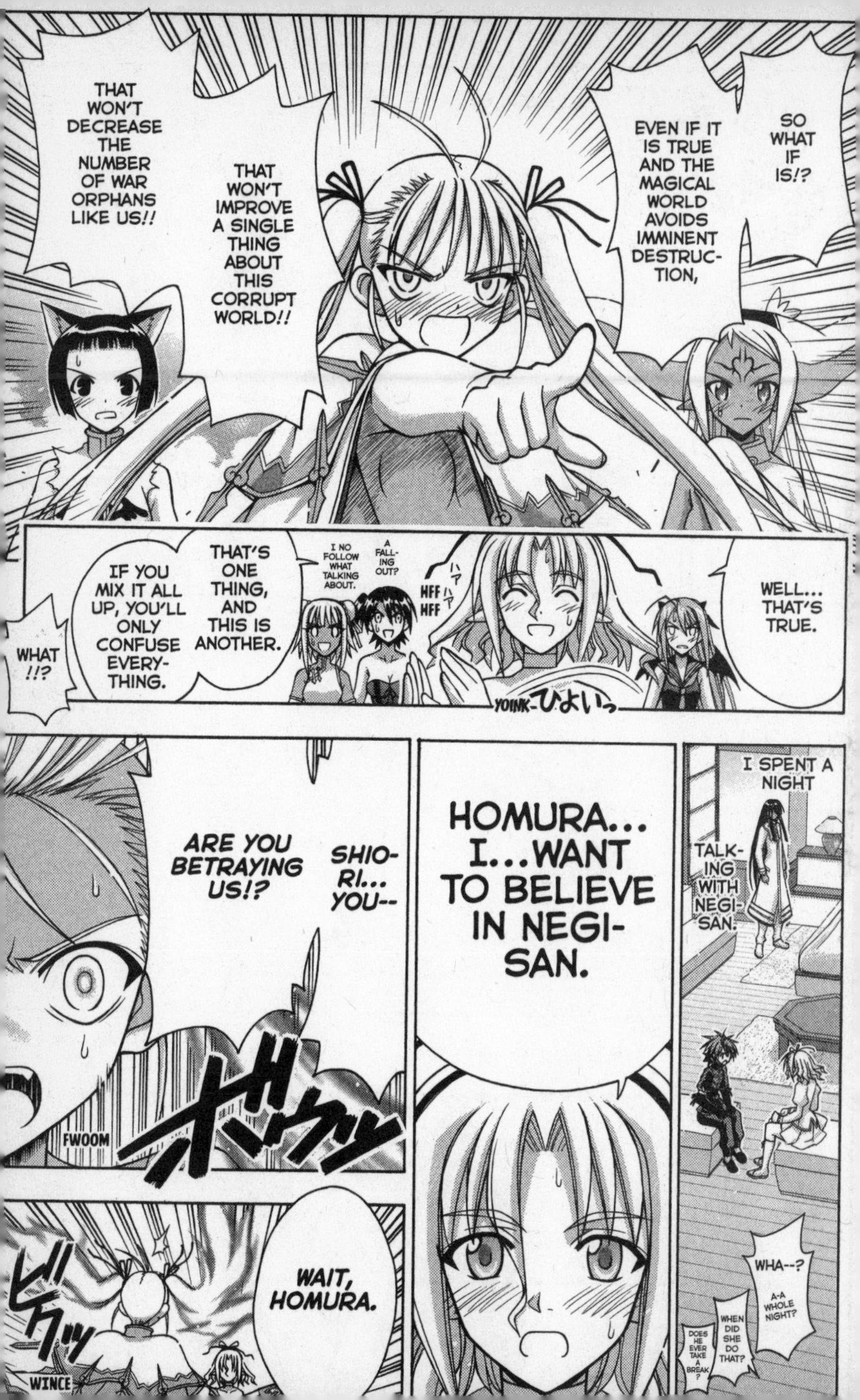
SO WHAT IF IS!?
EVEN IF IT IS TRUE AND THE MAGICAL WORLD AVOIDS IMMINENT DESTRUCTION,
THAT WON'T IMPROVE A SINGLE THING ABOUT THIS CORRUPT WORLD!!
THAT WON'T DECREASE THE NUMBER OF WAR ORPHANS LIKE US!!
WELL... THAT'S TRUE.
YOINK-ひょいっ
HFF HFF
A FALLING OUT?
I NO FOLLOW WHAT TALKING ABOUT.
THAT'S ONE THING, AND THIS IS ANOTHER.
IF YOU MIX IT ALL UP, YOU'LL ONLY CONFUSE EVERYTHING.
WHAT!!?
I SPENT A NIGHT TALKING WITH NEGI-SAN.
WHA--?
A-A WHOLE NIGHT?
WHEN DID SHE DO THAT?
DOES HE EVER TAKE A BREAK?
HOMURA... I...WANT TO BELIEVE IN NEGI-SAN.
SHIORI... YOU--
ARE YOU BETRAYING US!?
FWOOM
WAIT, HOMURA.
WINCE

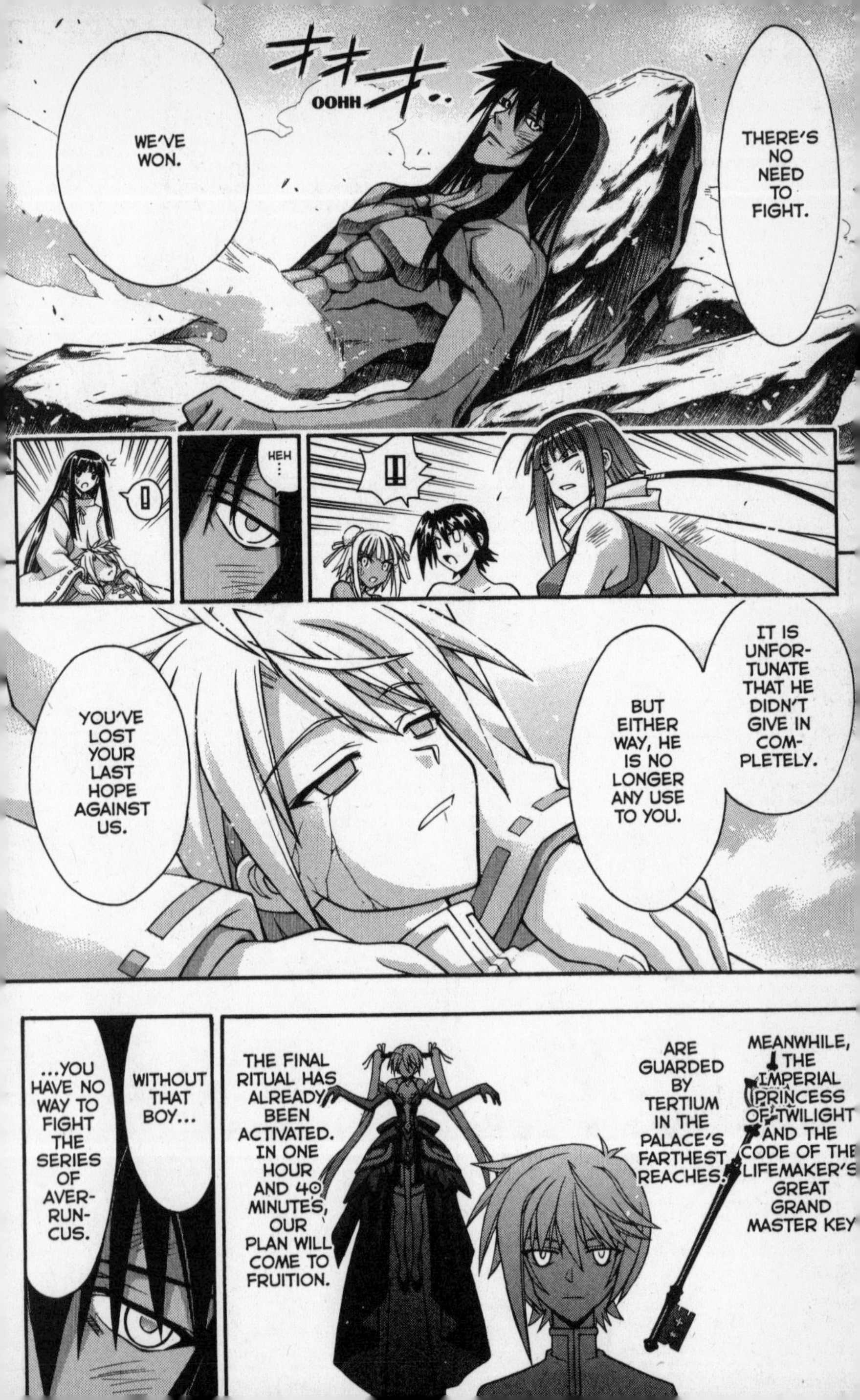
THERE'S NO NEED TO FIGHT.
OOHH
WE'VE WON.
!!
HEH...
!
IT IS UNFORTUNATE THAT HE DIDN'T GIVE IN COMPLETELY.
BUT EITHER WAY, HE IS NO LONGER ANY USE TO YOU.
YOU'VE LOST YOUR LAST HOPE AGAINST US.
MEANWHILE, THE IMPERIAL PRINCESS OF TWILIGHT AND THE CODE OF THE LIFEMAKER'S GREAT GRAND MASTER KEY
ARE GUARDED BY TERTIUM IN THE PALACE'S FARTHEST REACHES.
THE FINAL RITUAL HAS ALREADY BEEN ACTIVATED. IN ONE HOUR AND 40 MINUTES, OUR PLAN WILL COME TO FRUITION.
WITHOUT THAT BOY...
...YOU HAVE NO WAY TO FIGHT THE SERIES OF AVERRUNCUS.

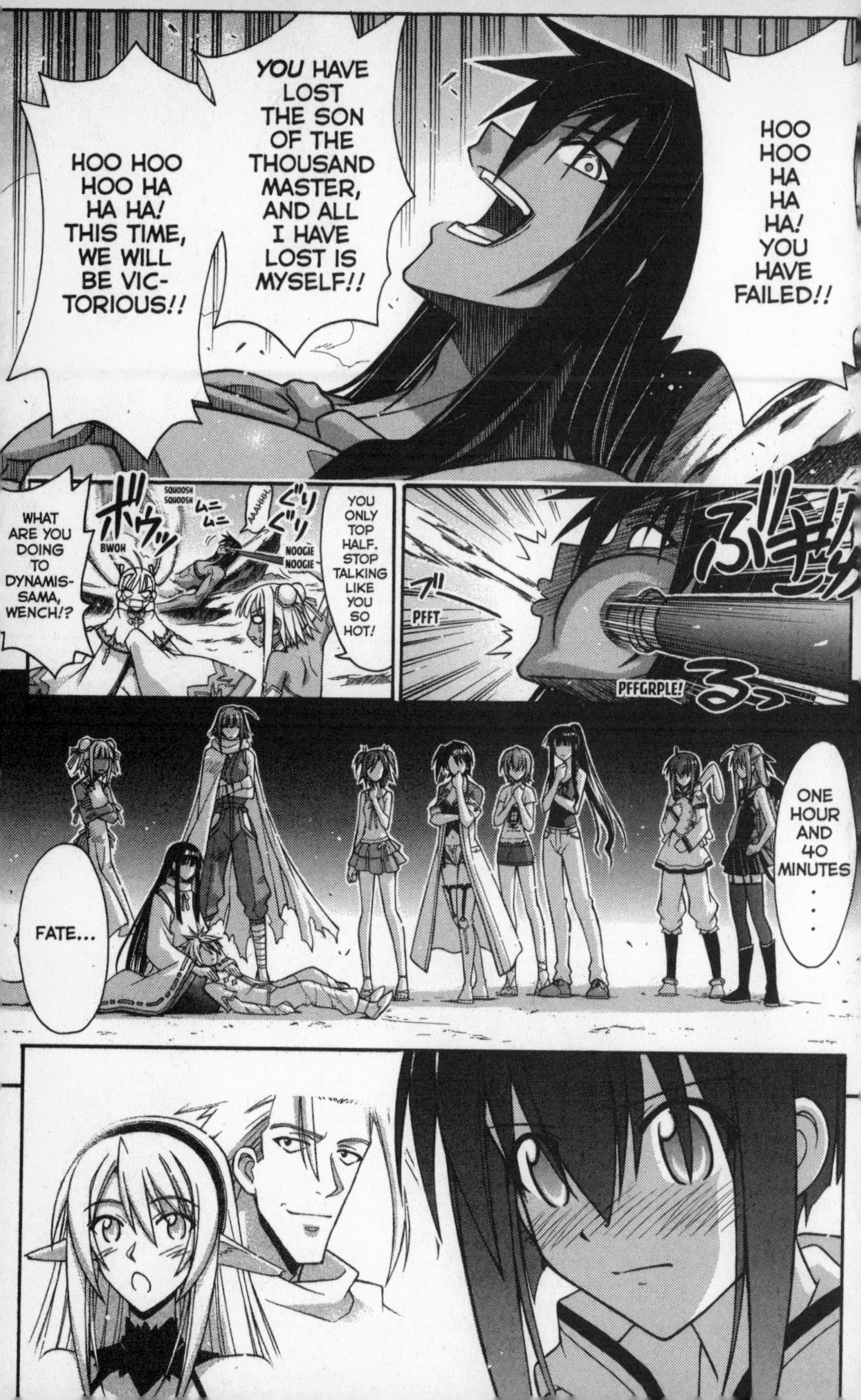
HOO HOO HA HA HA! YOU HAVE FAILED!!
YOU HAVE LOST THE SON OF THE THOUSAND MASTER, AND ALL I HAVE LOST IS MYSELF!!
HOO HOO HOO HA HA HA! THIS TIME, WE WILL BE VIC-TORIOUS!!
PFFT
PFFGRPLE!
YOU ONLY TOP HALF. STOP TALKING LIKE YOU SO HOT!
NOOGIE NOOGIE
AAAHHH
SQUOOSH SQUOOSH
BWOH
WHAT ARE YOU DOING TO DYNAMIS-SAMA, WENCH!?
ONE HOUR AND 40 MINUTES...
FATE...

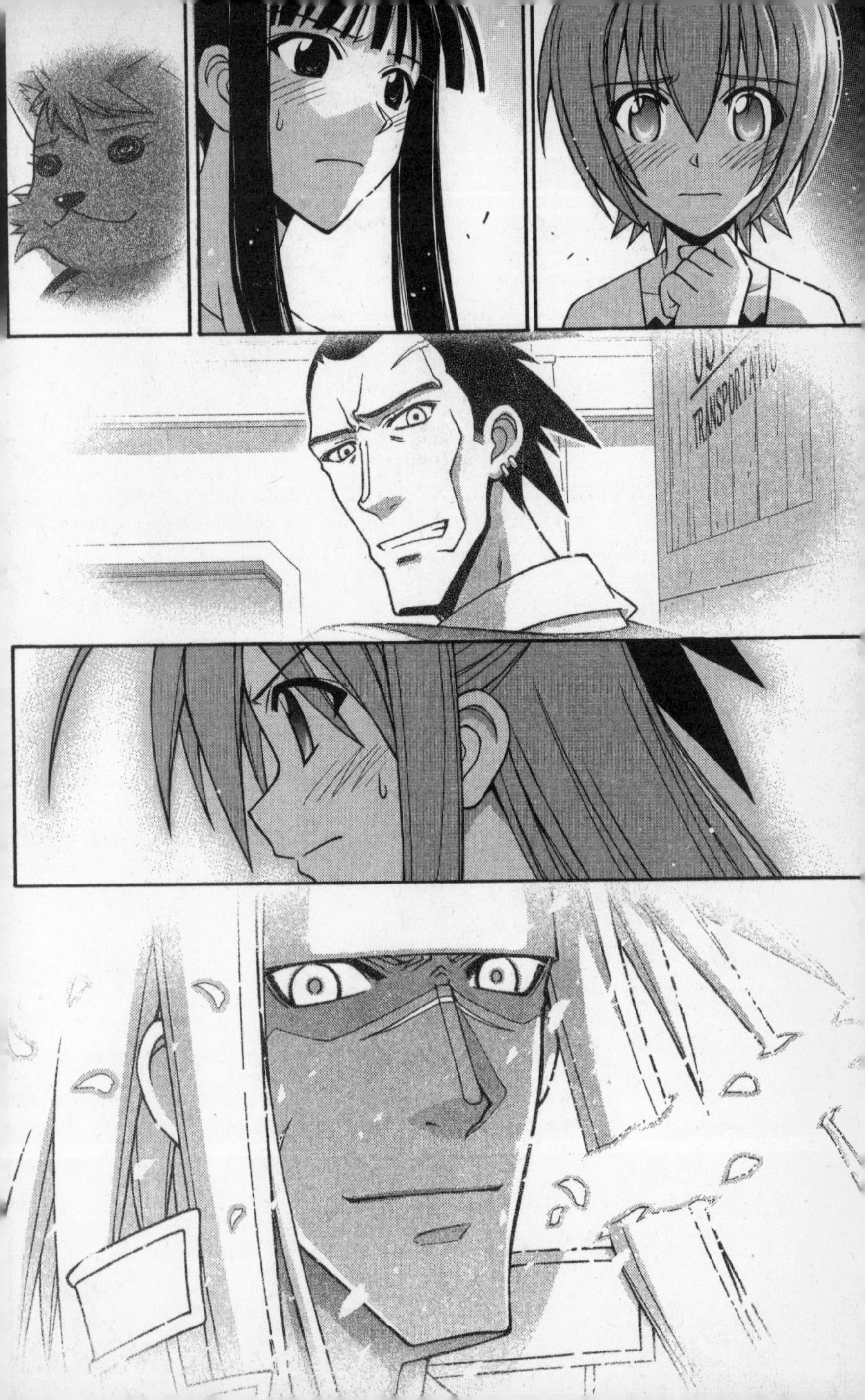
TRANSPORTATIO

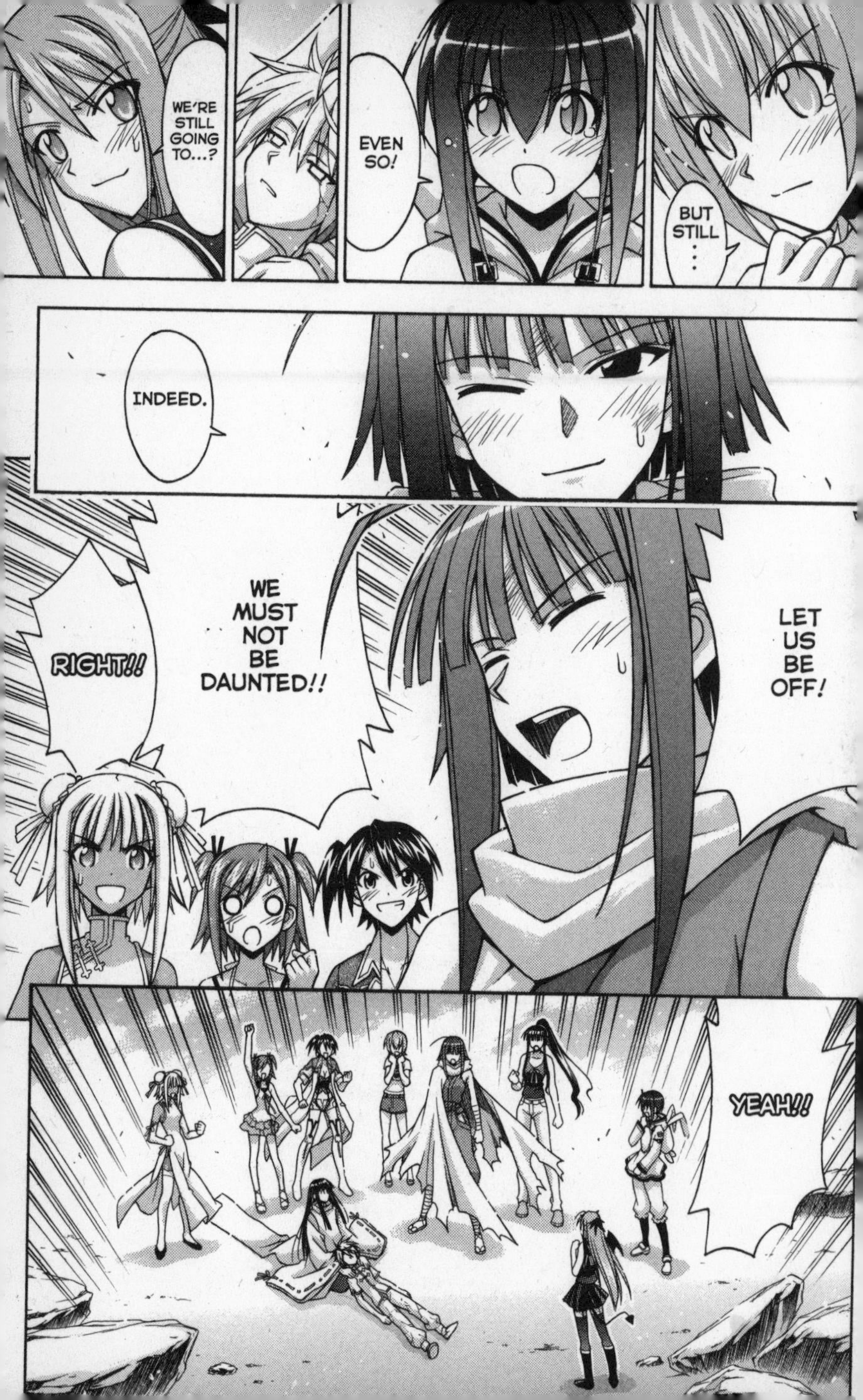

BUT STILL...
EVEN SO!
WE'RE STILL GOING TO...?
INDEED.
LET US BE OFF!
WE MUST NOT BE DAUNTED!!
RIGHT!!
YEAH!!

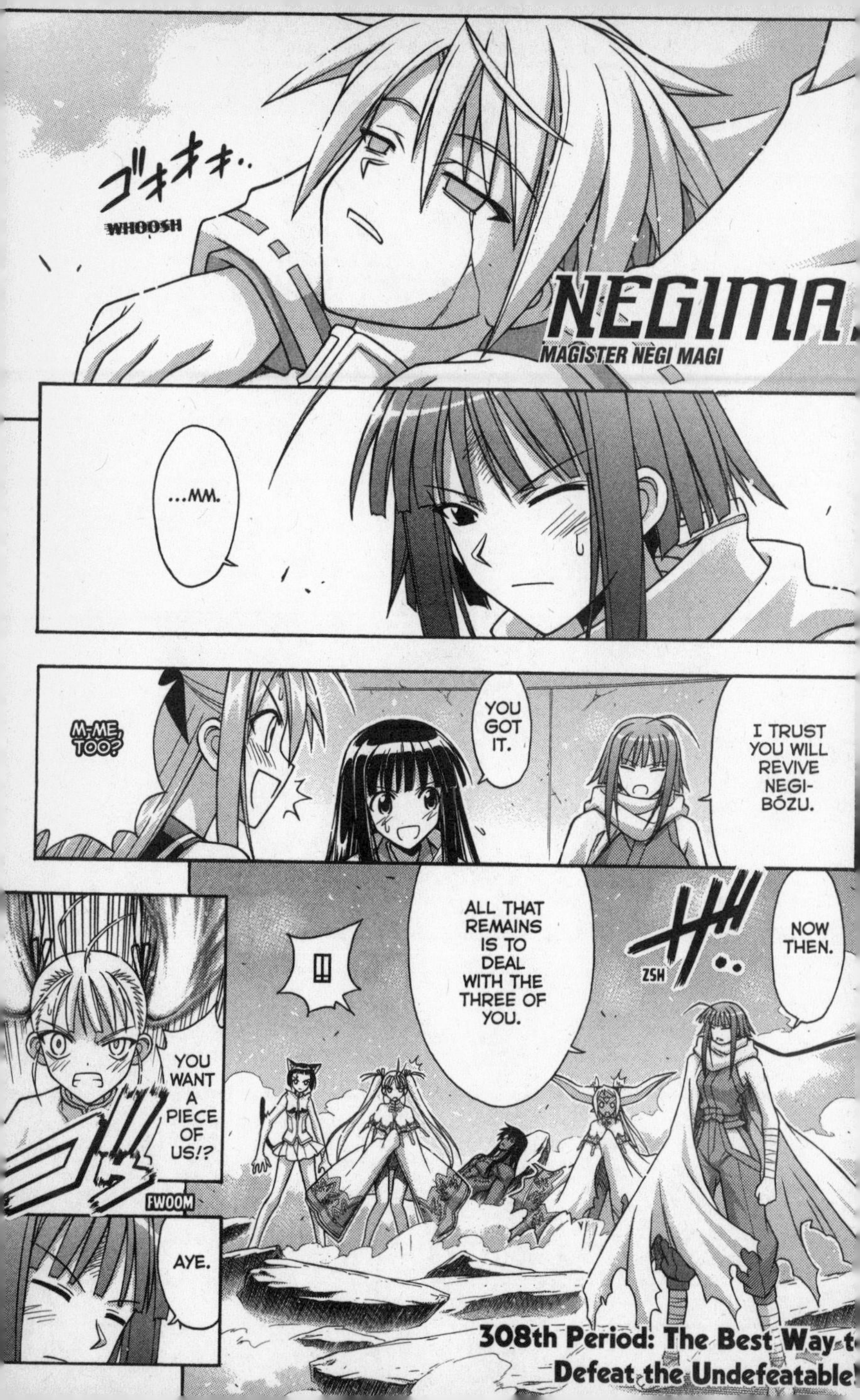
ゴオオオ..
WHOOSH
NEGIMA!
MAGISTER NEGI MAGI
...MM.
I TRUST YOU WILL REVIVE NEGI-BŌZU.
YOU GOT IT.
M-ME, TOO?
NOW THEN.
ZSH
ALL THAT REMAINS IS TO DEAL WITH THE THREE OF YOU.
!!
YOU WANT A PIECE OF US!?
FWOOM
AYE.
308th Period: The Best Way t
Defeat the Undefeatable

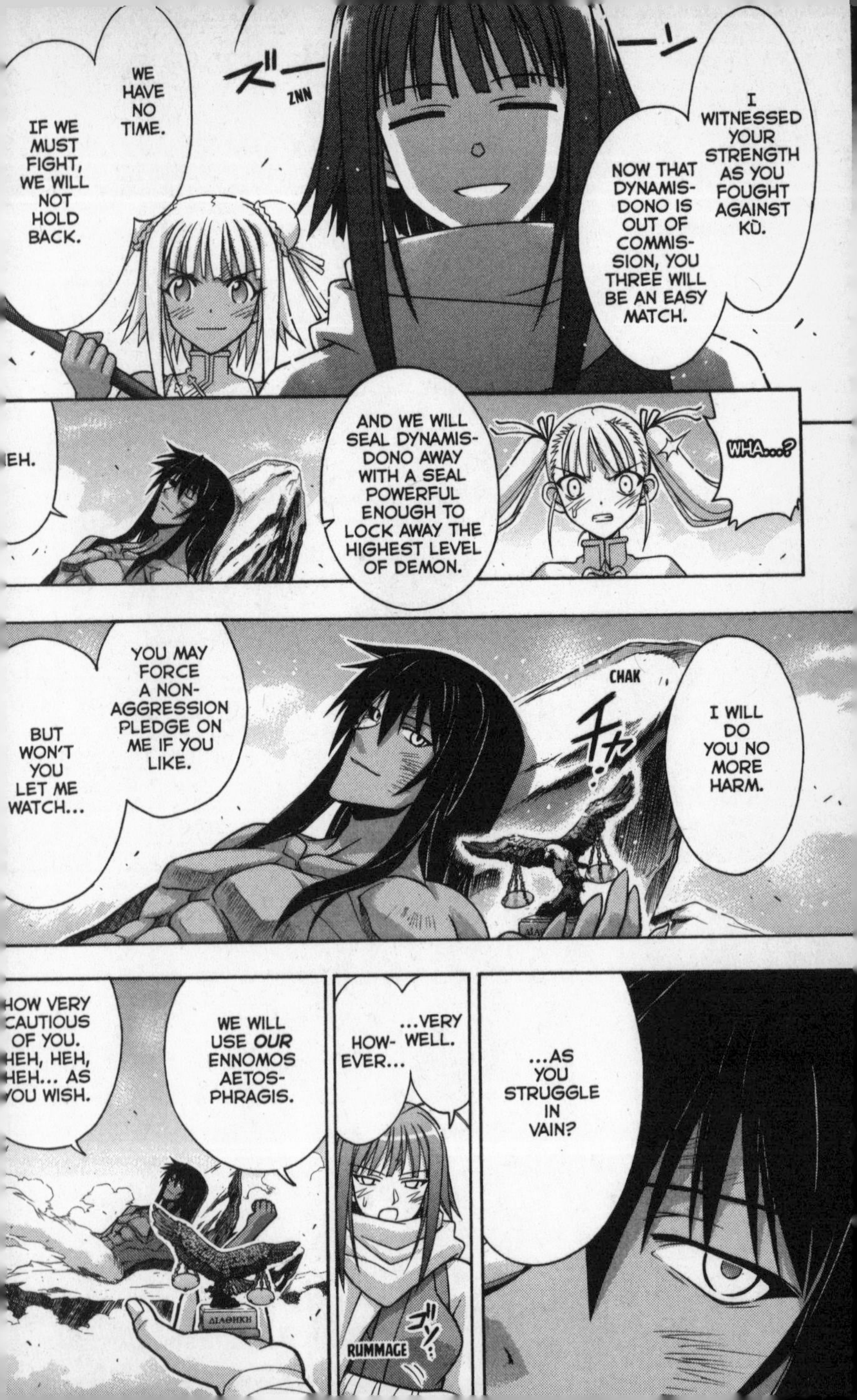
ZNN
I WITNESSED YOUR STRENGTH AS YOU FOUGHT AGAINST KŪ.
NOW THAT DYNAMIS-DONO IS OUT OF COMMISSION, YOU THREE WILL BE AN EASY MATCH.
WE HAVE NO TIME.
IF WE MUST FIGHT, WE WILL NOT HOLD BACK.
WHA...?
AND WE WILL SEAL DYNAMIS-DONO AWAY WITH A SEAL POWERFUL ENOUGH TO LOCK AWAY THE HIGHEST LEVEL OF DEMON.
EH.
I WILL DO YOU NO MORE HARM.
CHAK
YOU MAY FORCE A NON-AGGRESSION PLEDGE ON ME IF YOU LIKE.
BUT WON'T YOU LET ME WATCH...
...AS YOU STRUGGLE IN VAIN?
...VERY WELL.
HOW-EVER...
RUMMAGE
WE WILL USE *OUR* ENNOMOS AETOS-PHRAGIS.
HOW VERY CAUTIOUS OF YOU. HEH, HEH, HEH... AS YOU WISH.

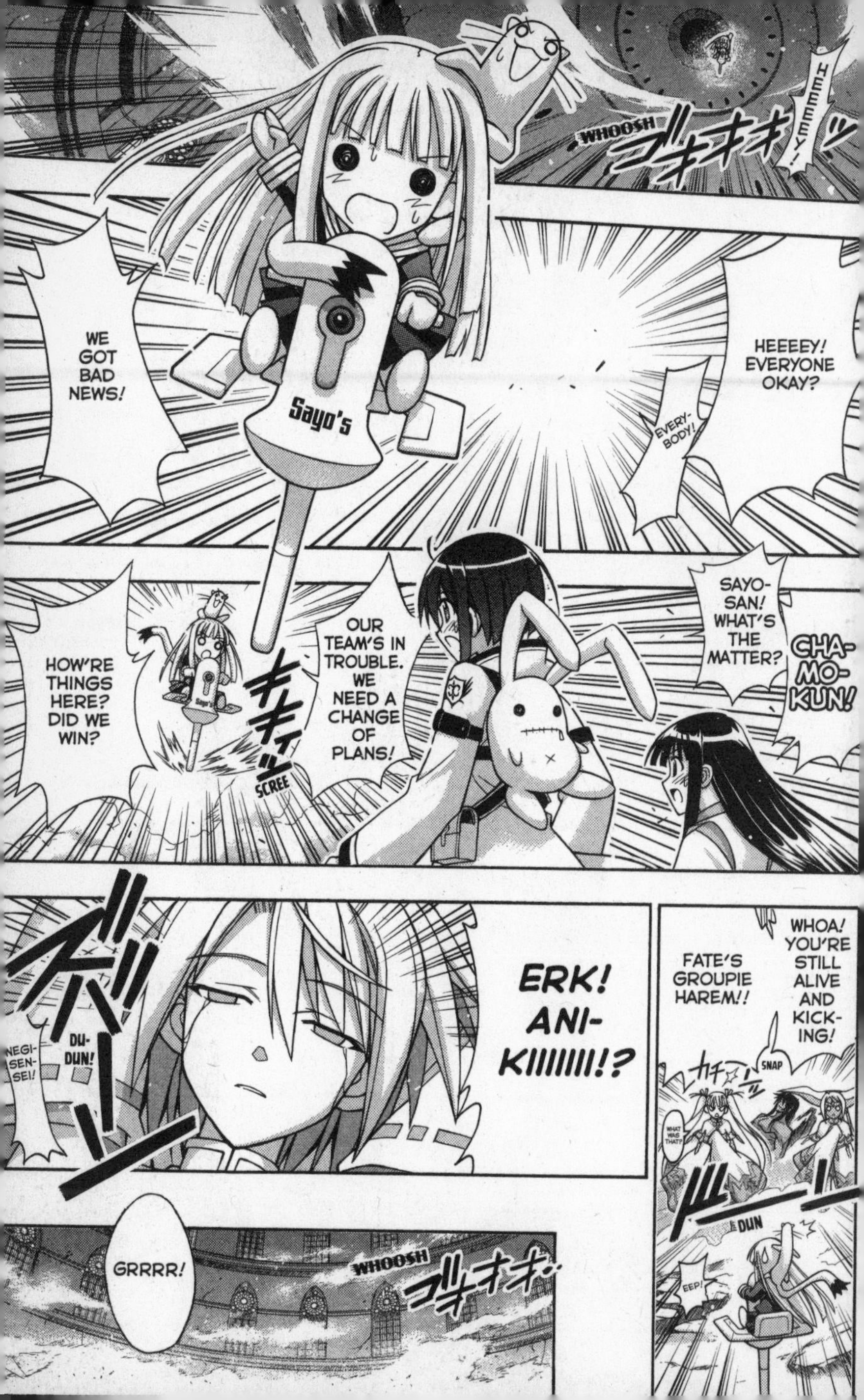

HEEEEY!
WHOOSH
HEEEEY! EVERYONE OKAY?
EVERY-BODY!
WE GOT BAD NEWS!
CHA-MO-KUN!
SAYO-SAN! WHAT'S THE MATTER?
OUR TEAM'S IN TROUBLE. WE NEED A CHANGE OF PLANS!
SCREE
HOW'RE THINGS HERE? DID WE WIN?
WHOA! YOU'RE STILL ALIVE AND KICK-ING!
FATE'S GROUPIE HAREM!!
SNAP
WHAT WAS THAT?
DUN
EEP!
ERK! ANI-KIIIIIII!?
DU-DUN!
NEGI-SEN-SEI!
WHOOSH
GRRRR!

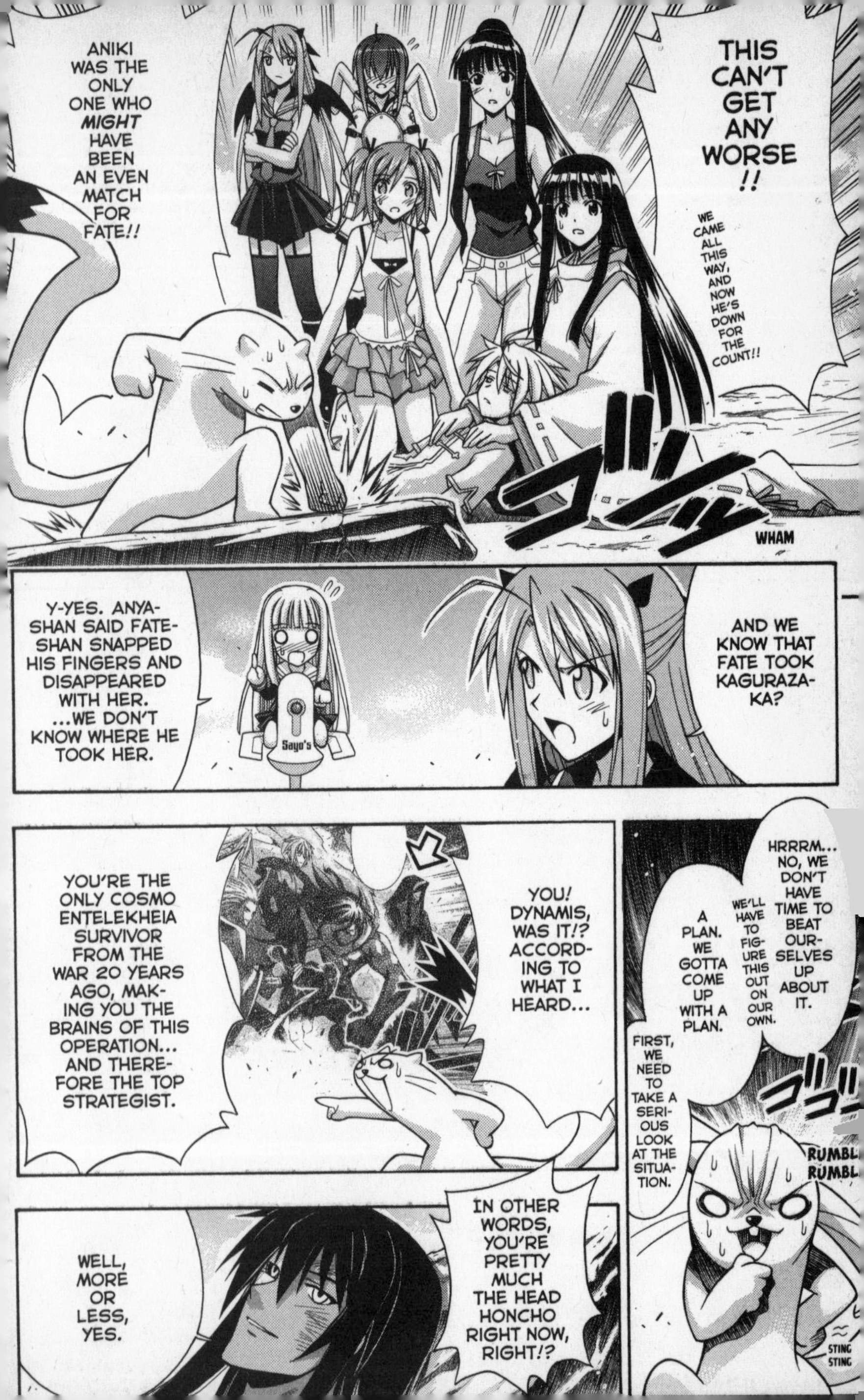
THIS CAN'T GET ANY WORSE!!
WE CAME ALL THIS WAY, AND NOW HE'S DOWN FOR THE COUNT!!
ANIKI WAS THE ONLY ONE WHO *MIGHT* HAVE BEEN AN EVEN MATCH FOR FATE!!
WHAM
AND WE KNOW THAT FATE TOOK KAGURAZAKA?
Y-YES. ANYA-SHAN SAID FATE-SHAN SNAPPED HIS FINGERS AND DISAPPEARED WITH HER. ...WE DON'T KNOW WHERE HE TOOK HER.
Sayo's
HRRRM... NO, WE DON'T HAVE TIME TO BEAT OURSELVES UP ABOUT IT.
WE'LL HAVE TO FIGURE THIS OUT ON OUR OWN.
A PLAN. WE GOTTA COME UP WITH A PLAN.
FIRST, WE NEED TO TAKE A SERIOUS LOOK AT THE SITUATION.
RUMBL
RUMBL
STING
STING
YOU! DYNAMIS, WAS IT!? ACCORDING TO WHAT I HEARD...
YOU'RE THE ONLY COSMO ENTELEKHEIA SURVIVOR FROM THE WAR 20 YEARS AGO, MAKING YOU THE BRAINS OF THIS OPERATION... AND THEREFORE THE TOP STRATEGIST.
IN OTHER WORDS, YOU'RE PRETTY MUCH THE HEAD HONCHO RIGHT NOW, RIGHT!?
WELL, MORE OR LESS, YES.

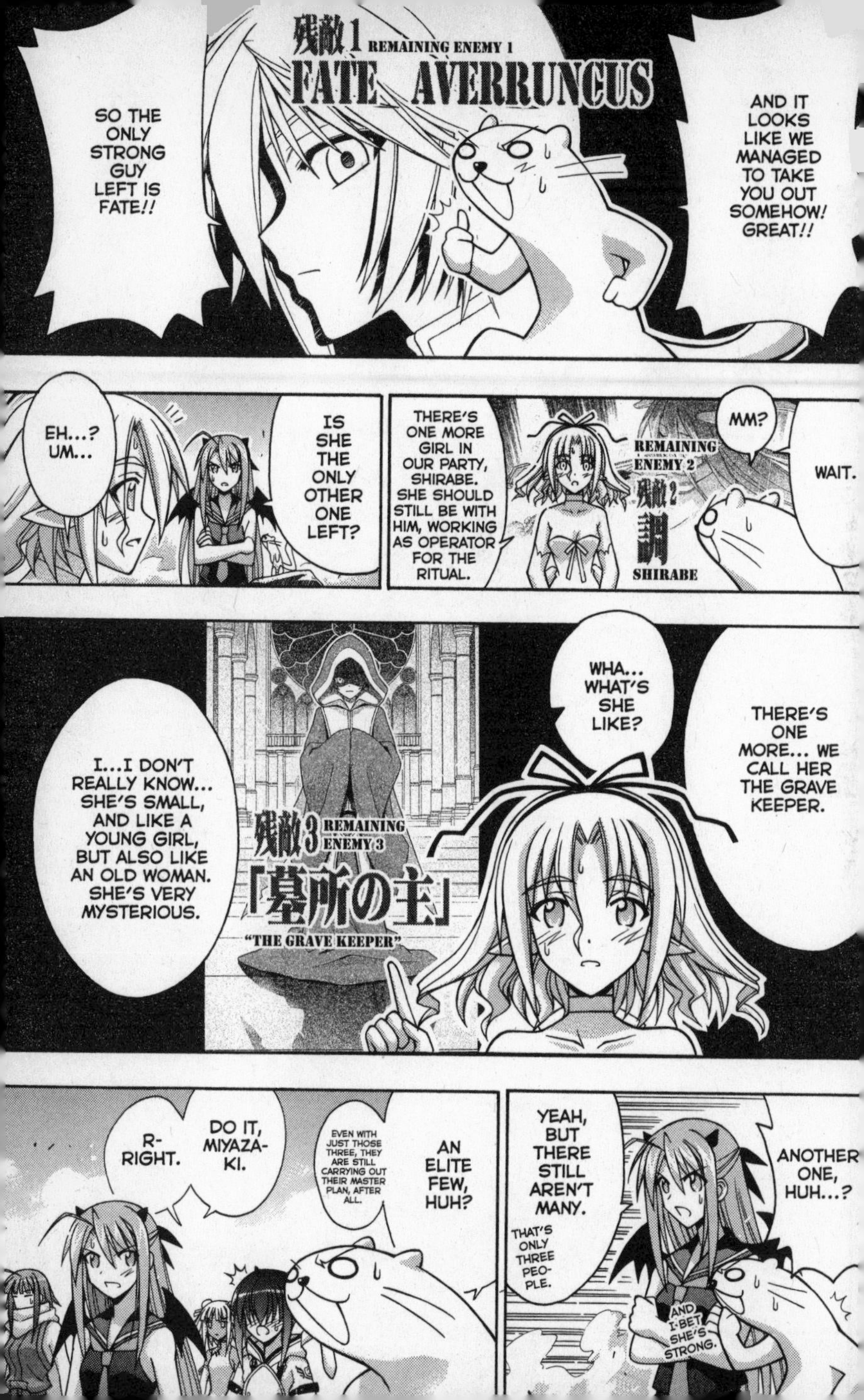
残敵1 REMAINING ENEMY 1
FATE AVERRUNCUS
AND IT LOOKS LIKE WE MANAGED TO TAKE YOU OUT SOMEHOW! GREAT!!
SO THE ONLY STRONG GUY LEFT IS FATE!!
WAIT.
MM?
THERE'S ONE MORE GIRL IN OUR PARTY, SHIRABE. SHE SHOULD STILL BE WITH HIM, WORKING AS OPERATOR FOR THE RITUAL.
REMAINING ENEMY 2 残敵2 調 SHIRABE
IS SHE THE ONLY OTHER ONE LEFT?
EH...? UM...
THERE'S ONE MORE... WE CALL HER THE GRAVE KEEPER.
WHA... WHAT'S SHE LIKE?
残敵3 REMAINING ENEMY 3 「墓所の主」 "THE GRAVE KEEPER"
I...I DON'T REALLY KNOW... SHE'S SMALL, AND LIKE A YOUNG GIRL, BUT ALSO LIKE AN OLD WOMAN. SHE'S VERY MYSTERIOUS.
ANOTHER ONE, HUH...?
AND I BET SHE'S STRONG.
YEAH, BUT THERE STILL AREN'T MANY.
THAT'S ONLY THREE PEO-PLE.
AN ELITE FEW, HUH?
EVEN WITH JUST THOSE THREE, THEY ARE STILL CARRYING OUT THEIR MASTER PLAN, AFTER ALL.
DO IT, MIYAZA-KI.
R-RIGHT.

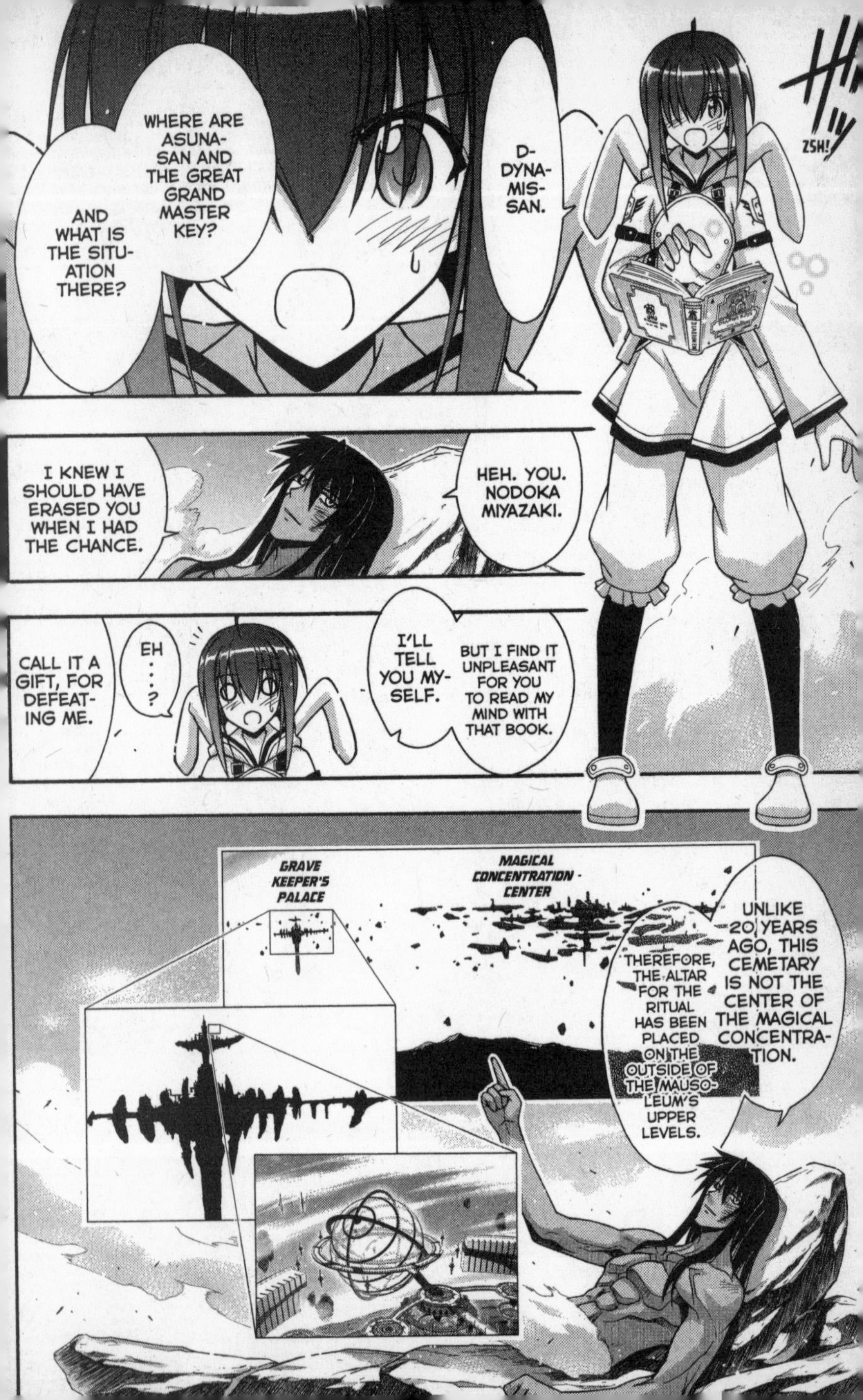
ZSH!
D-DYNAMIS-SAN.
WHERE ARE ASUNA-SAN AND THE GREAT GRAND MASTER KEY?
AND WHAT IS THE SITUATION THERE?
HEH. YOU. NODOKA MIYAZAKI.
I KNEW I SHOULD HAVE ERASED YOU WHEN I HAD THE CHANCE.
BUT I FIND IT UNPLEASANT FOR YOU TO READ MY MIND WITH THAT BOOK.
I'LL TELL YOU MYSELF.
EH...?
CALL IT A GIFT, FOR DEFEATING ME.
MAGICAL CONCENTRATION CENTER
GRAVE KEEPER'S PALACE
UNLIKE 20 YEARS AGO, THIS CEMETARY IS NOT THE CENTER OF THE MAGICAL CONCENTRATION.
THEREFORE, THE ALTAR FOR THE RITUAL HAS BEEN PLACED ON THE OUTSIDE OF THE MAUSOLEUM'S UPPER LEVELS.

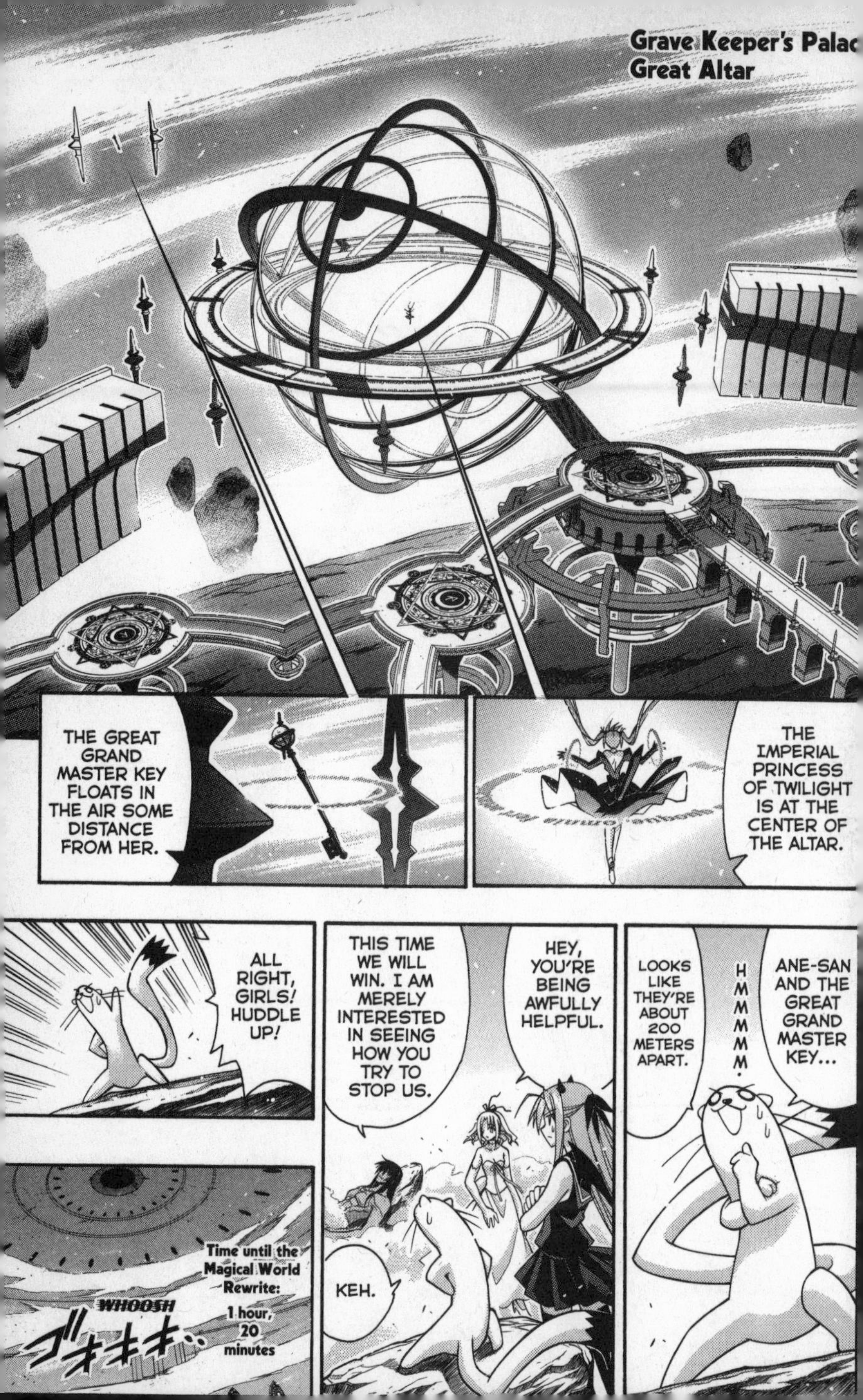
Grave Keeper's Palac
Great Altar
THE IMPERIAL PRINCESS OF TWILIGHT IS AT THE CENTER OF THE ALTAR.
THE GREAT GRAND MASTER KEY FLOATS IN THE AIR SOME DISTANCE FROM HER.
ANE-SAN AND THE GREAT GRAND MASTER KEY...
HMMMMM.
LOOKS LIKE THEY'RE ABOUT 200 METERS APART.
HEY, YOU'RE BEING AWFULLY HELPFUL.
THIS TIME WE WILL WIN. I AM MERELY INTERESTED IN SEEING HOW YOU TRY TO STOP US.
KEH.
ALL RIGHT, GIRLS! HUDDLE UP!
Time until the Magical World Rewrite:
1 hour, 20 minutes
WHOOSH

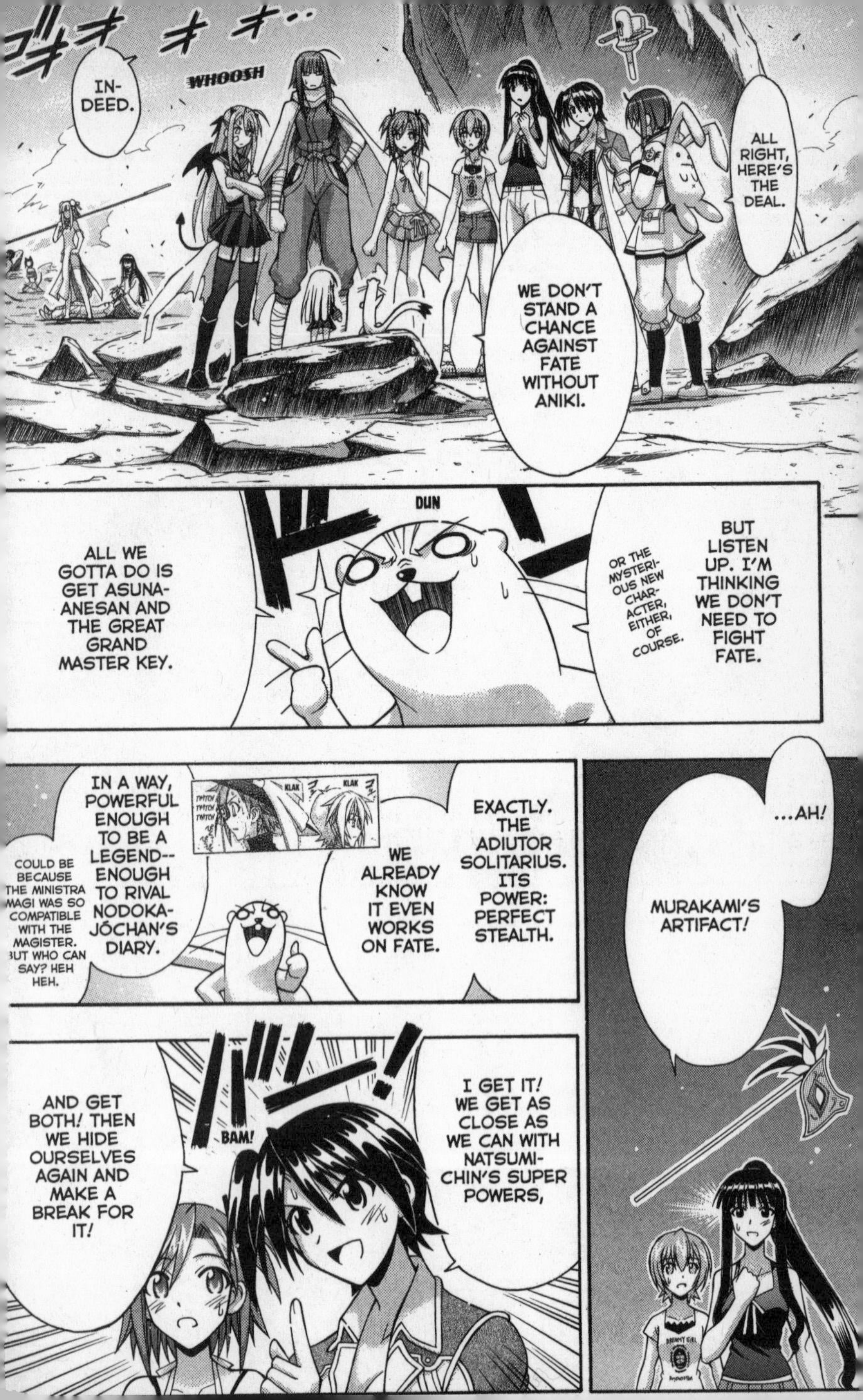
ALL RIGHT, HERE'S THE DEAL.
WE DON'T STAND A CHANCE AGAINST FATE WITHOUT ANIKI.
IN-DEED.
WHOOSH
BUT LISTEN UP. I'M THINKING WE DON'T NEED TO FIGHT FATE.
OR THE MYSTERIOUS NEW CHARACTER, EITHER, OF COURSE.
DUN
ALL WE GOTTA DO IS GET ASUNA-ANESAN AND THE GREAT GRAND MASTER KEY.
...AH!
MURAKAMI'S ARTIFACT!
EXACTLY. THE ADIUTOR SOLITARIUS. ITS POWER: PERFECT STEALTH.
WE ALREADY KNOW IT EVEN WORKS ON FATE.
KLAK
KLAK
TWITCH TWITCH TWITCH
IN A WAY, POWERFUL ENOUGH TO BE A LEGEND-- ENOUGH TO RIVAL NODOKA-JÓCHAN'S DIARY.
COULD BE BECAUSE THE MINISTRA MAGI WAS SO COMPATIBLE WITH THE MAGISTER. BUT WHO CAN SAY? HEH HEH.
I GET IT! WE GET AS CLOSE AS WE CAN WITH NATSUMI-CHIN'S SUPER POWERS,
BAM!
AND GET BOTH! THEN WE HIDE OURSELVES AGAIN AND MAKE A BREAK FOR IT!

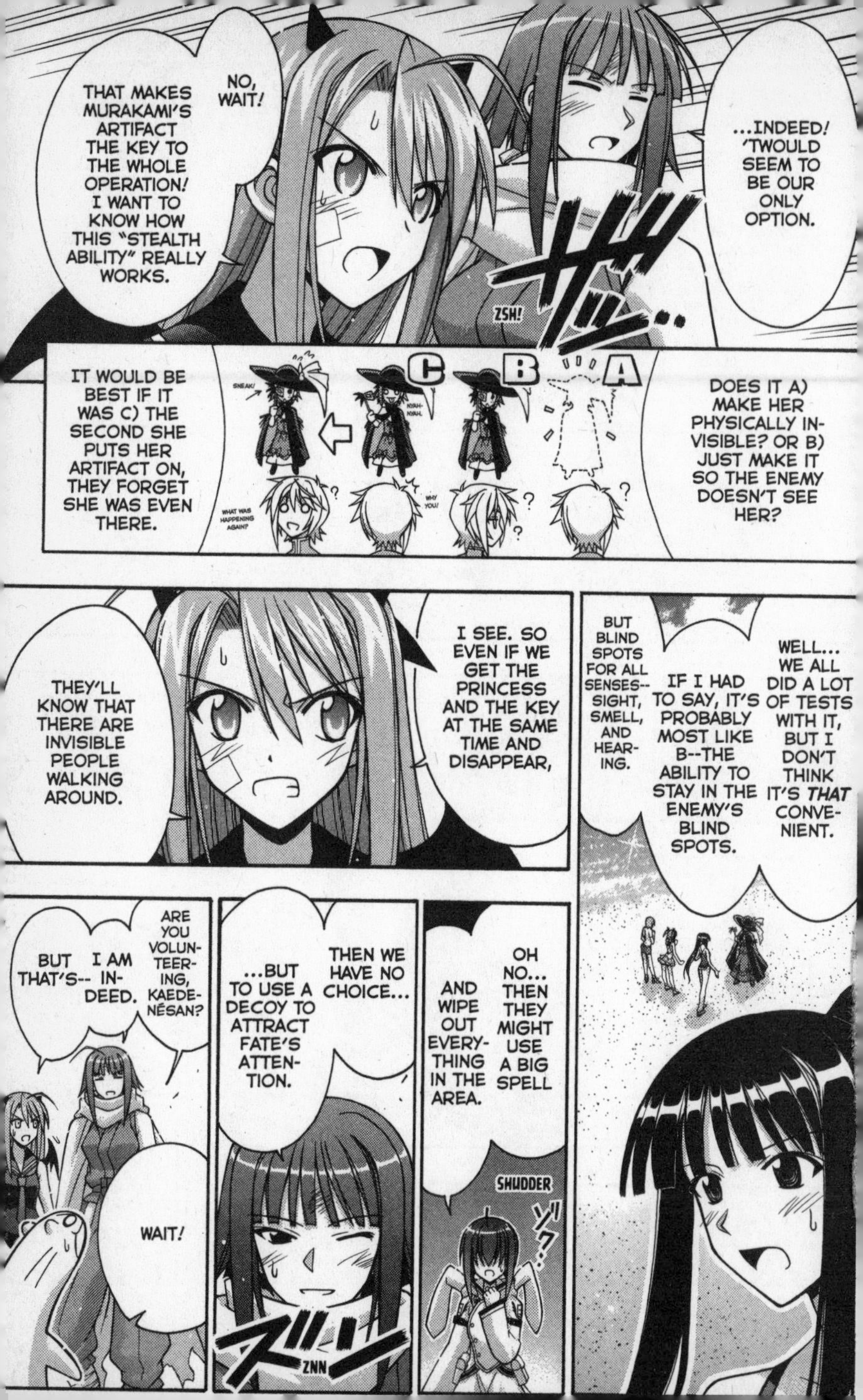
...INDEED! 'TWOULD SEEM TO BE OUR ONLY OPTION.
ZSH!
NO, WAIT!
THAT MAKES MURAKAMI'S ARTIFACT THE KEY TO THE WHOLE OPERATION! I WANT TO KNOW HOW THIS "STEALTH ABILITY" REALLY WORKS.
DOES IT A) MAKE HER PHYSICALLY INVISIBLE? OR B) JUST MAKE IT SO THE ENEMY DOESN'T SEE HER?
A
B
C
WHY YOU!
KYAH-NYAH
SNEAK!
WHAT WAS HAPPENING AGAIN?
IT WOULD BE BEST IF IT WAS C) THE SECOND SHE PUTS HER ARTIFACT ON, THEY FORGET SHE WAS EVEN THERE.
WELL... WE ALL DID A LOT OF TESTS WITH IT, BUT I DON'T THINK IT'S *THAT* CONVENIENT.
IF I HAD TO SAY, IT'S PROBABLY MOST LIKE B--THE ABILITY TO STAY IN THE ENEMY'S BLIND SPOTS.
BUT BLIND SPOTS FOR ALL SENSES--SIGHT, SMELL, AND HEARING.
I SEE. SO EVEN IF WE GET THE PRINCESS AND THE KEY AT THE SAME TIME AND DISAPPEAR,
THEY'LL KNOW THAT THERE ARE INVISIBLE PEOPLE WALKING AROUND.
OH NO... THEN THEY MIGHT USE A BIG SPELL
AND WIPE OUT EVERYTHING IN THE AREA.
SHUDDER
THEN WE HAVE NO CHOICE...
...BUT TO USE A DECOY TO ATTRACT FATE'S ATTENTION.
ZNN
ARE YOU VOLUNTEERING, KAEDE-NÉSAN?
I AM INDEED.
BUT THAT'S--
WAIT!

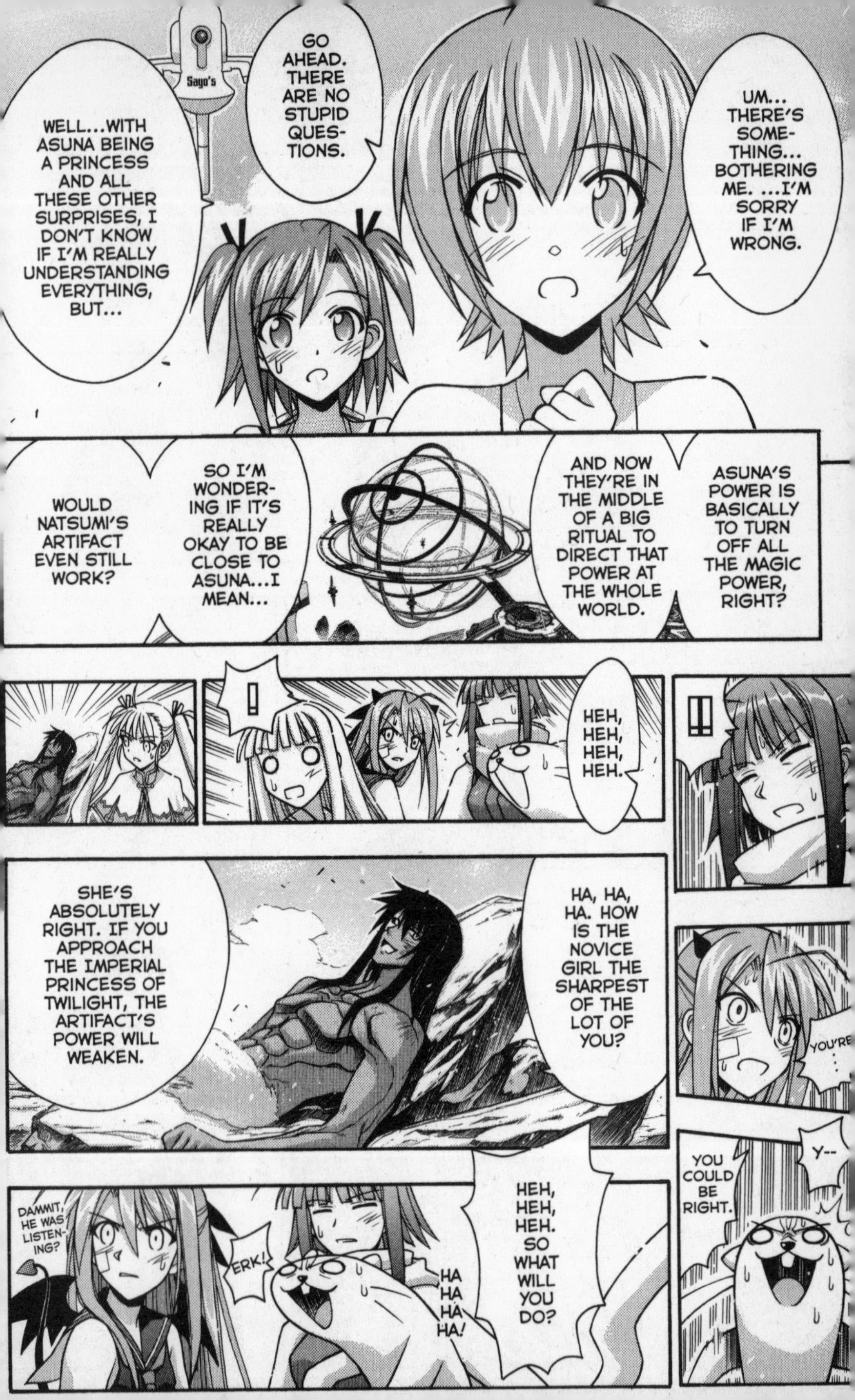
UM... THERE'S SOMETHING... BOTHERING ME. ...I'M SORRY IF I'M WRONG.
GO AHEAD. THERE ARE NO STUPID QUESTIONS.
Sayo's
WELL...WITH ASUNA BEING A PRINCESS AND ALL THESE OTHER SURPRISES, I DON'T KNOW IF I'M REALLY UNDERSTANDING EVERYTHING, BUT...
ASUNA'S POWER IS BASICALLY TO TURN OFF ALL THE MAGIC POWER, RIGHT?
AND NOW THEY'RE IN THE MIDDLE OF A BIG RITUAL TO DIRECT THAT POWER AT THE WHOLE WORLD.
SO I'M WONDERING IF IT'S REALLY OKAY TO BE CLOSE TO ASUNA...I MEAN...
WOULD NATSUMI'S ARTIFACT EVEN STILL WORK?
!!
HEH, HEH, HEH, HEH.
!
YOU'RE...
Y--
YOU COULD BE RIGHT.
HA, HA, HA. HOW IS THE NOVICE GIRL THE SHARPEST OF THE LOT OF YOU?
SHE'S ABSOLUTELY RIGHT. IF YOU APPROACH THE IMPERIAL PRINCESS OF TWILIGHT, THE ARTIFACT'S POWER WILL WEAKEN.
HEH, HEH, HEH. SO WHAT WILL YOU DO?
HA HA HA HA!
ERK!
DAMMIT, HE WAS LISTENING?

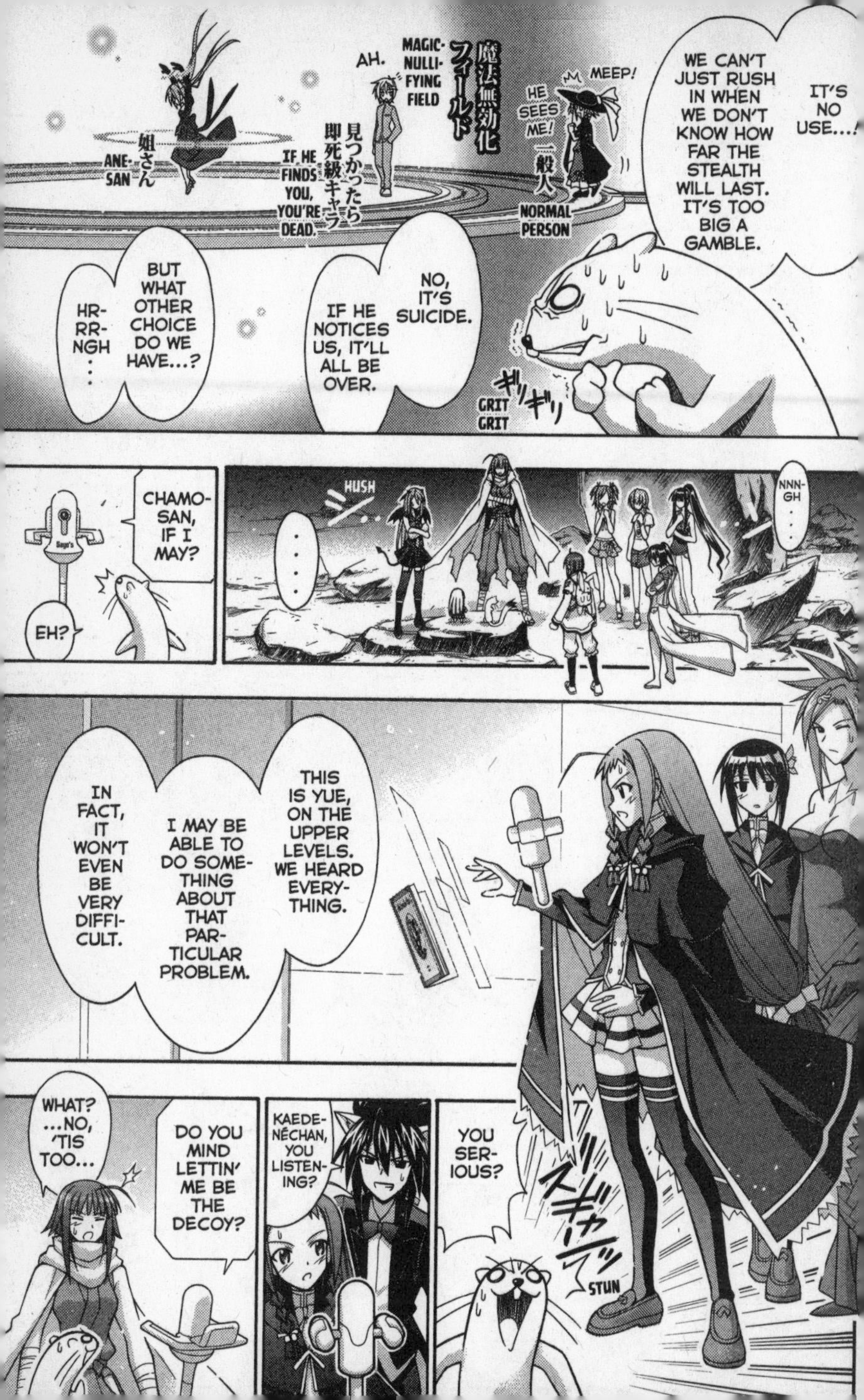
IT'S NO USE...!
WE CAN'T JUST RUSH IN WHEN WE DON'T KNOW HOW FAR THE STEALTH WILL LAST. IT'S TOO BIG A GAMBLE.
MEEP!
HE SEES ME!
一般人
NORMAL PERSON
魔法無効化フィールド
MAGIC-NULLIFYING FIELD
AH.
見つかったら即死級キャラ
IF HE FINDS YOU, YOU'RE DEAD.
姐さん
ANE-SAN
ギリギリ
GRIT GRIT
NO, IT'S SUICIDE.
IF HE NOTICES US, IT'LL ALL BE OVER.
BUT WHAT OTHER CHOICE DO WE HAVE...?
HR-RR-NGH...
NNN-GH...
HUSH
....
CHAMO-SAN, IF I MAY?
EH?
THIS IS YUE, ON THE UPPER LEVELS. WE HEARD EVERYTHING.
I MAY BE ABLE TO DO SOMETHING ABOUT THAT PARTICULAR PROBLEM.
IN FACT, IT WON'T EVEN BE VERY DIFFICULT.
STUN
YOU SERIOUS?
KAEDE-NÉCHAN, YOU LISTENING?
DO YOU MIND LETTIN' ME BE THE DECOY?
WHAT? ...NO, 'TIS TOO...

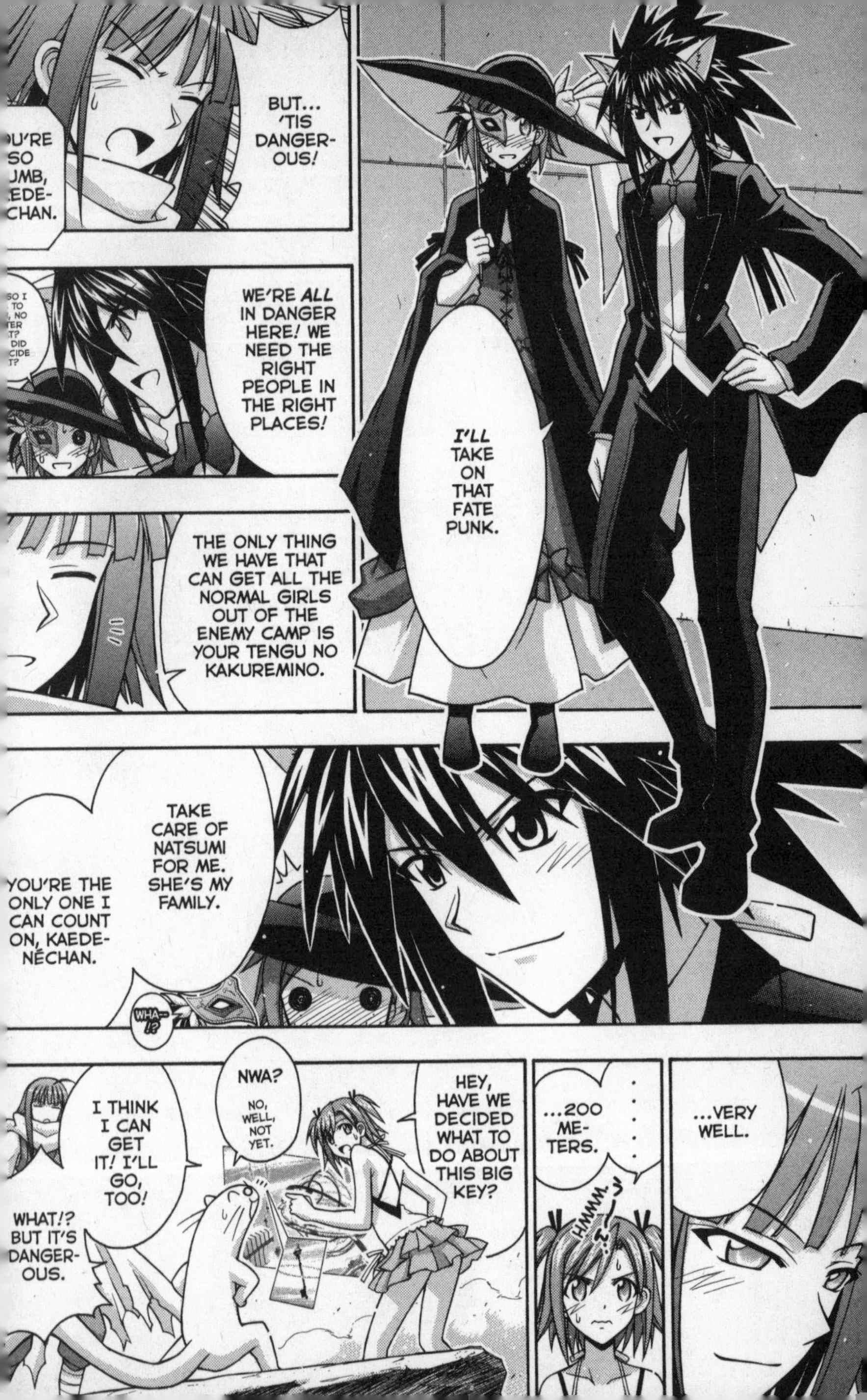
I'LL TAKE ON THAT FATE PUNK.
BUT... 'TIS DANGEROUS!
OU'RE SO UMB, EDE-CHAN.
WE'RE ALL IN DANGER HERE! WE NEED THE RIGHT PEOPLE IN THE RIGHT PLACES!
THE ONLY THING WE HAVE THAT CAN GET ALL THE NORMAL GIRLS OUT OF THE ENEMY CAMP IS YOUR TENGU NO KAKUREMINO.
TAKE CARE OF NATSUMI FOR ME. SHE'S MY FAMILY.
YOU'RE THE ONLY ONE I CAN COUNT ON, KAEDE-NÉCHAN.
WHA-!?
...VERY WELL.
...200 METERS.
HMMM.
HEY, HAVE WE DECIDED WHAT TO DO ABOUT THIS BIG KEY?
NWA?
NO, WELL, NOT YET.
I THINK I CAN GET IT! I'LL GO, TOO!
WHAT!? BUT IT'S DANGEROUS.

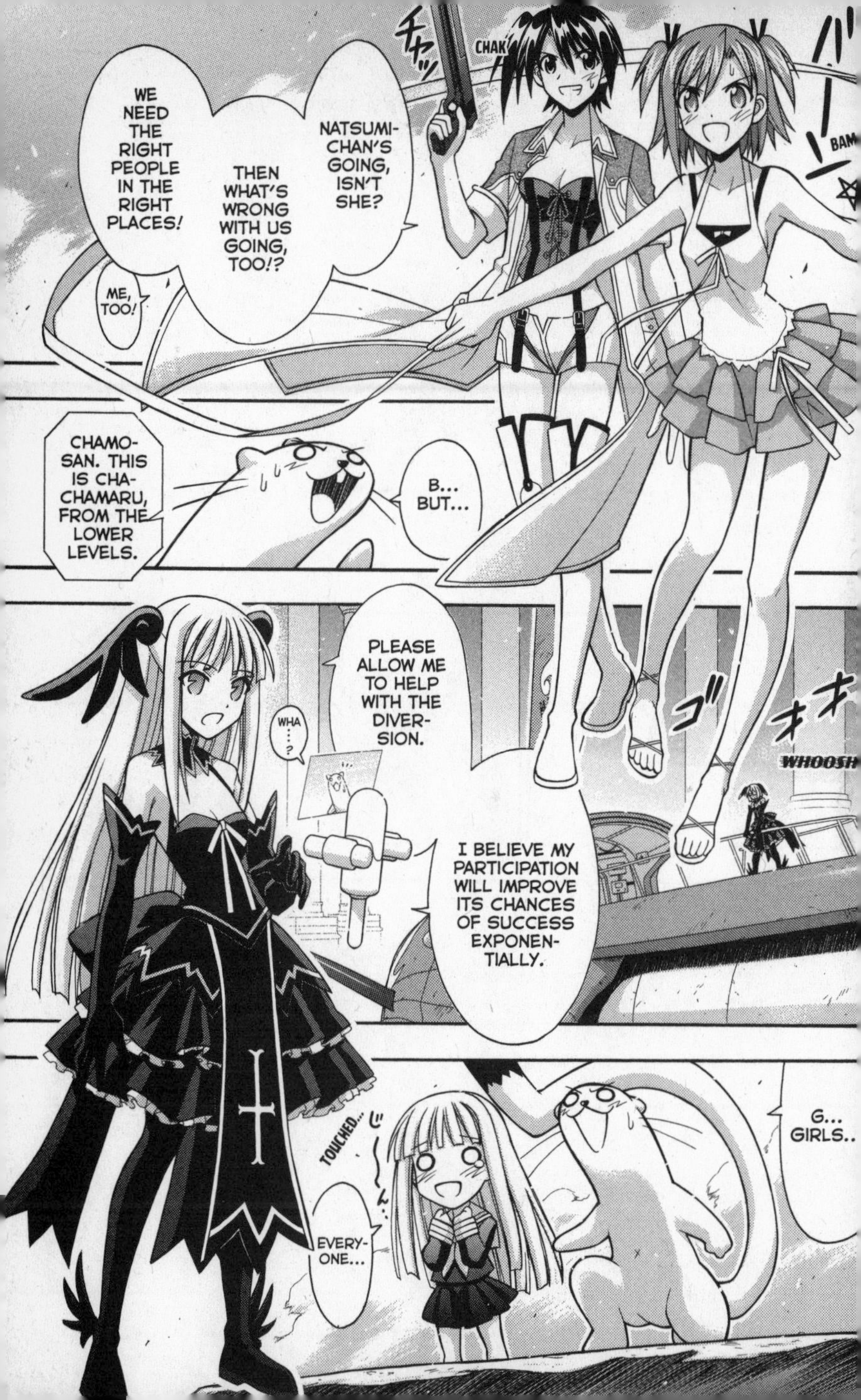
BAM
CHAK
NATSUMI-CHAN'S GOING, ISN'T SHE?
THEN WHAT'S WRONG WITH US GOING, TOO!?
WE NEED THE RIGHT PEOPLE IN THE RIGHT PLACES!
ME, TOO!
B... BUT...
CHAMO-SAN. THIS IS CHA-CHAMARU, FROM THE LOWER LEVELS.
WHOOSH
PLEASE ALLOW ME TO HELP WITH THE DIVERSION.
WHA...?
I BELIEVE MY PARTICIPATION WILL IMPROVE ITS CHANCES OF SUCCESS EXPONENTIALLY.
G... GIRLS...
TOUCHED...
EVERY-ONE...

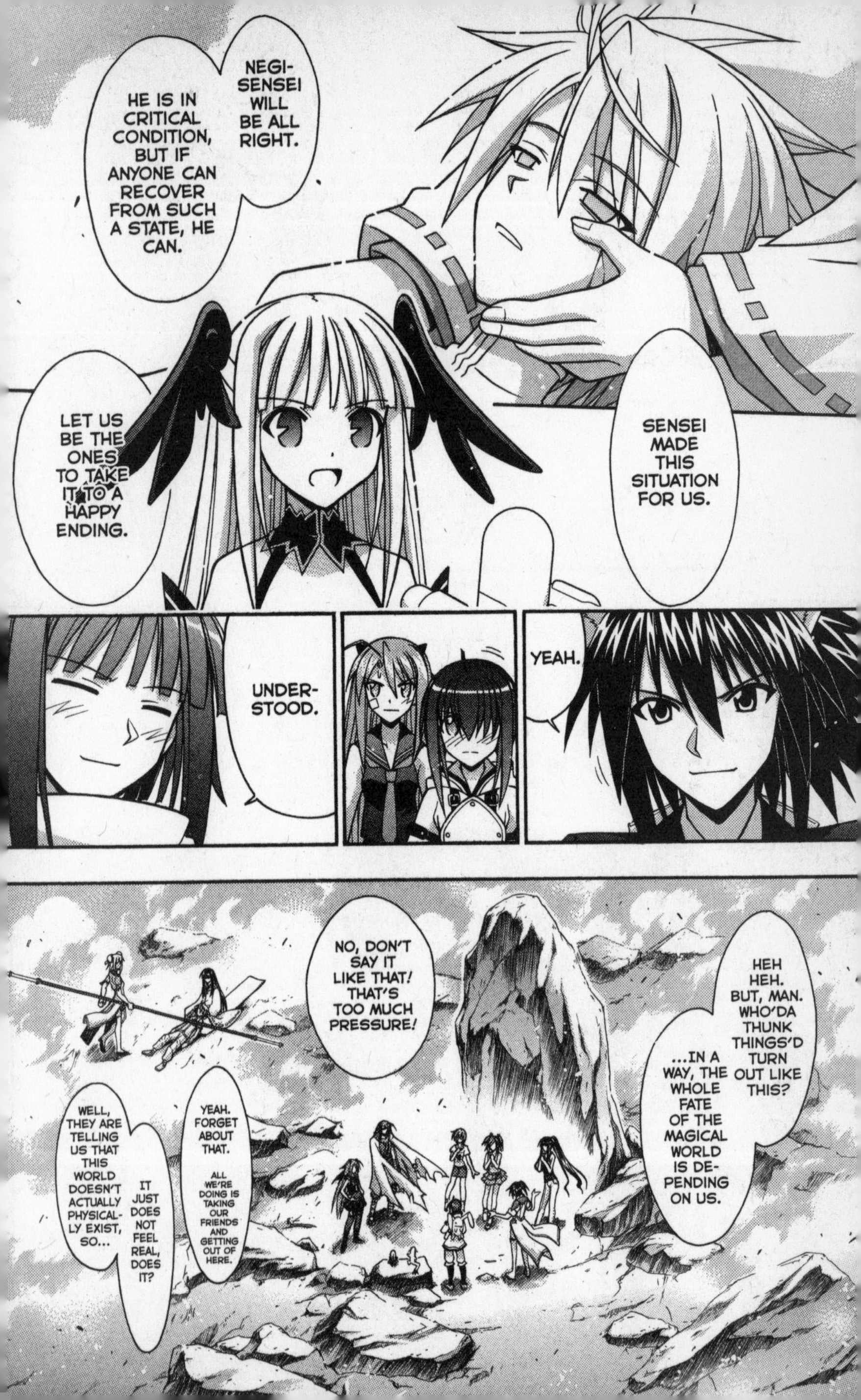
NEGI-SENSEI WILL BE ALL RIGHT.
HE IS IN CRITICAL CONDITION, BUT IF ANYONE CAN RECOVER FROM SUCH A STATE, HE CAN.
SENSEI MADE THIS SITUATION FOR US.
LET US BE THE ONES TO TAKE IT TO A HAPPY ENDING.
YEAH.
UNDER-STOOD.
HEH HEH. BUT, MAN. WHO'DA THUNK THINGS'D TURN OUT LIKE THIS?
...IN A WAY, THE WHOLE FATE OF THE MAGICAL WORLD IS DE-PENDING ON US.
NO, DON'T SAY IT LIKE THAT! THAT'S TOO MUCH PRESSURE!
YEAH. FORGET ABOUT THAT.
ALL WE'RE DOING IS TAKING OUR FRIENDS AND GETTING OUT OF HERE.
WELL, THEY ARE TELLING US THAT THIS WORLD DOESN'T ACTUALLY PHYSICAL-LY EXIST, SO...
IT JUST DOES NOT FEEL REAL, DOES IT?

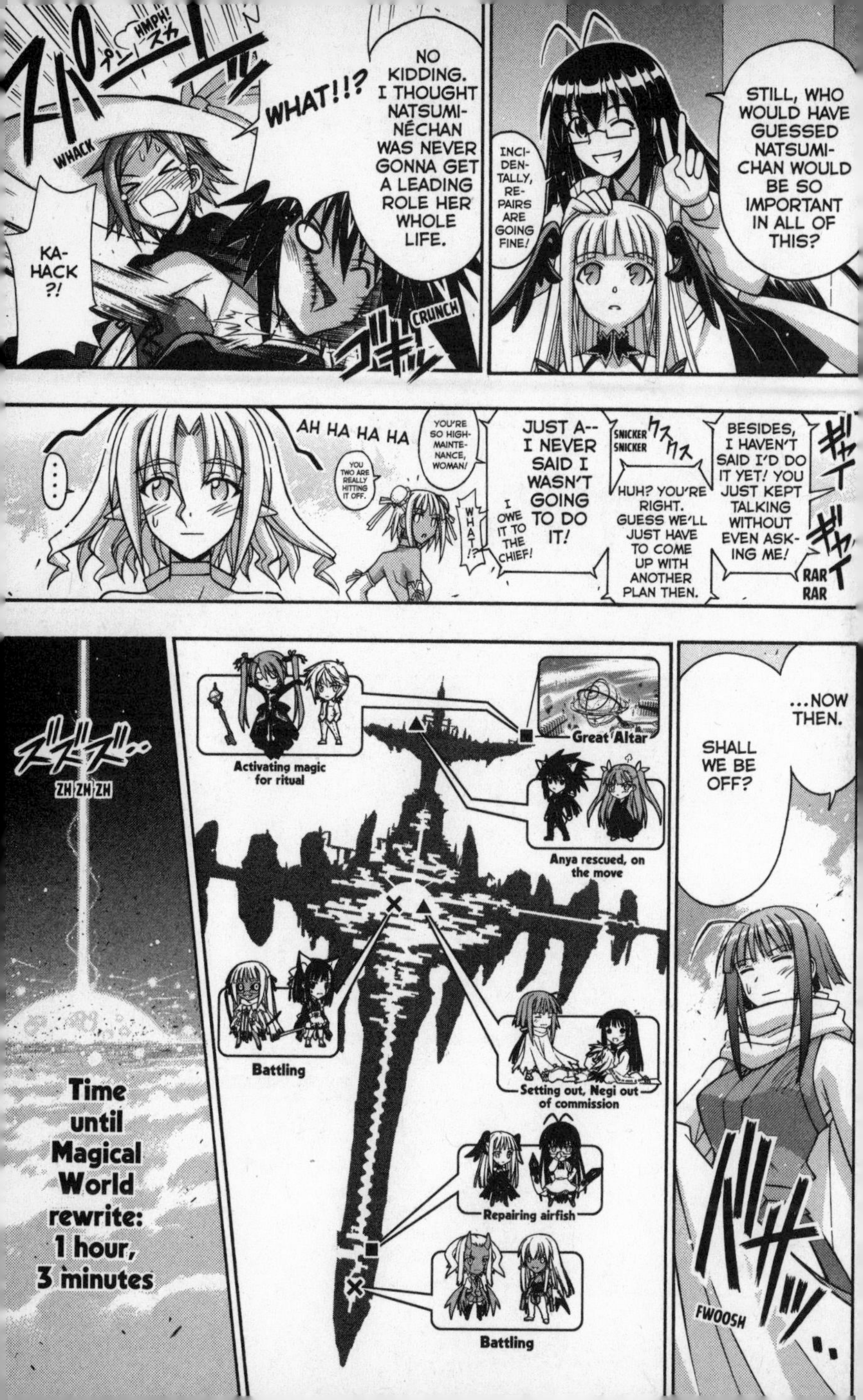
STILL, WHO WOULD HAVE GUESSED NATSUMI-CHAN WOULD BE SO IMPORTANT IN ALL OF THIS?
INCI-DENTALLY, RE-PAIRS ARE GOING FINE!
NO KIDDING. I THOUGHT NATSUMI-NÉCHAN WAS NEVER GONNA GET A LEADING ROLE HER WHOLE LIFE.
HMPH!
WHAT!!?
WHACK
KA-HACK ?!
CRUNCH
RAR RAR
BESIDES, I HAVEN'T SAID I'D DO IT YET! YOU JUST KEPT TALKING WITHOUT EVEN ASK-ING ME!
SNICKER SNICKER
HUH? YOU'RE RIGHT. GUESS WE'LL JUST HAVE TO COME UP WITH ANOTHER PLAN THEN.
JUST A-- I NEVER SAID I WASN'T GOING TO DO IT!
I OWE IT TO THE CHIEF!
WHAT!?
YOU'RE SO HIGH-MAINTE-NANCE, WOMAN!
YOU TWO ARE REALLY HITTING IT OFF.
AH HA HA HA
....
...NOW THEN.
SHALL WE BE OFF?
FWOOSH
Great Altar
Activating magic for ritual
Anya rescued, on the move
Battling
Setting out, Negi out of commission
Repairing airfish
Battling
ZH ZH ZH
Time until Magical World rewrite: 1 hour, 3 minutes

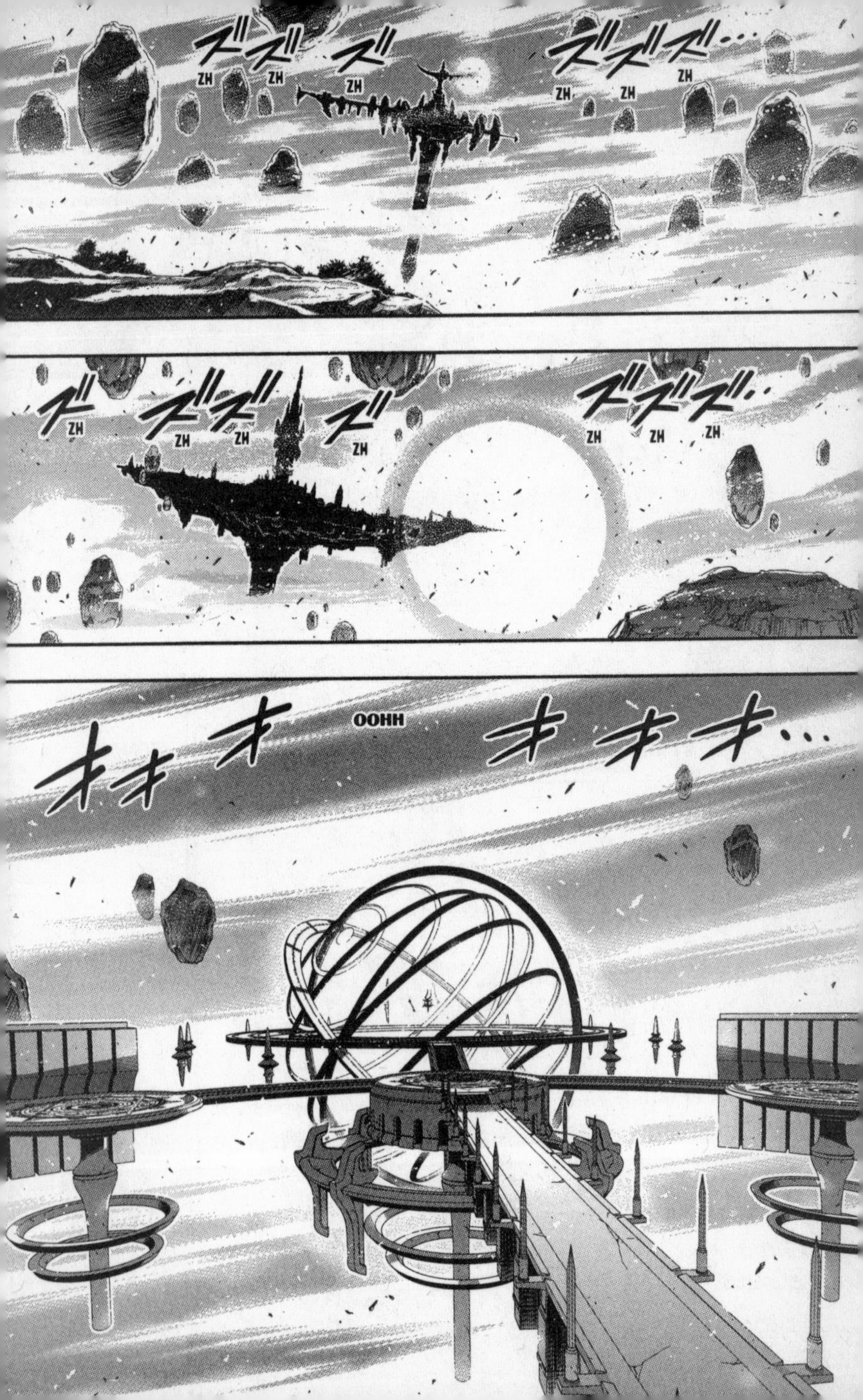
ズズズ…
ZH ZH ZH
ズズズ
ZH ZH ZH
ズズズ…
ZH ZH ZH
ズズズズ
ZH ZH ZH ZH
オオオ…
OOHH
オオオ

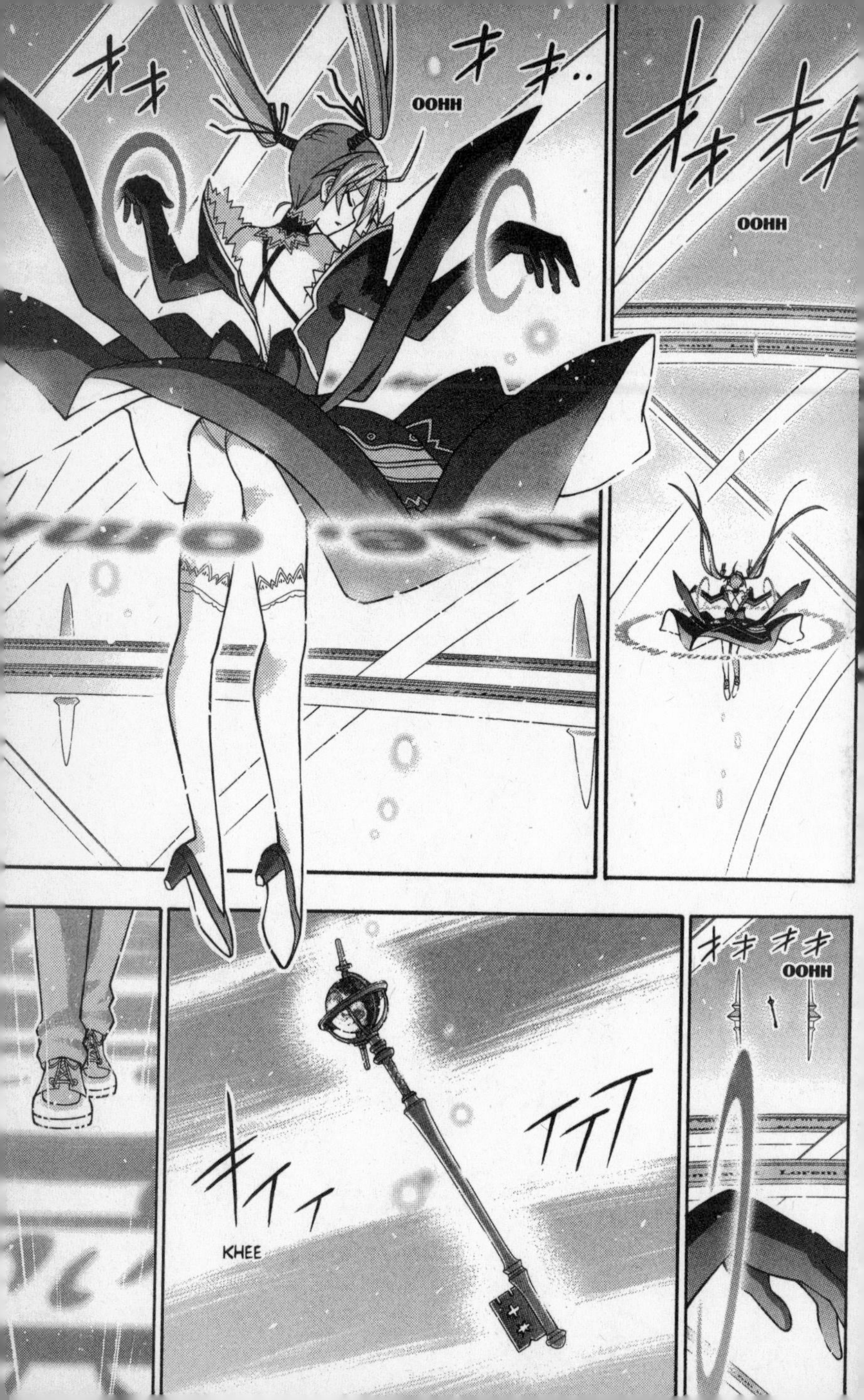

OOHH
OOHH
OOHH
KHEE

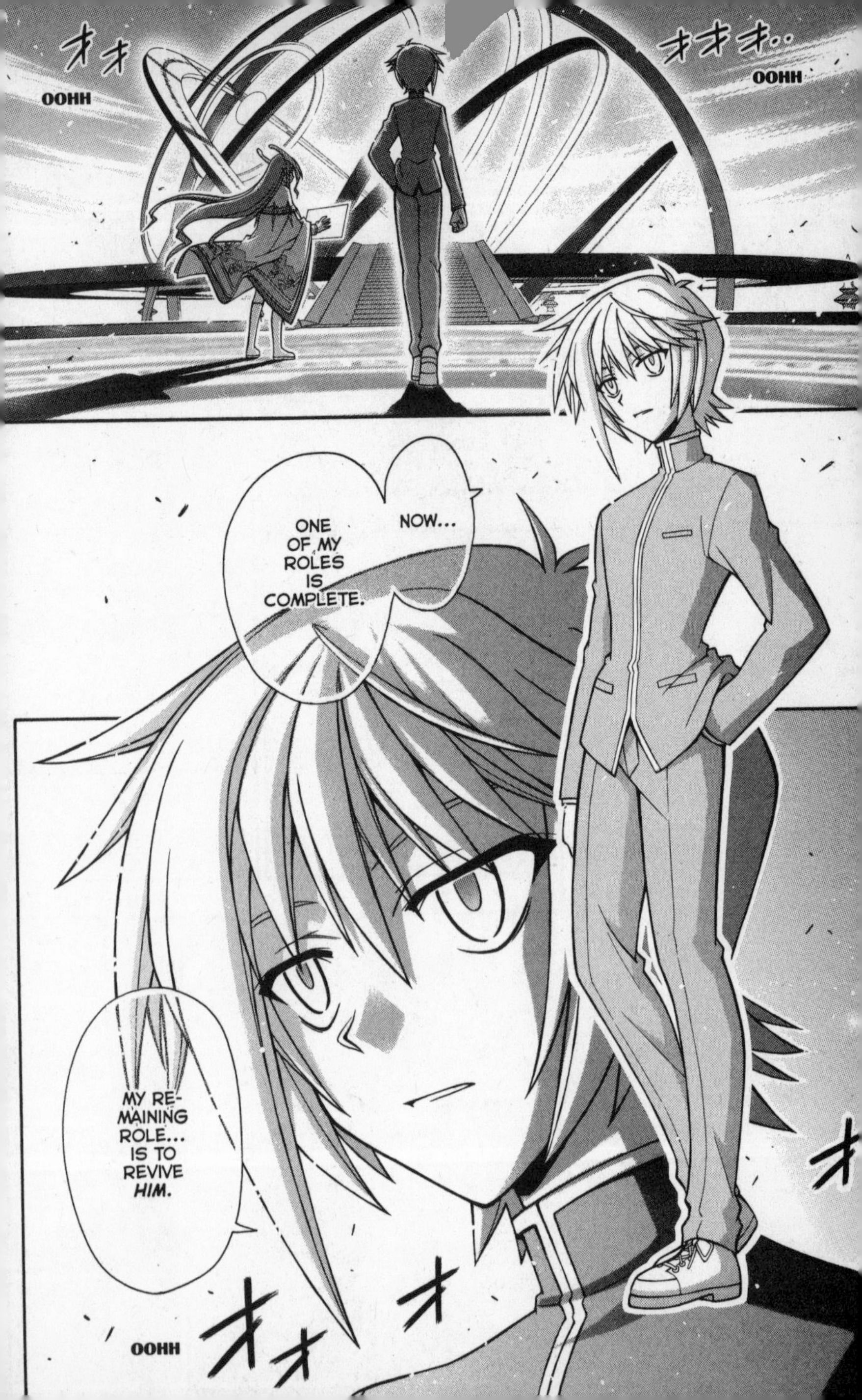
オオオ..
OOHH
オオ
OOHH
NOW...
ONE OF MY ROLES IS COMPLETE.
MY RE-MAINING ROLE... IS TO REVIVE *HIM*.
オ
オオ
OOHH

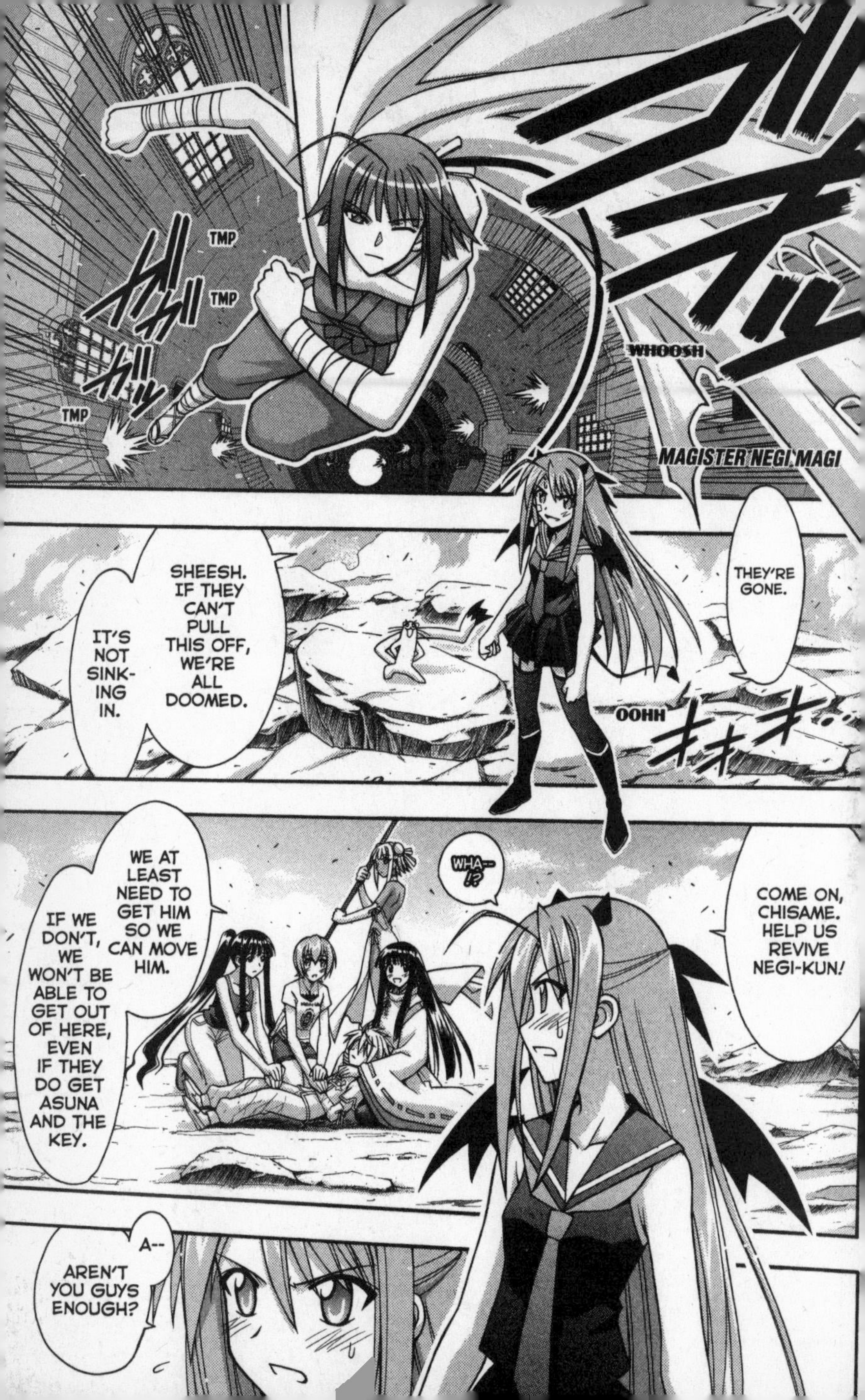
WHOOSH
MAGISTER NEGI MAGI
TMP
TMP
TMP
THEY'RE GONE.
OOHH
SHEESH. IF THEY CAN'T PULL THIS OFF, WE'RE ALL DOOMED.
IT'S NOT SINKING IN.
COME ON, CHISAME. HELP US REVIVE NEGI-KUN!
WHA-- !?
WE AT LEAST NEED TO GET HIM SO WE CAN MOVE HIM.
IF WE DON'T, WE WON'T BE ABLE TO GET OUT OF HERE, EVEN IF THEY DO GET ASUNA AND THE KEY.
A-- AREN'T YOU GUYS ENOUGH?

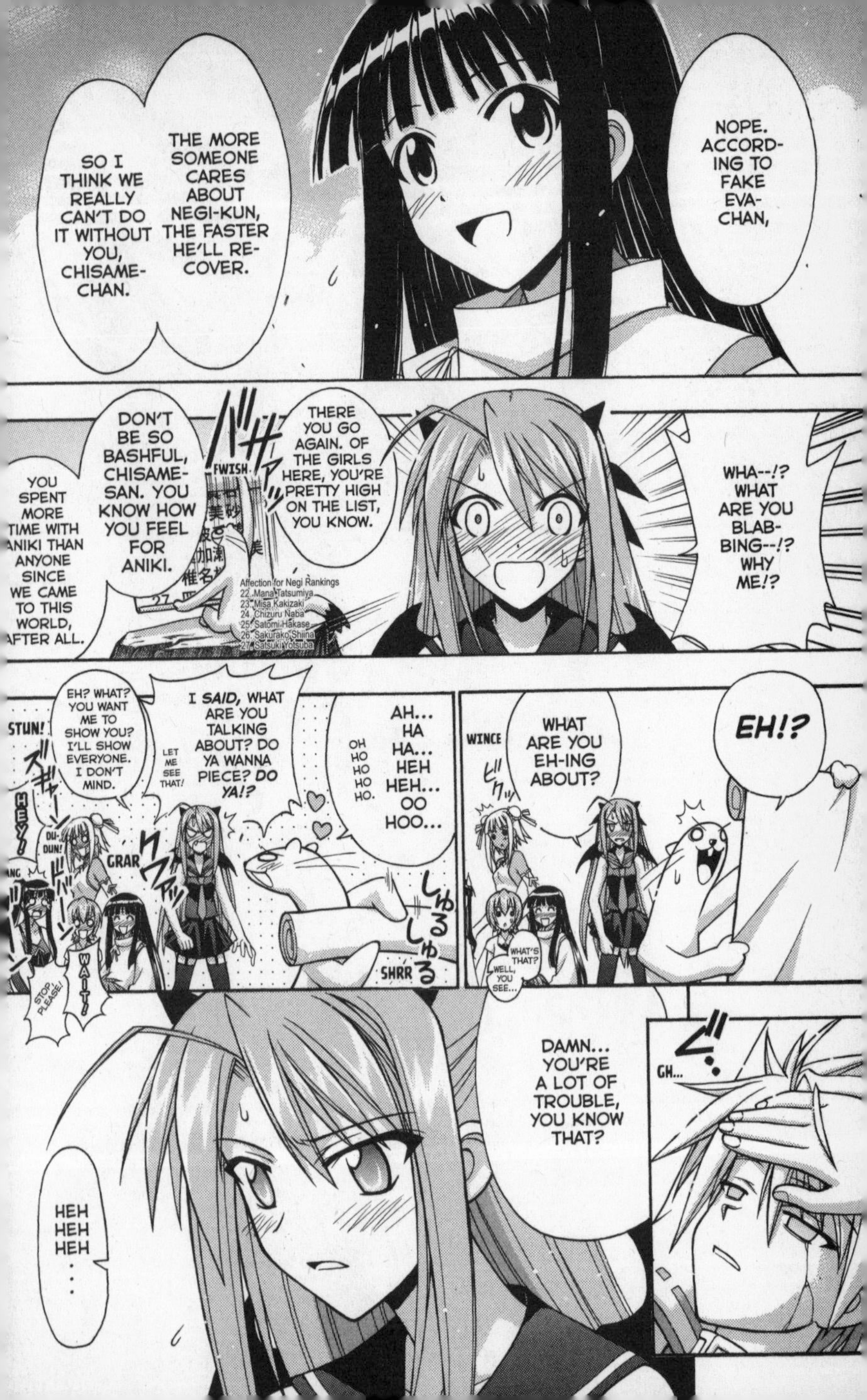
NOPE. ACCORDING TO FAKE EVA-CHAN,
THE MORE SOMEONE CARES ABOUT NEGI-KUN, THE FASTER HE'LL RECOVER.
SO I THINK WE REALLY CAN'T DO IT WITHOUT YOU, CHISAME-CHAN.
WHA--!? WHAT ARE YOU BLABBING--!? WHY ME!?
THERE YOU GO AGAIN. OF THE GIRLS HERE, YOU'RE PRETTY HIGH ON THE LIST, YOU KNOW.
FWISH
DON'T BE SO BASHFUL, CHISAME-SAN. YOU KNOW HOW YOU FEEL FOR ANIKI.
Affection for Negi Rankings
22. Mana Tatsumiya
23. Misa Kakizaki
24. Chizuru Naba
25. Satomi Hakase
26. Sakurako Shiina
27. Satsuki Yotsuba
YOU SPENT MORE TIME WITH ANIKI THAN ANYONE SINCE WE CAME TO THIS WORLD, AFTER ALL.
EH!?
WHAT ARE YOU EH-ING ABOUT?
WINCE
WHAT'S THAT?
WELL, YOU SEE...
AH... HA HA... HEH HEH... OO HOO...
OH HO HO HO HO.
SHRR
I SAID, WHAT ARE YOU TALKING ABOUT? DO YA WANNA PIECE? DO YA!?
GRAR
LET ME SEE THAT!
EH? WHAT? YOU WANT ME TO SHOW YOU? I'LL SHOW EVERYONE. I DON'T MIND.
STUN!
HEY!
DU-DUN!
WAIT!
STOP, PLEASE!
GH...
DAMN... YOU'RE A LOT OF TROUBLE, YOU KNOW THAT?
HEH HEH HEH...

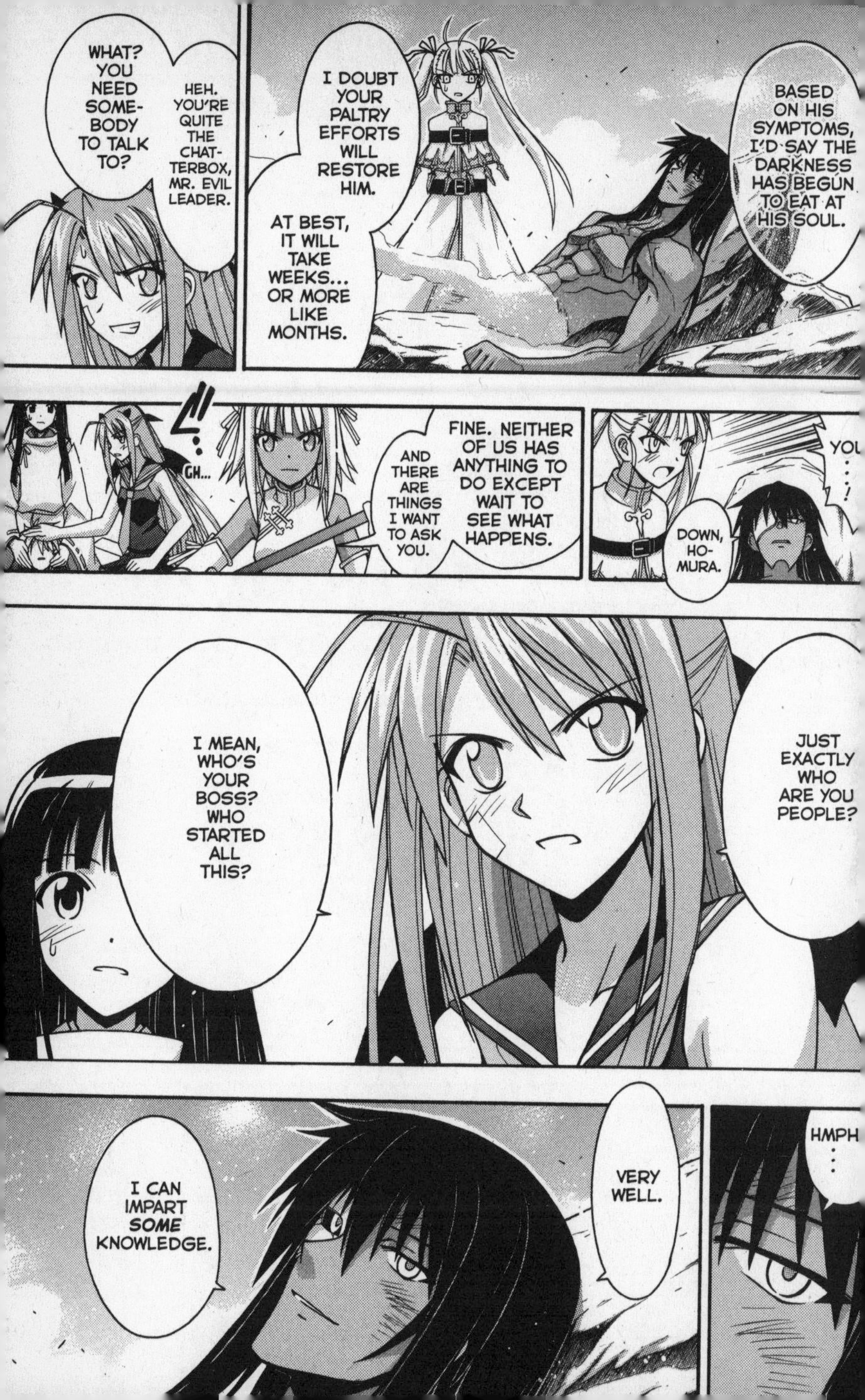
BASED ON HIS SYMPTOMS, I'D SAY THE DARKNESS HAS BEGUN TO EAT AT HIS SOUL.
I DOUBT YOUR PALTRY EFFORTS WILL RESTORE HIM.
AT BEST, IT WILL TAKE WEEKS... OR MORE LIKE MONTHS.
HEH. YOU'RE QUITE THE CHATTERBOX, MR. EVIL LEADER.
WHAT? YOU NEED SOMEBODY TO TALK TO?
YOU...!
DOWN, HOMURA.
FINE. NEITHER OF US HAS ANYTHING TO DO EXCEPT WAIT TO SEE WHAT HAPPENS.
AND THERE ARE THINGS I WANT TO ASK YOU.
GH...
JUST EXACTLY WHO ARE YOU PEOPLE?
I MEAN, WHO'S YOUR BOSS? WHO STARTED ALL THIS?
HMPH...
VERY WELL.
I CAN IMPART *SOME* KNOWLEDGE.

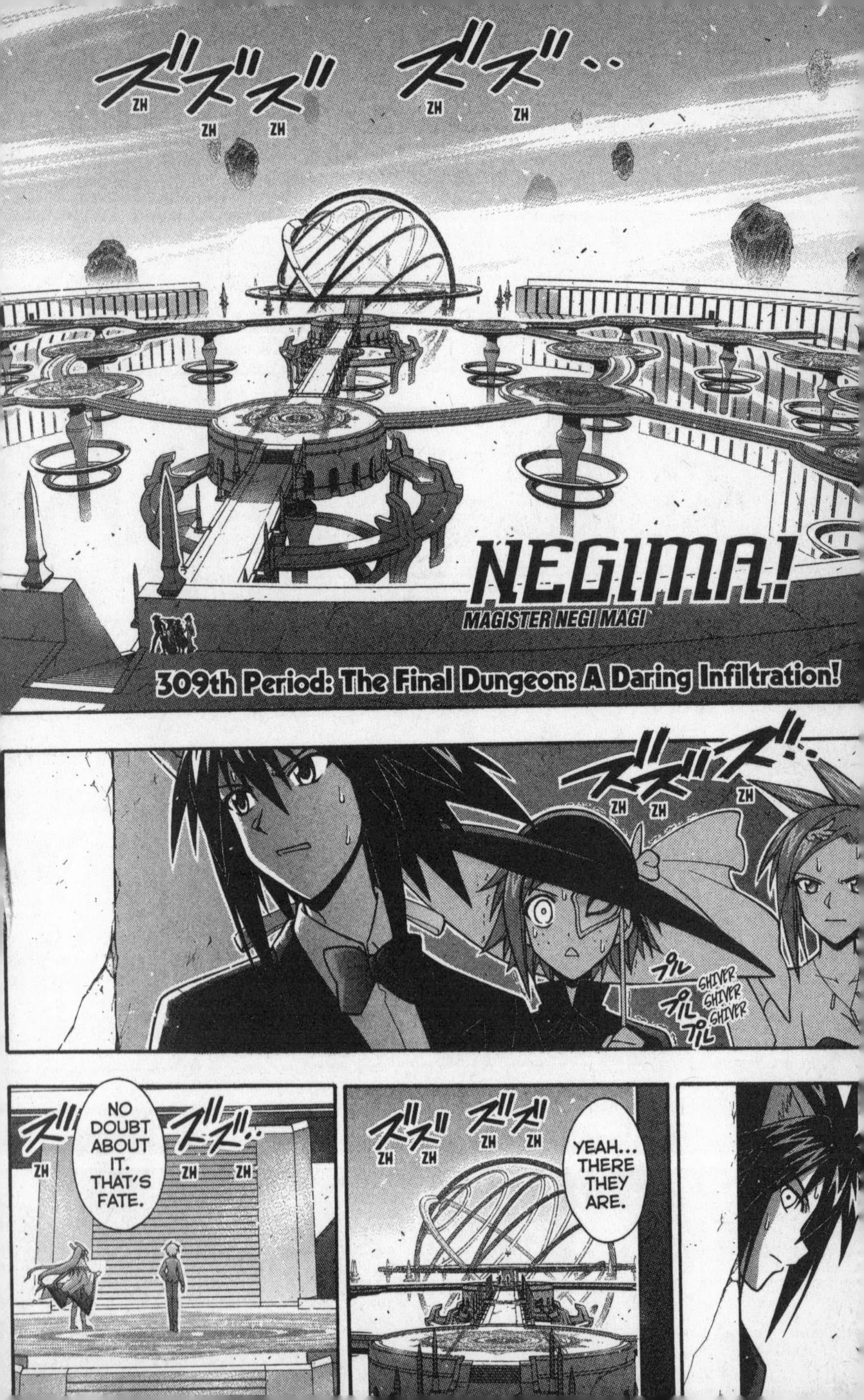
ZH ZH
ZH ZH ZH
NEGIMA!
MAGISTER NEGI MAGI
309th Period: The Final Dungeon: A Daring Infiltration!
ZH ZH ZH
SHIVER SHIVER SHIVER
YEAH... THERE THEY ARE.
ZH ZH ZH ZH
NO DOUBT ABOUT IT. THAT'S FATE.
ZH ZH ZH

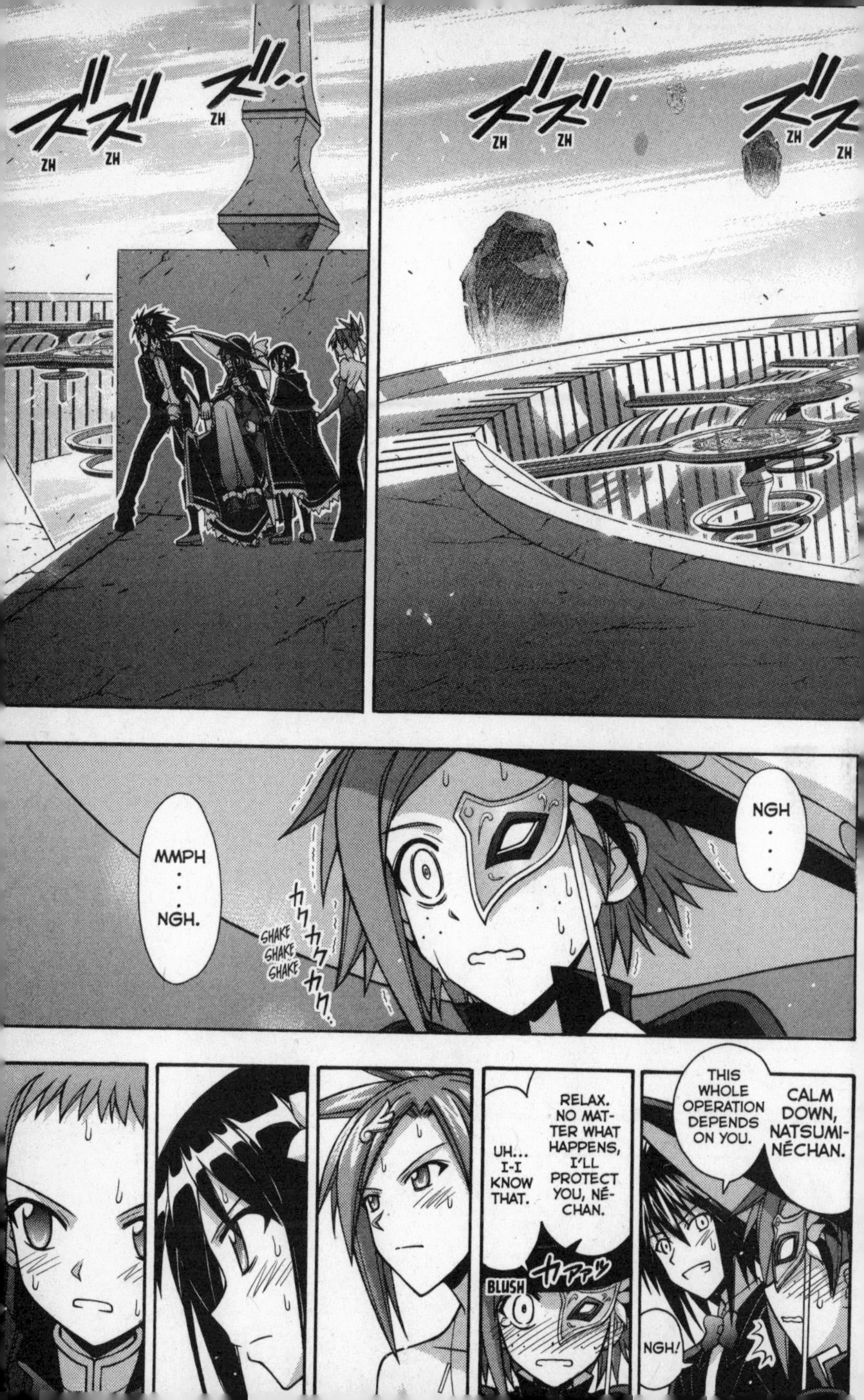
ZH
ZH
ZH
ZH
ZH
ZH
ZH
NGH . . .
MMPH . . . NGH.
SHAKE SHAKE SHAKE
CALM DOWN, NATSUMI-NÉCHAN.
THIS WHOLE OPERATION DEPENDS ON YOU.
NGH!
RELAX. NO MATTER WHAT HAPPENS, I'LL PROTECT YOU, NÉ-CHAN.
UH... I-I KNOW THAT.
BLUSH

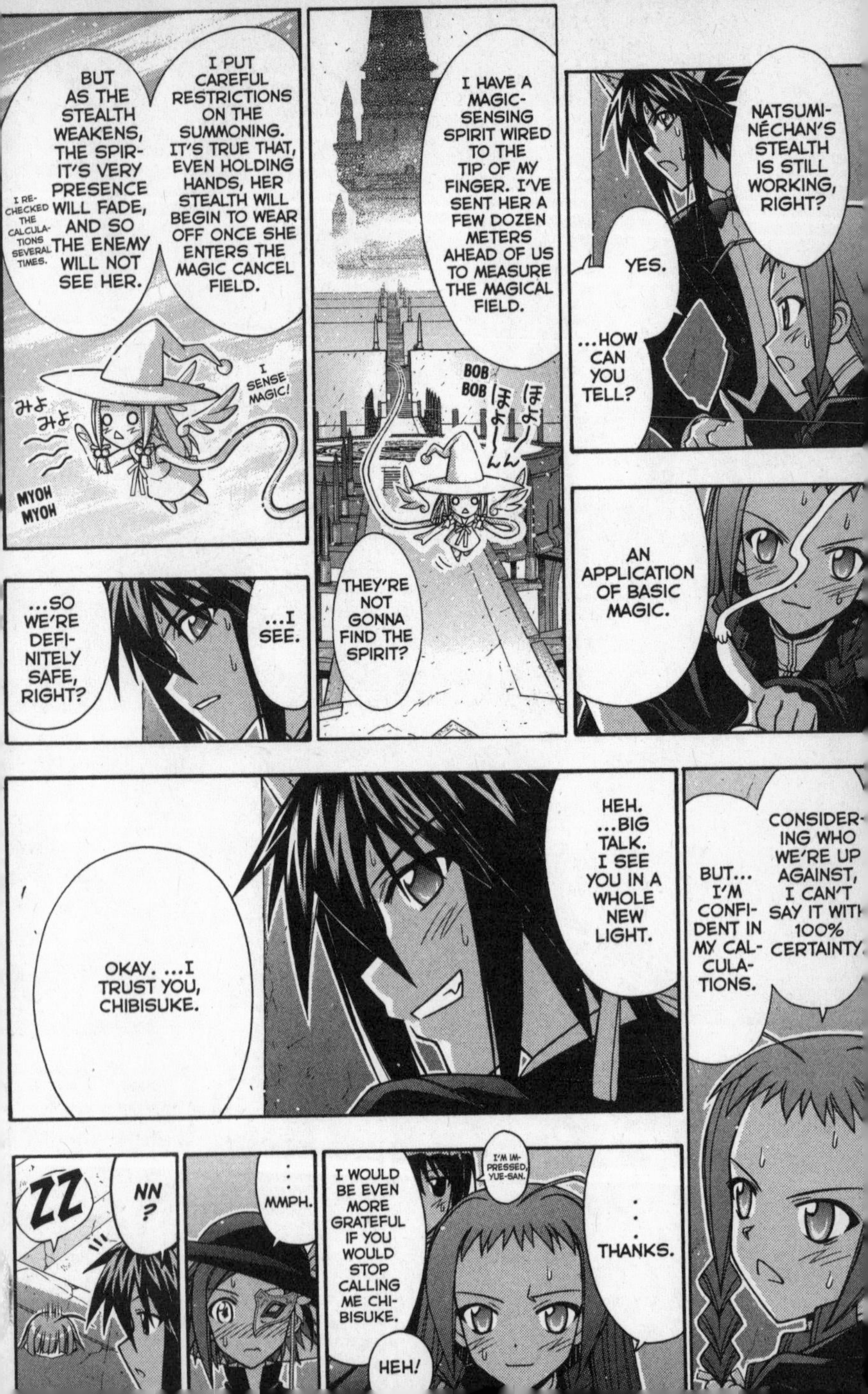
NATSUMI-NÉCHAN'S STEALTH IS STILL WORKING, RIGHT?
YES.
...HOW CAN YOU TELL?
AN APPLICATION OF BASIC MAGIC.
I HAVE A MAGIC-SENSING SPIRIT WIRED TO THE TIP OF MY FINGER. I'VE SENT HER A FEW DOZEN METERS AHEAD OF US TO MEASURE THE MAGICAL FIELD.
BOB BOB
ほよ〜ん ほよ〜ん
THEY'RE NOT GONNA FIND THE SPIRIT?
I PUT CAREFUL RESTRICTIONS ON THE SUMMONING. IT'S TRUE THAT, EVEN HOLDING HANDS, HER STEALTH WILL BEGIN TO WEAR OFF ONCE SHE ENTERS THE MAGIC CANCEL FIELD.
BUT AS THE STEALTH WEAKENS, THE SPIRIT'S VERY PRESENCE WILL FADE, AND SO THE ENEMY WILL NOT SEE HER.
I RE-CHECKED THE CALCULATIONS SEVERAL TIMES.
I SENSE MAGIC!
みよみよ
MYOH MYOH
...I SEE.
...SO WE'RE DEFINITELY SAFE, RIGHT?
CONSIDERING WHO WE'RE UP AGAINST, I CAN'T SAY IT WITH 100% CERTAINTY.
BUT... I'M CONFIDENT IN MY CALCULATIONS.
HEH. ...BIG TALK. I SEE YOU IN A WHOLE NEW LIGHT.
OKAY. ...I TRUST YOU, CHIBISUKE.
...THANKS.
I'M IMPRESSED, YUE-SAN.
I WOULD BE EVEN MORE GRATEFUL IF YOU WOULD STOP CALLING ME CHIBISUKE.
HEH!
...MMPH.
NN?
ZZ

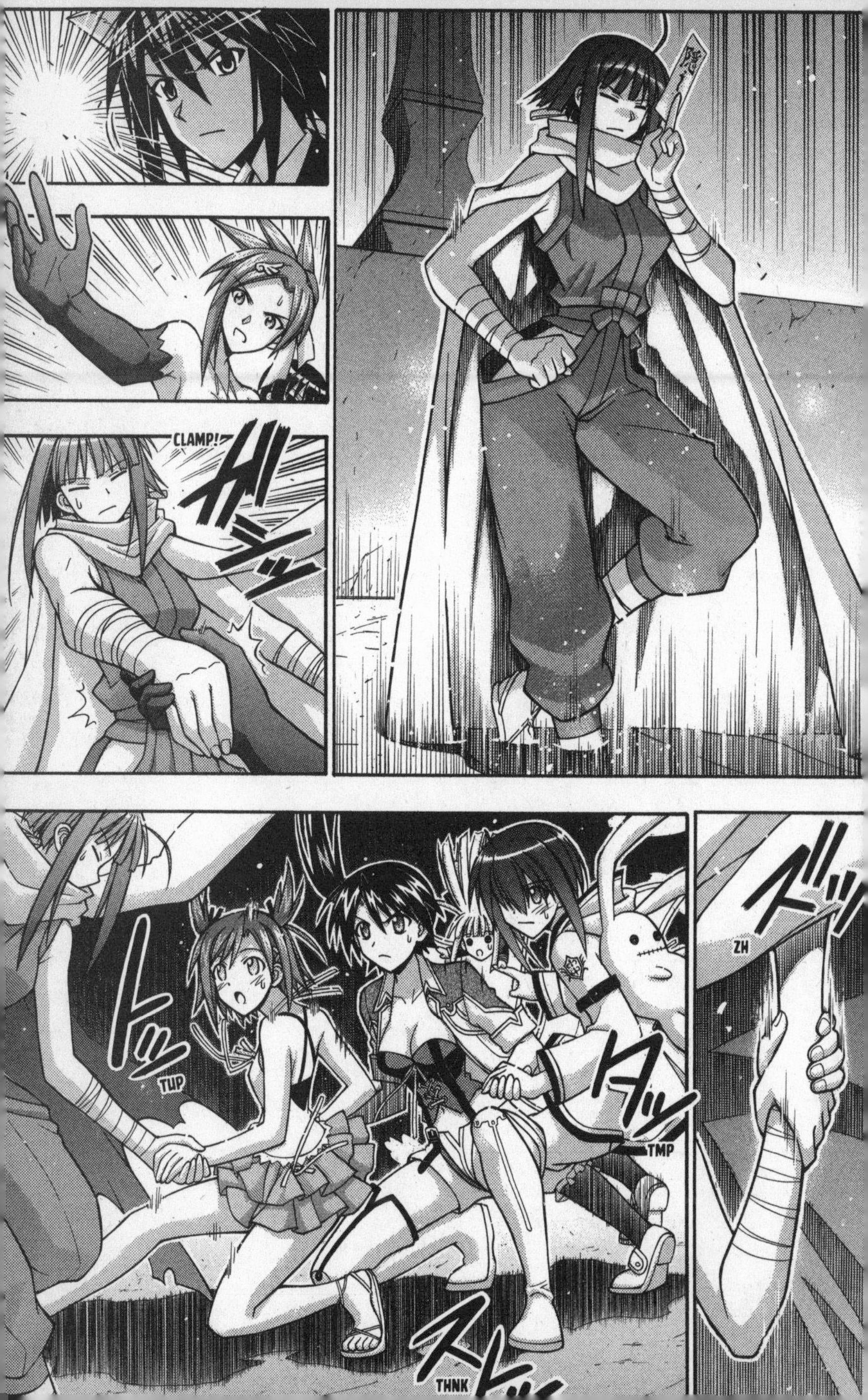
CLAMP!
ZH
TMP
TUP
THNK

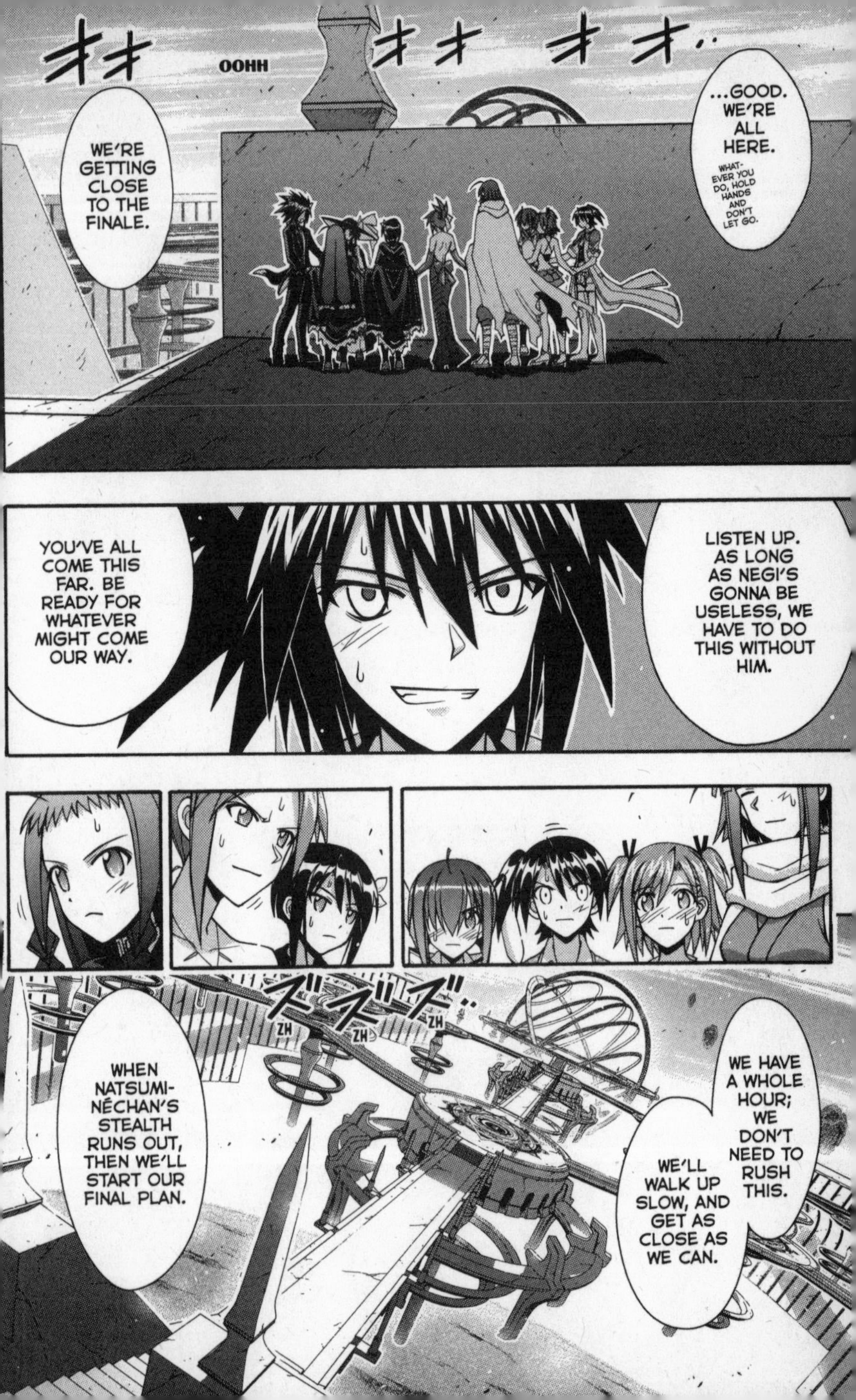
オオ
OOHH
オオオオ..
...GOOD. WE'RE ALL HERE.
WHATEVER YOU DO, HOLD HANDS AND DON'T LET GO.
WE'RE GETTING CLOSE TO THE FINALE.
LISTEN UP. AS LONG AS NEGI'S GONNA BE USELESS, WE HAVE TO DO THIS WITHOUT HIM.
YOU'VE ALL COME THIS FAR. BE READY FOR WHATEVER MIGHT COME OUR WAY.
ズズズ..
ZH ZH ZH
WE HAVE A WHOLE HOUR; WE DON'T NEED TO RUSH THIS.
WE'LL WALK UP SLOW, AND GET AS CLOSE AS WE CAN.
WHEN NATSUMI-NÉCHAN'S STEALTH RUNS OUT, THEN WE'LL START OUR FINAL PLAN.

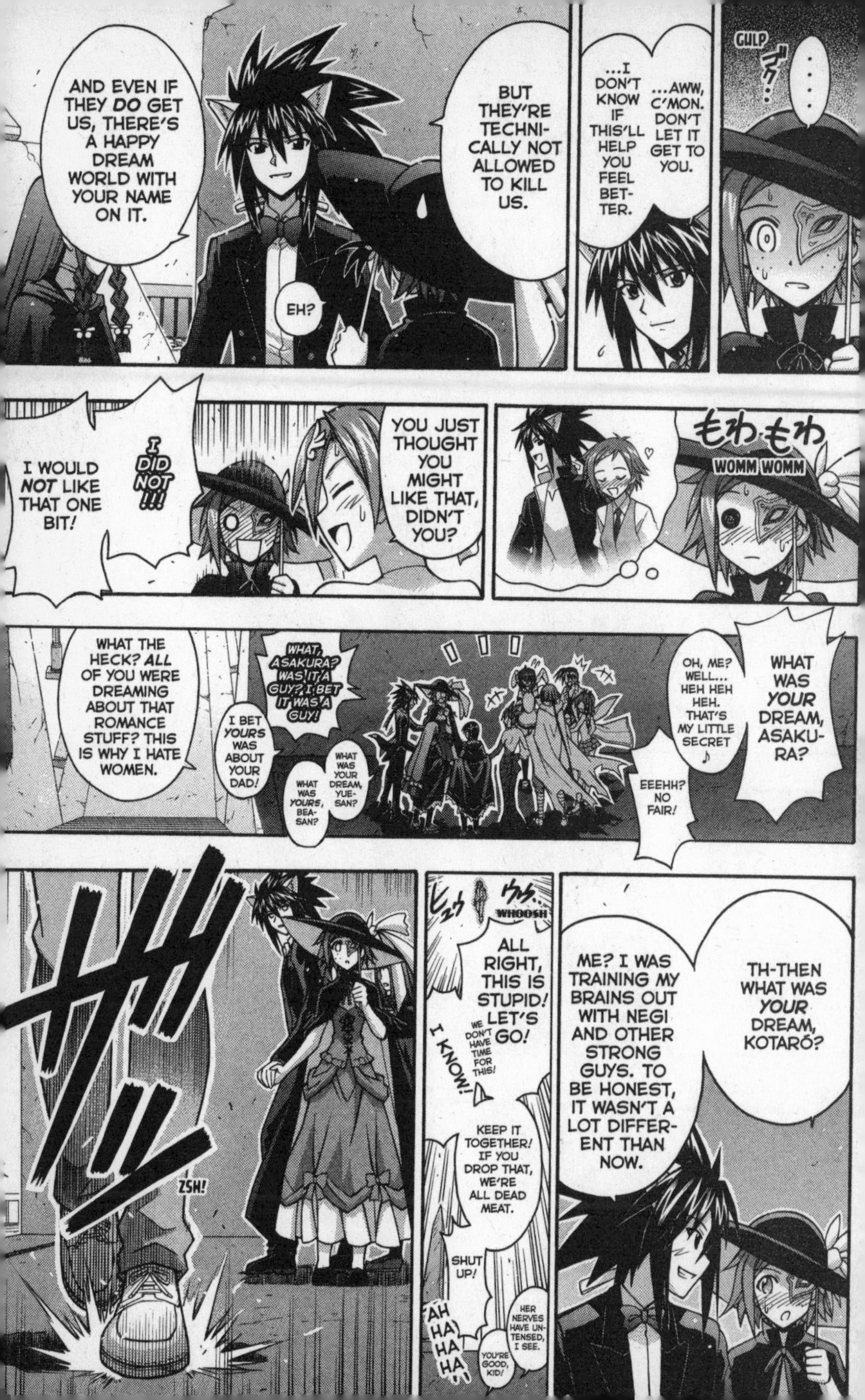

GULP
......
...AWW, C'MON. DON'T LET IT GET TO YOU.
...I DON'T KNOW IF THIS'LL HELP YOU FEEL BETTER.
BUT THEY'RE TECHNICALLY NOT ALLOWED TO KILL US.
EH?
AND EVEN IF THEY *DO* GET US, THERE'S A HAPPY DREAM WORLD WITH YOUR NAME ON IT.
もわもわ
WOMM WOMM
YOU JUST THOUGHT YOU MIGHT LIKE THAT, DIDN'T YOU?
I DID NOT!!!
I WOULD *NOT* LIKE THAT ONE BIT!
WHAT WAS *YOUR* DREAM, ASAKURA?
OH, ME? WELL... HEH HEH HEH. THAT'S MY LITTLE SECRET ♪
EEEHH? NO FAIR!
WHAT, ASAKURA? WAS IT A GUY? I BET IT WAS A GUY!
WHAT WAS YOUR DREAM, YUE-SAN?
WHAT WAS *YOURS*, BEA-SAN?
I BET *YOURS* WAS ABOUT YOUR DAD!
WHAT THE HECK? *ALL* OF YOU WERE DREAMING ABOUT THAT ROMANCE STUFF? THIS IS WHY I HATE WOMEN.
TH-THEN WHAT WAS *YOUR* DREAM, KOTARŌ?
ME? I WAS TRAINING MY BRAINS OUT WITH NEGI AND OTHER STRONG GUYS. TO BE HONEST, IT WASN'T A LOT DIFFERENT THAN NOW.
WHOOSH
ALL RIGHT, THIS IS STUPID! LET'S GO!
WE DON'T HAVE TIME FOR THIS!
I KNOW!
KEEP IT TOGETHER! IF YOU DROP THAT, WE'RE ALL DEAD MEAT.
SHUT UP!
AH HA HA HA!
HER NERVES HAVE UNTENSED, I SEE.
YOU'RE GOOD, KID!
ZSH!

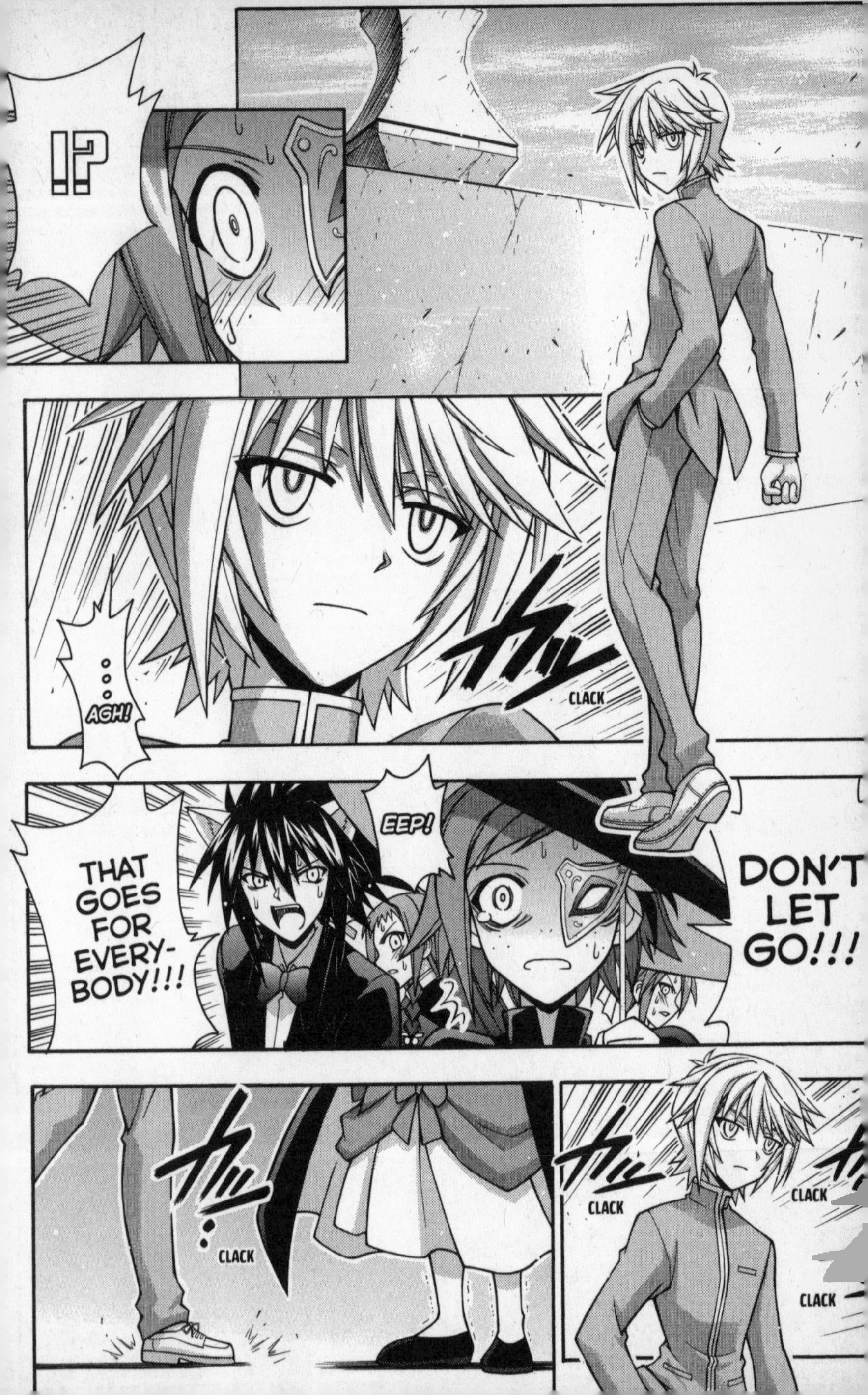

!?
CLACK
...AGH!
DON'T LET GO!!!
EEP!
THAT GOES FOR EVERY-BODY!!!
CLACK
CLACK
CLACK
CLACK

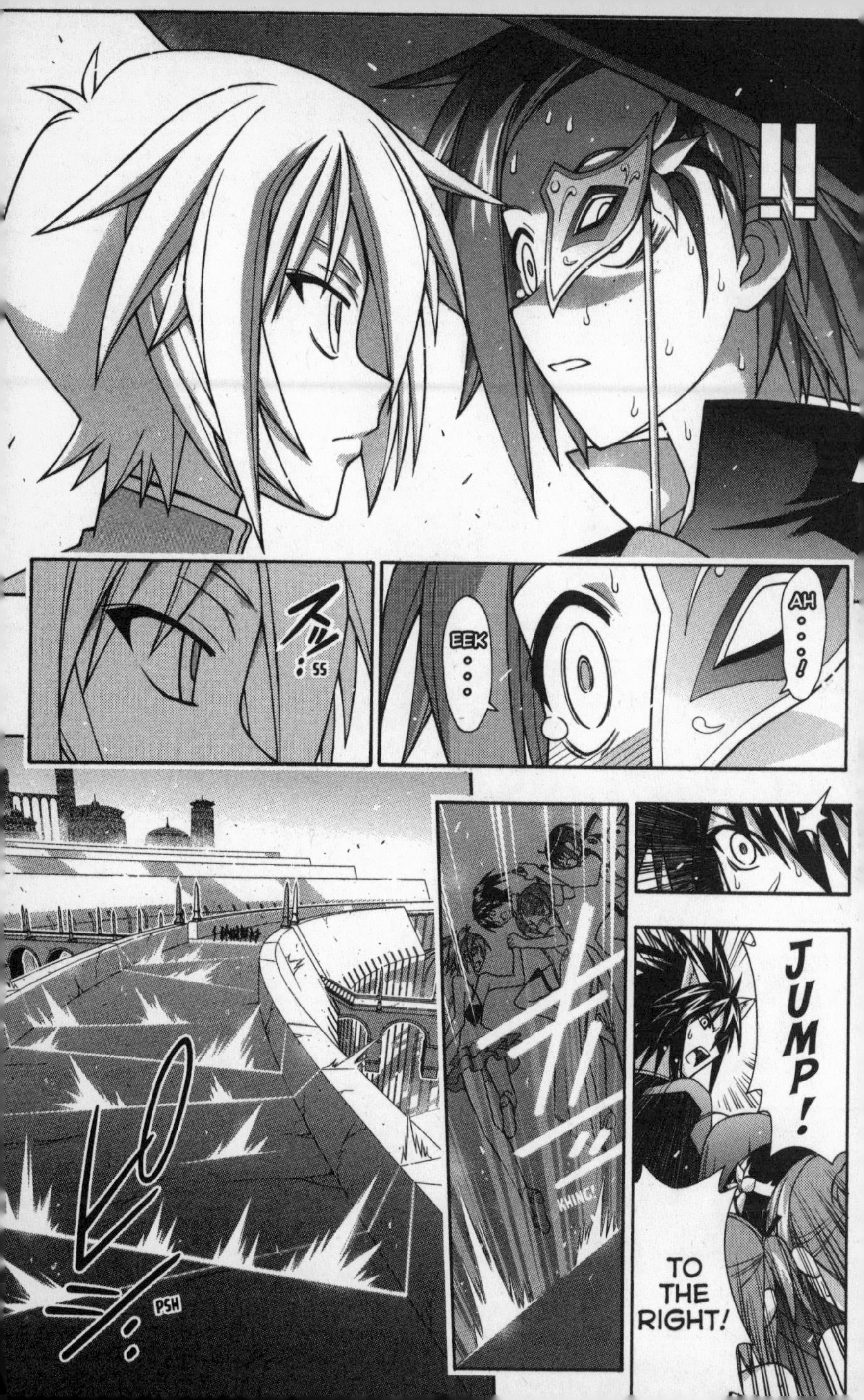
!!
AH...!
EEK...
スッ
SS
JUMP!
TO THE RIGHT!
KHING!
PSH

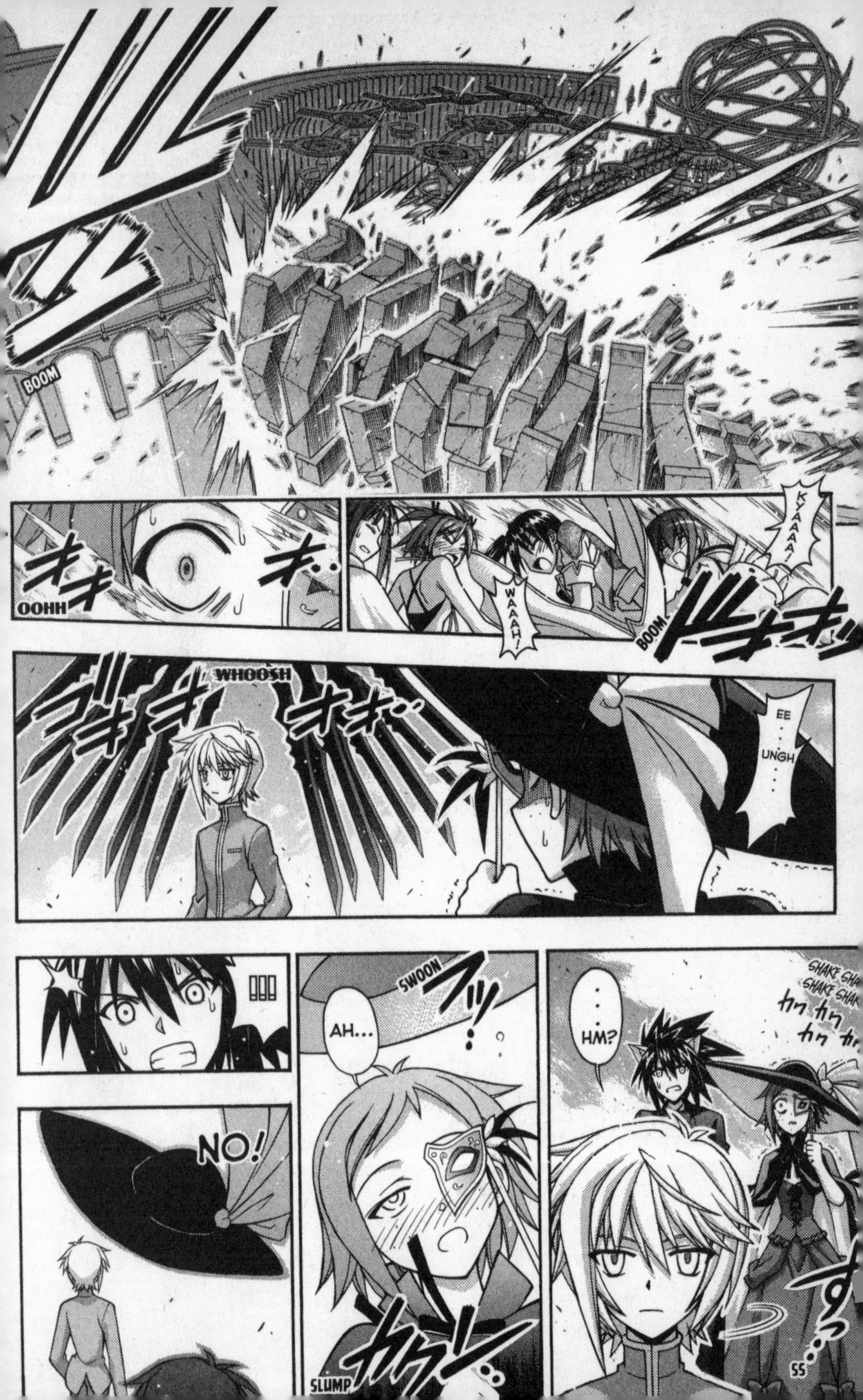
BOOM
KYAAAA!
WAAAH!
BOOM
OOHH
WHOOSH
EE... UNGH...
SHAKE SHAKE
SHAKE SHAKE
...HM?
SS
SWOON
AH...
SLUMP
!!!
NO!

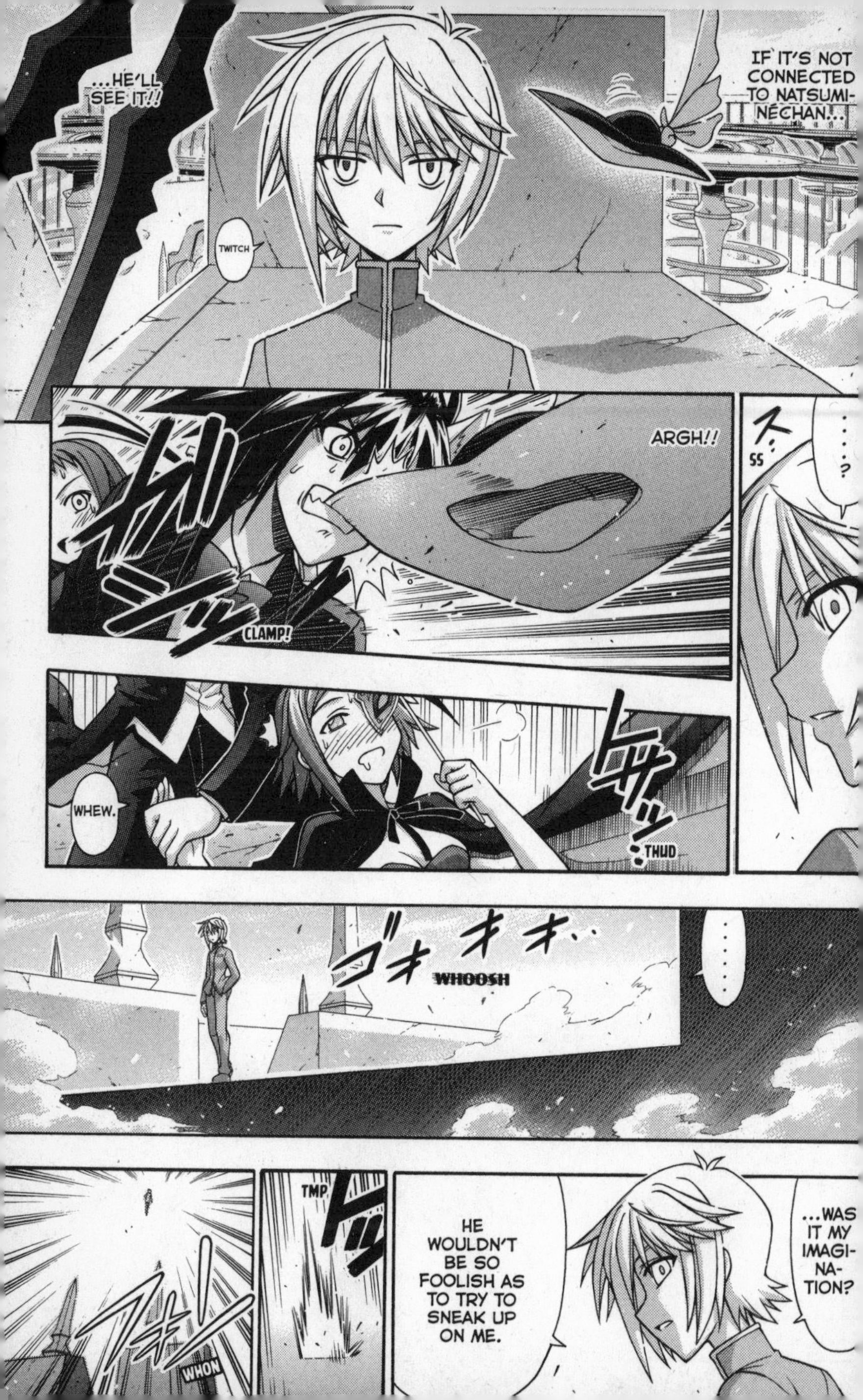
IF IT'S NOT CONNECTED TO NATSUMI-NÉCHAN...
...HE'LL SEE IT!!
TWITCH
SS
...?
ARGH!!
CLAMP!
THUD
WHEW.
...
WHOOSH
...WAS IT MY IMAGINATION?
HE WOULDN'T BE SO FOOLISH AS TO TRY TO SNEAK UP ON ME.
TMP
WHON

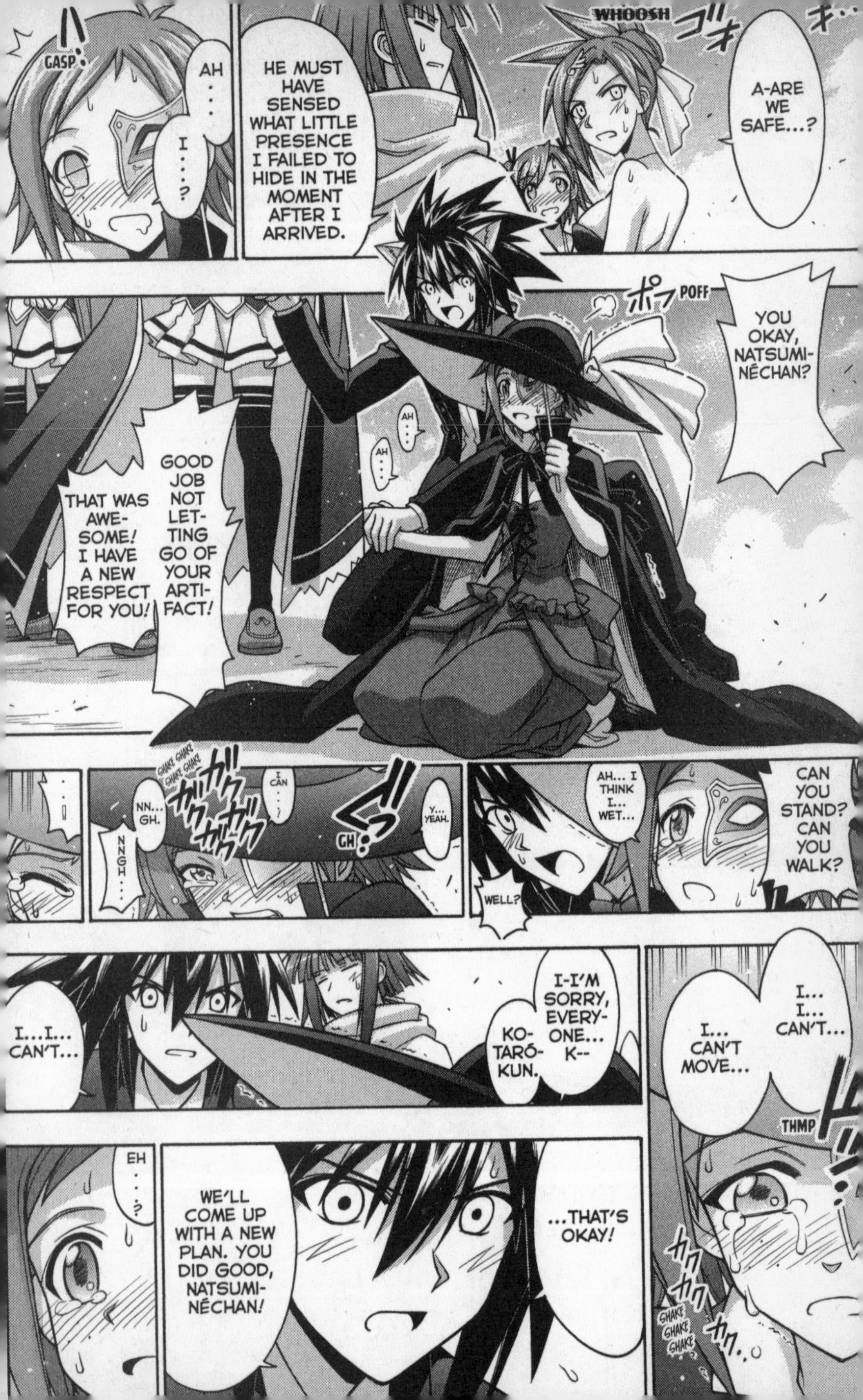
WHOOSH
A-ARE WE SAFE...?
HE MUST HAVE SENSED WHAT LITTLE PRESENCE I FAILED TO HIDE IN THE MOMENT AFTER I ARRIVED.
GASP
AH... I...?
POFF
YOU OKAY, NATSUMI-NÉCHAN?
AH...
AH...
GOOD JOB NOT LETTING GO OF YOUR ARTIFACT!
THAT WAS AWESOME! I HAVE A NEW RESPECT FOR YOU!
CAN YOU STAND? CAN YOU WALK?
AH... I THINK I... WET...
WELL?
Y... YEAH.
GH
I CAN...?
SHAKE SHAKE SHAKE SHAKE
NN... GH.
NNGH...
...!
I... I... CAN'T...
I... CAN'T MOVE...
THMP
SHAKE SHAKE SHAKE
I-I'M SORRY, EVERYONE... K--
KOTARŌ-KUN.
I...I... CAN'T...
...THAT'S OKAY!
WE'LL COME UP WITH A NEW PLAN. YOU DID GOOD, NATSUMI-NÉCHAN!
EH...?

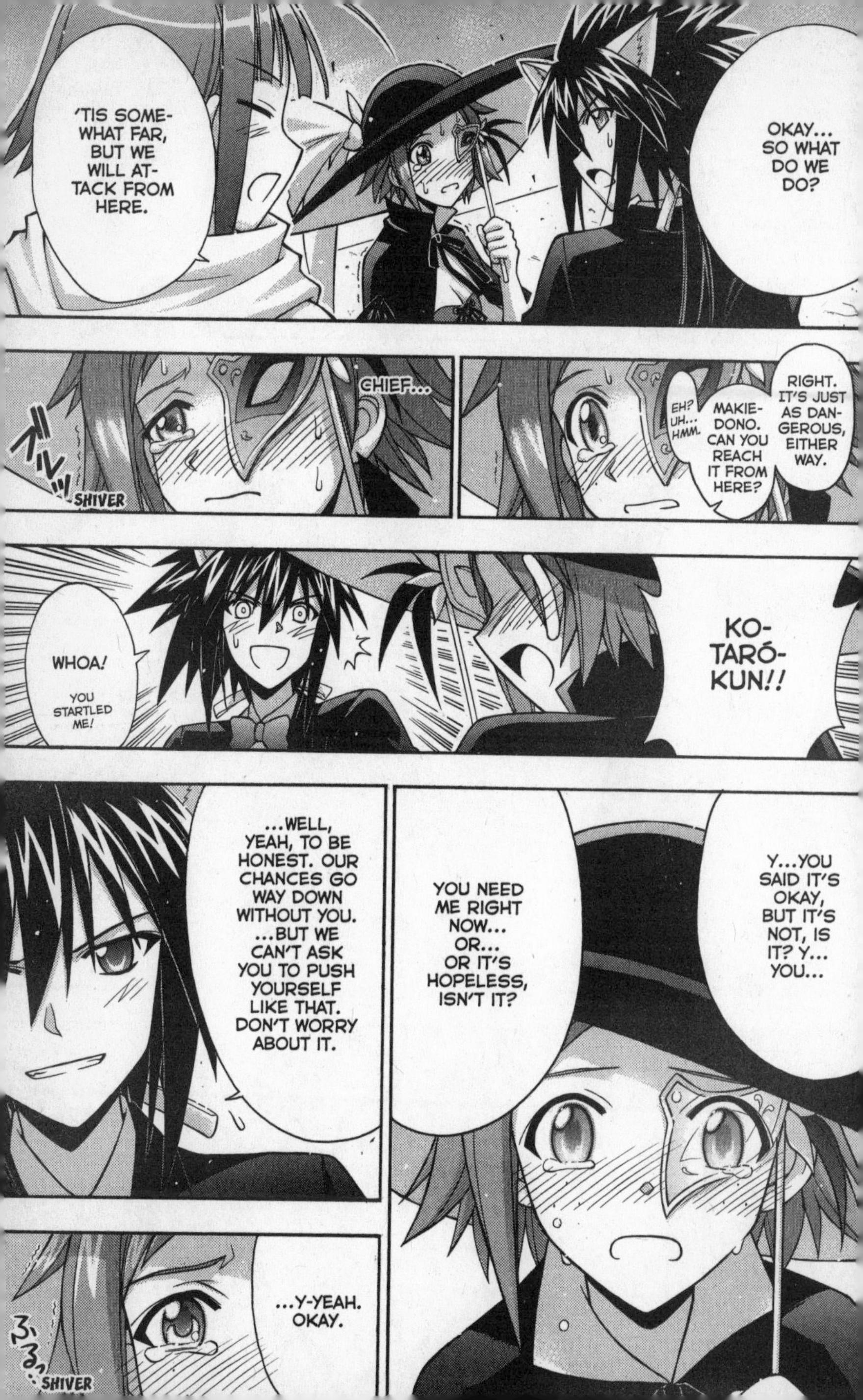
OKAY... SO WHAT DO WE DO?
'TIS SOME-WHAT FAR, BUT WE WILL AT-TACK FROM HERE.
RIGHT. IT'S JUST AS DAN-GEROUS, EITHER WAY.
MAKIE-DONO. CAN YOU REACH IT FROM HERE?
EH? UH... HMM.
CHIEF...
SHIVER
KO-TARÓ-KUN!!
WHOA!
YOU STARTLED ME!
Y...YOU SAID IT'S OKAY, BUT IT'S NOT, IS IT? Y... YOU...
YOU NEED ME RIGHT NOW... OR... OR IT'S HOPELESS, ISN'T IT?
...WELL, YEAH, TO BE HONEST. OUR CHANCES GO WAY DOWN WITHOUT YOU. ...BUT WE CAN'T ASK YOU TO PUSH YOURSELF LIKE THAT. DON'T WORRY ABOUT IT.
...Y-YEAH. OKAY.
SHIVER

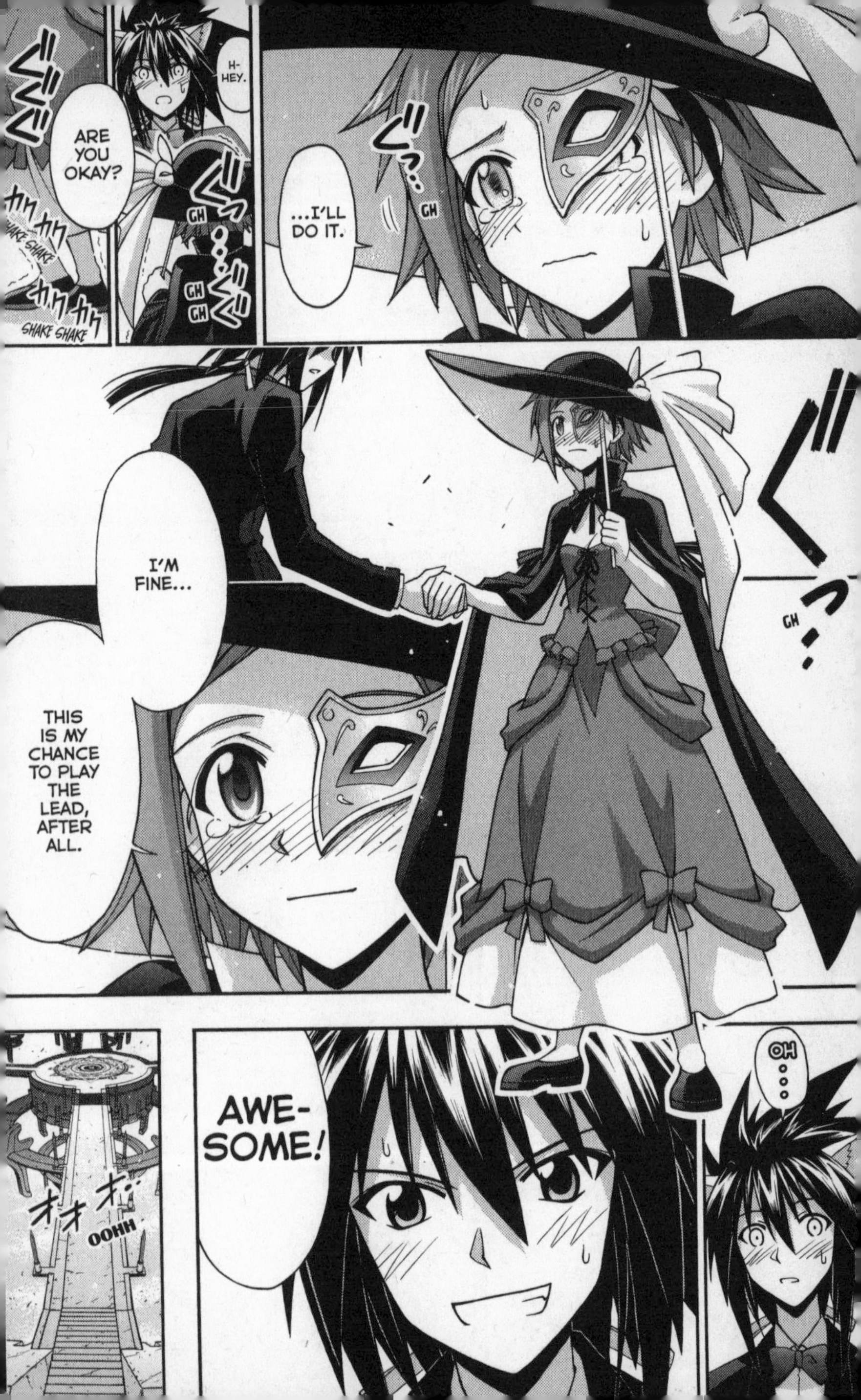
GH
...I'LL DO IT.
GH
GH
GH
H-HEY.
ARE YOU OKAY?
SHAKE SHAKE
SHAKE SHAKE
GH
I'M FINE...
THIS IS MY CHANCE TO PLAY THE LEAD, AFTER ALL.
OH...
AWE-SOME!
OOHH

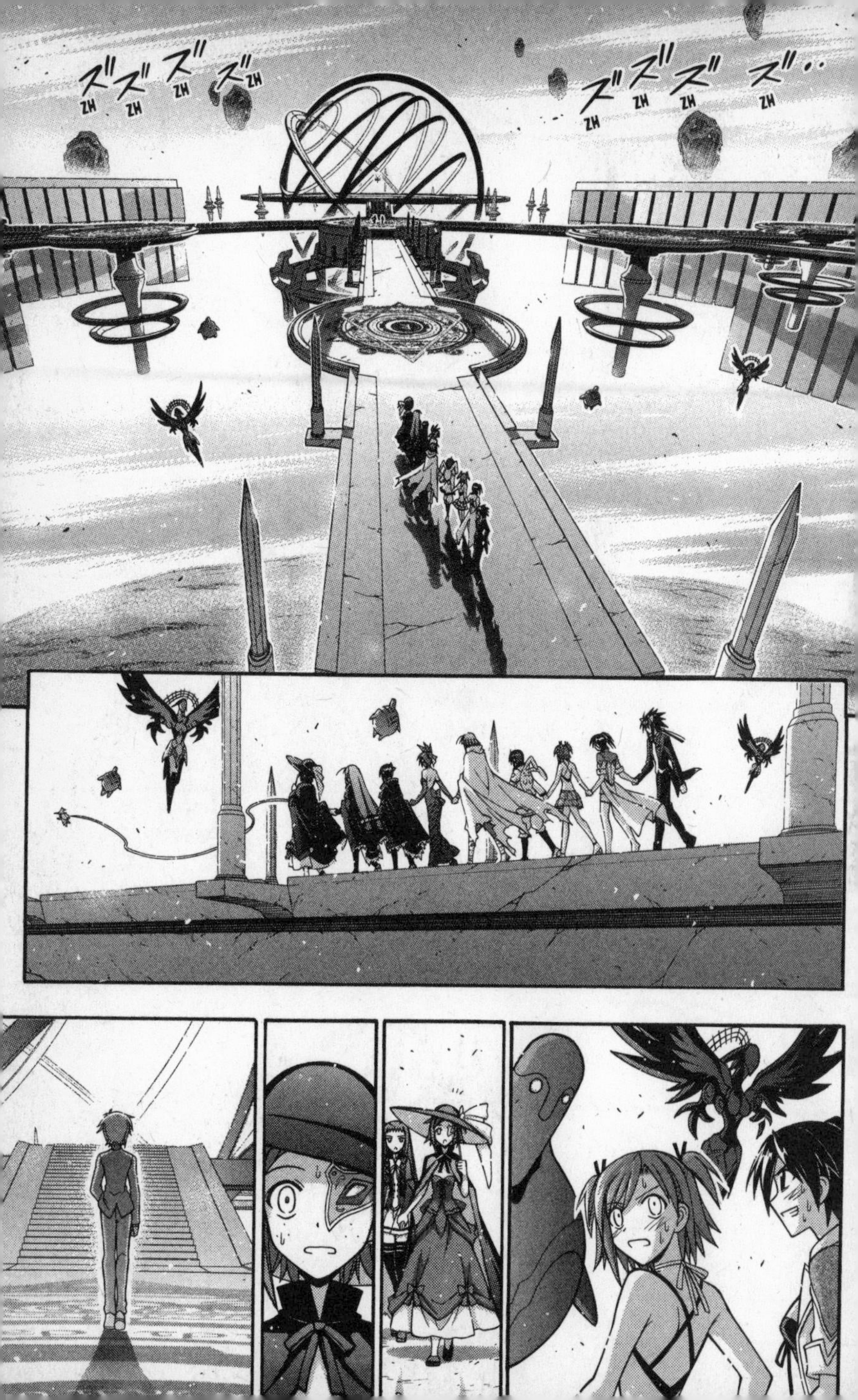
ズズズズ..
ZH ZH ZH ZH
ズズズズ
ZH ZH ZH ZH

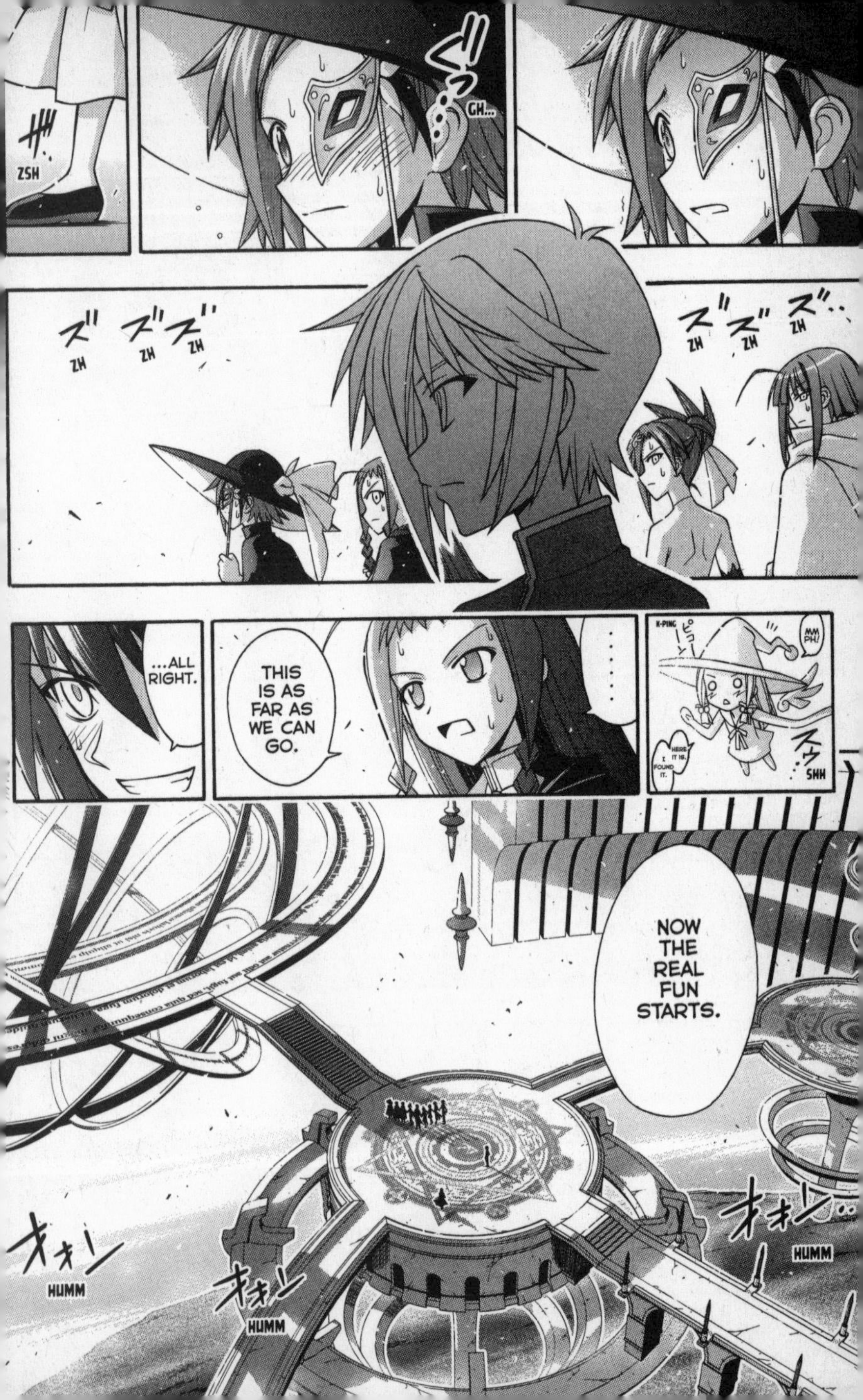
GH...
ZSH
ZH ZH ZH...
ZH ZH ZH
K-PING
MM PH!
HERE IT IS. I FOUND IT.
SHH
......
THIS IS AS FAR AS WE CAN GO.
...ALL RIGHT.
NOW THE REAL FUN STARTS.
HUMM
HUMM
HUMM

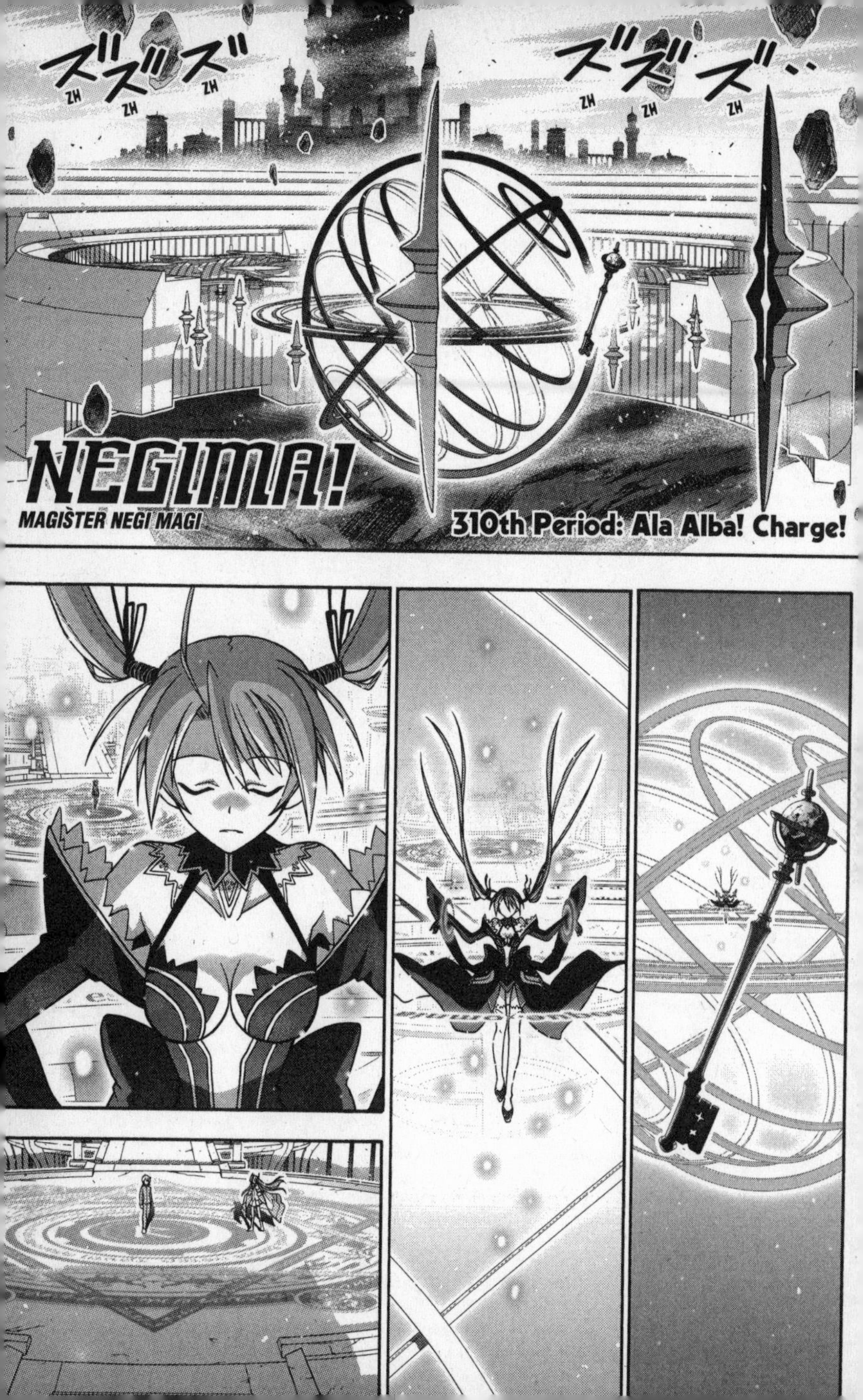
ズズズ‥
ZH ZH ZH
ズズズ
ZH ZH ZH
NEGIMA!
MAGISTER NEGI MAGI
310th Period: Ala Alba! Charge!

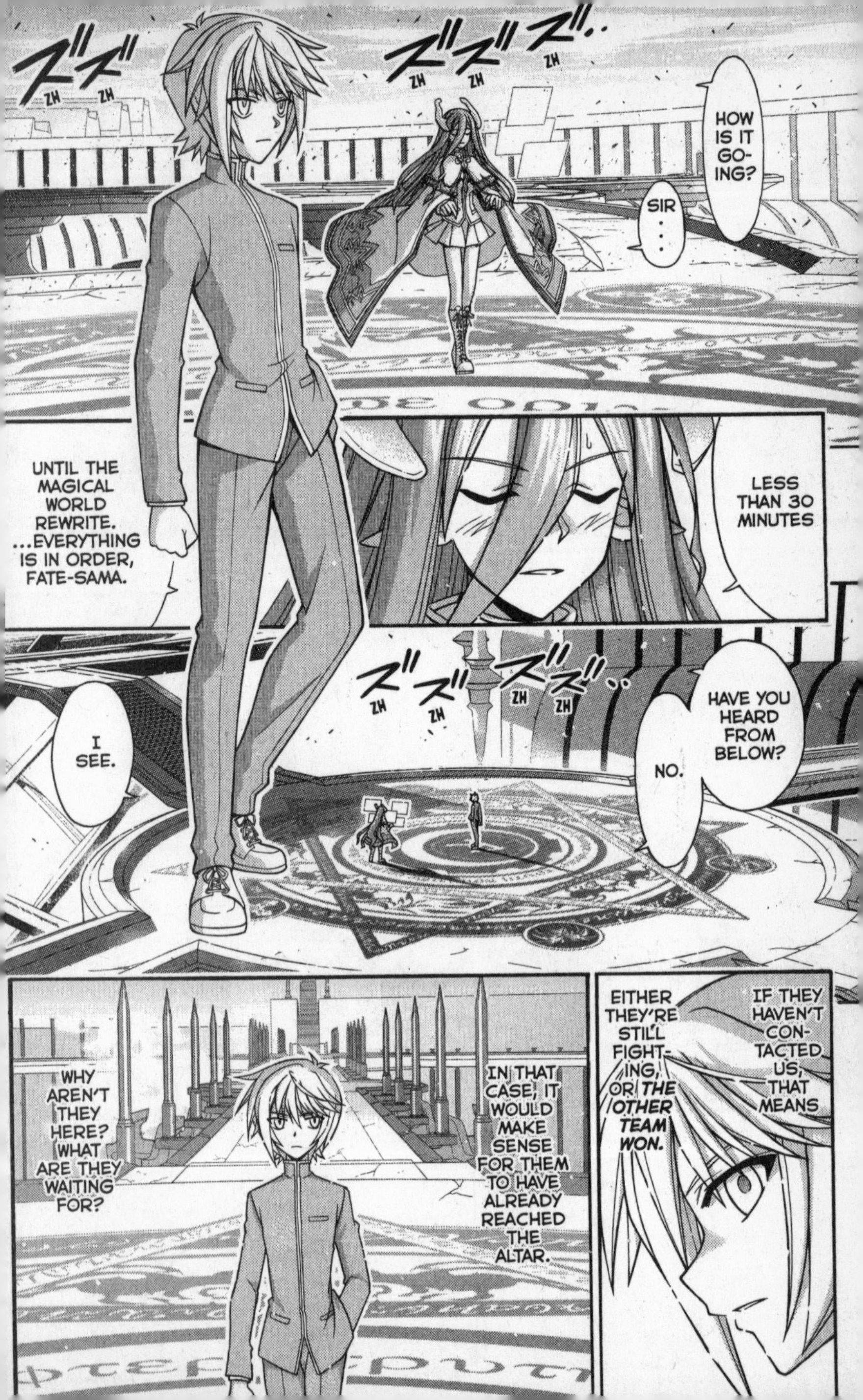
ZH ZH ZH
ZH ZH
HOW IS IT GOING?
SIR...
LESS THAN 30 MINUTES
UNTIL THE MAGICAL WORLD REWRITE. ...EVERYTHING IS IN ORDER, FATE-SAMA.
ZH ZH ZH ZH
HAVE YOU HEARD FROM BELOW?
NO.
I SEE.
IF THEY HAVEN'T CONTACTED US, THAT MEANS
EITHER THEY'RE STILL FIGHTING, OR *THE OTHER TEAM WON.*
IN THAT CASE, IT WOULD MAKE SENSE FOR THEM TO HAVE ALREADY REACHED THE ALTAR.
WHY AREN'T THEY HERE? WHAT ARE THEY WAITING FOR?

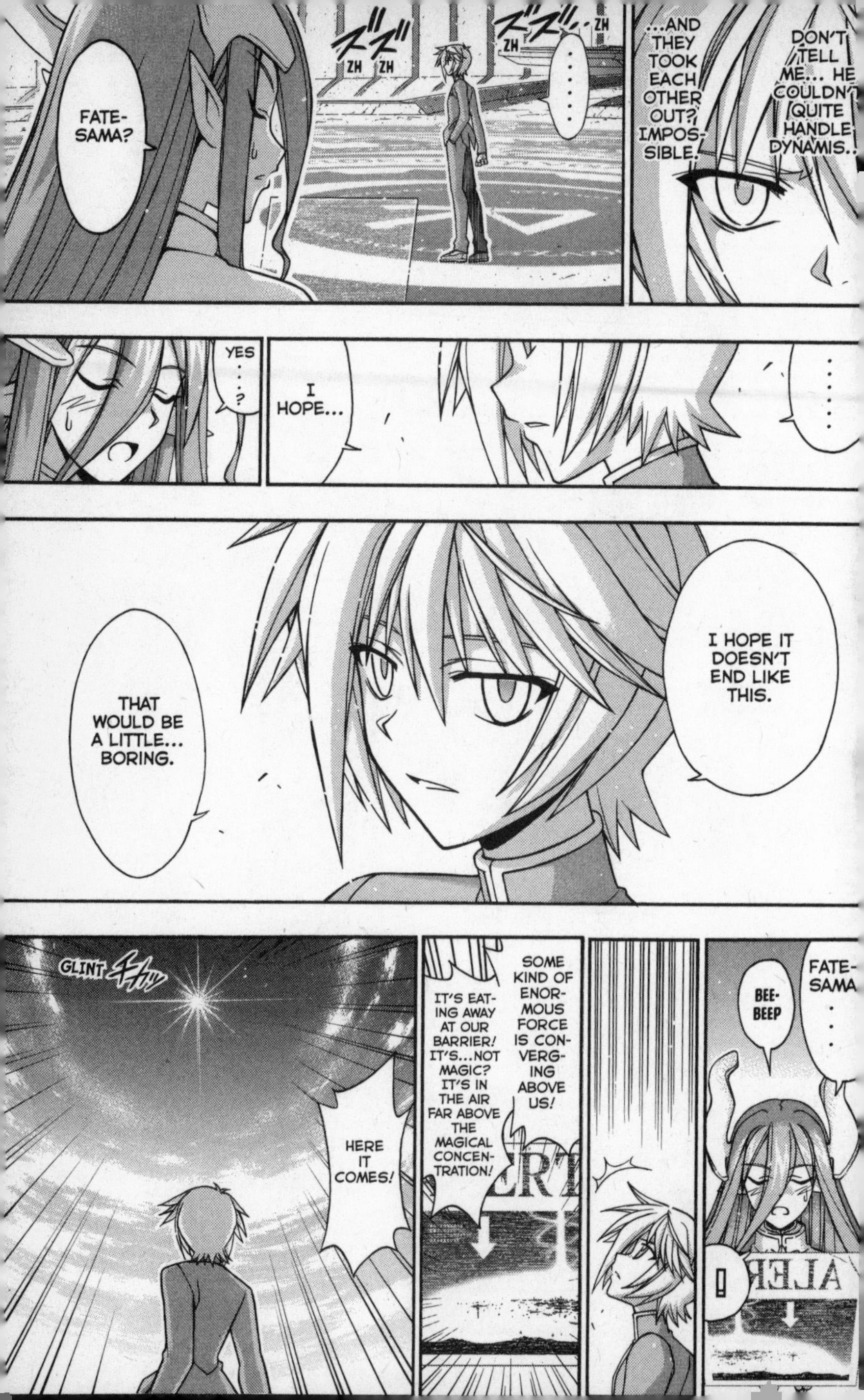
DON'T TELL ME... HE COULDN'T QUITE HANDLE DYNAMIS...
...AND THEY TOOK EACH OTHER OUT? IMPOSSIBLE.
ZH
......
ZH ZH
FATE-SAMA?
......
I HOPE...
YES...?
I HOPE IT DOESN'T END LIKE THIS.
THAT WOULD BE A LITTLE... BORING.
FATE-SAMA...
BEE-BEEP
SOME KIND OF ENORMOUS FORCE IS CONVERGING ABOVE US!
IT'S EATING AWAY AT OUR BARRIER! IT'S...NOT MAGIC? IT'S IN THE AIR FAR ABOVE THE MAGICAL CONCENTRATION!
GLINT
HERE IT COMES!

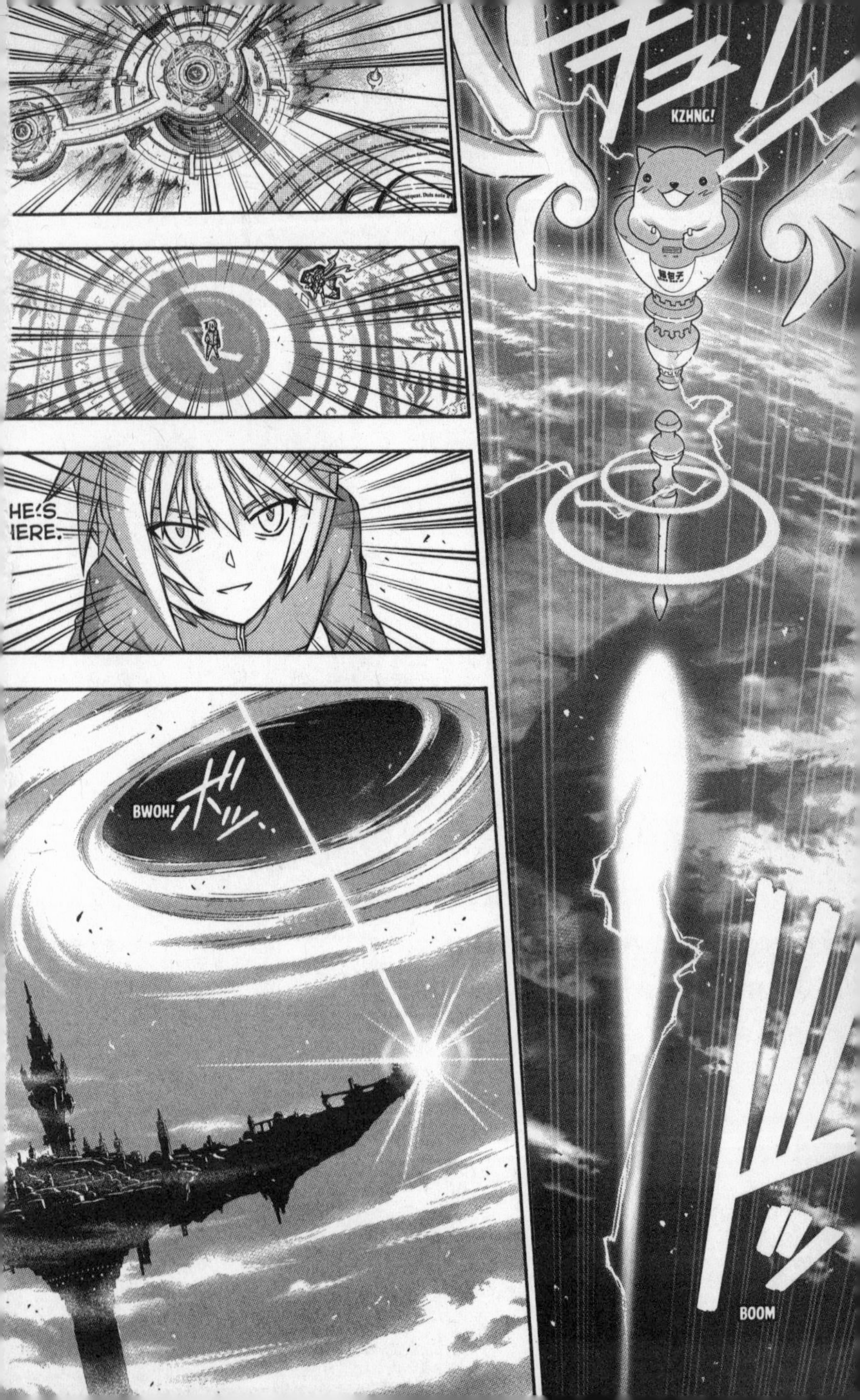
KZHNG!
BOOM
HE'S HERE.
BWOH!

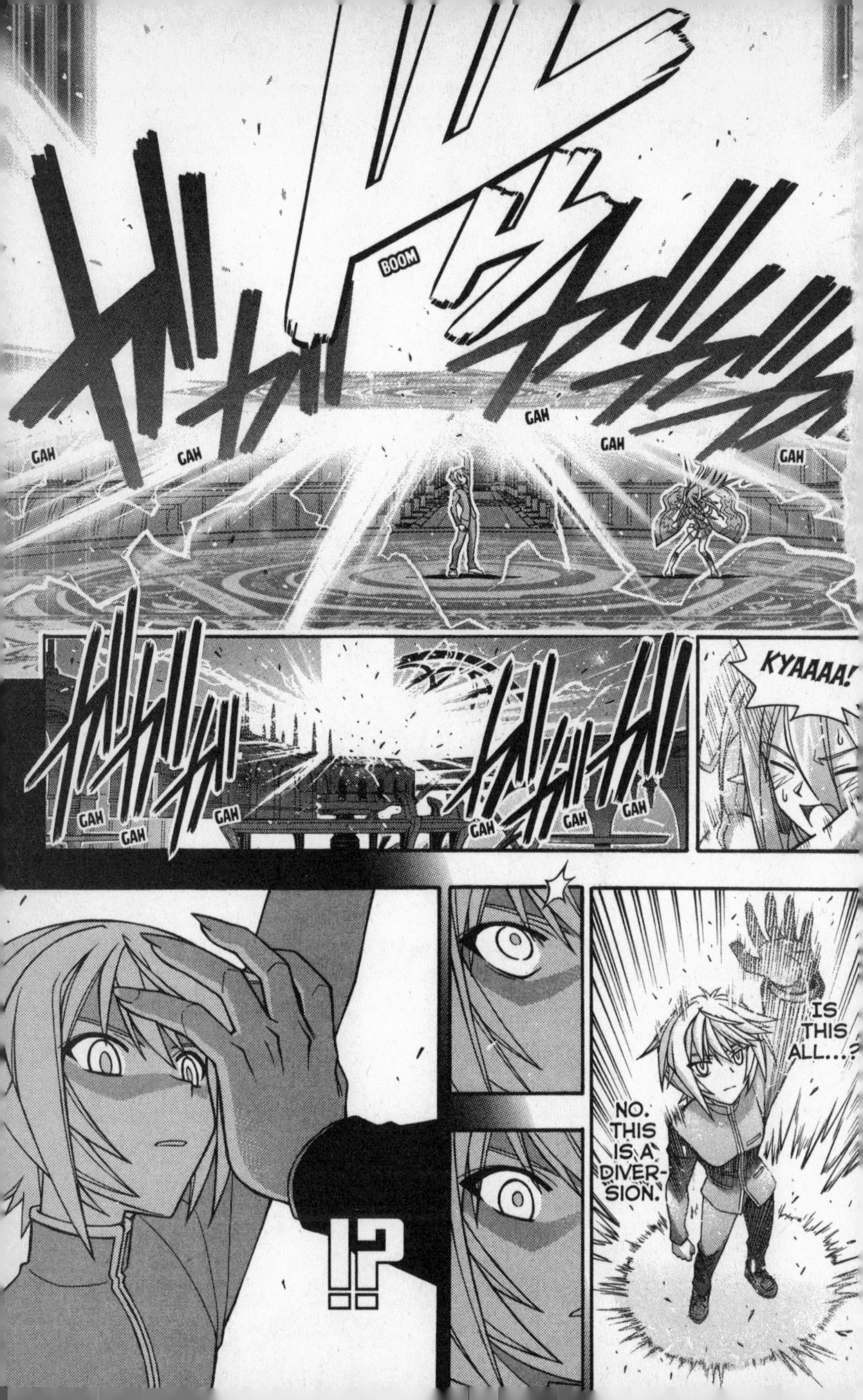
BOOM
GAH
GAH
GAH
GAH
GAH
KYAAAA!
GAH
GAH
GAH
GAH
GAH
GAH
IS THIS ALL...?
NO. THIS IS A DIVERSION.
!?

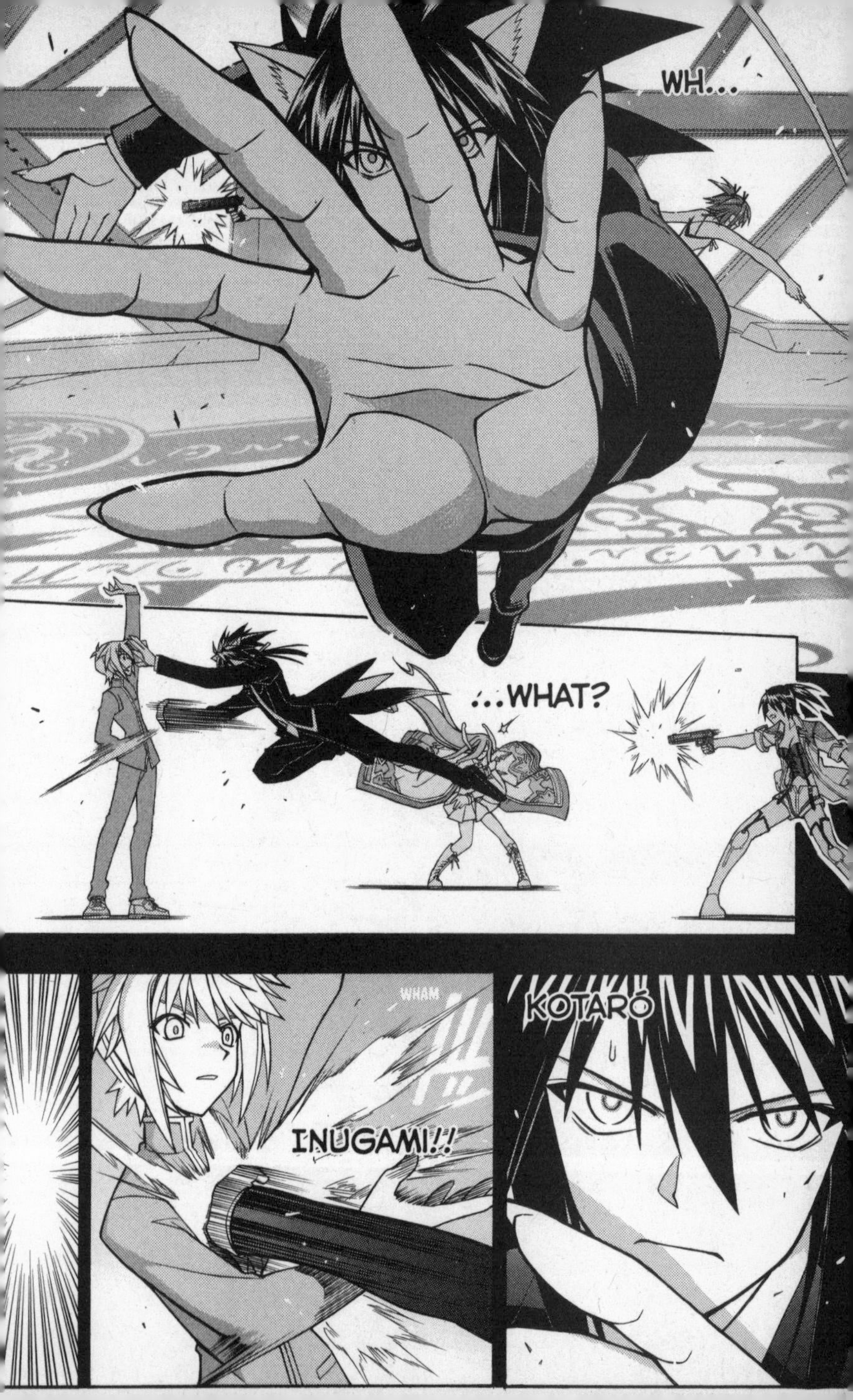
WH...
...WHAT?
KOTARŌ
WHAM
INUGAMI!!

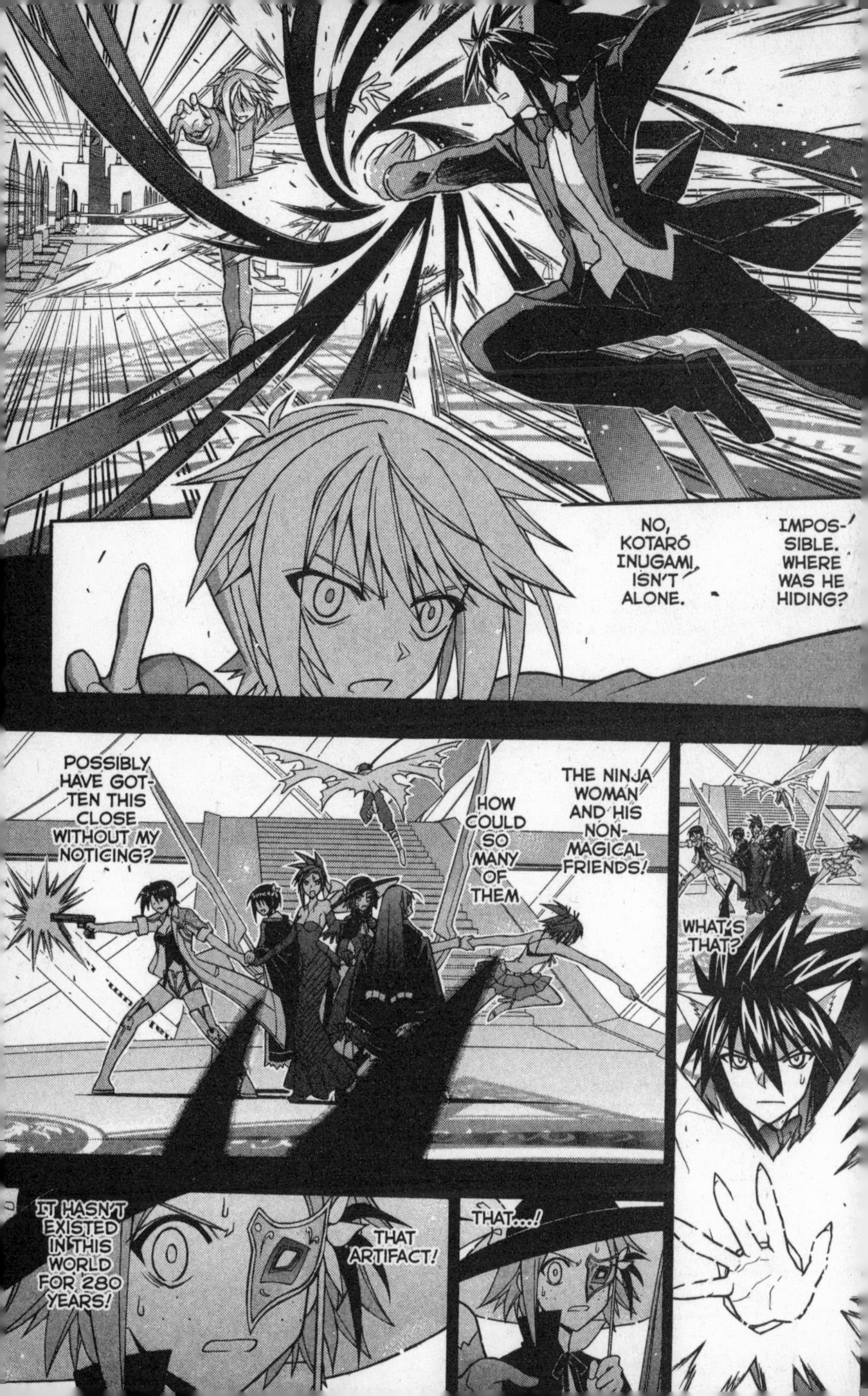
IMPOSSIBLE. WHERE WAS HE HIDING?
NO, KOTARŌ INUGAMI ISN'T ALONE.
WHAT'S THAT?
THE NINJA WOMAN AND HIS NON-MAGICAL FRIENDS!
HOW COULD SO MANY OF THEM
POSSIBLY HAVE GOTTEN THIS CLOSE WITHOUT MY NOTICING?
THAT...!
THAT ARTIFACT!
IT HASN'T EXISTED IN THIS WORLD FOR 280 YEARS!

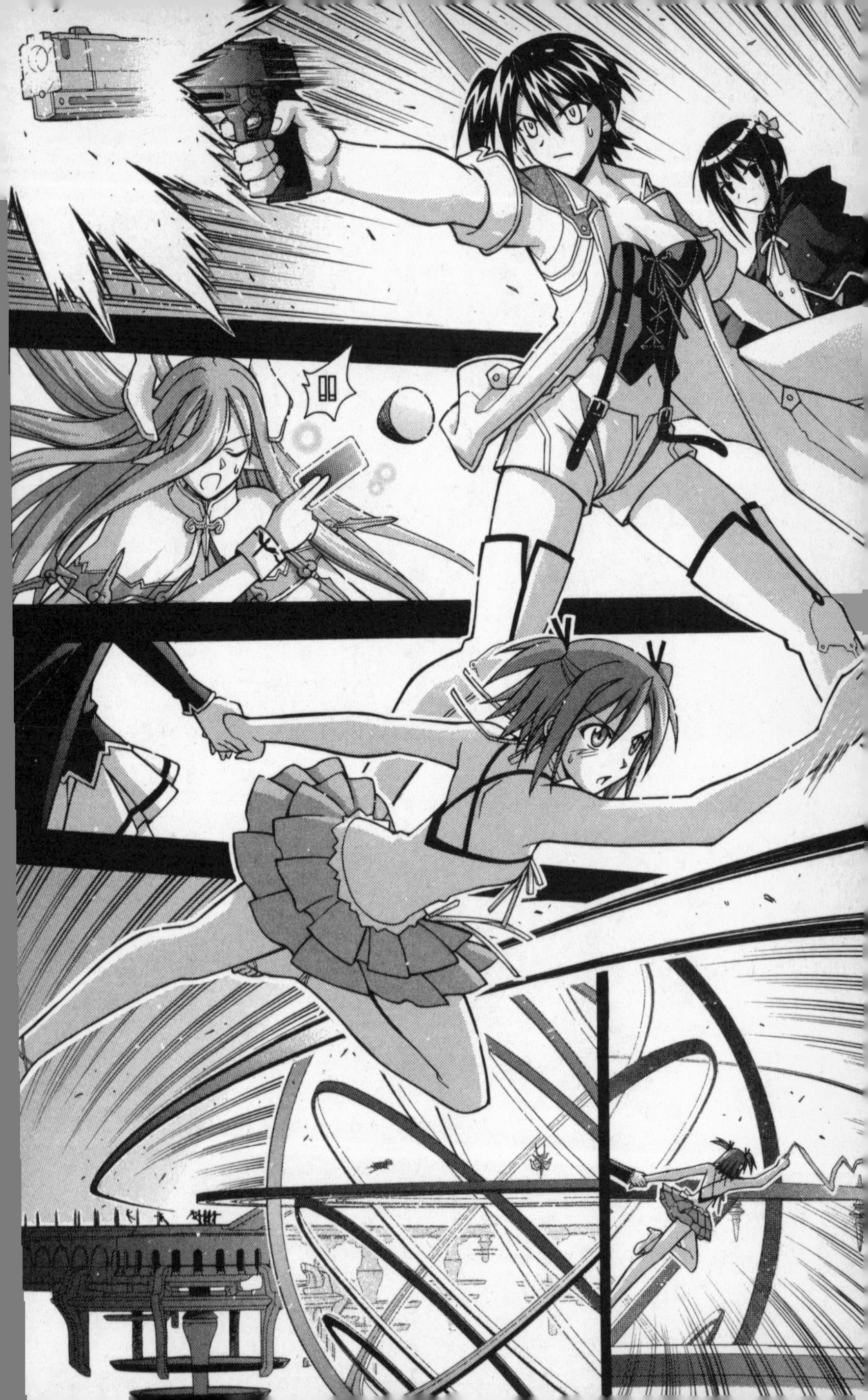
!!

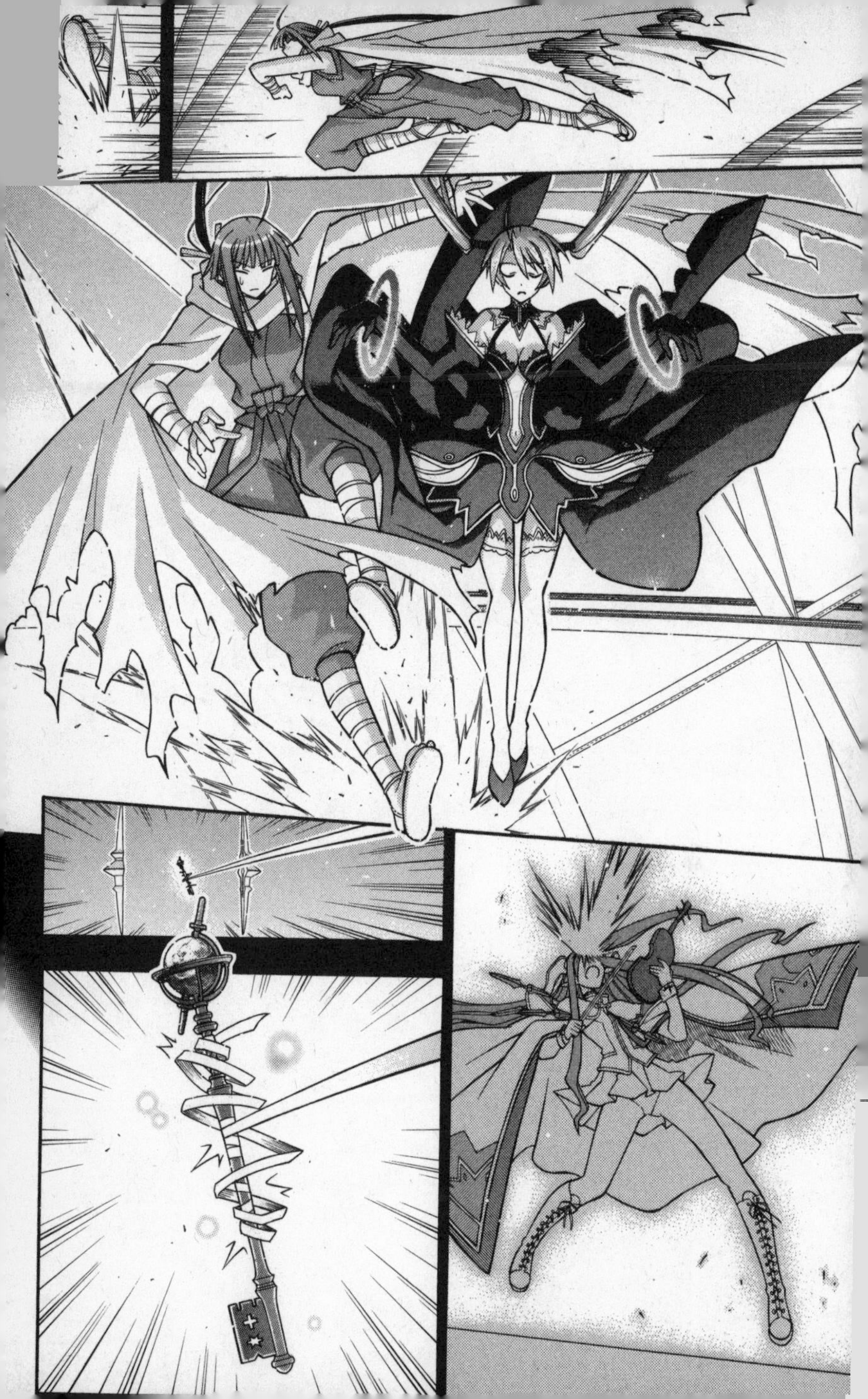

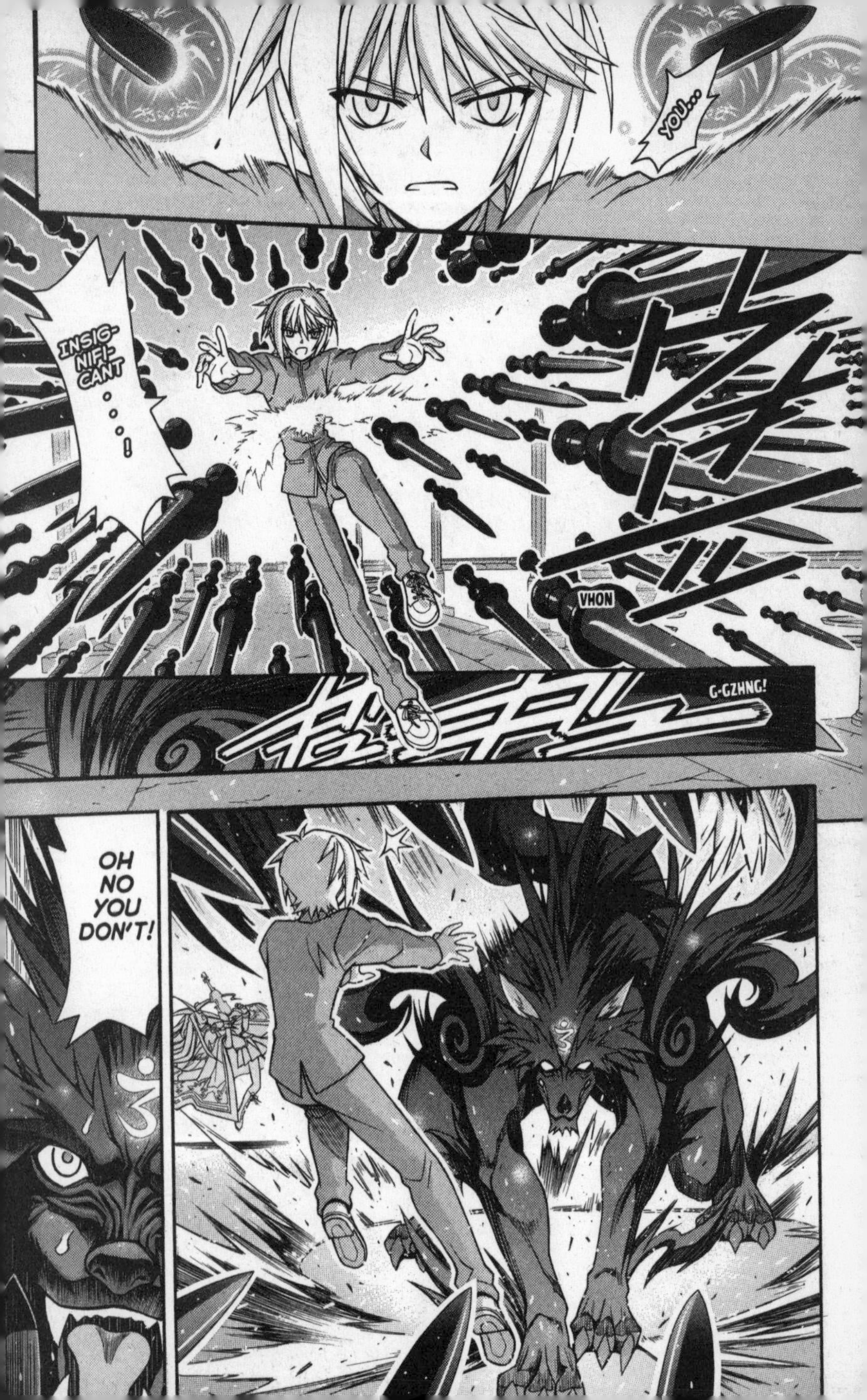
YOU...
INSIG-NIFI-CANT....!
VHON
G-GZHNG!
OH NO YOU DON'T!

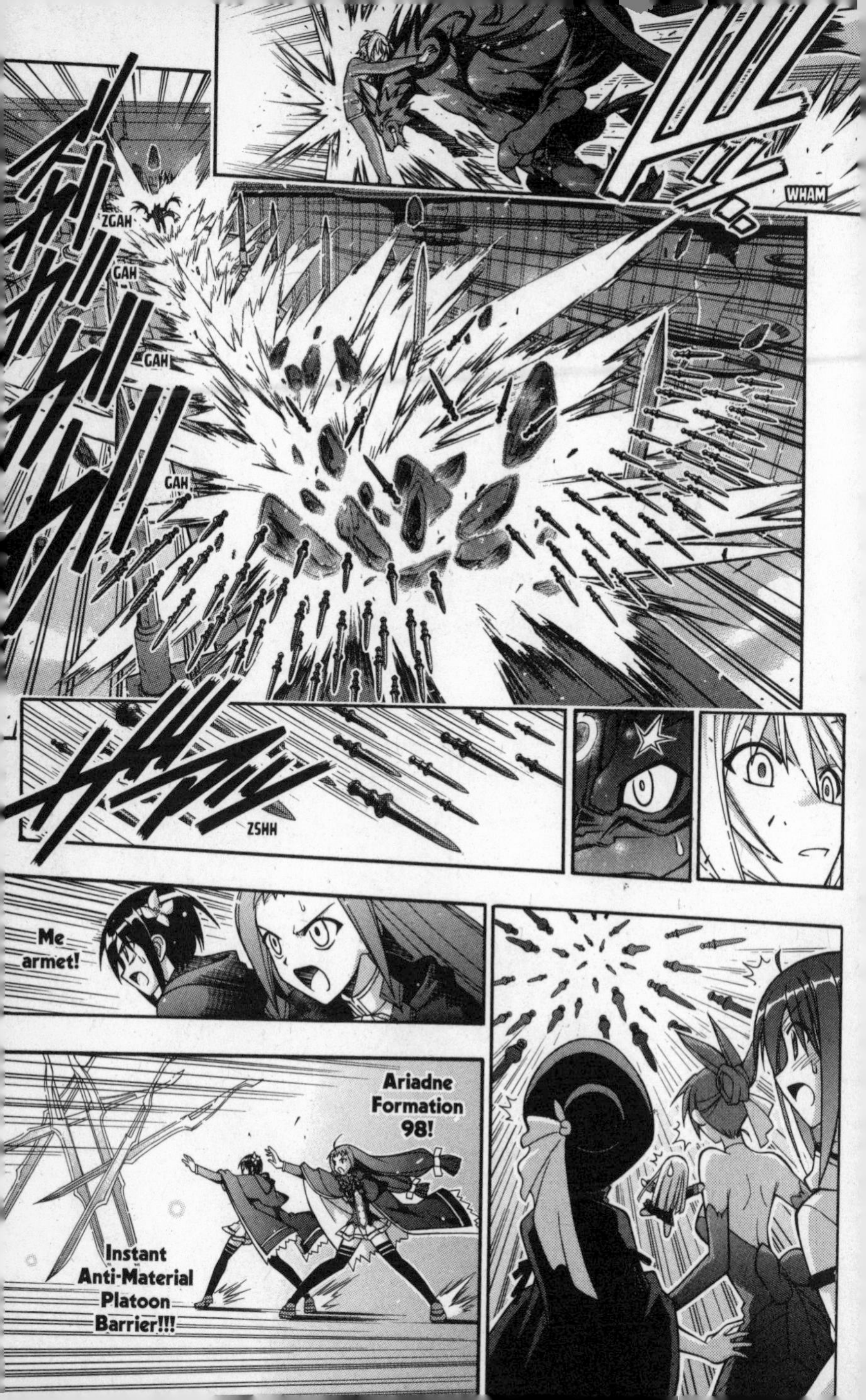
WHAM
ZGAH
GAH
GAH
GAH
ZSHH
Me armet!
Ariadne Formation 98!
Instant Anti-Material Platoon Barrier!!!

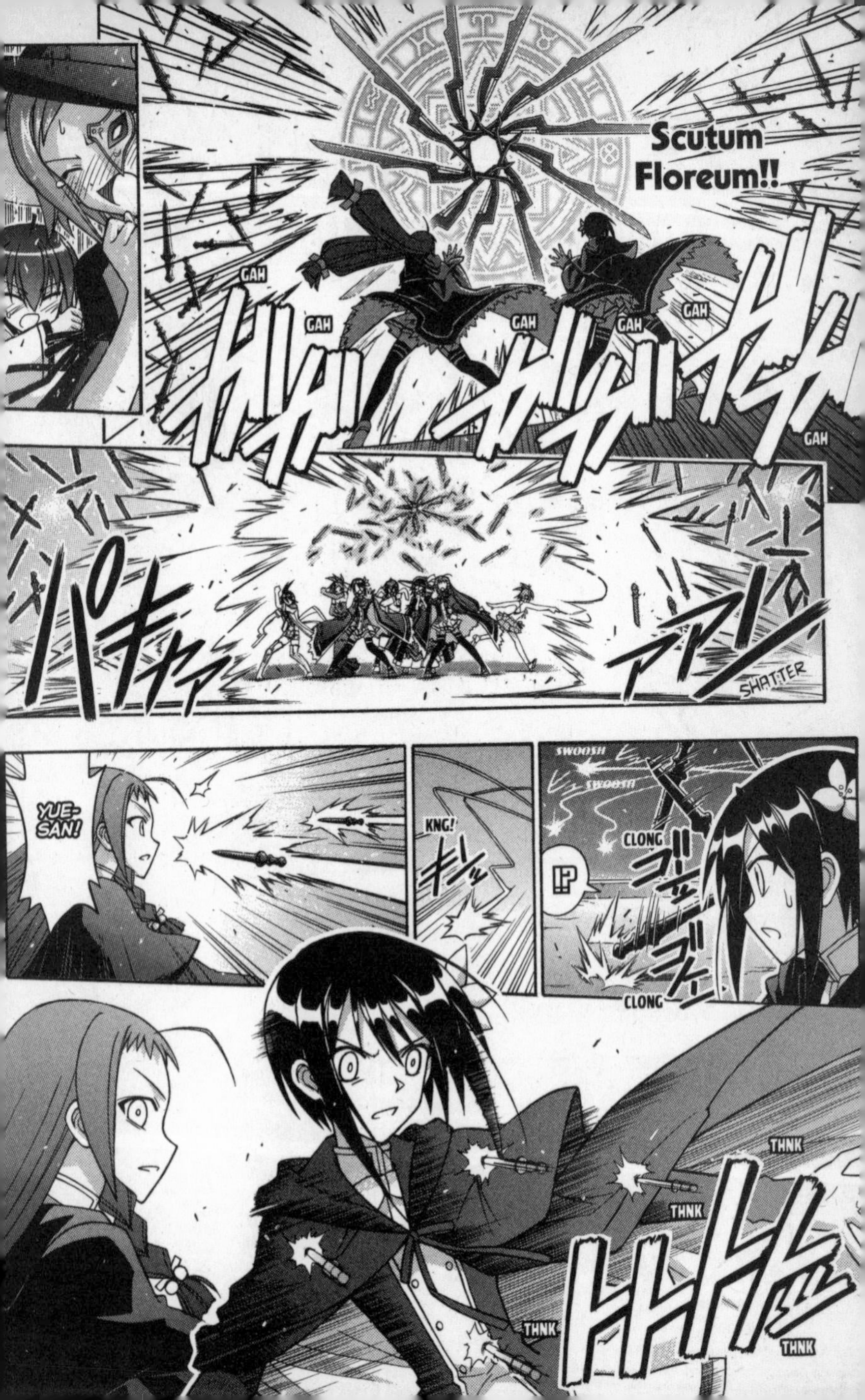
Scutum Floreum!!
GAH
GAH
GAH
GAH
GAH
GAH
SHATTER
SWOOSH
SWOOSH
CLONG
!?
CLONG
KNG!
YUE-SAN!
THNK
THNK
THNK
THNK

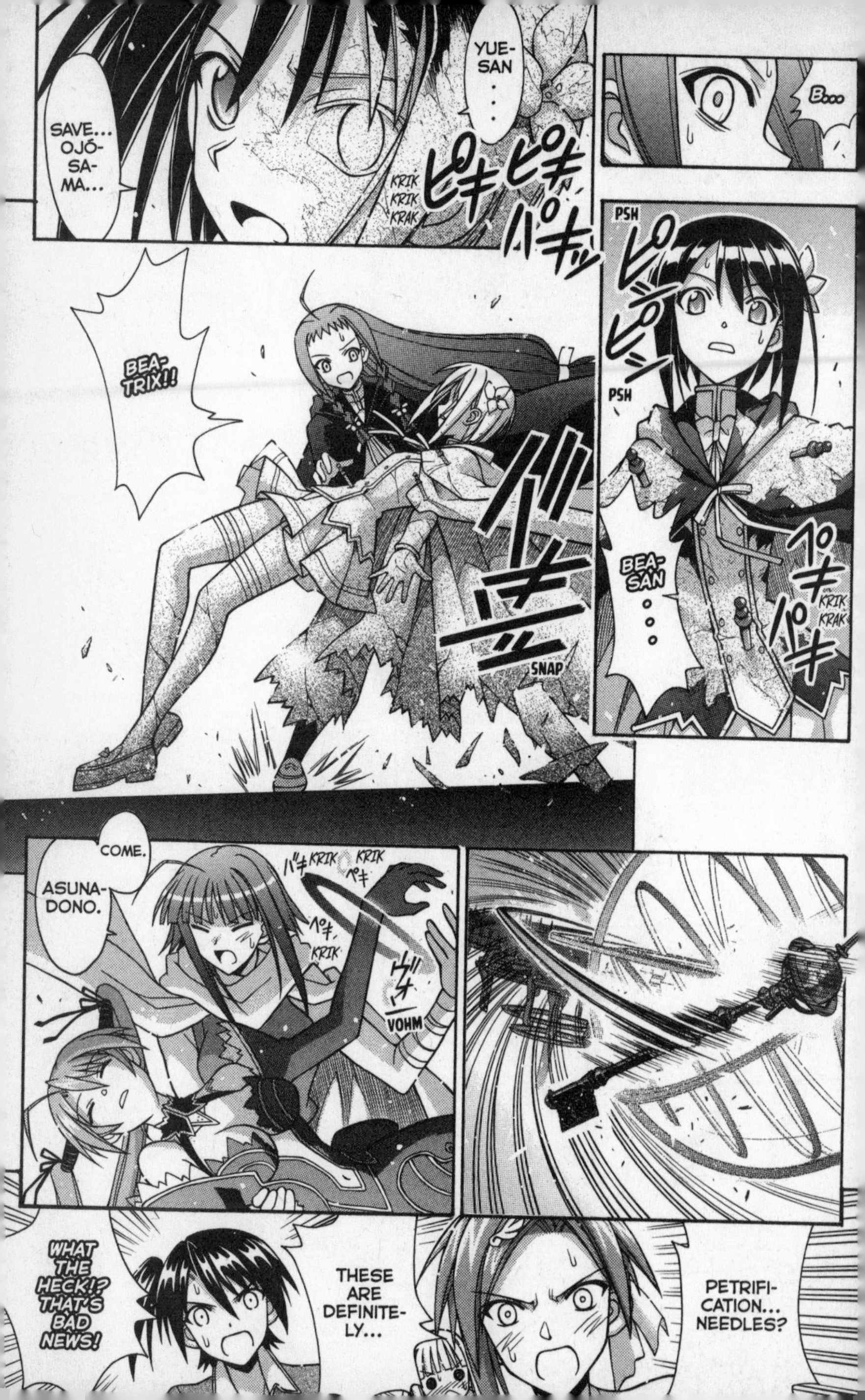
B...
YUE-SAN...
SAVE... OJŌ-SAMA...
KRIK KRIK KRAK
PSH
PSH
BEA-SAN...
KRIK KRAK
BEA-TRIX!!
SNAP
COME.
ASUNA-DONO.
KRIK KRIK
KRIK
VOHM
PETRIFI-CATION... NEEDLES?
THESE ARE DEFINITE-LY...
WHAT THE HECK!? THAT'S BAD NEWS!

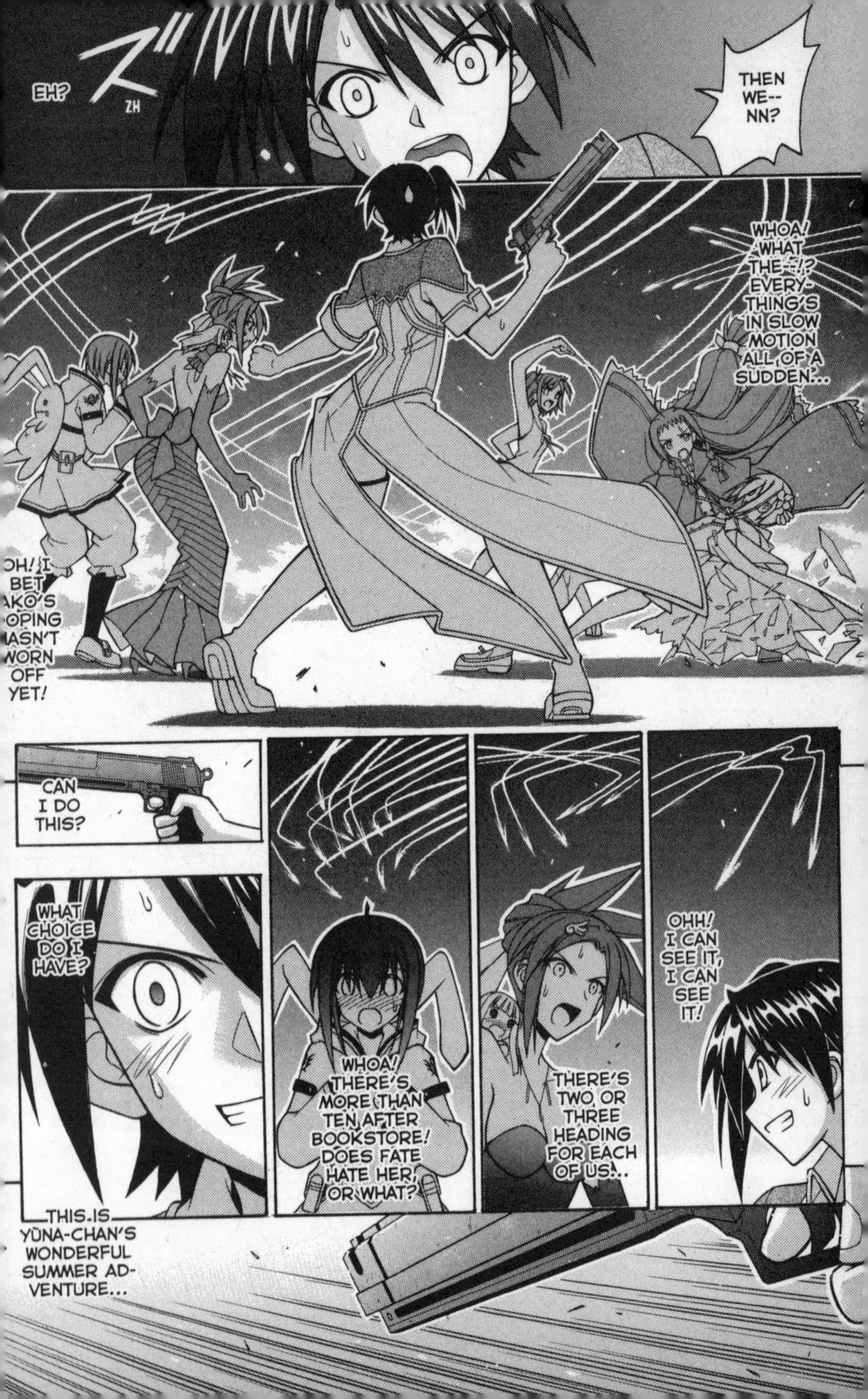
THEN WE-- NN?
ZH
EH?
WHOA! WHAT THE--!? EVERYTHING'S IN SLOW MOTION ALL OF A SUDDEN...
OH! I BET AKO'S OPING ASN'T WORN OFF YET!
OHH! I CAN SEE IT, I CAN SEE IT!
THERE'S TWO OR THREE HEADING FOR EACH OF US...
WHOA! THERE'S MORE THAN TEN AFTER BOOKSTORE! DOES FATE HATE HER, OR WHAT?
CAN I DO THIS?
WHAT CHOICE DO I HAVE?
THIS IS YUNA-CHAN'S WONDERFUL SUMMER ADVENTURE...

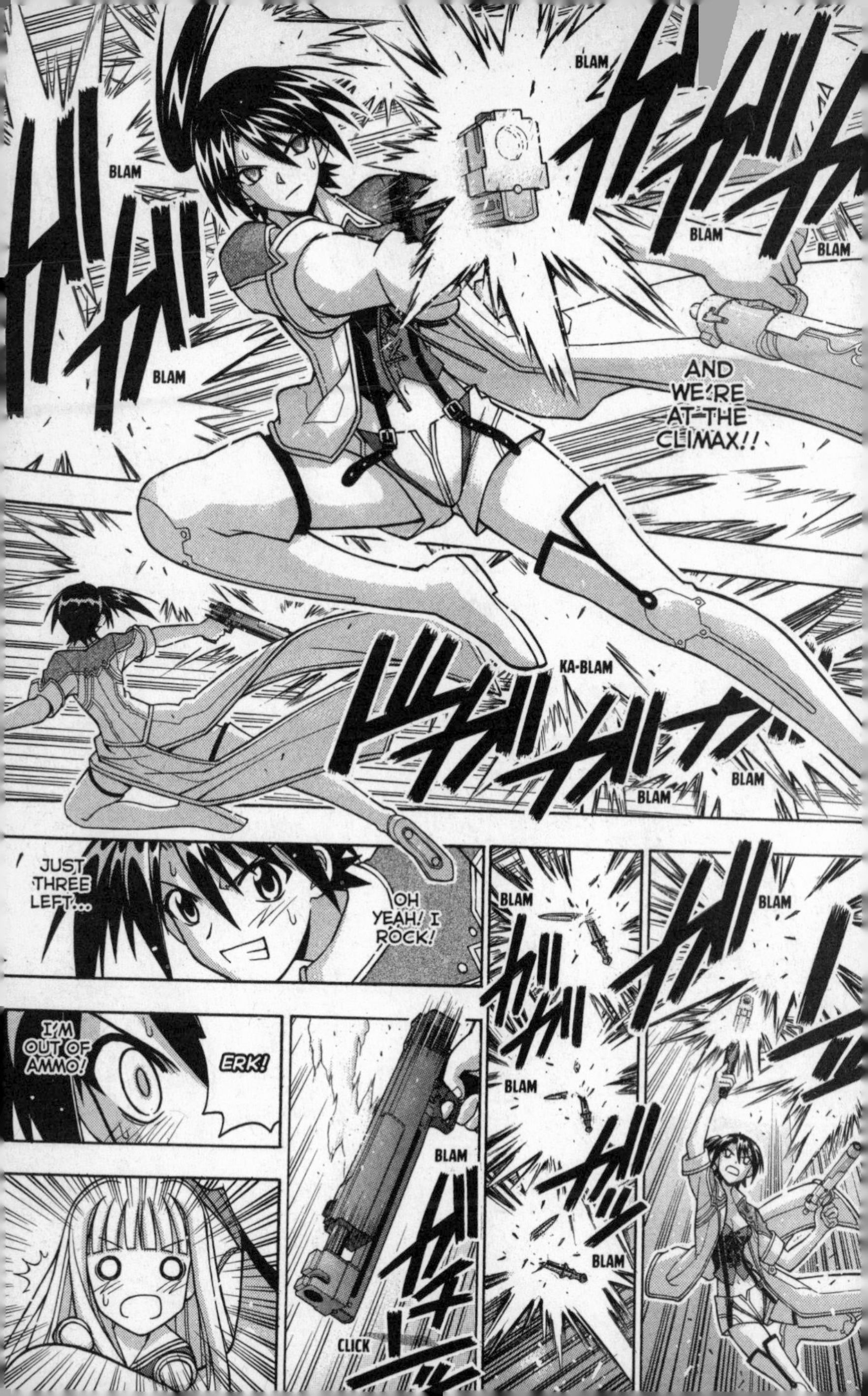
BLAM
BLAM
BLAM
BLAM
BLAM
AND WE'RE AT THE CLIMAX!!
KA-BLAM
BLAM
BLAM
BLAM
BLAM
BLAM
BLAM
BLAM
OH YEAH! I ROCK!
JUST THREE LEFT...
BLAM
CLICK
ERK!
I'M OUT OF AMMO!

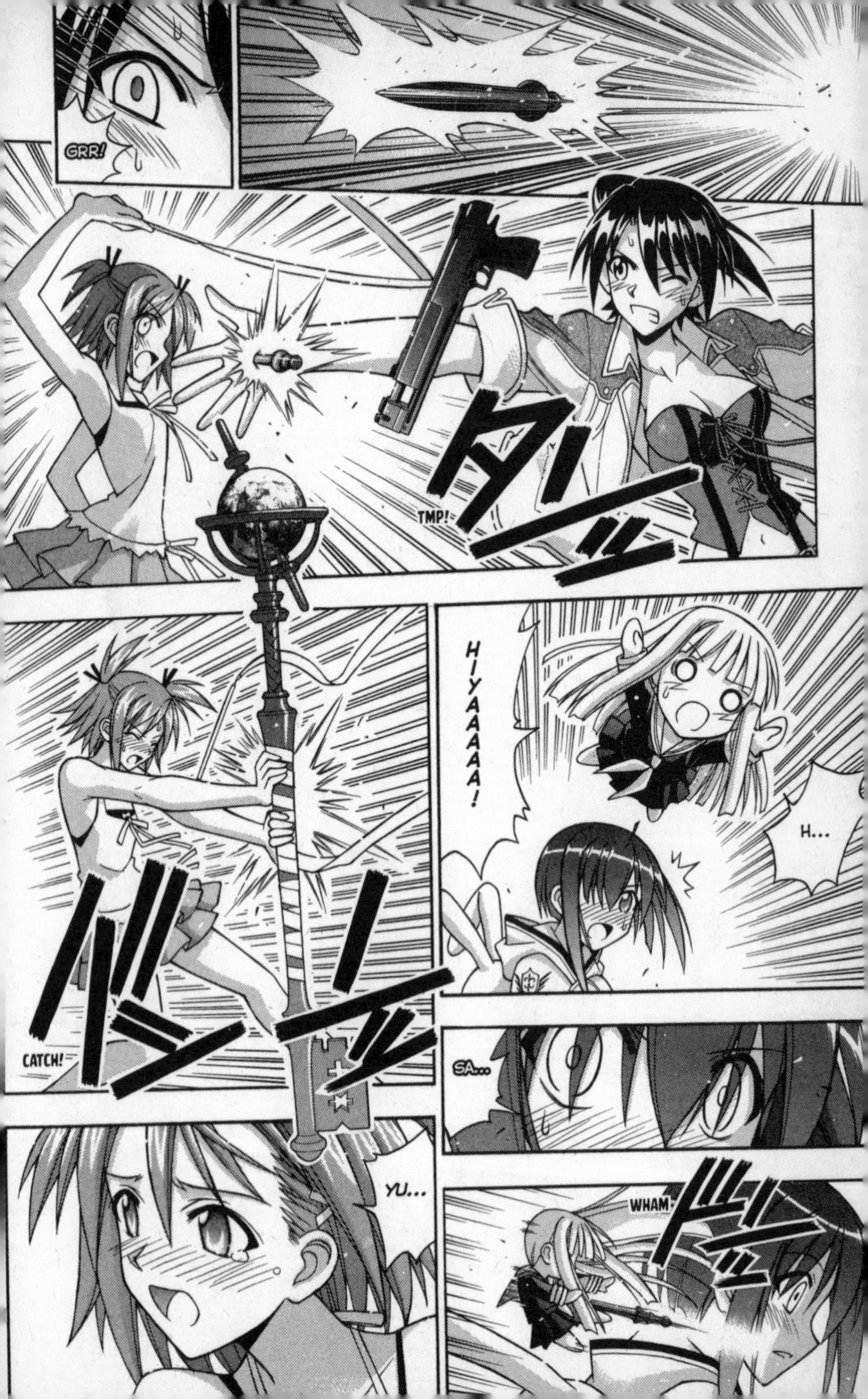
GRR!
TMP!
HIYAAAAAA!
H...
CATCH!
SA...
YU...
WHAM

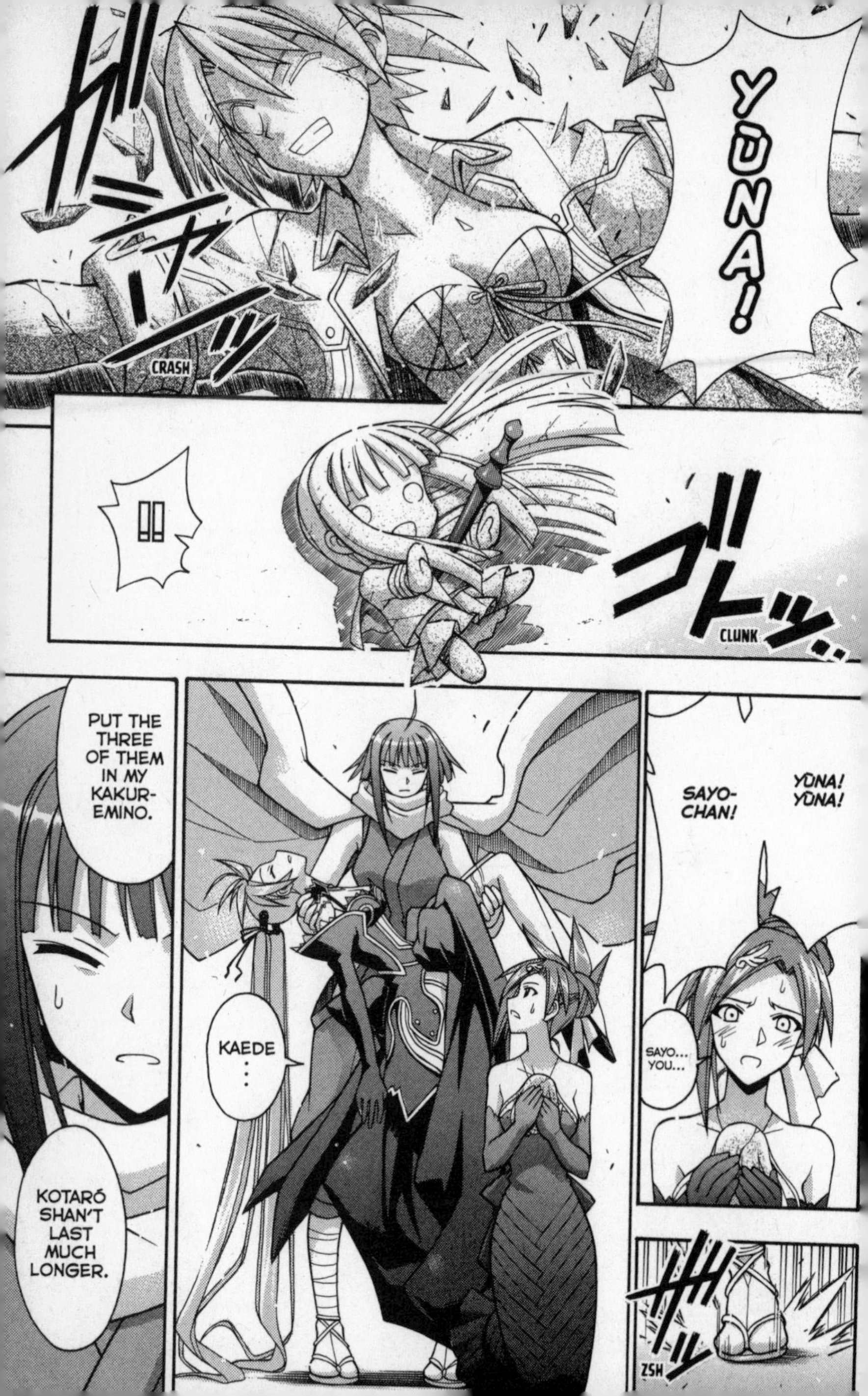
YŪNA!
CRASH
!!
CLUNK
YŪNA! YŪNA!
SAYO-CHAN!
SAYO... YOU...
ZSH
KAEDE . . .
PUT THE THREE OF THEM IN MY KAKUR-EMINO.
KOTARŌ SHAN'T LAST MUCH LONGER.

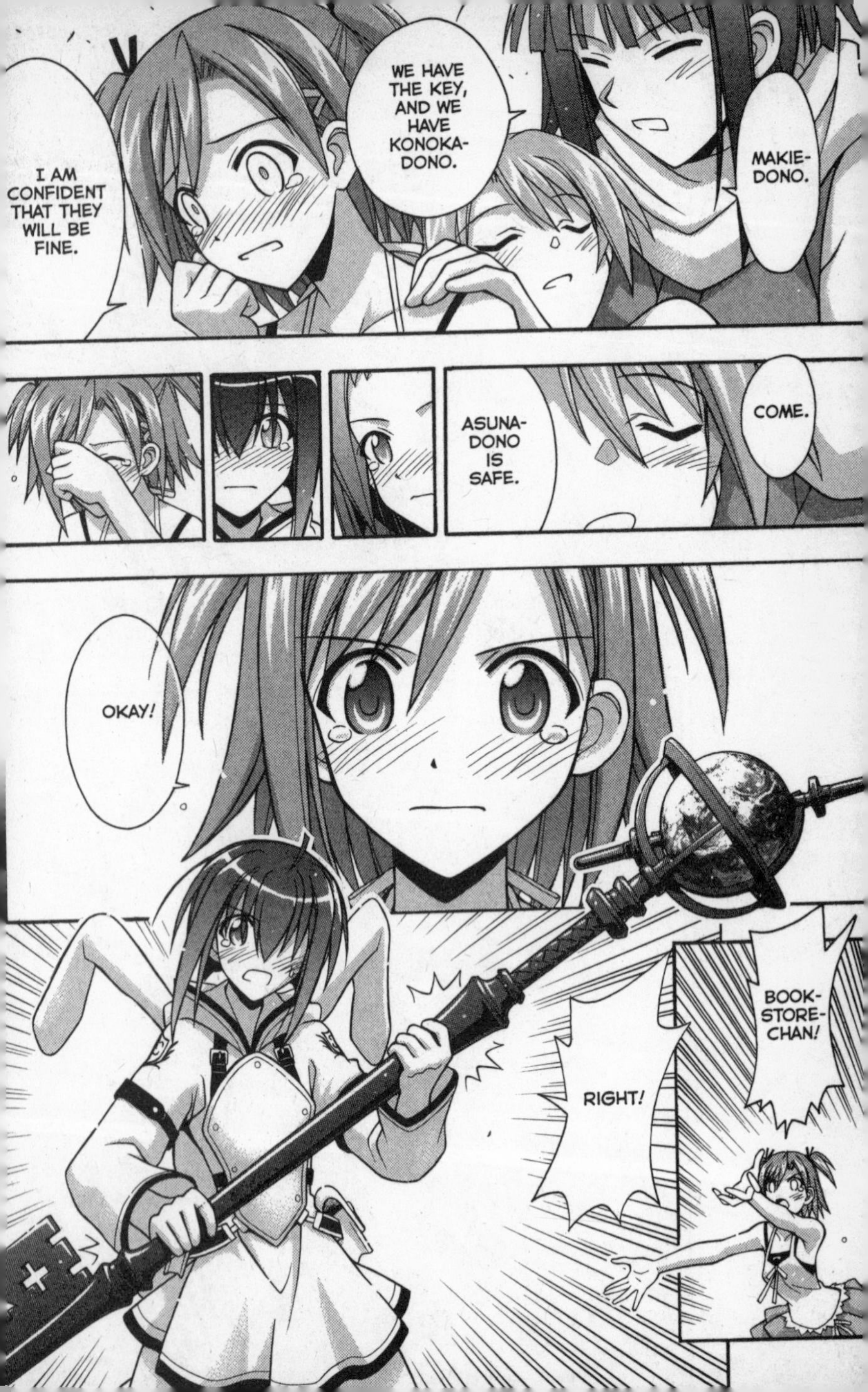
MAKIE-DONO.
WE HAVE THE KEY, AND WE HAVE KONOKA-DONO.
I AM CONFIDENT THAT THEY WILL BE FINE.
COME.
ASUNA-DONO IS SAFE.
OKAY!
BOOK-STORE-CHAN!
RIGHT!

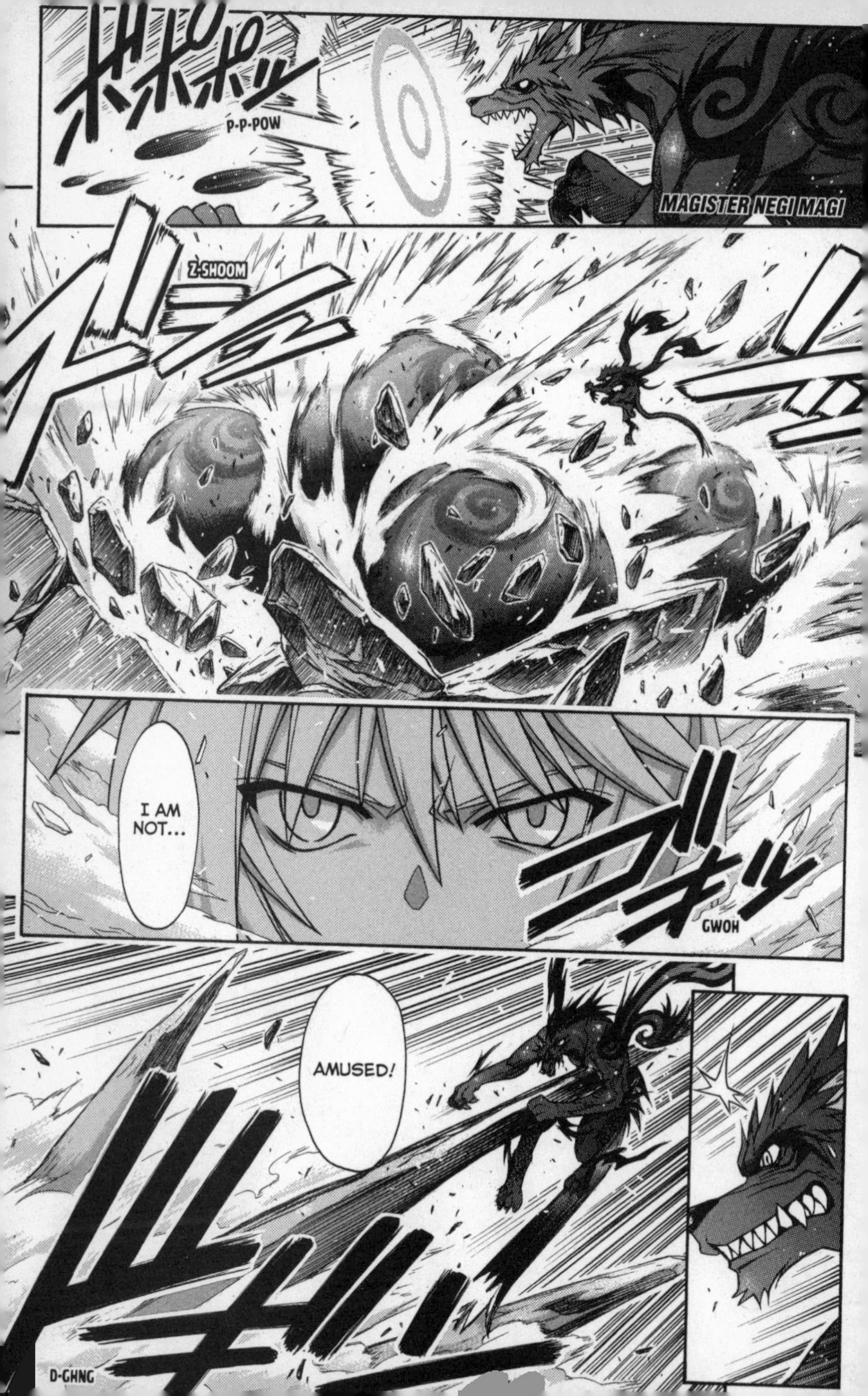

P-P-POW
MAGISTER NEGI MAGI
Z-SHOOM
I AM NOT...
GWOH
AMUSED!
D-GHNG

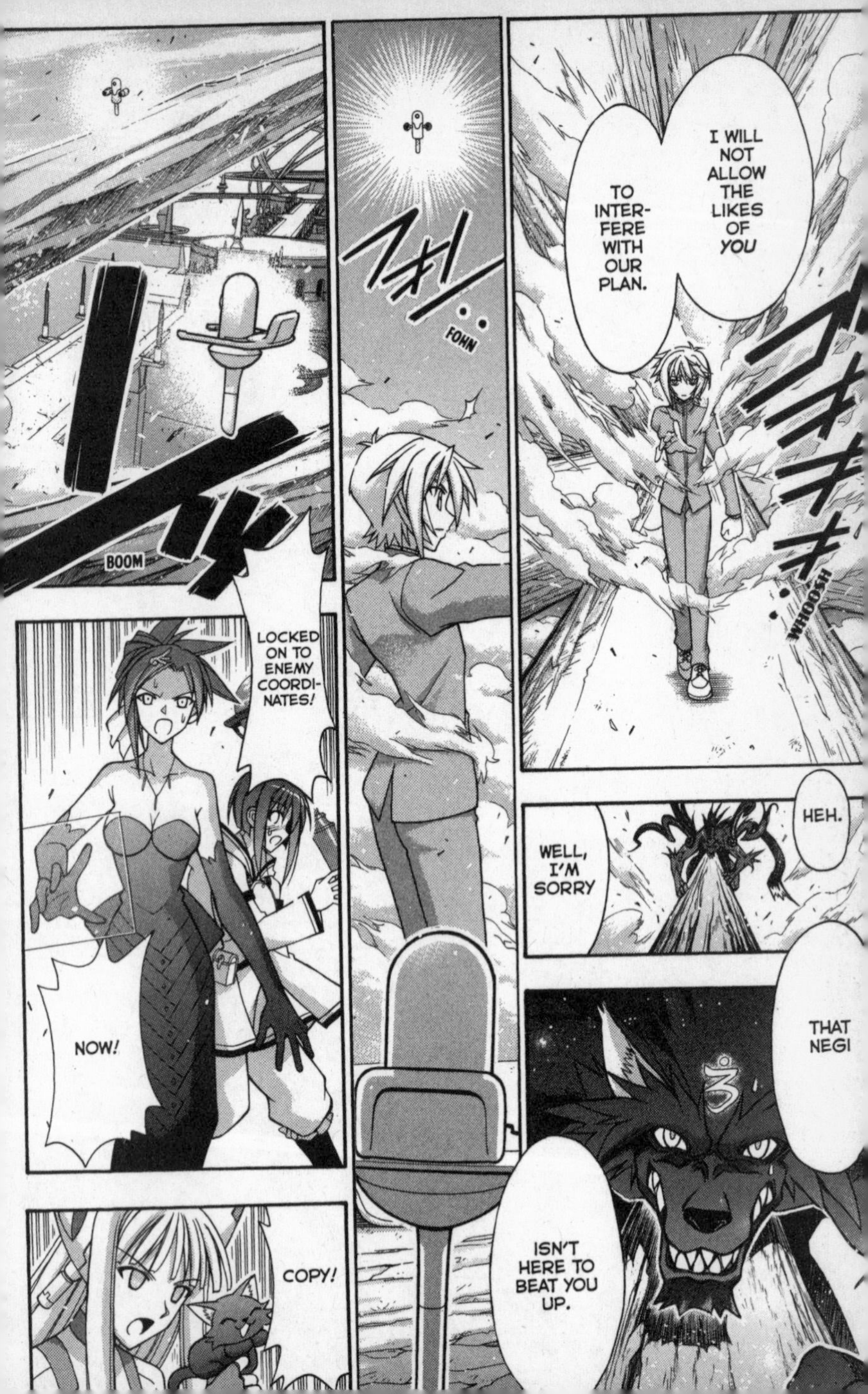

I WILL NOT ALLOW THE LIKES OF *YOU*
TO INTERFERE WITH OUR PLAN.
WHOOSH
HEH.
WELL, I'M SORRY
THAT NEGI
ISN'T HERE TO BEAT YOU UP.
FOHN
BOOM
LOCKED ON TO ENEMY COORDINATES!
NOW!
COPY!

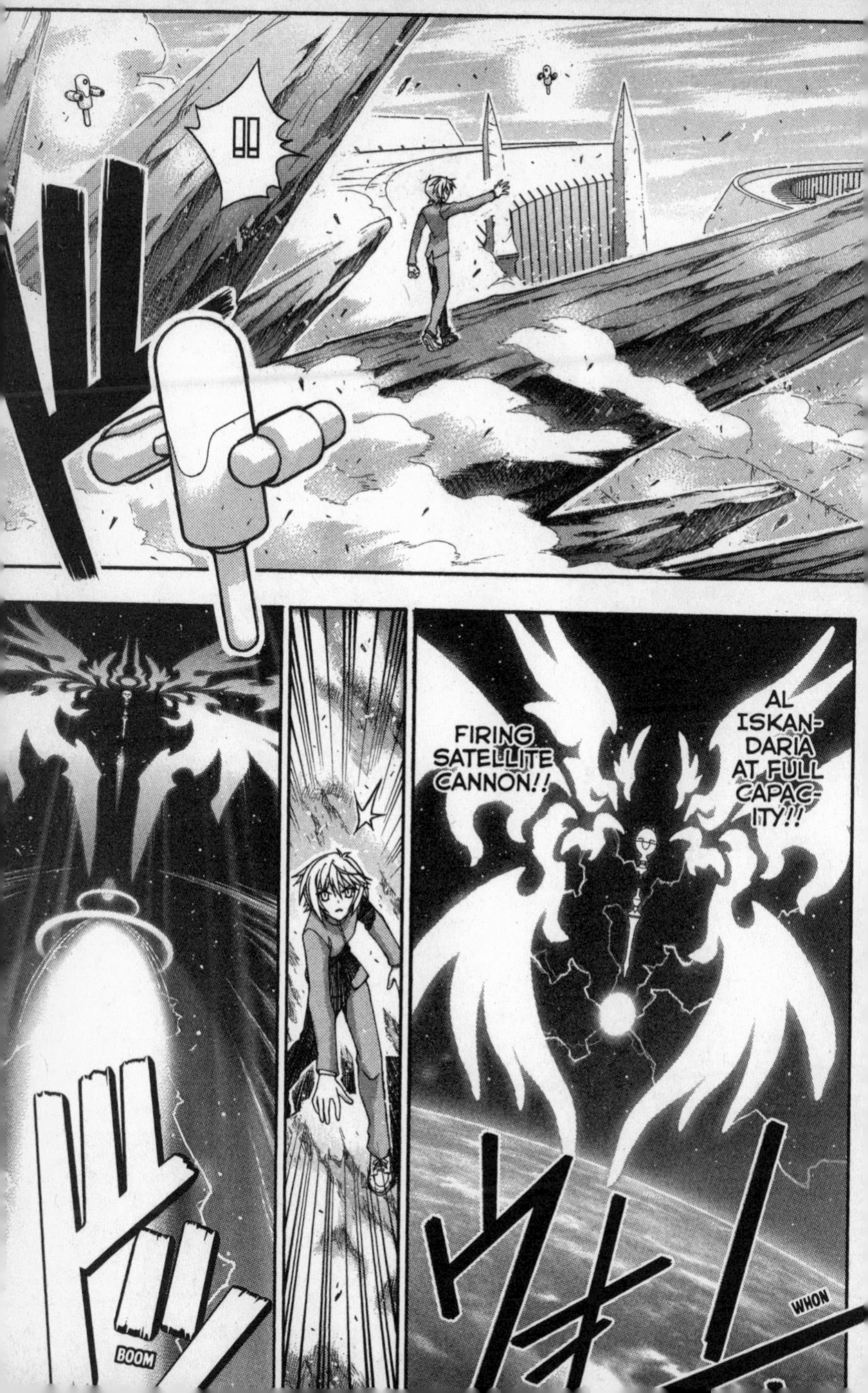
!!
AL ISKAN-DARIA AT FULL CAPAC-ITY!!
FIRING SATELLITE CANNON!!
WHON
BOOM

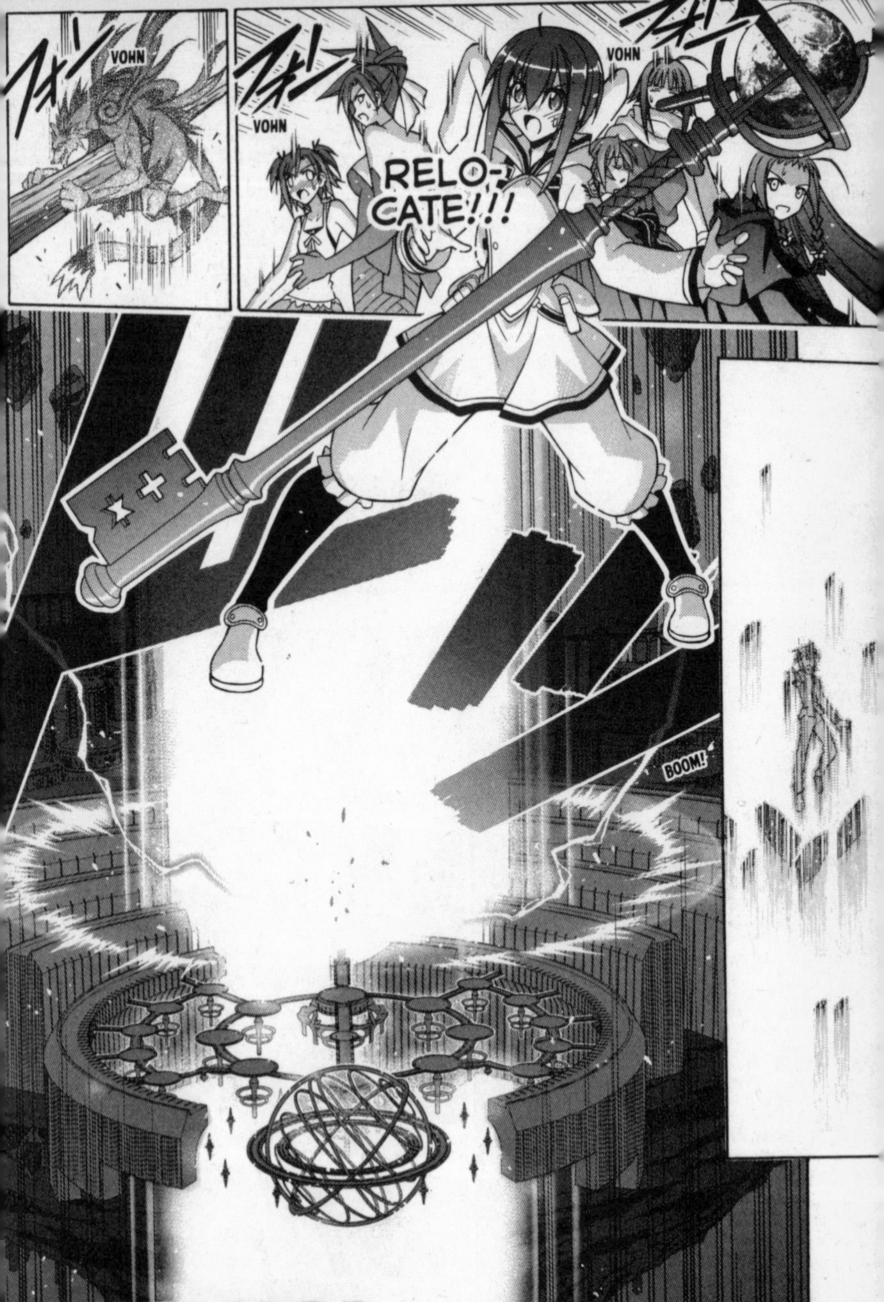
VOHN
VOHN
RELO-CATE!!!
VOHN
BOOM!

NEGIMA!

MAGISTER NEGI MAGI

311th Chapter: Fate Strikes Back

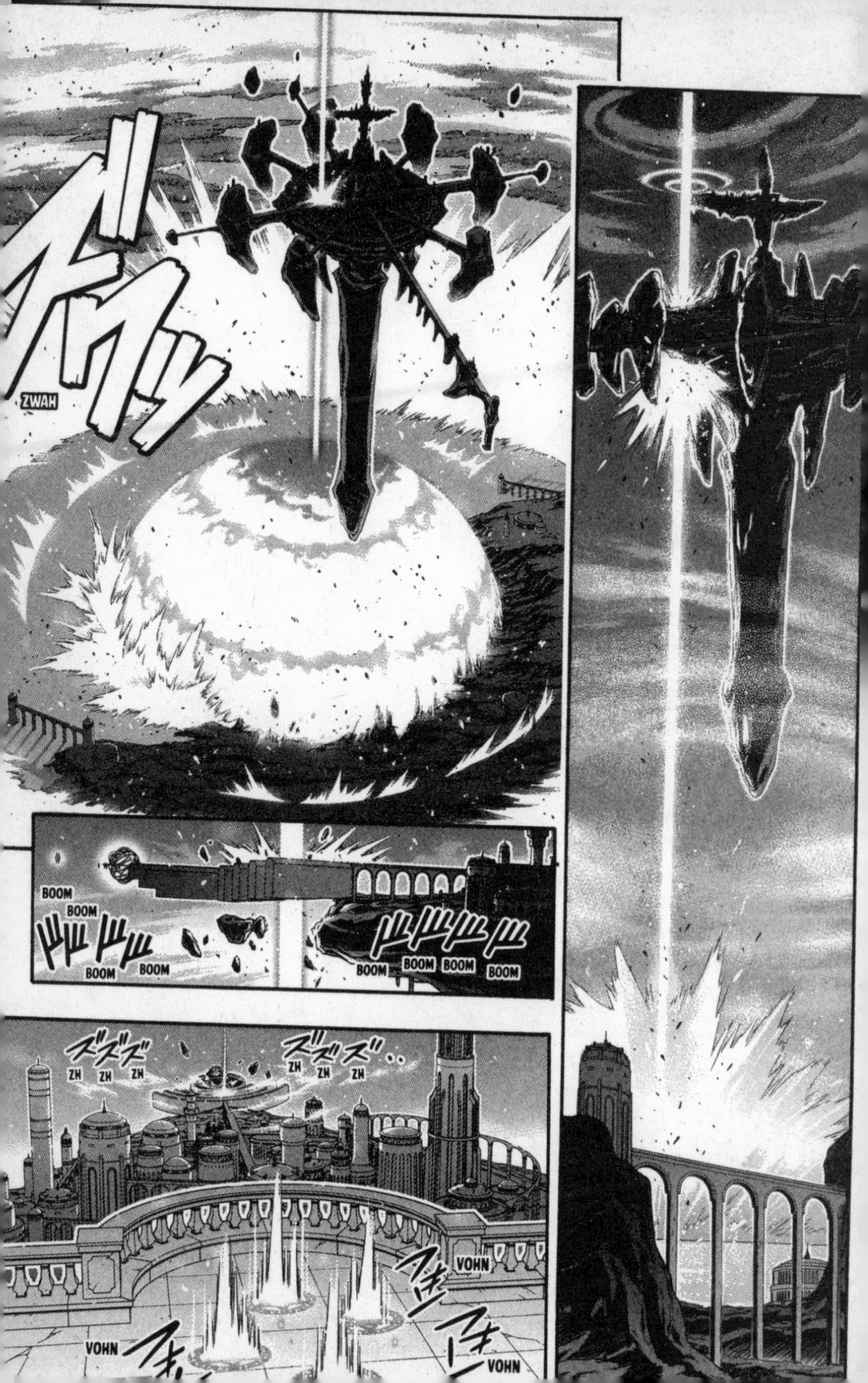
ZWAH
BOOM
BOOM
BOOM
BOOM
BOOM
BOOM
BOOM
BOOM
ZH ZH ZH
ZH ZH ZH
VOHN
VOHN
VOHN

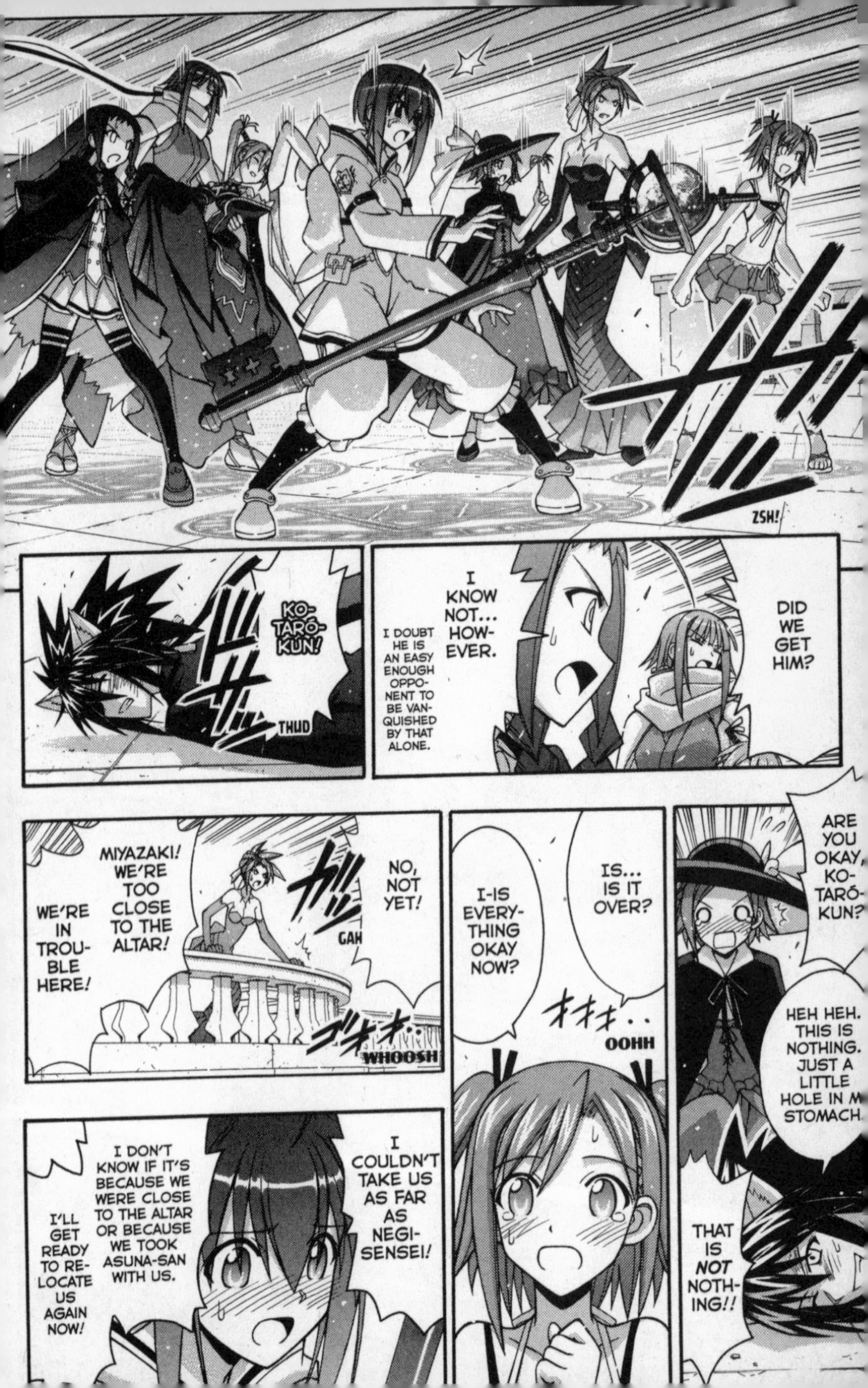
ZSH!
DID WE GET HIM?
I KNOW NOT... HOWEVER.
I DOUBT HE IS AN EASY ENOUGH OPPONENT TO BE VANQUISHED BY THAT ALONE.
KOTARŌ-KUN!
THUD
ARE YOU OKAY, KOTARŌ-KUN?
HEH HEH. THIS IS NOTHING. JUST A LITTLE HOLE IN M STOMACH.
THAT IS *NOT* NOTHING!!
IS... IS IT OVER?
I-IS EVERYTHING OKAY NOW?
OOHH
NO, NOT YET!
GAH
MIYAZAKI! WE'RE TOO CLOSE TO THE ALTAR!
WE'RE IN TROUBLE HERE!
WHOOSH
I COULDN'T TAKE US AS FAR AS NEGI-SENSEI!
I DON'T KNOW IF IT'S BECAUSE WE WERE CLOSE TO THE ALTAR OR BECAUSE WE TOOK ASUNA-SAN WITH US.
I'LL GET READY TO RELOCATE US AGAIN NOW!

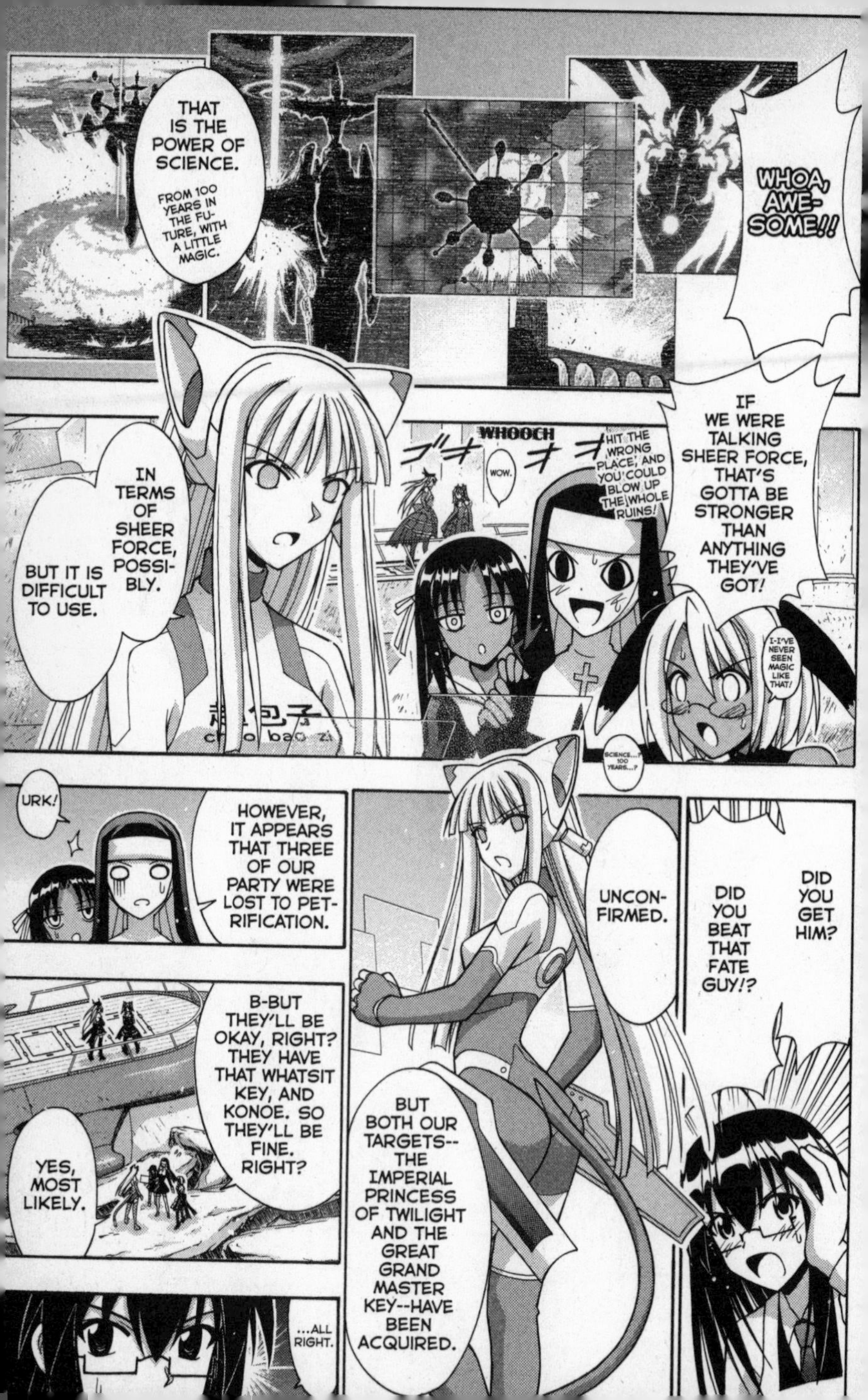
WHOA, AWE-SOME!!
THAT IS THE POWER OF SCIENCE.
FROM 100 YEARS IN THE FU-TURE, WITH A LITTLE MAGIC.
IF WE WERE TALKING SHEER FORCE, THAT'S GOTTA BE STRONGER THAN ANYTHING THEY'VE GOT!
HIT THE WRONG PLACE, AND YOU COULD BLOW UP THE WHOLE RUINS!
WHOOCH
WOW.
I-I'VE NEVER SEEN MAGIC LIKE THAT!
SCIENCE...? 100 YEARS...?
IN TERMS OF SHEER FORCE, POSSI-BLY.
BUT IT IS DIFFICULT TO USE.
DID YOU GET HIM?
DID YOU BEAT THAT FATE GUY!?
UNCON-FIRMED.
BUT BOTH OUR TARGETS--THE IMPERIAL PRINCESS OF TWILIGHT AND THE GREAT GRAND MASTER KEY--HAVE BEEN ACQUIRED.
HOWEVER, IT APPEARS THAT THREE OF OUR PARTY WERE LOST TO PET-RIFICATION.
URK!
B-BUT THEY'LL BE OKAY, RIGHT? THEY HAVE THAT WHATSIT KEY, AND KONOE. SO THEY'LL BE FINE. RIGHT?
YES, MOST LIKELY.
...ALL RIGHT.

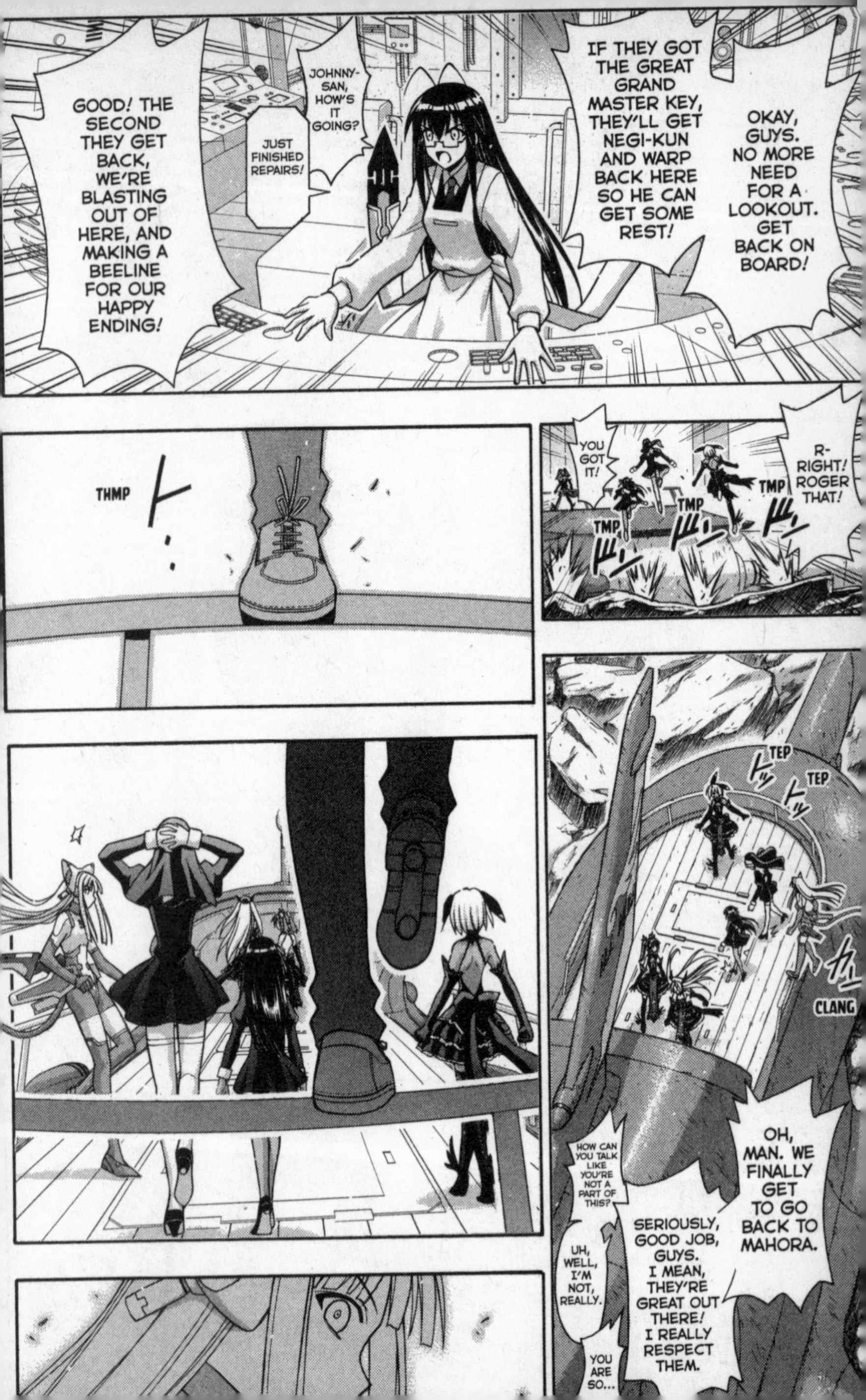
OKAY, GUYS. NO MORE NEED FOR A LOOKOUT. GET BACK ON BOARD!
IF THEY GOT THE GREAT GRAND MASTER KEY, THEY'LL GET NEGI-KUN AND WARP BACK HERE SO HE CAN GET SOME REST!
JOHNNY-SAN, HOW'S IT GOING?
JUST FINISHED REPAIRS!
GOOD! THE SECOND THEY GET BACK, WE'RE BLASTING OUT OF HERE, AND MAKING A BEELINE FOR OUR HAPPY ENDING!
R-RIGHT! ROGER THAT!
YOU GOT IT!
TMP
TMP
TMP
THMP
TEP
TEP
CLANG
OH, MAN. WE FINALLY GET TO GO BACK TO MAHORA.
SERIOUSLY, GOOD JOB, GUYS. I MEAN, THEY'RE GREAT OUT THERE! I REALLY RESPECT THEM.
HOW CAN YOU TALK LIKE YOU'RE NOT A PART OF THIS?
UH, WELL, I'M NOT, REALLY.
YOU ARE SO...

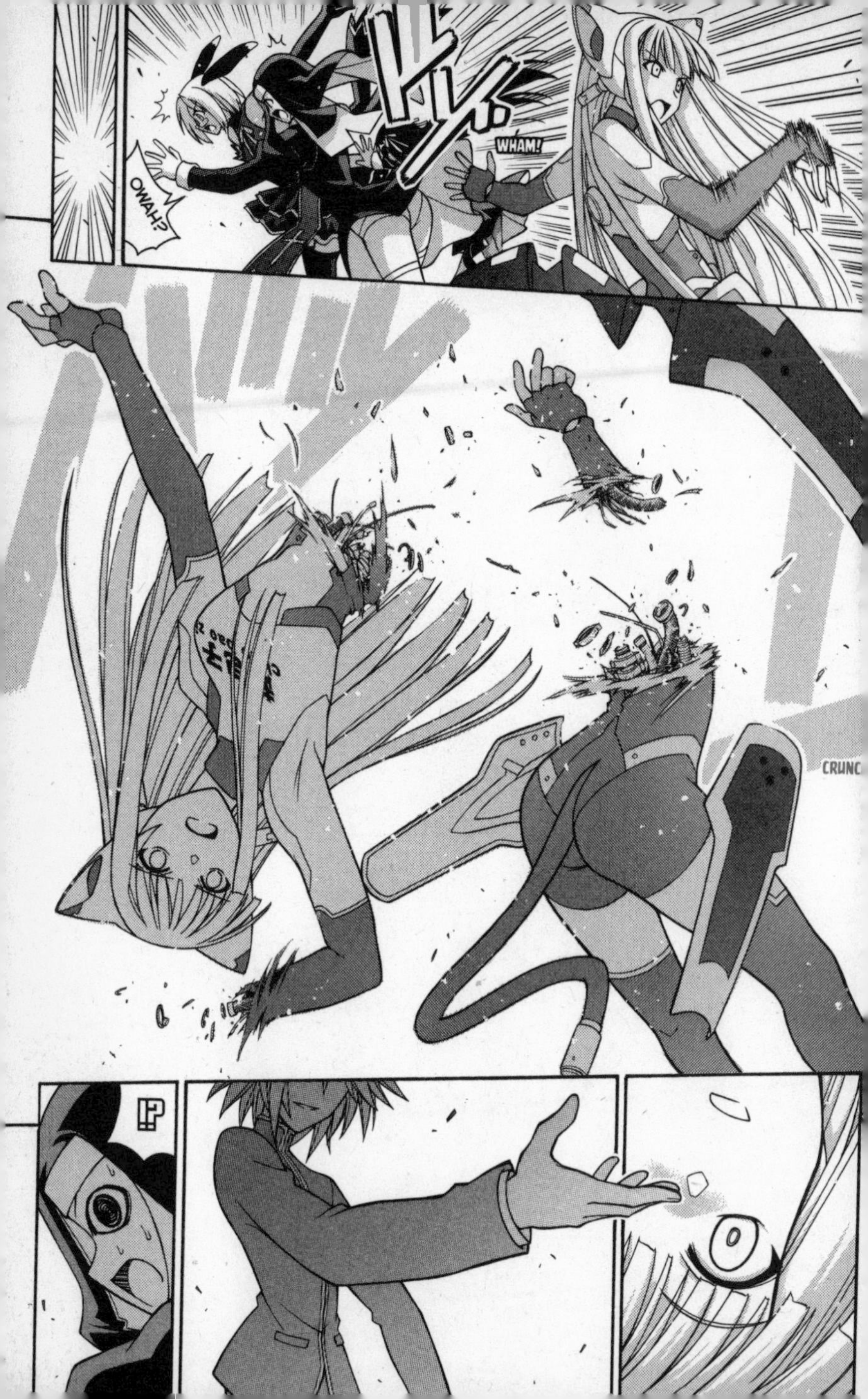
WHAM!
OWAH?
CRUNC
!?

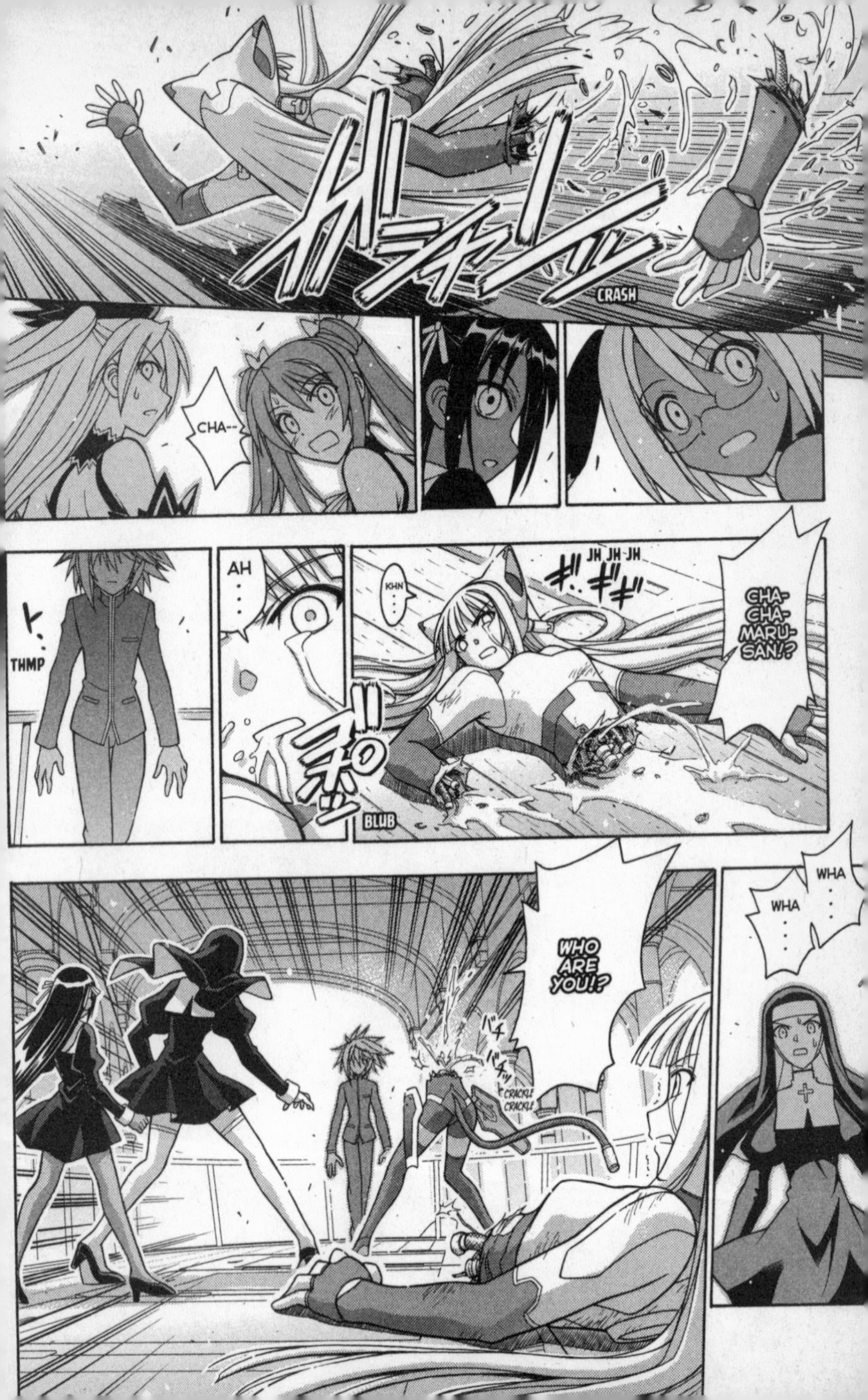
CRASH
CHA--
CHA-CHA-MARU-SAN!?
JH JH JH
KHN...
BLUB
AH...
THMP
WHA...
WHA...
WHO ARE YOU!?
CRACKLE CRACKLE

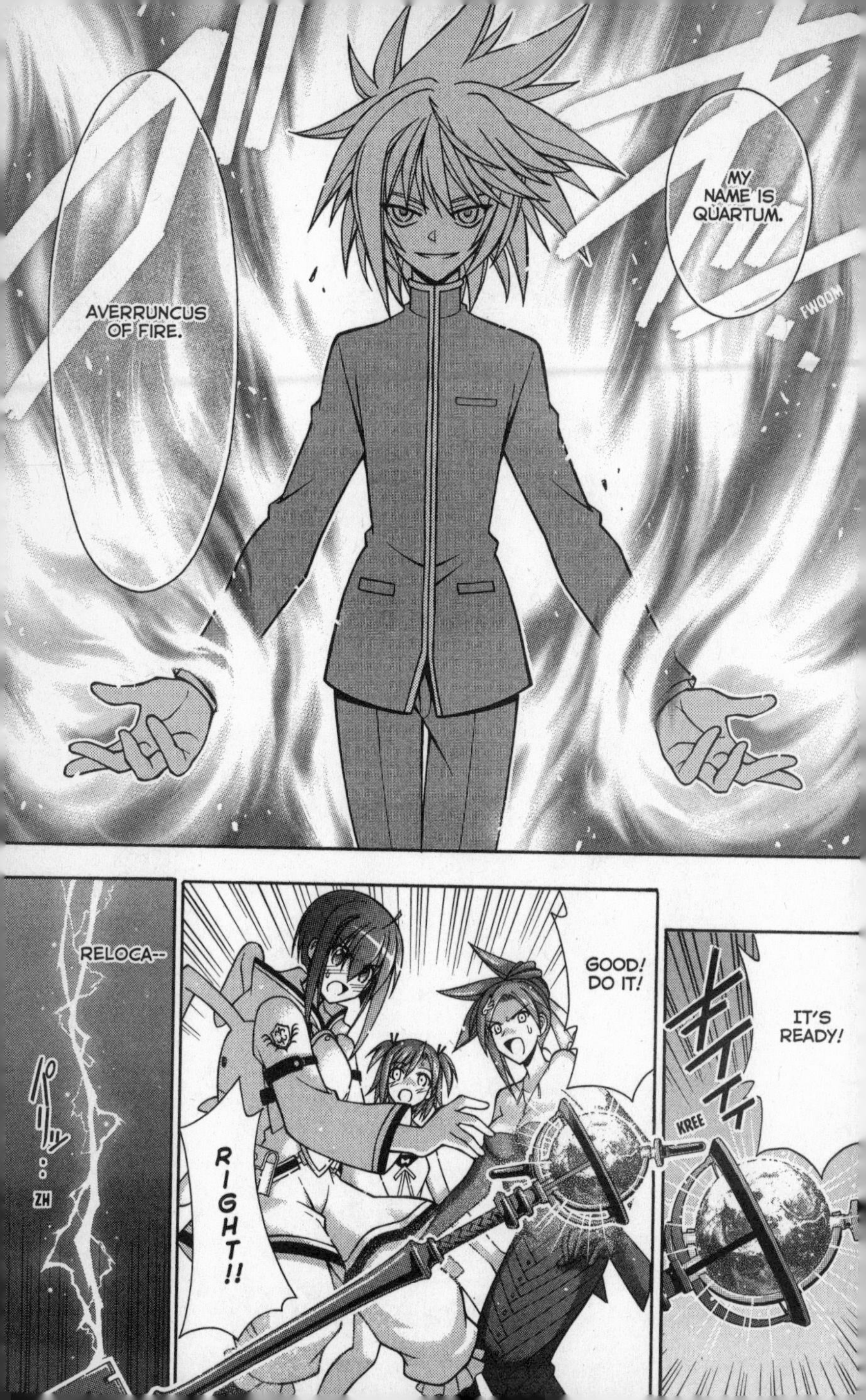
MY NAME IS QUARTUM.
FWOOM
AVERRUNCUS OF FIRE.
IT'S READY!
KREE
GOOD! DO IT!
RIGHT!!
RELOCA--
ZH

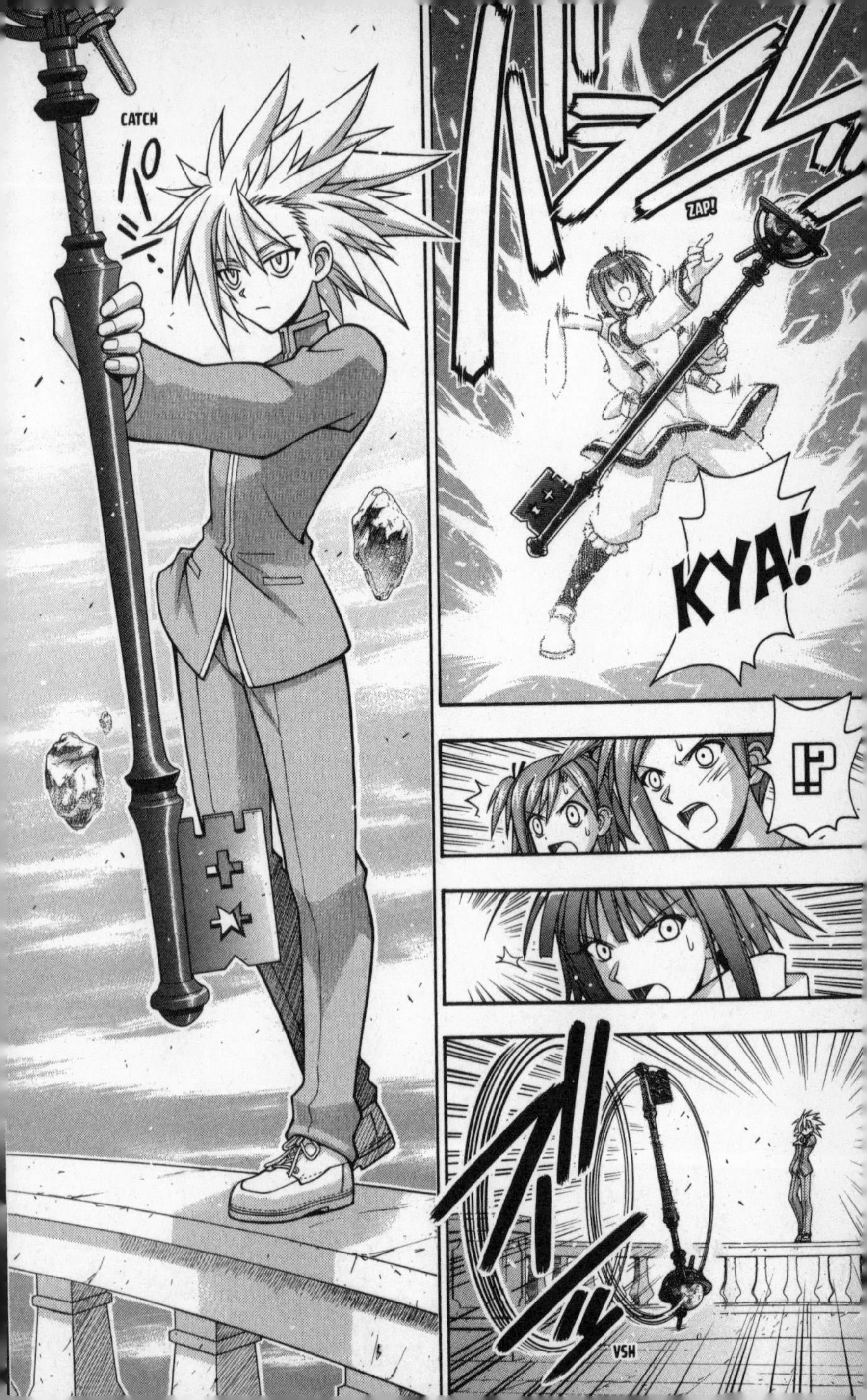
ZAP!
KYA!
!?
VSH
CATCH

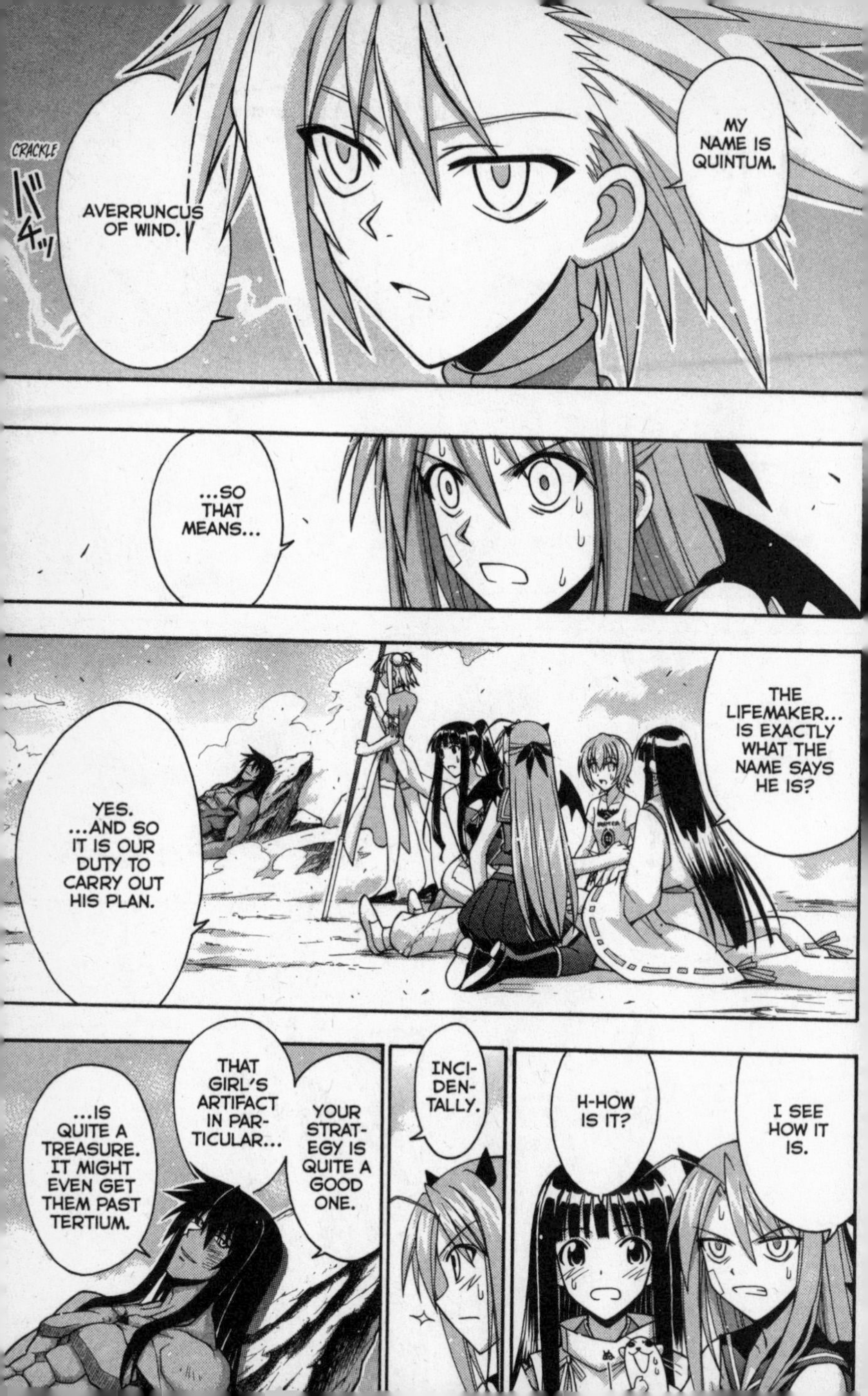
MY NAME IS QUINTUM.
AVERRUNCUS OF WIND.
CRACKLE
バチッ
...SO THAT MEANS...
THE LIFEMAKER... IS EXACTLY WHAT THE NAME SAYS HE IS?
YES. ...AND SO IT IS OUR DUTY TO CARRY OUT HIS PLAN.
I SEE HOW IT IS.
H-HOW IS IT?
INCI-DEN-TALLY.
YOUR STRAT-EGY IS QUITE A GOOD ONE.
THAT GIRL'S ARTIFACT IN PAR-TICULAR...
...IS QUITE A TREASURE. IT MIGHT EVEN GET THEM PAST TERTIUM.

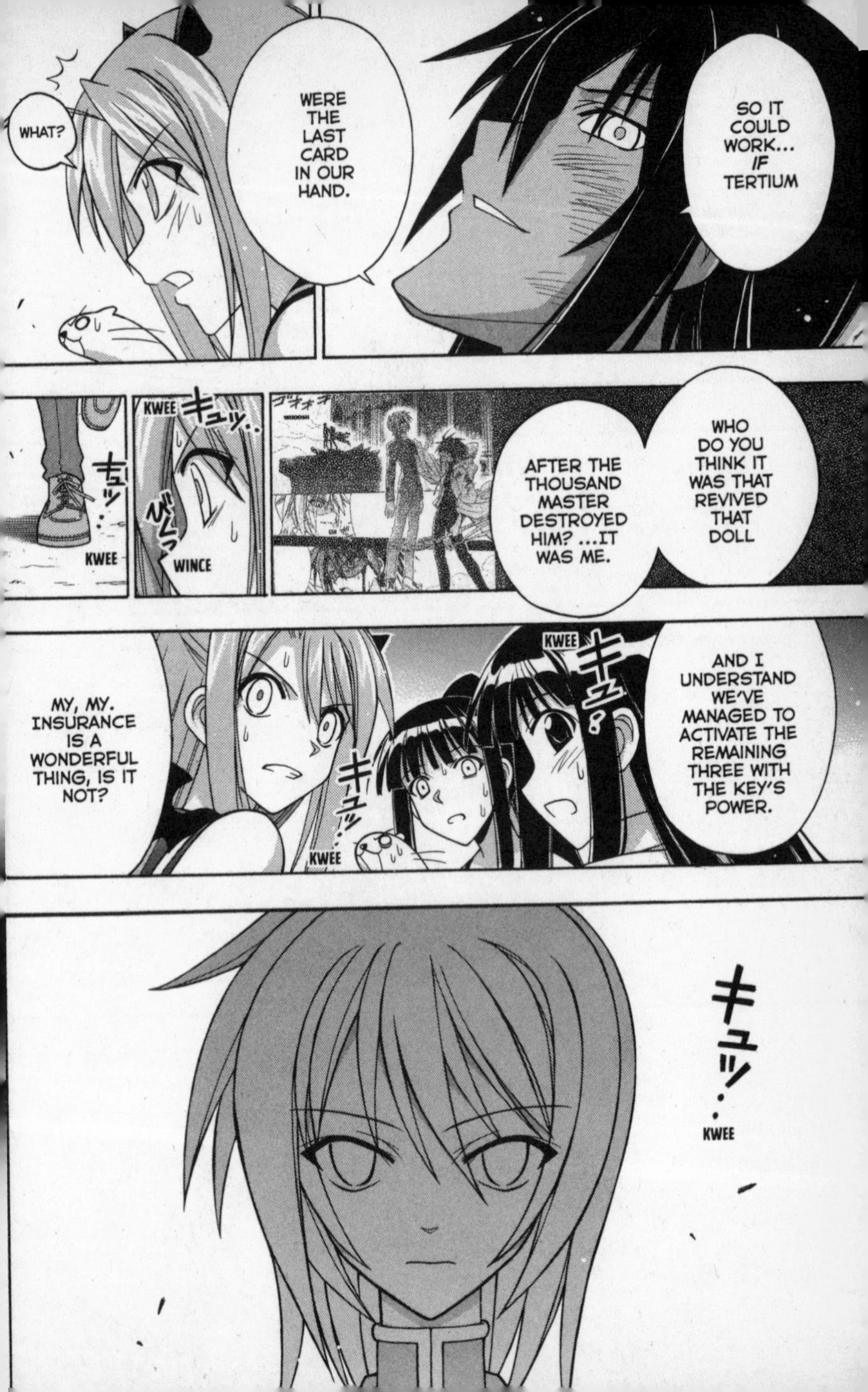
SO IT COULD WORK... IF TERTIUM
WERE THE LAST CARD IN OUR HAND.
WHAT?
WHO DO YOU THINK IT WAS THAT REVIVED THAT DOLL
AFTER THE THOUSAND MASTER DESTROYED HIM? ...IT WAS ME.
キュッ
KWEE
びくっ
WINCE
キュッ
KWEE
キュ
KWEE
AND I UNDERSTAND WE'VE MANAGED TO ACTIVATE THE REMAINING THREE WITH THE KEY'S POWER.
MY, MY. INSURANCE IS A WONDERFUL THING, IS IT NOT?
キュッ
KWEE
キュッ
KWEE

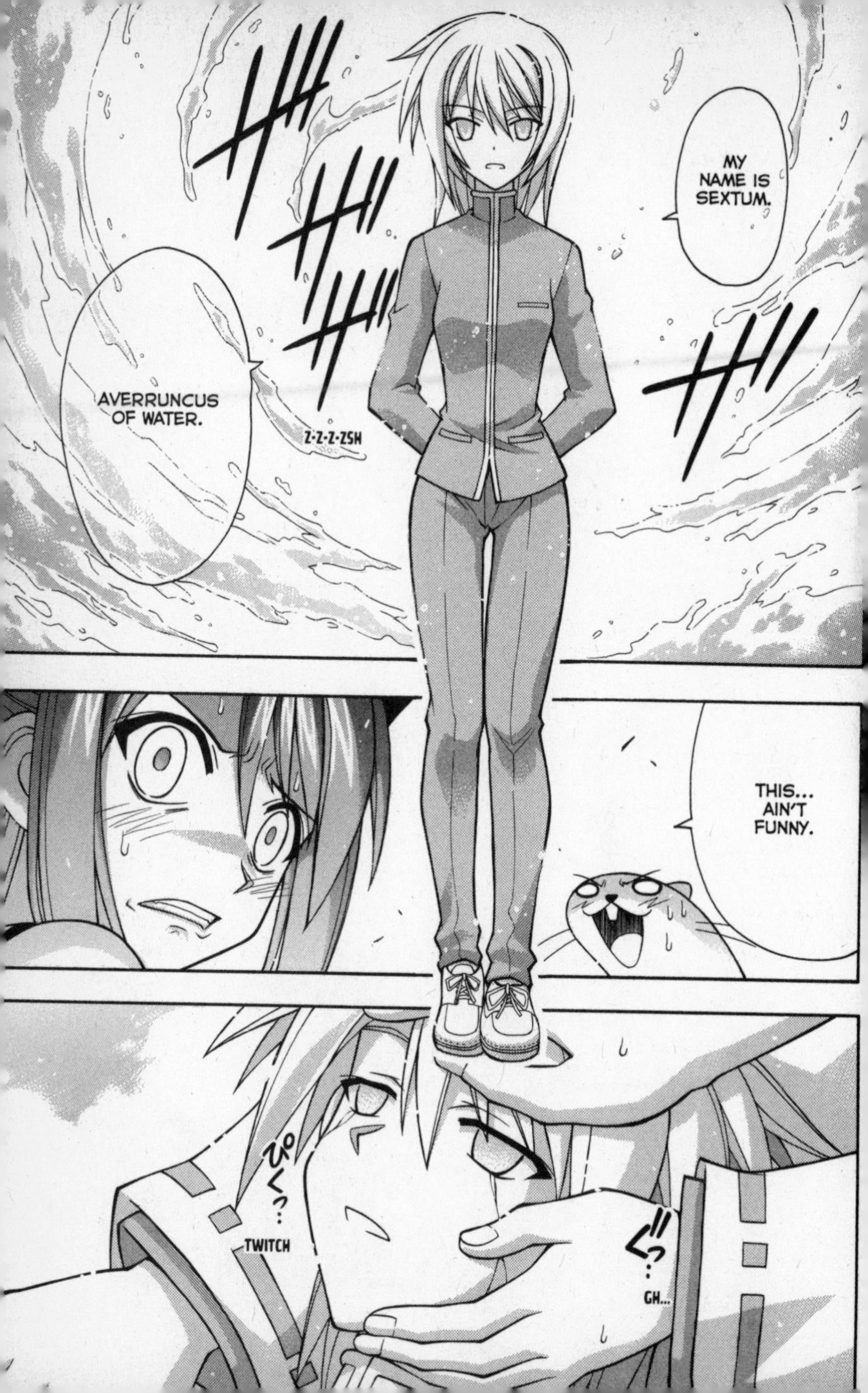
MY NAME IS SEXTUM.
AVERRUNCUS OF WATER.
Z-Z-Z-ZSH
THIS... AIN'T FUNNY.
GH...
ぐっ…
ぴくっ…
TWITCH

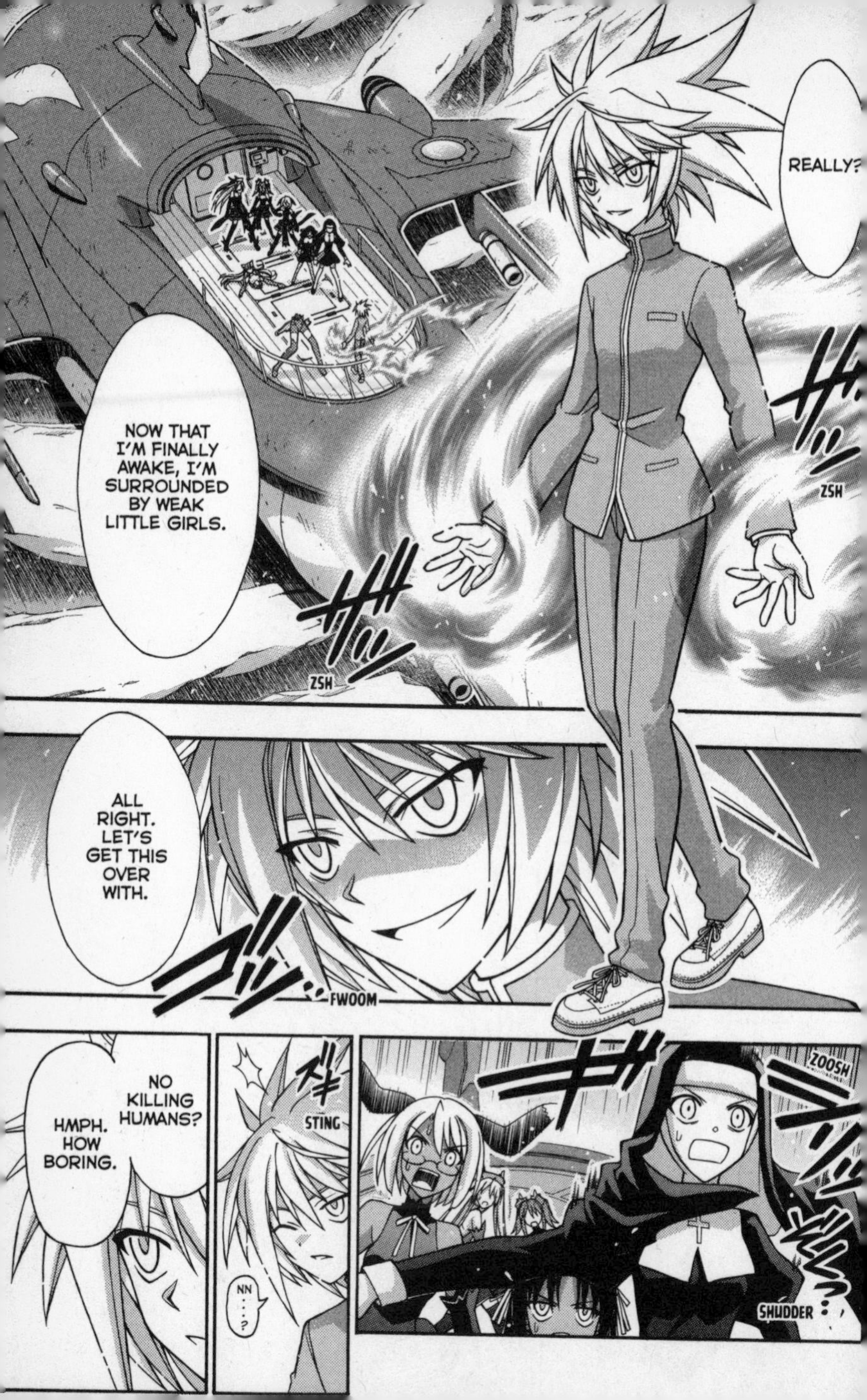
REALLY?
ZSH
NOW THAT I'M FINALLY AWAKE, I'M SURROUNDED BY WEAK LITTLE GIRLS.
ZSH
ALL RIGHT. LET'S GET THIS OVER WITH.
FWOOM
ZOOSH
SHUDDER
STING
NN...?
NO KILLING HUMANS?
HMPH. HOW BORING.

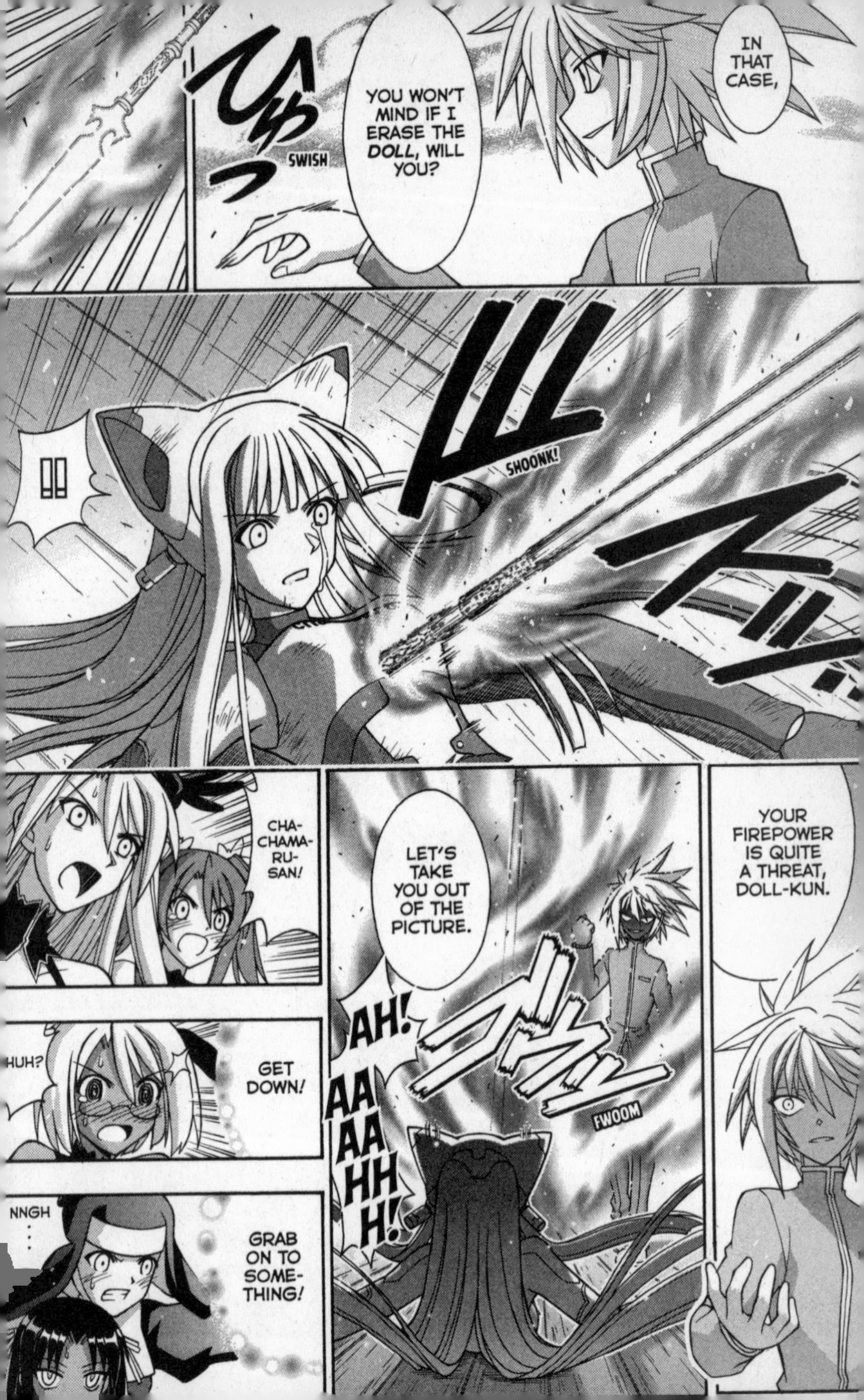

IN THAT CASE,
YOU WON'T MIND IF I ERASE THE *DOLL*, WILL YOU?
SWISH
!!
SHOONK!
YOUR FIREPOWER IS QUITE A THREAT, DOLL-KUN.
LET'S TAKE YOU OUT OF THE PICTURE.
FWOOM
AH! AAAAHHH!
CHA-CHAMA-RU-SAN!
GET DOWN!
HUH?
GRAB ON TO SOME-THING!
NNGH...

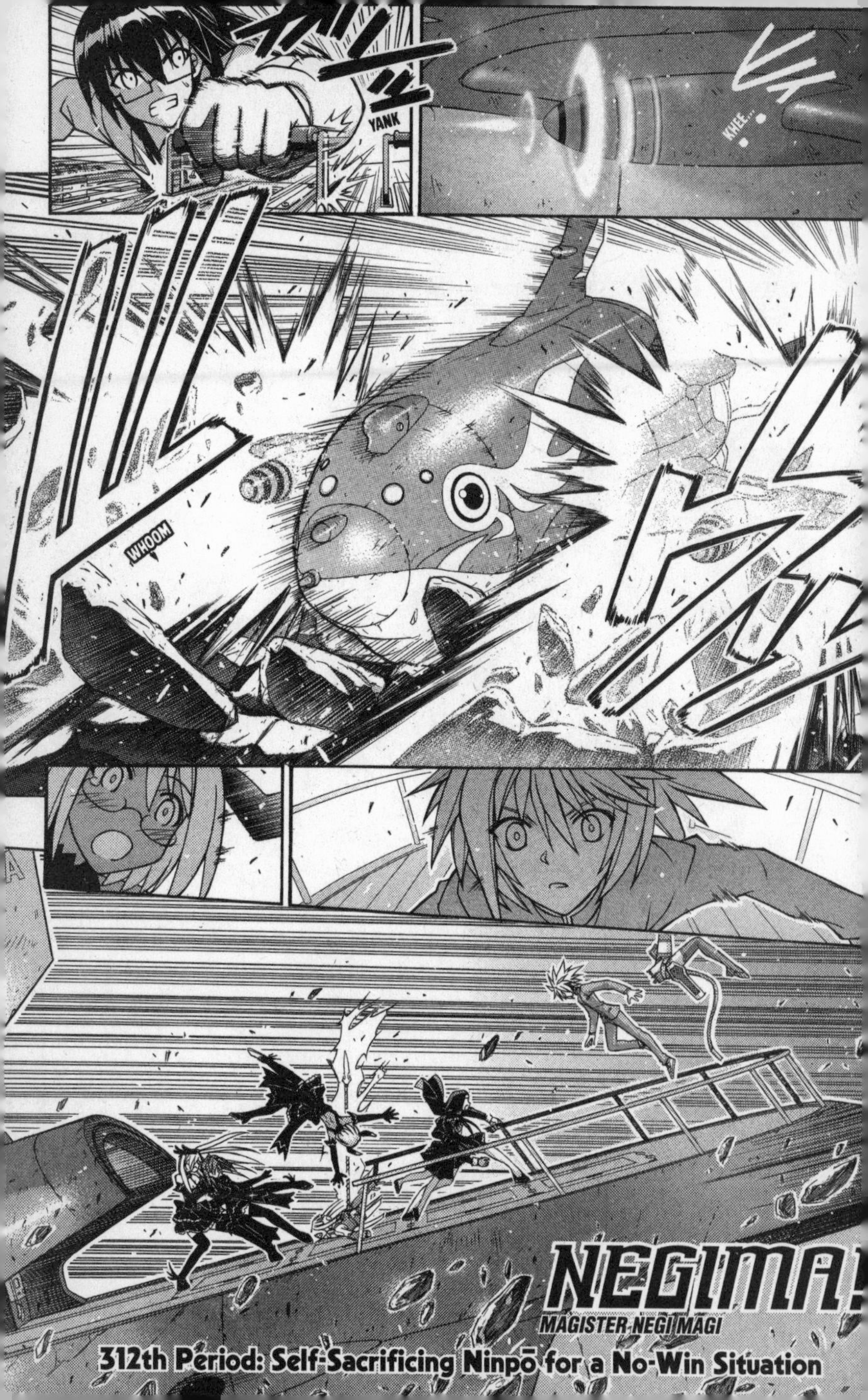
KHEE...
YANK
WHOOM

NEGIMA!

MAGISTER NEGI MAGI

312th Period: Self-Sacrificing Ninpō for a No-Win Situation

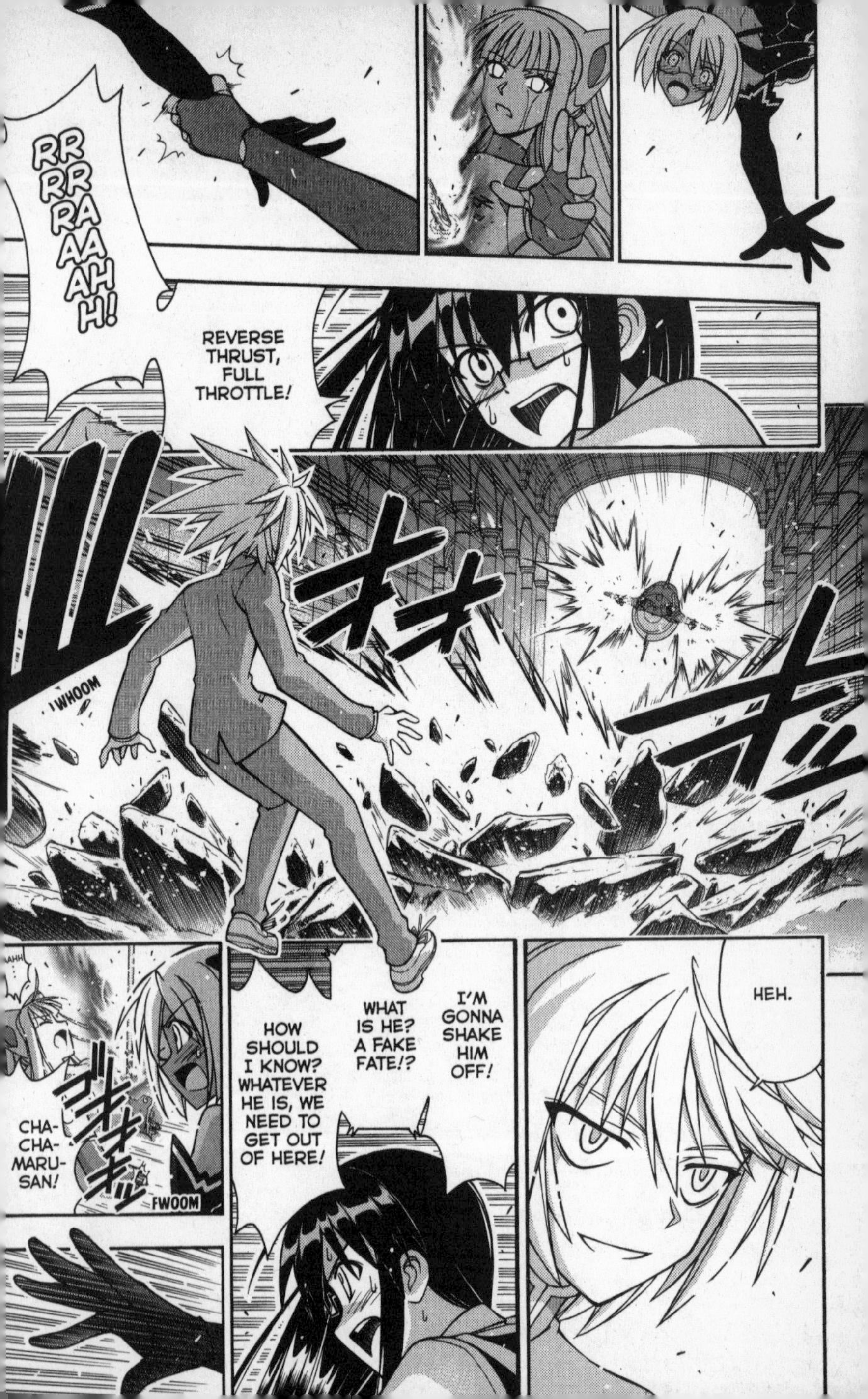
RRRRRAAAAHH!
REVERSE THRUST, FULL THROTTLE!
WHOOM
HEH.
I'M GONNA SHAKE HIM OFF!
WHAT IS HE? A FAKE FATE!?
HOW SHOULD I KNOW? WHATEVER HE IS, WE NEED TO GET OUT OF HERE!
CHA-CHA-MARU-SAN!
FWOOM

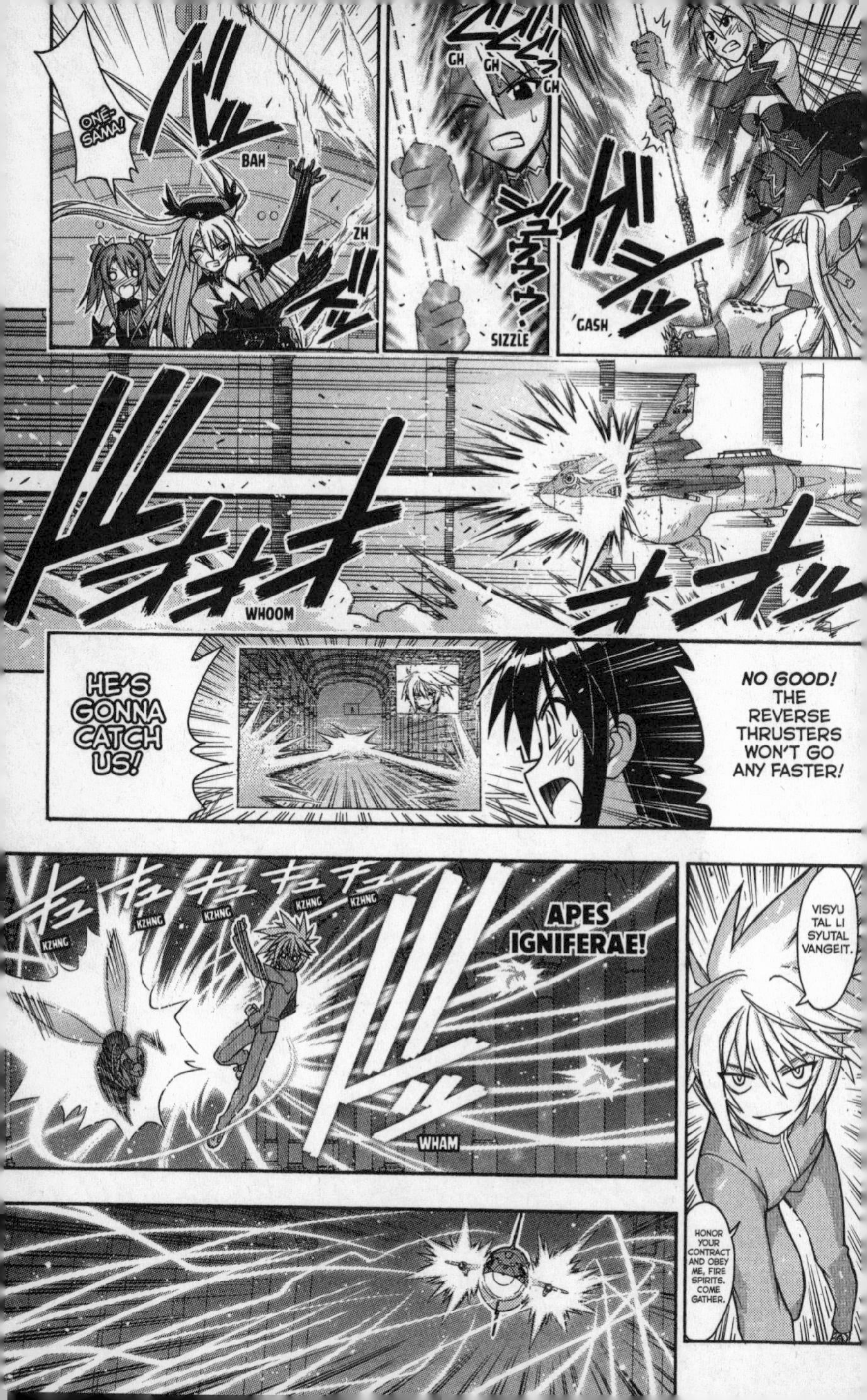
GASH
GH GH GH
SIZZLE
ONE-SAMA!
BAH
ZH
WHOOM
NO GOOD! THE REVERSE THRUSTERS WON'T GO ANY FASTER!
HE'S GONNA CATCH US!
VISYU TAL LI SYUTAL VANGEIT.
HONOR YOUR CONTRACT AND OBEY ME, FIRE SPIRITS. COME GATHER.
APES IGNIFERAE!
KZHNG
KZHNG
KZHNG
KZHNG
KZHNG
WHAM

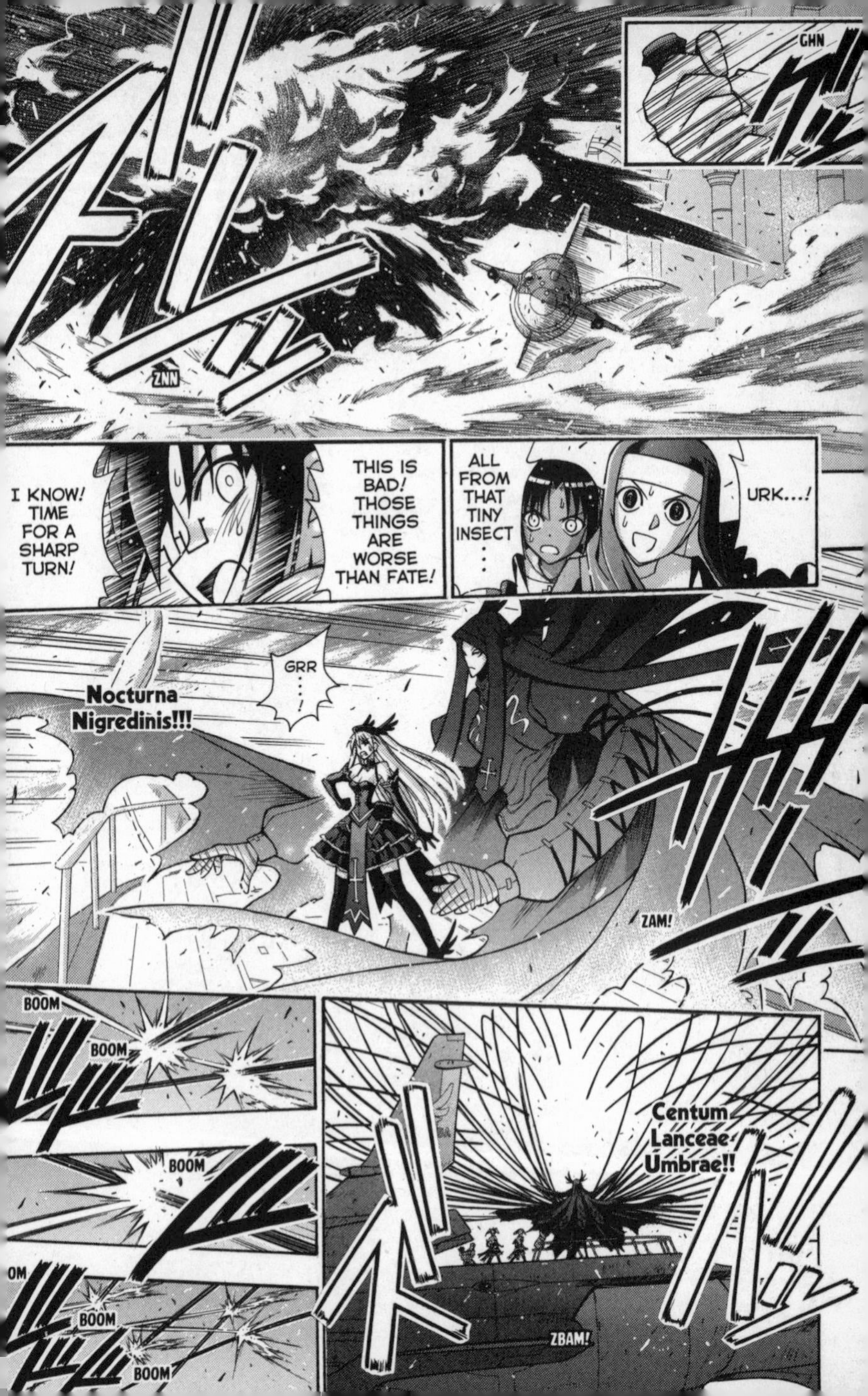
GHN
ZNN
URK...!
ALL FROM THAT TINY INSECT...
THIS IS BAD! THOSE THINGS ARE WORSE THAN FATE!
I KNOW! TIME FOR A SHARP TURN!
GRR...!
Nocturna Nigredinis!!!
ZAM!
Centum Lanceae Umbrae!!
ZBAM!
BOOM
BOOM
BOOM
OM
BOOM
BOOM

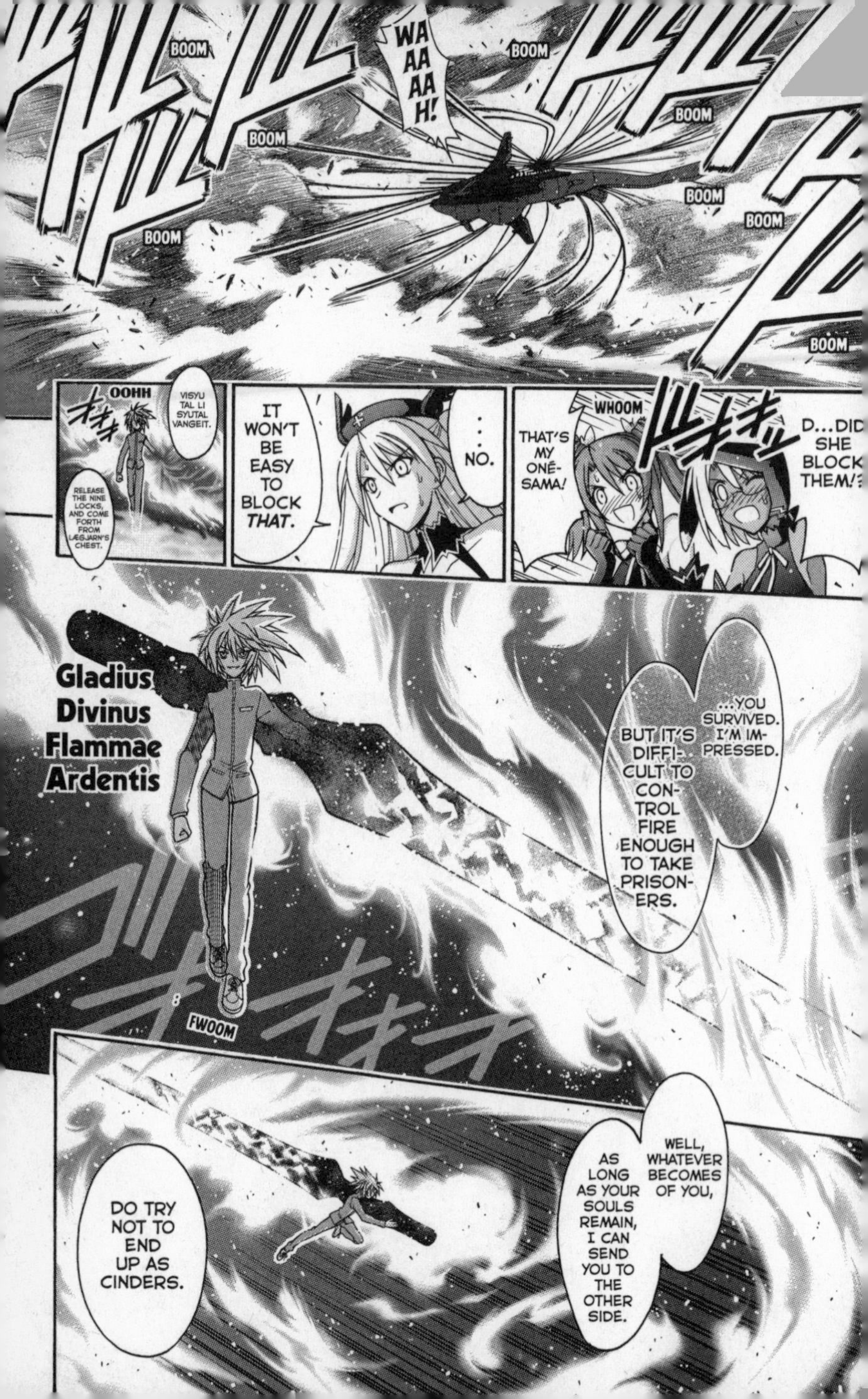
BOOM
BOOM
BOOM
BOOM
WA AA AA H!
BOOM
BOOM
BOOM
WHOOM
D...DID SHE BLOCK THEM!?
THAT'S MY ONÉ-SAMA!
...NO.
IT WON'T BE EASY TO BLOCK THAT.
VISYU TAL LI SYUTAL VANGEIT.
Release the nine locks, and come forth from Lægjarn's chest.
OOHH
...YOU SURVIVED. I'M IMPRESSED.
BUT IT'S DIFFI-CULT TO CON-TROL FIRE ENOUGH TO TAKE PRISON-ERS.
Gladius Divinus Flammae Ardentis
FWOOM
WELL, WHATEVER BECOMES OF YOU,
AS LONG AS YOUR SOULS REMAIN, I CAN SEND YOU TO THE OTHER SIDE.
DO TRY NOT TO END UP AS CINDERS.

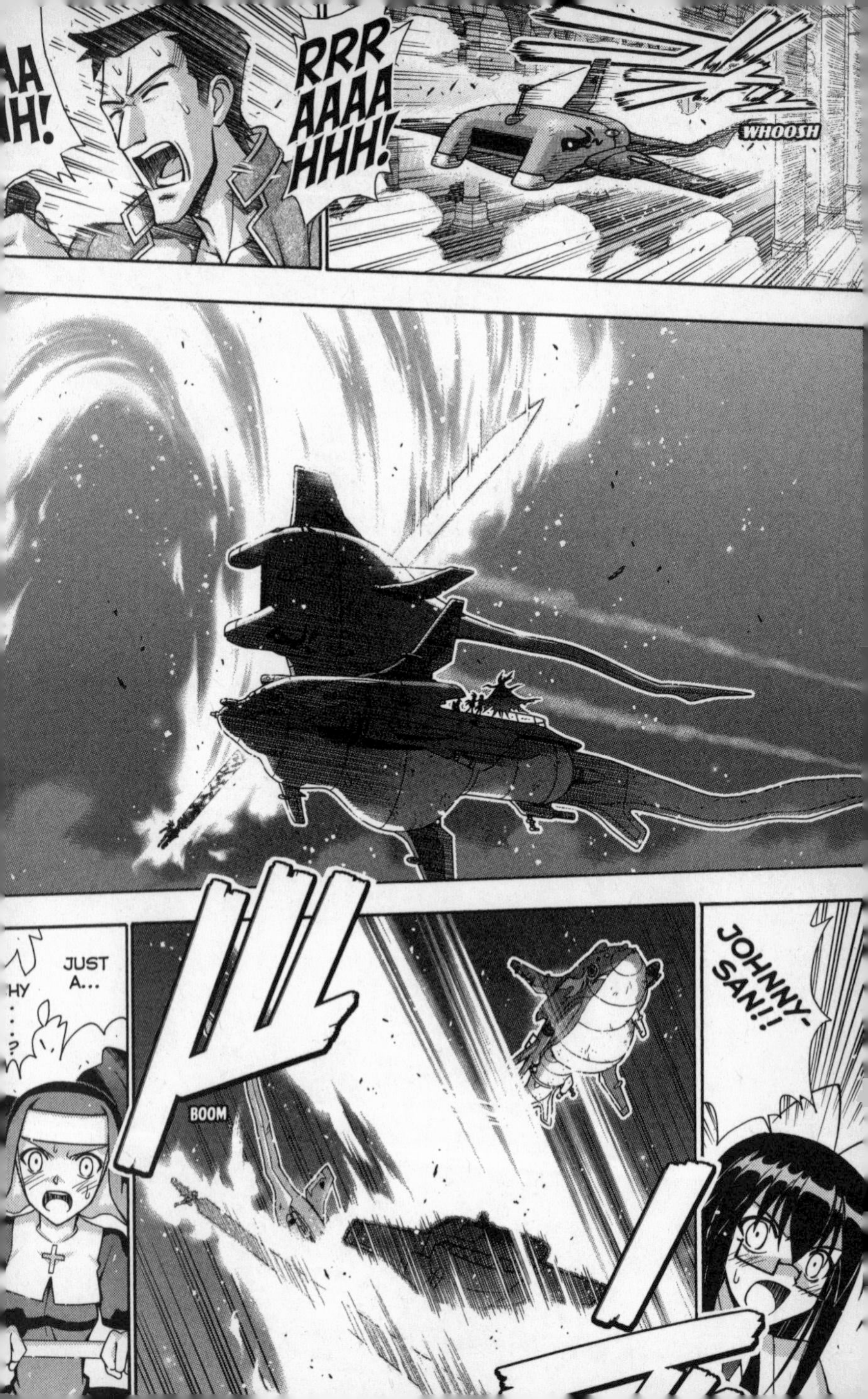

WHOOSH
RRR AAAA HHH!
JOHNNY-SAN!!
BOOM
JUST A...

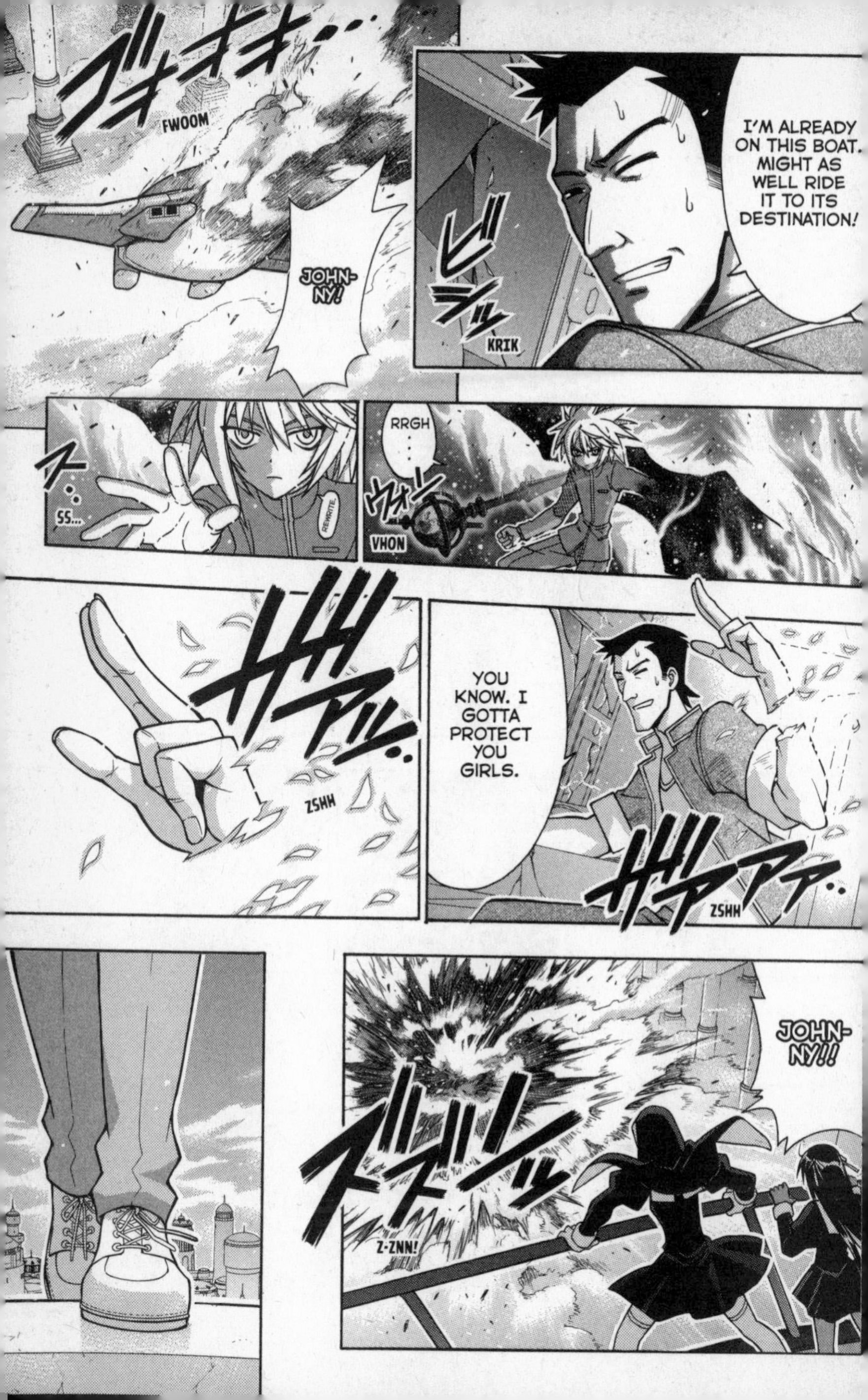
I'M ALREADY ON THIS BOAT. MIGHT AS WELL RIDE IT TO ITS DESTINATION!
KRIK
FWOOM
JOHN-NY!
RRGH...
VHON
SS...
REWRITE.
YOU KNOW. I GOTTA PROTECT YOU GIRLS.
ZSHH
ZSHH
JOHN-NY!!
Z-ZNN!

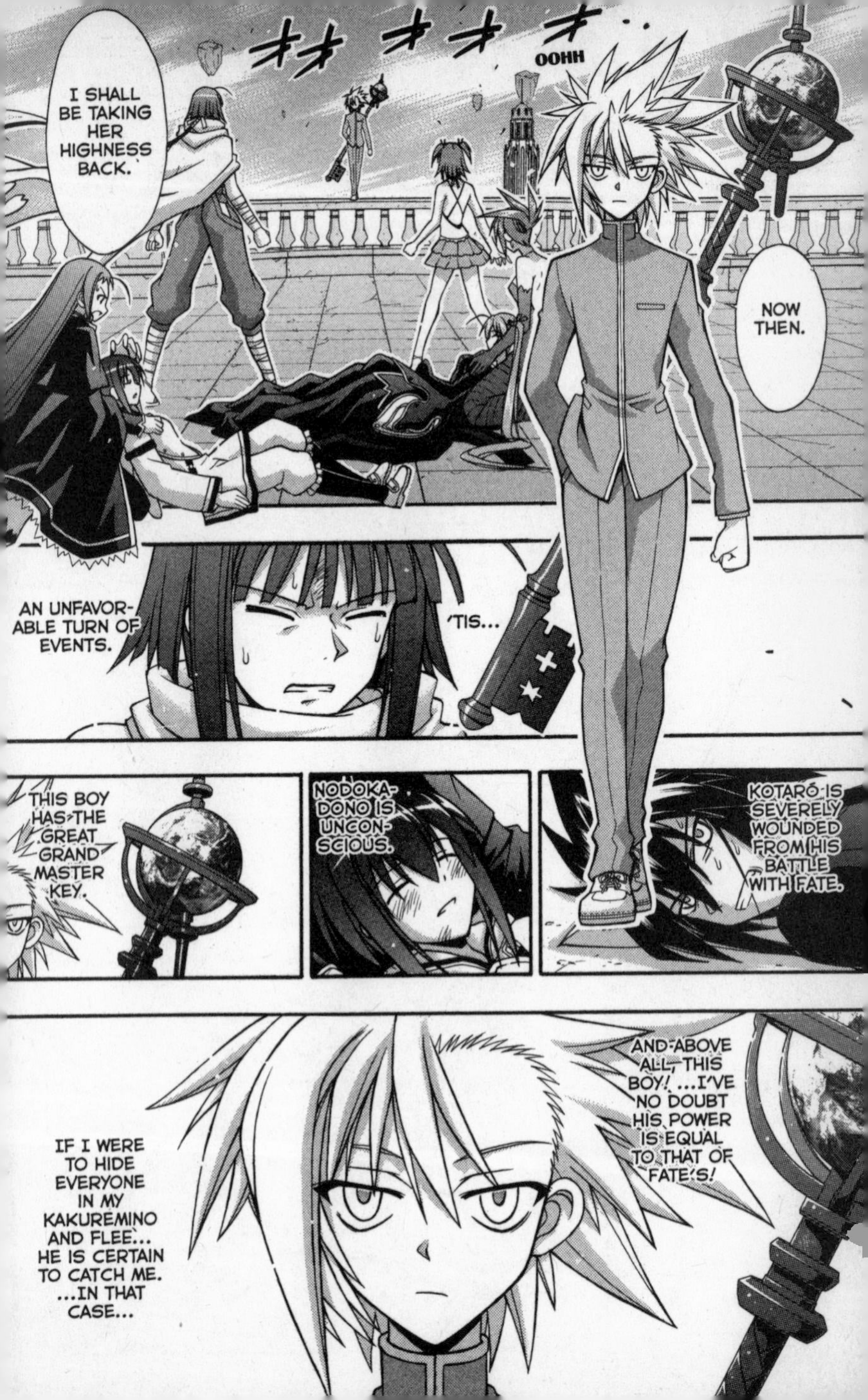
OOHH
NOW THEN.
I SHALL BE TAKING HER HIGHNESS BACK.
'TIS...
AN UNFAVORABLE TURN OF EVENTS.
KOTARŌ IS SEVERELY WOUNDED FROM HIS BATTLE WITH FATE.
NODOKA-DONO IS UNCONSCIOUS.
THIS BOY HAS THE GREAT GRAND MASTER KEY.
AND ABOVE ALL, THIS BOY! ...I'VE NO DOUBT HIS POWER IS EQUAL TO THAT OF FATE'S!
IF I WERE TO HIDE EVERYONE IN MY KAKUREMINO AND FLEE... HE IS CERTAIN TO CATCH ME. ...IN THAT CASE...

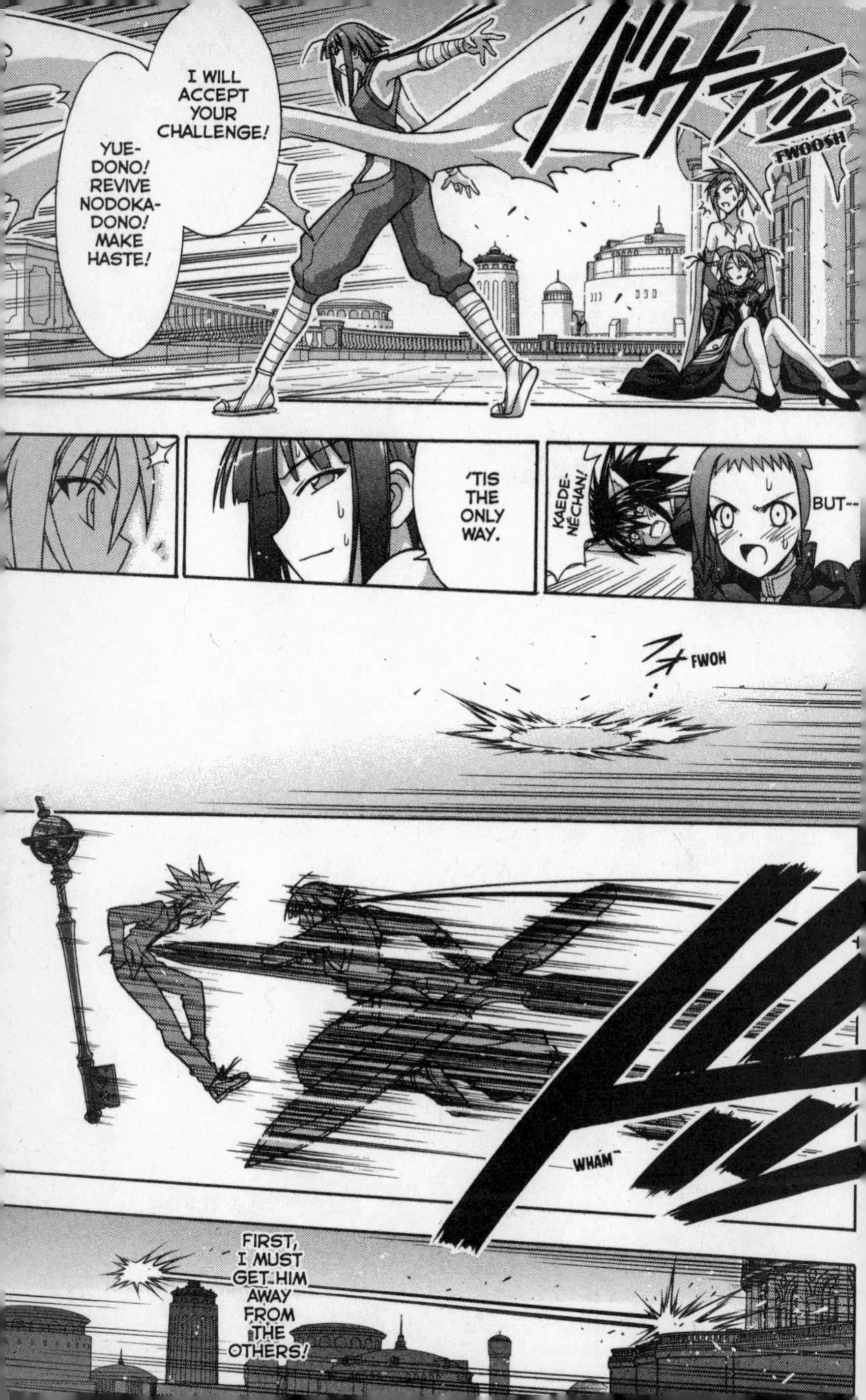
FWOOSH
I WILL ACCEPT YOUR CHALLENGE!
YUE-DONO! REVIVE NODOKA-DONO! MAKE HASTE!
BUT--
KAEDE-NECHAN!
'TIS THE ONLY WAY.
FWOH
WHAM
FIRST, I MUST GET HIM AWAY FROM THE OTHERS!

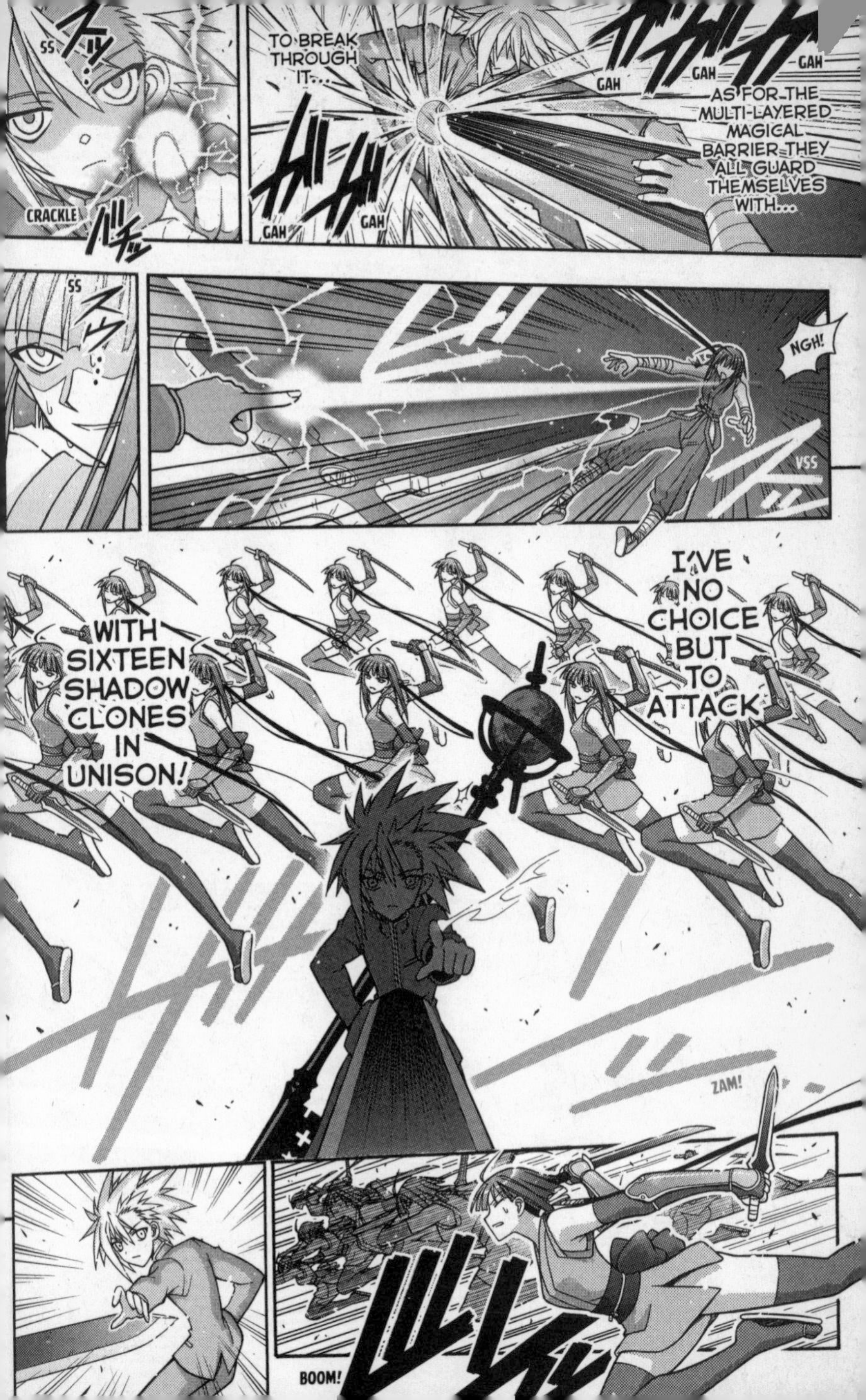
GAH
GAH
GAH
AS FOR THE MULTI-LAYERED MAGICAL BARRIER THEY ALL GUARD THEMSELVES WITH...
TO BREAK THROUGH IT...
GAH
GAH
SS
CRACKLE
NGH!
VSS
SS
I'VE NO CHOICE BUT TO ATTACK
WITH SIXTEEN SHADOW CLONES IN UNISON!
ZAM!
BOOM!

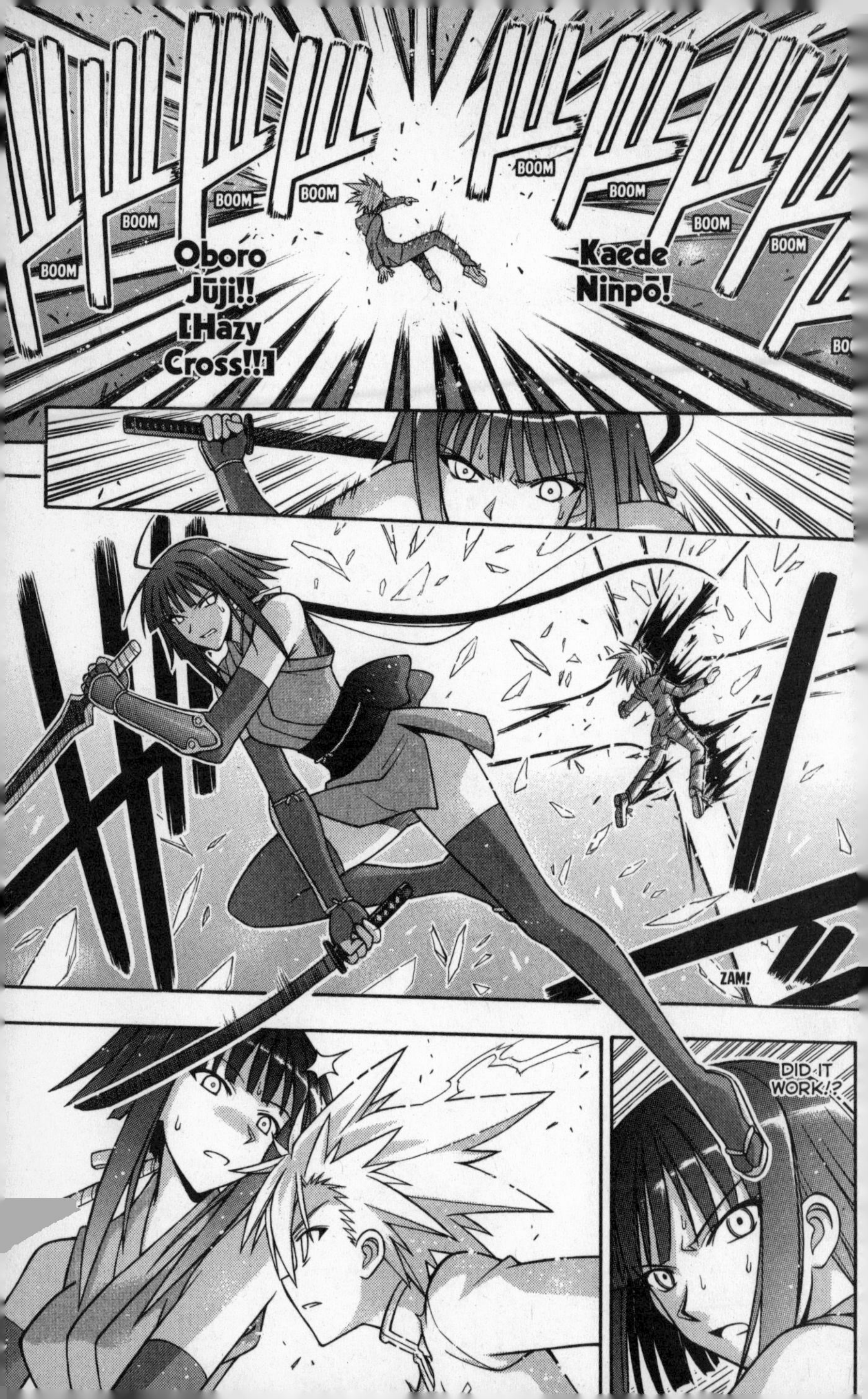

BOOM
BOOM
BOOM
BOOM
Kaede Ninpō!
Oboro Jūji!! [Hazy Cross!!]
BOOM
BOOM
BOOM
BOOM
ZAM!
DID IT WORK!?

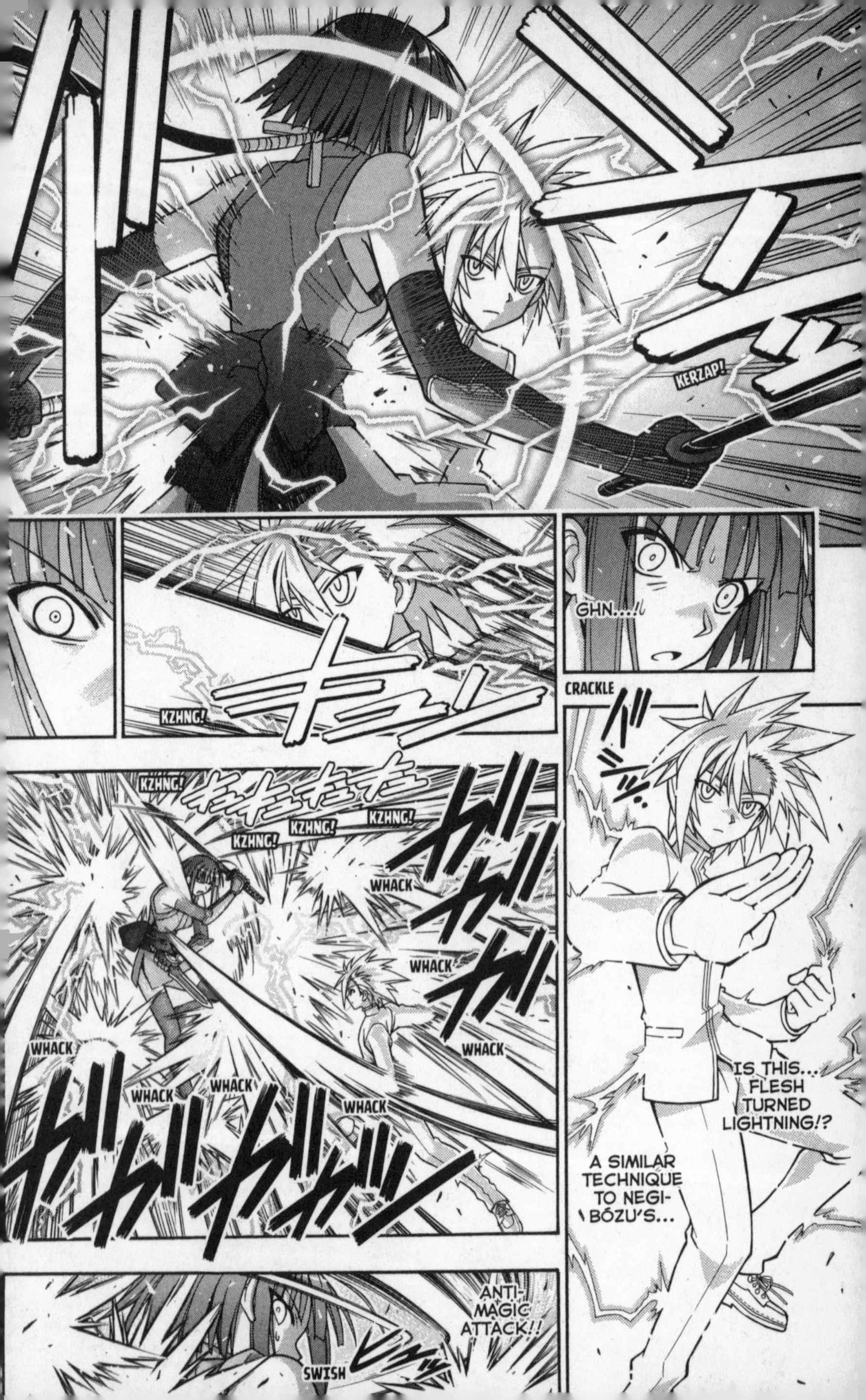
KERZAP!
GHN...!!
KZHNG!
CRACKLE
IS THIS... FLESH TURNED LIGHTNING!?
A SIMILAR TECHNIQUE TO NEGI-BŌZU'S...
KZHNG!
KZHNG!
KZHNG!
KZHNG!
WHACK
WHACK
WHACK
WHACK
WHACK
WHACK
WHACK
ANTI-MAGIC ATTACK!!
SWISH

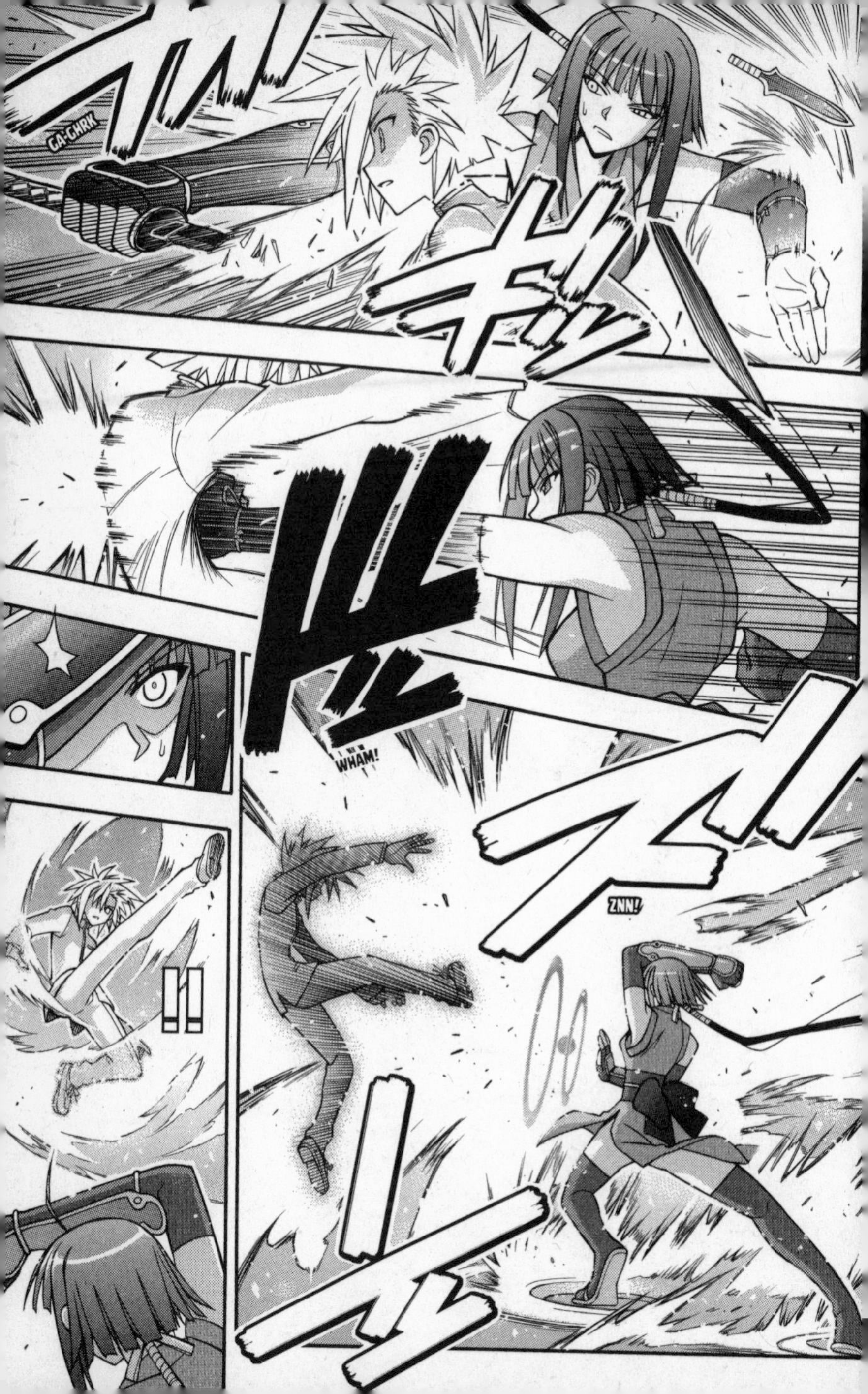
GA-GHRK
WHAM!
ZNN!
!!

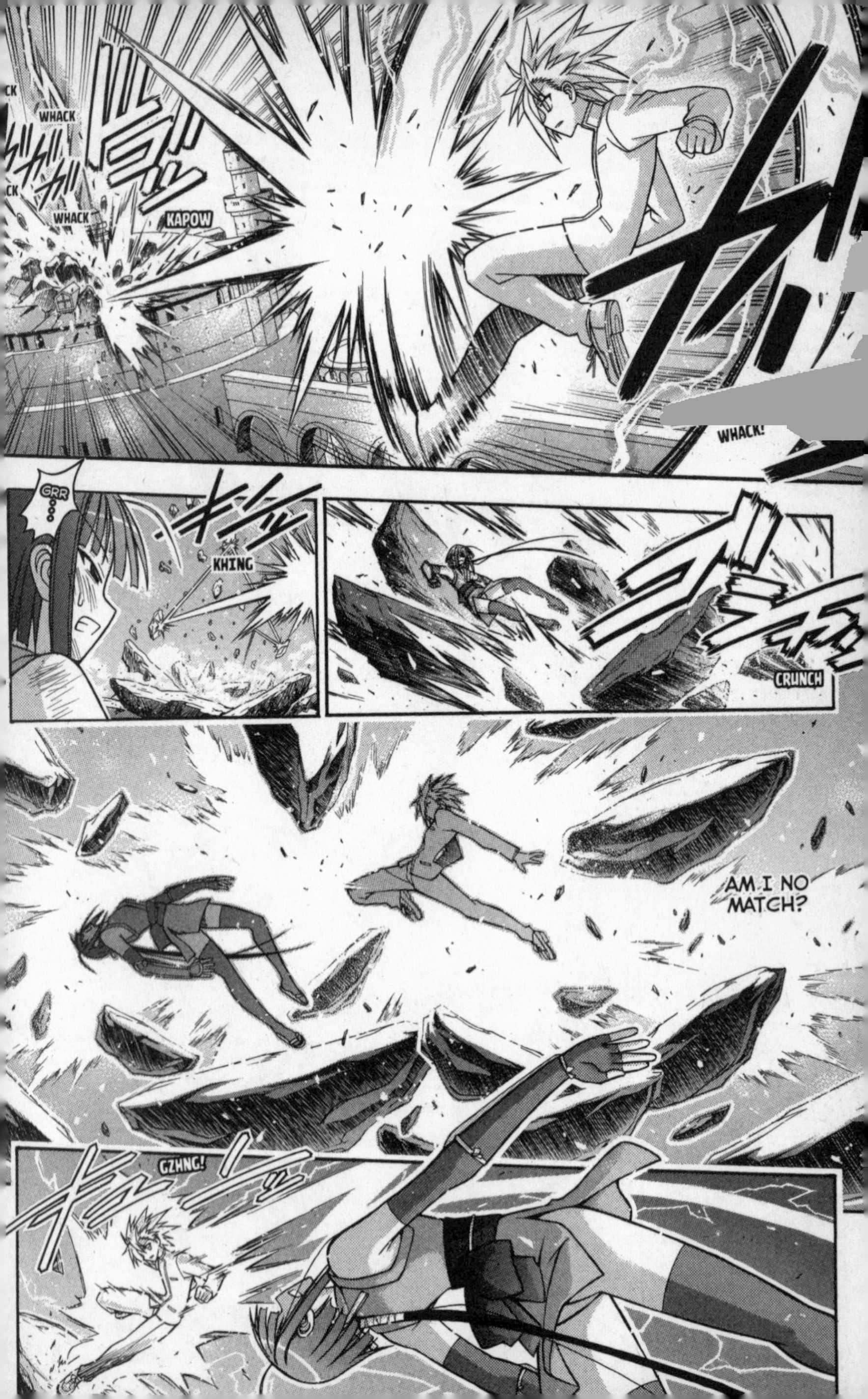
WHACK!
KAPOW
WHACK
WHACK
CRUNCH
GRR...
KHING
AM I NO MATCH?
GZHNG!

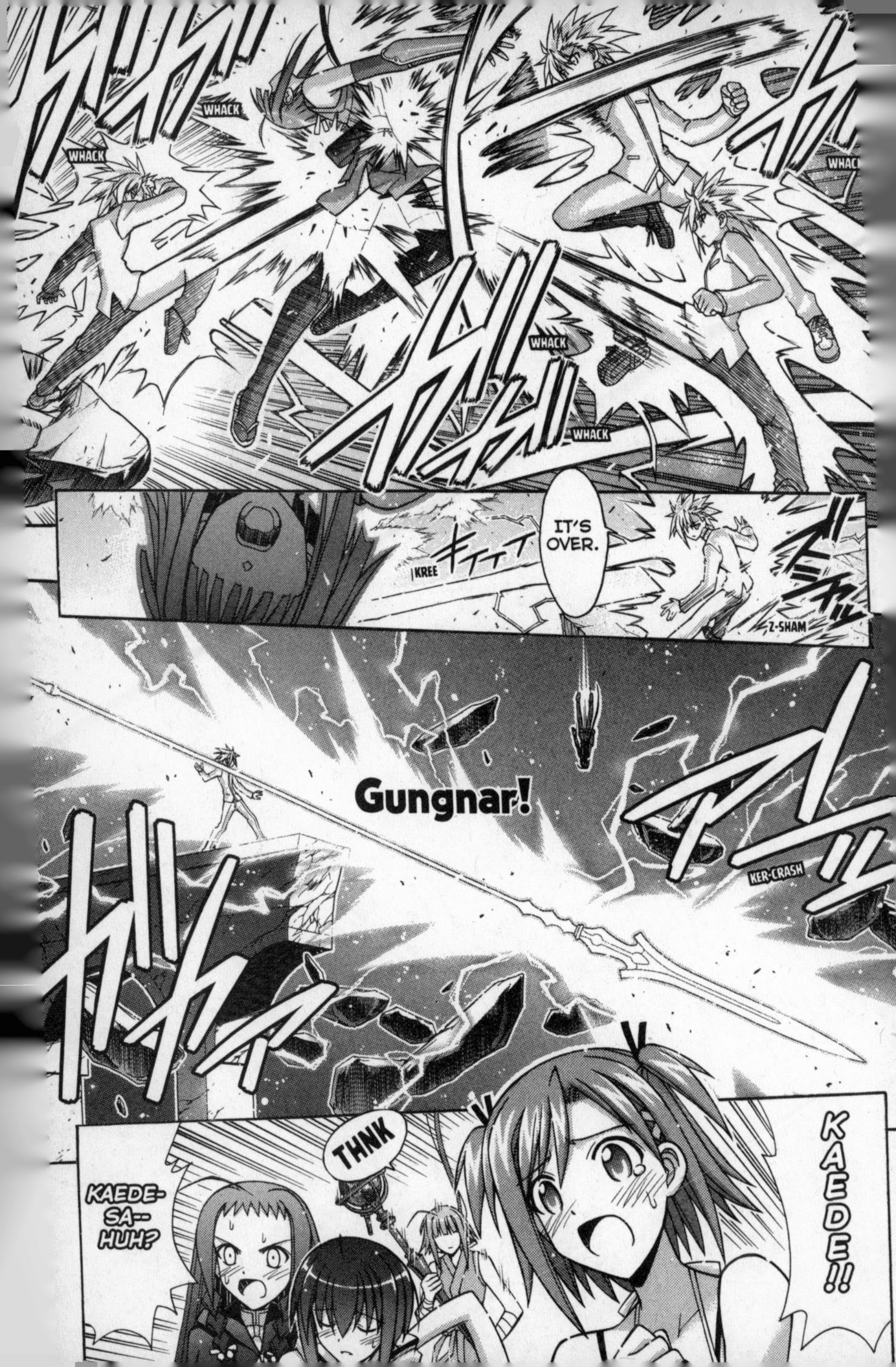
WHACK
WHACK
WHACK
WHACK
WHACK
Z-SHAM
IT'S OVER.
KREE
KER-CRASH
Gungnar!
KAEDE!!
THNK
KAEDE-SA-- HUH?

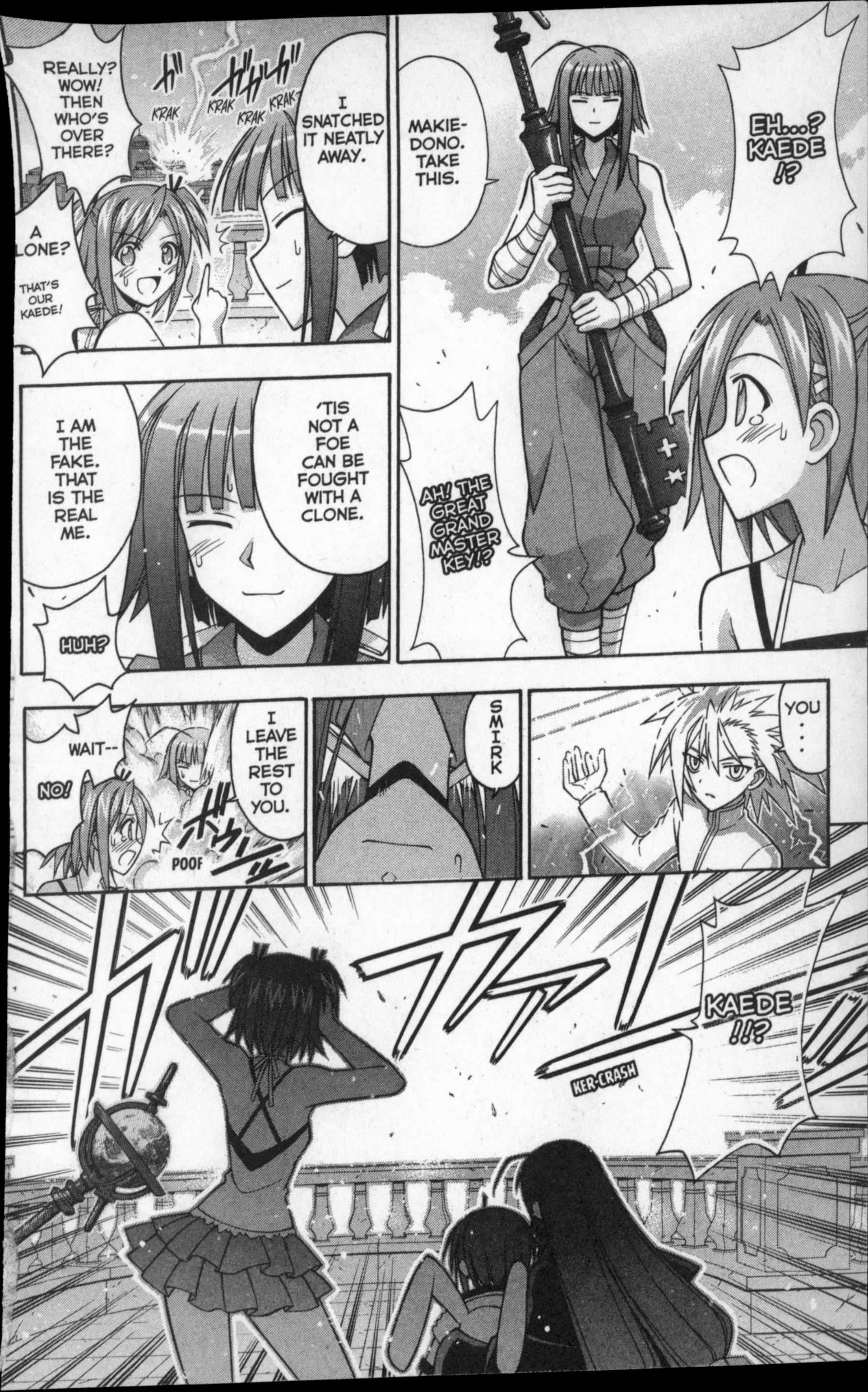
EH...? KAEDE !?
MAKIE-DONO. TAKE THIS.
AH! THE GREAT GRAND MASTER KEY!?
KRAK KRAK KRAK KRAK
I SNATCHED IT NEATLY AWAY.
REALLY? WOW! THEN WHO'S OVER THERE?
A CLONE?
THAT'S OUR KAEDE!
'TIS NOT A FOE CAN BE FOUGHT WITH A CLONE.
I AM THE FAKE. THAT IS THE REAL ME.
HUH?
YOU...
SMIRK
I LEAVE THE REST TO YOU.
WAIT--
NO!
POOF
KAEDE !!?
KER-CRASH

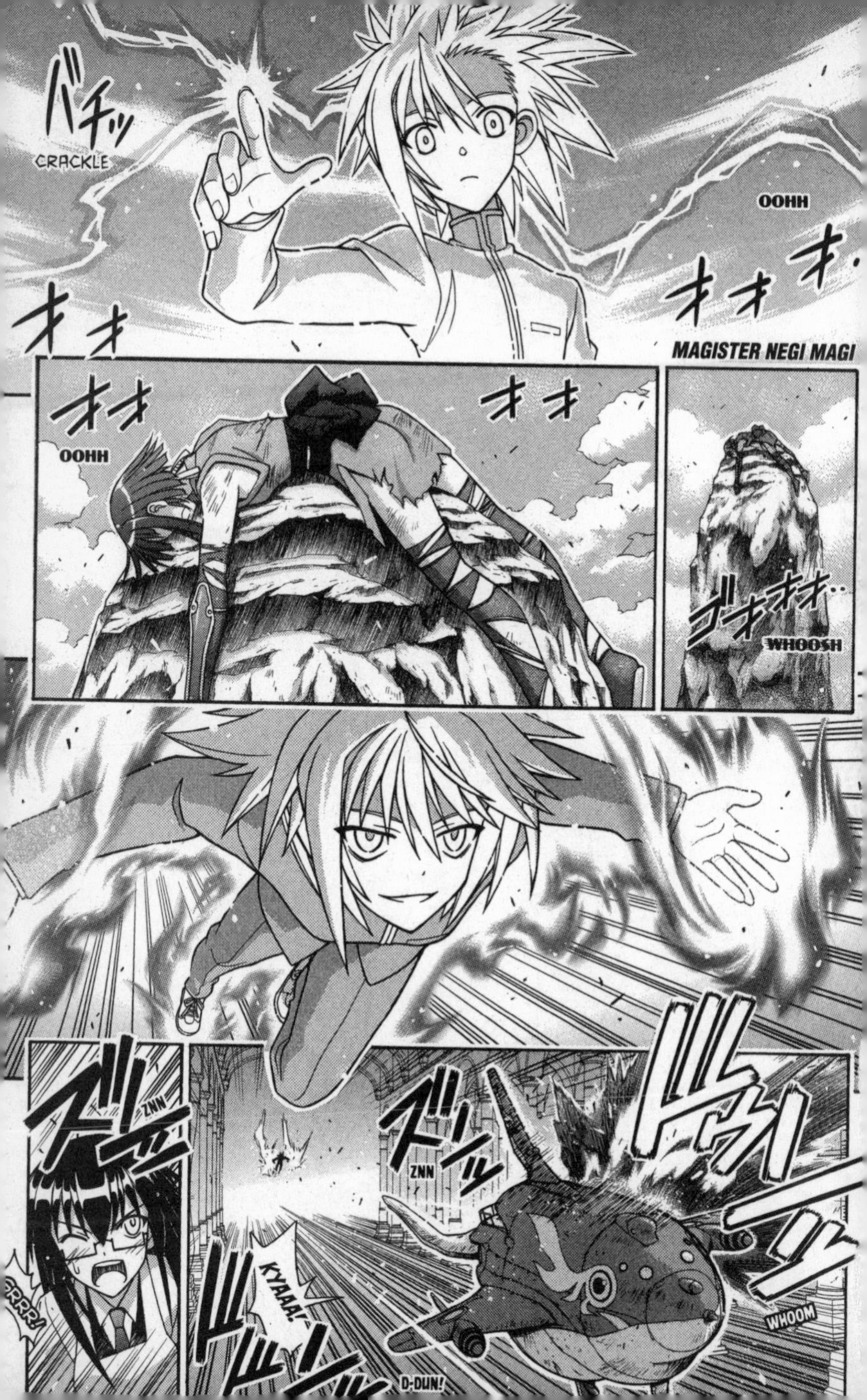
OOHH
オオオ
バチッ
CRACKLE
オオ
ゴオオオ…
WHOOSH
オオ
オオ
OOHH
ドゥン
WHOOM
ズンッ
ZNN
KYAAA!
D-DUN!
ズン
ZNN
GRRR!

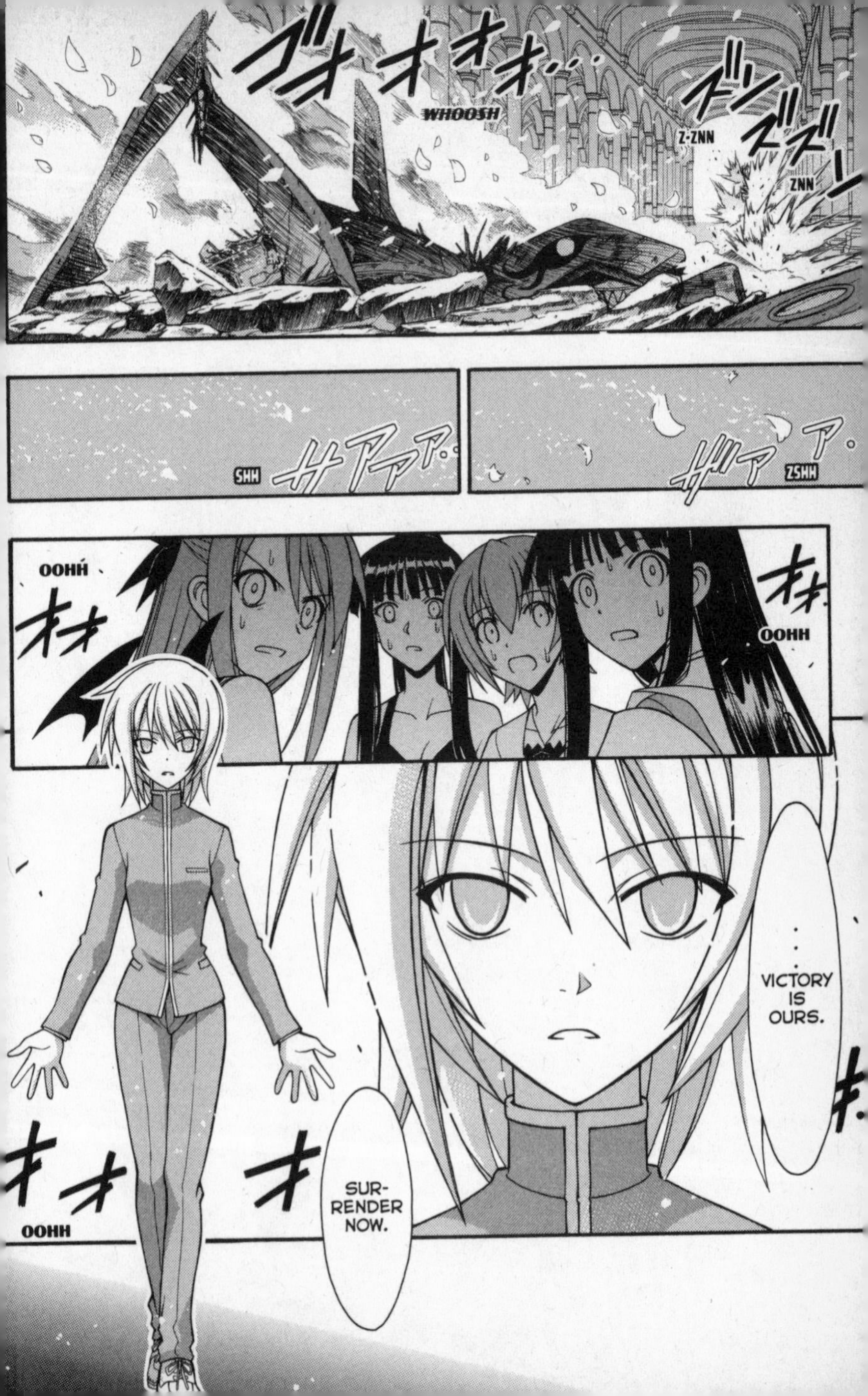

ズン
Z-ZNN
ズズン
ZNN
ゴオオオオ...
WHOOSH
ザァア.
ZSHH
サアァア.
SHH
オォ.
OOHH
オォ
OOHH
... VICTORY IS OURS.
SUR-RENDER NOW.
オ
オォ オ
OOHH

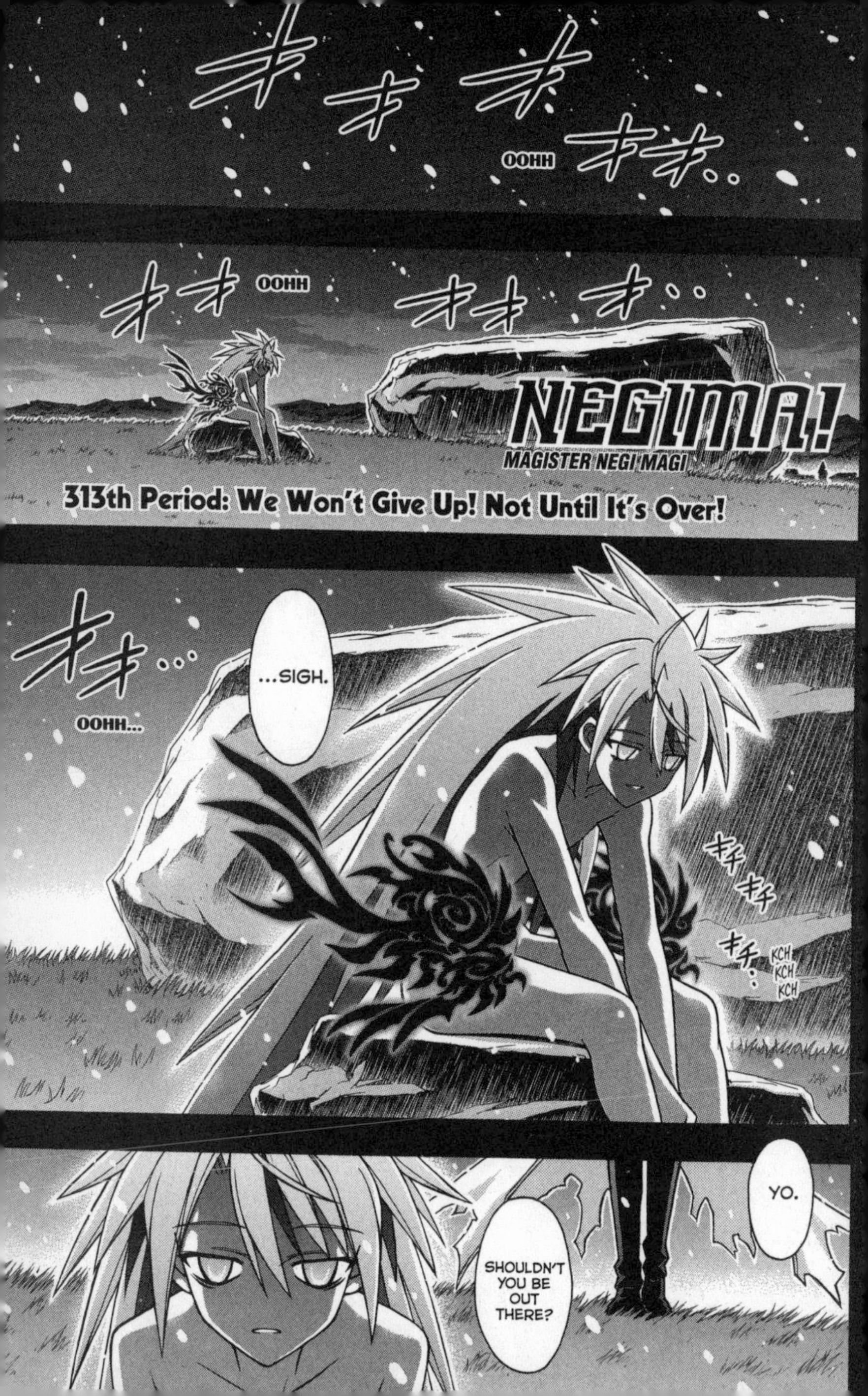
OOHH
OOHH
NEGIMA!
MAGISTER NEGI MAGI
313th Period: We Won't Give Up! Not Until It's Over!
...SIGH.
OOHH...
KCH KCH KCH
YO.
SHOULDN'T YOU BE OUT THERE?

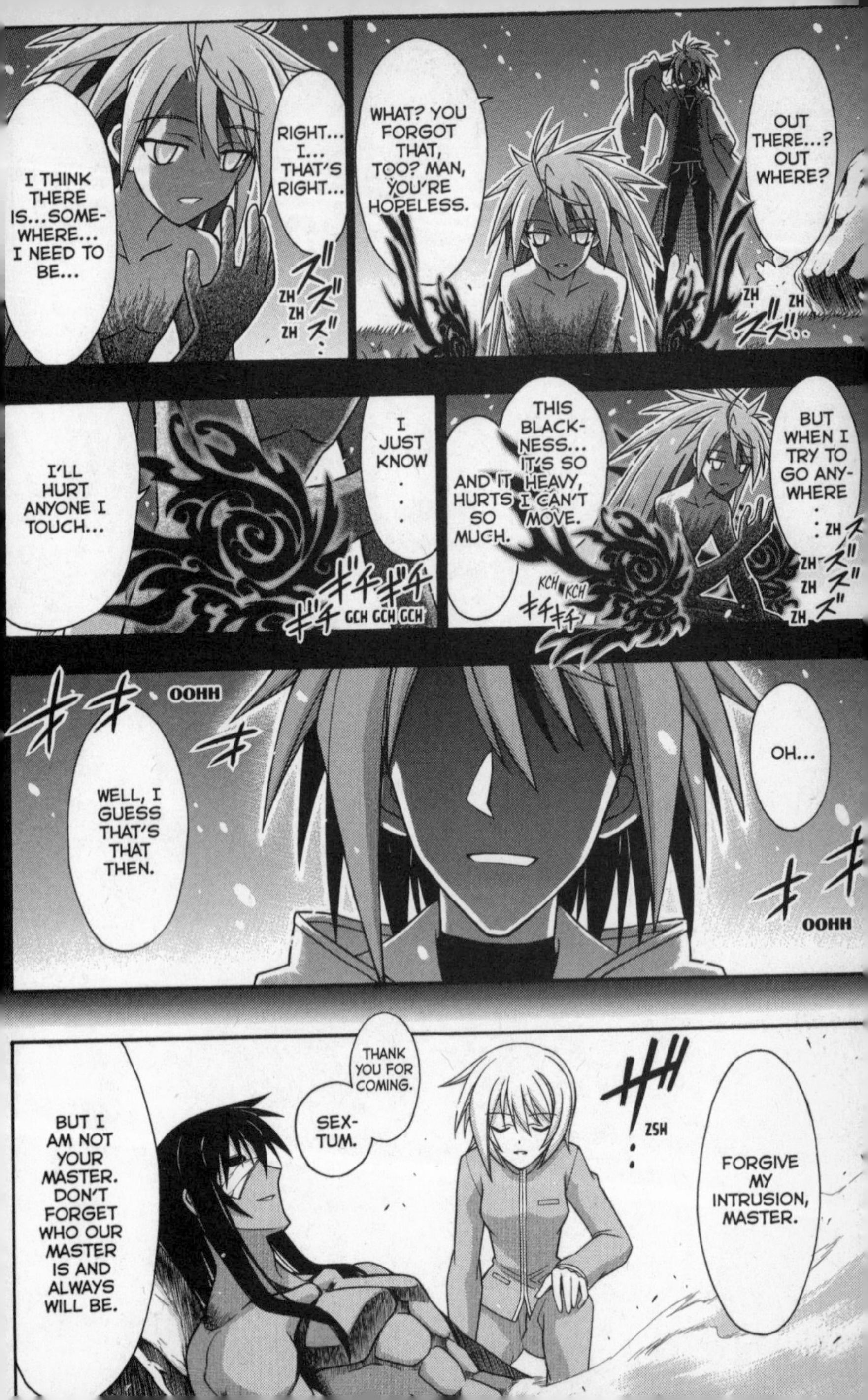
OUT THERE...? OUT WHERE?
ZH ZH
WHAT? YOU FORGOT THAT, TOO? MAN, YOU'RE HOPELESS.
RIGHT... I... THAT'S RIGHT...
ZH ZH ZH
I THINK THERE IS...SOME-WHERE... I NEED TO BE...
BUT WHEN I TRY TO GO ANY-WHERE . . .
ZH ZH ZH ZH
THIS BLACK-NESS... IT'S SO HEAVY, I CAN'T MOVE.
AND IT HURTS SO MUCH.
KCH KCH
I JUST KNOW . . .
GCH GCH GCH
I'LL HURT ANYONE I TOUCH...
OH...
OOHH
WELL, I GUESS THAT'S THAT THEN.
OOHH
FORGIVE MY INTRUSION, MASTER.
ZSH
THANK YOU FOR COMING.
SEX-TUM.
BUT I AM NOT YOUR MASTER. DON'T FORGET WHO OUR MASTER IS AND ALWAYS WILL BE.

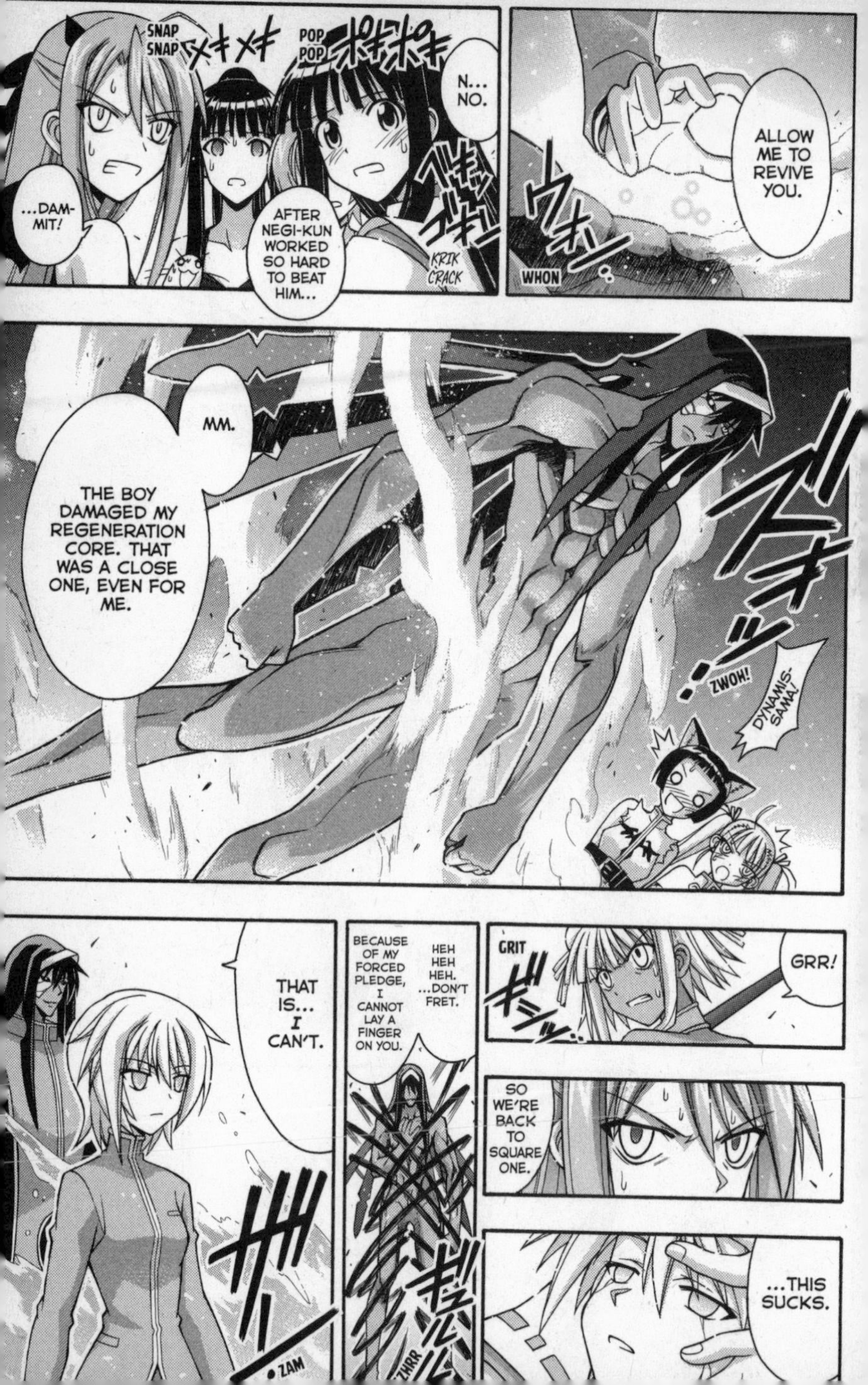
ALLOW ME TO REVIVE YOU.
WHON
POP POP
N... NO.
KRIK CRACK
SNAP SNAP
AFTER NEGI-KUN WORKED SO HARD TO BEAT HIM...
...DAM-MIT!
ZWOH!
DYNAMIS-SAMA!
MM.
THE BOY DAMAGED MY REGENERATION CORE. THAT WAS A CLOSE ONE, EVEN FOR ME.
GRR!
GRIT
SO WE'RE BACK TO SQUARE ONE.
...THIS SUCKS.
HEH HEH HEH. ...DON'T FRET.
BECAUSE OF MY FORCED PLEDGE, I CANNOT LAY A FINGER ON YOU.
ZHRR
THAT IS... I CAN'T.
ZAM

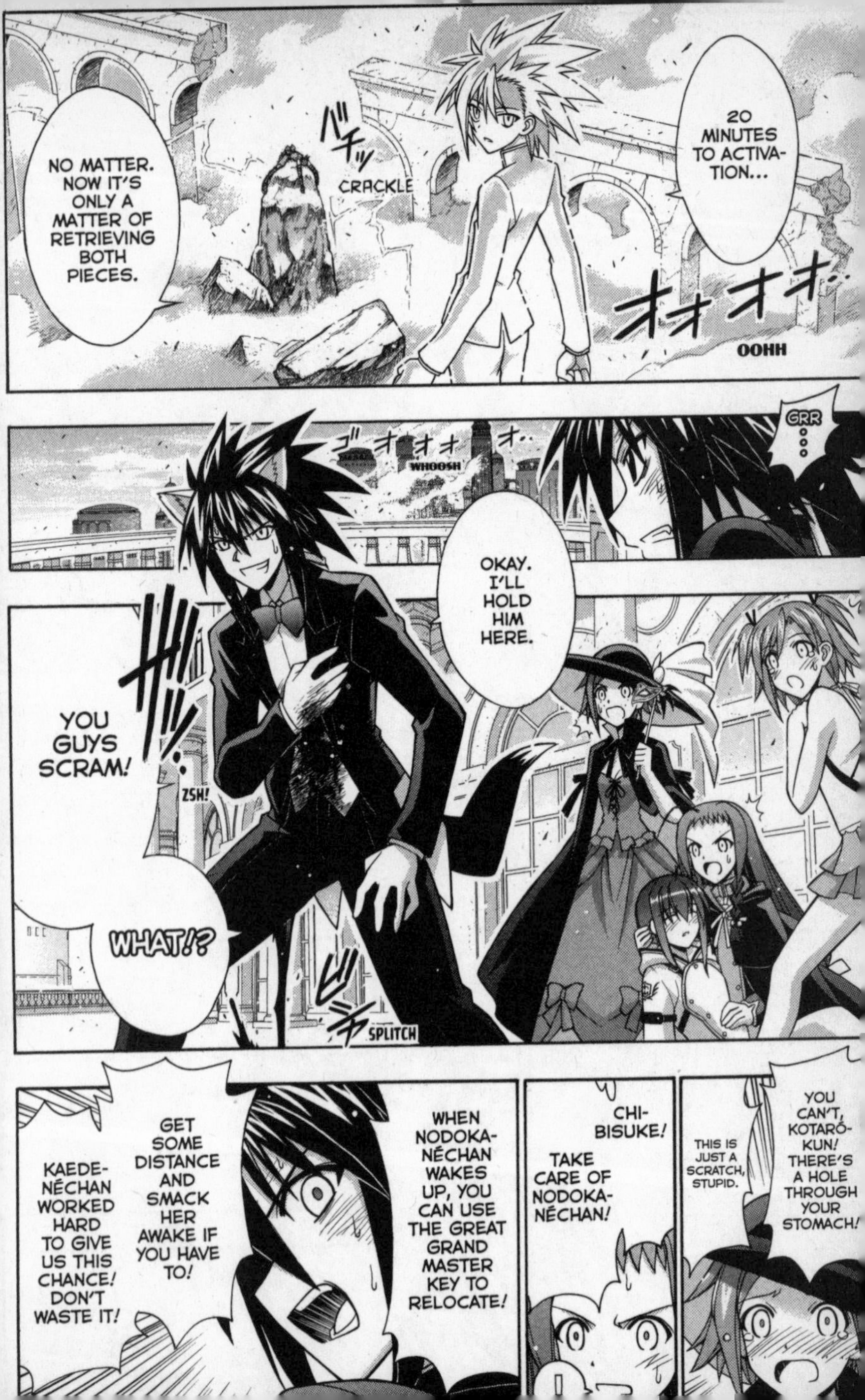
20 MINUTES TO ACTIVATION...
OOHH
CRACKLE
NO MATTER. NOW IT'S ONLY A MATTER OF RETRIEVING BOTH PIECES.
GRR...
WHOOSH
OKAY. I'LL HOLD HIM HERE.
YOU GUYS SCRAM!
ZSH!
WHAT!?
SPLITCH
YOU CAN'T, KOTARŌ-KUN! THERE'S A HOLE THROUGH YOUR STOMACH!
THIS IS JUST A SCRATCH, STUPID.
CHIBISUKE!
TAKE CARE OF NODOKA-NÉCHAN!
WHEN NODOKA-NÉCHAN WAKES UP, YOU CAN USE THE GREAT GRAND MASTER KEY TO RELOCATE!
GET SOME DISTANCE AND SMACK HER AWAKE IF YOU HAVE TO!
KAEDE-NÉCHAN WORKED HARD TO GIVE US THIS CHANCE! DON'T WASTE IT!

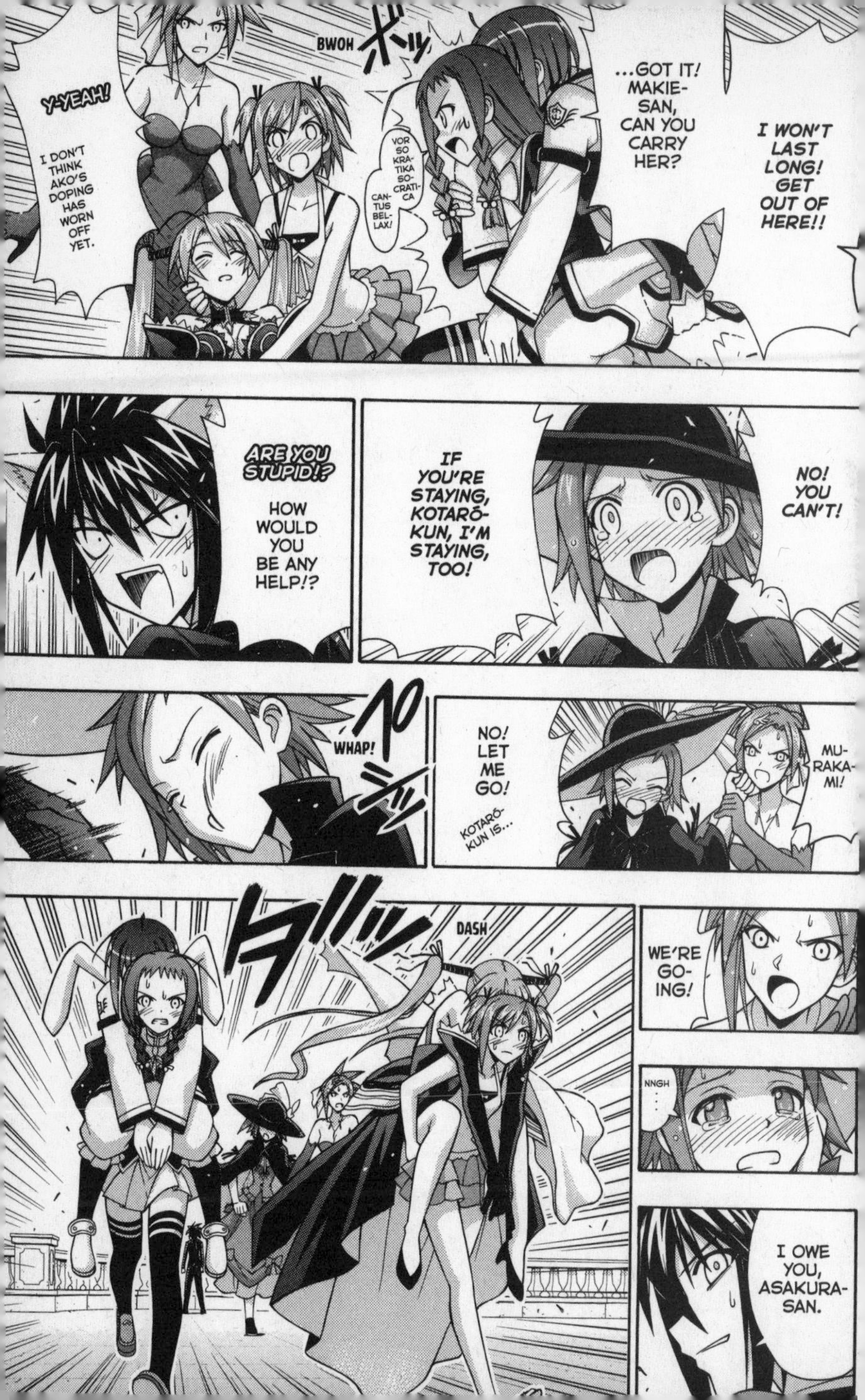
I WON'T LAST LONG! GET OUT OF HERE!!
...GOT IT! MAKIE-SAN, CAN YOU CARRY HER?
VOR SO KRATIKA SOCRATICA CANTUS BELLAX!
BWOH
Y-YEAH!
I DON'T THINK AKO'S DOPING HAS WORN OFF YET.
NO! YOU CAN'T!
IF YOU'RE STAYING, KOTARŌ-KUN, I'M STAYING, TOO!
ARE YOU STUPID!?
HOW WOULD YOU BE ANY HELP!?
MURAKAMI!
NO! LET ME GO!
KOTARŌ-KUN IS...
WHAP!
WE'RE GOING!
NNGH...
I OWE YOU, ASAKURA-SAN.
DASH

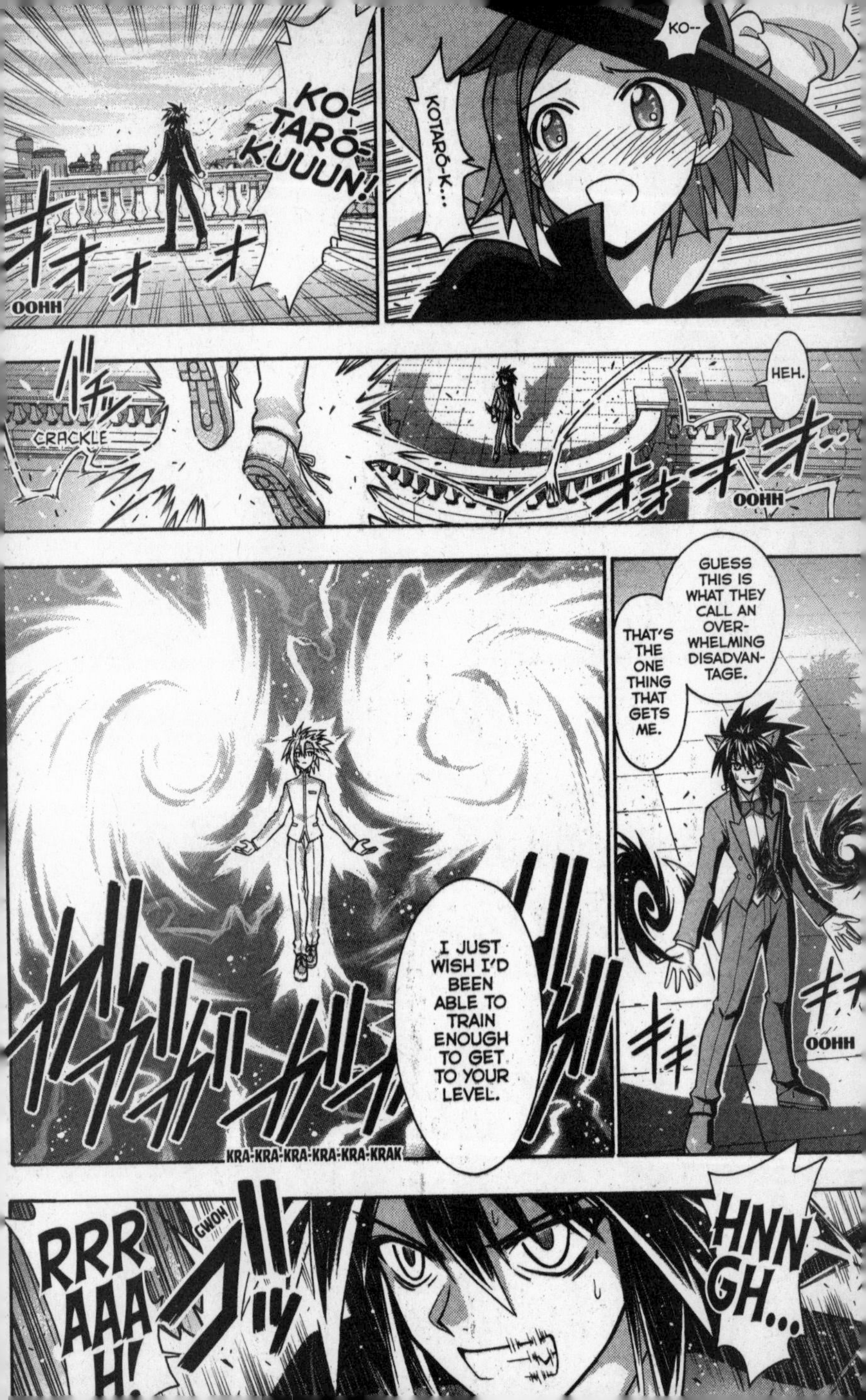
KO--
KOTARÔ-K...
KO-TARÔ-KUUUN!
OOHH
HEH.
OOHH
CRACKLE
GUESS THIS IS WHAT THEY CALL AN OVER-WHELMING DISADVAN-TAGE.
THAT'S THE ONE THING THAT GETS ME.
OOHH
I JUST WISH I'D BEEN ABLE TO TRAIN ENOUGH TO GET TO YOUR LEVEL.
KRA-KRA-KRA-KRA-KRA-KRAK
HNNGH...
GWOH
RRRAAAH!

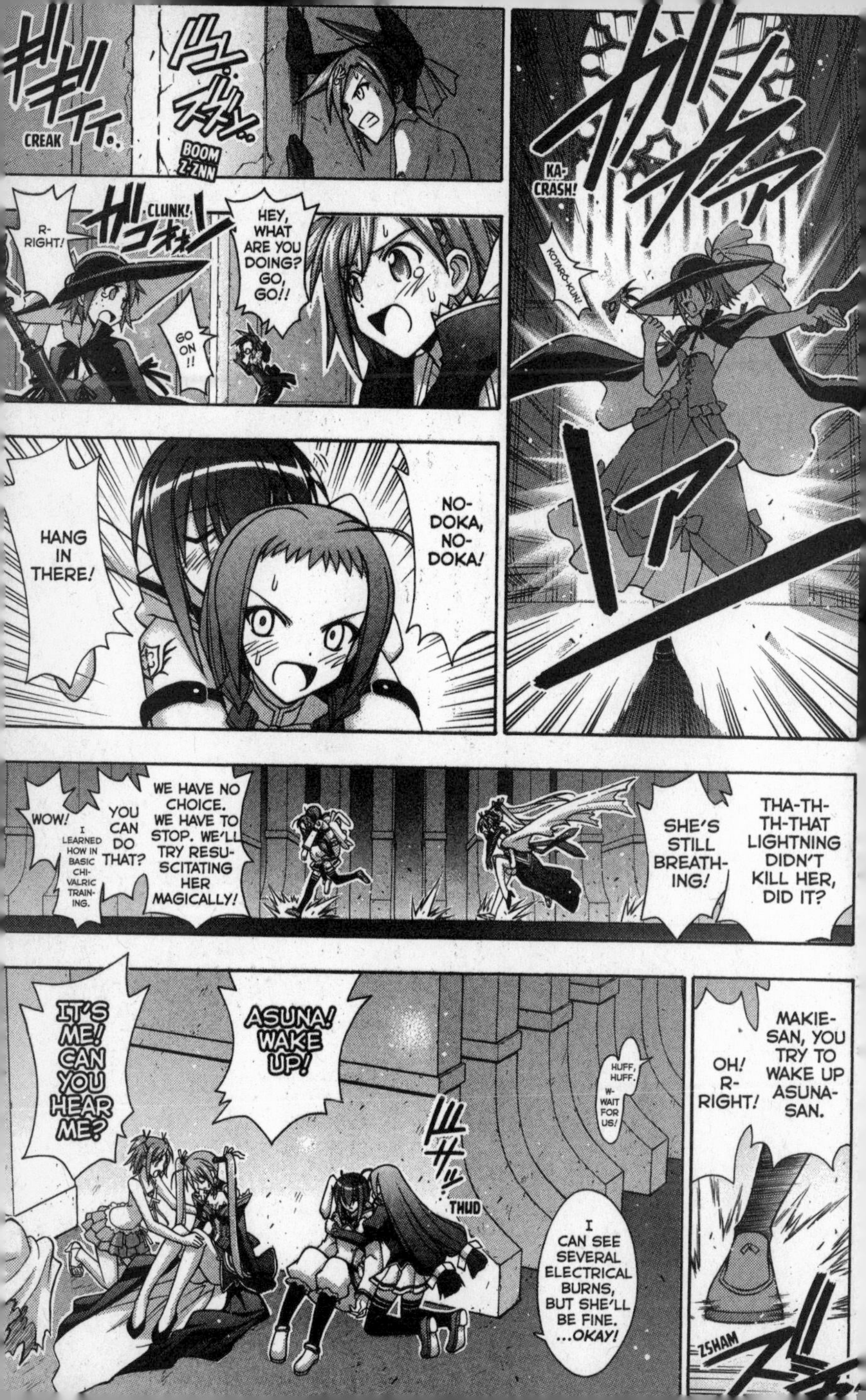
KA-CRASH!
KOTARŌ-KUN!
BOOM Z-ZNN
CREAK
HEY, WHAT ARE YOU DOING? GO, GO!!
GO ON!!
CLUNK!
R-RIGHT!
NO-DOKA, NO-DOKA!
HANG IN THERE!
THA-TH-TH-THAT LIGHTNING DIDN'T KILL HER, DID IT?
SHE'S STILL BREATHING!
WE HAVE NO CHOICE. WE HAVE TO STOP. WE'LL TRY RESUSCITATING HER MAGICALLY!
YOU CAN DO THAT?
WOW!
I LEARNED HOW IN BASIC CHIVALRIC TRAINING.
MAKIE-SAN, YOU TRY TO WAKE UP ASUNA-SAN.
OH! R-RIGHT!
ZSHAM
HUFF, HUFF.
W-WAIT FOR US!
THUD
I CAN SEE SEVERAL ELECTRICAL BURNS, BUT SHE'LL BE FINE. ...OKAY!
ASUNA! WAKE UP!
IT'S ME! CAN YOU HEAR ME?

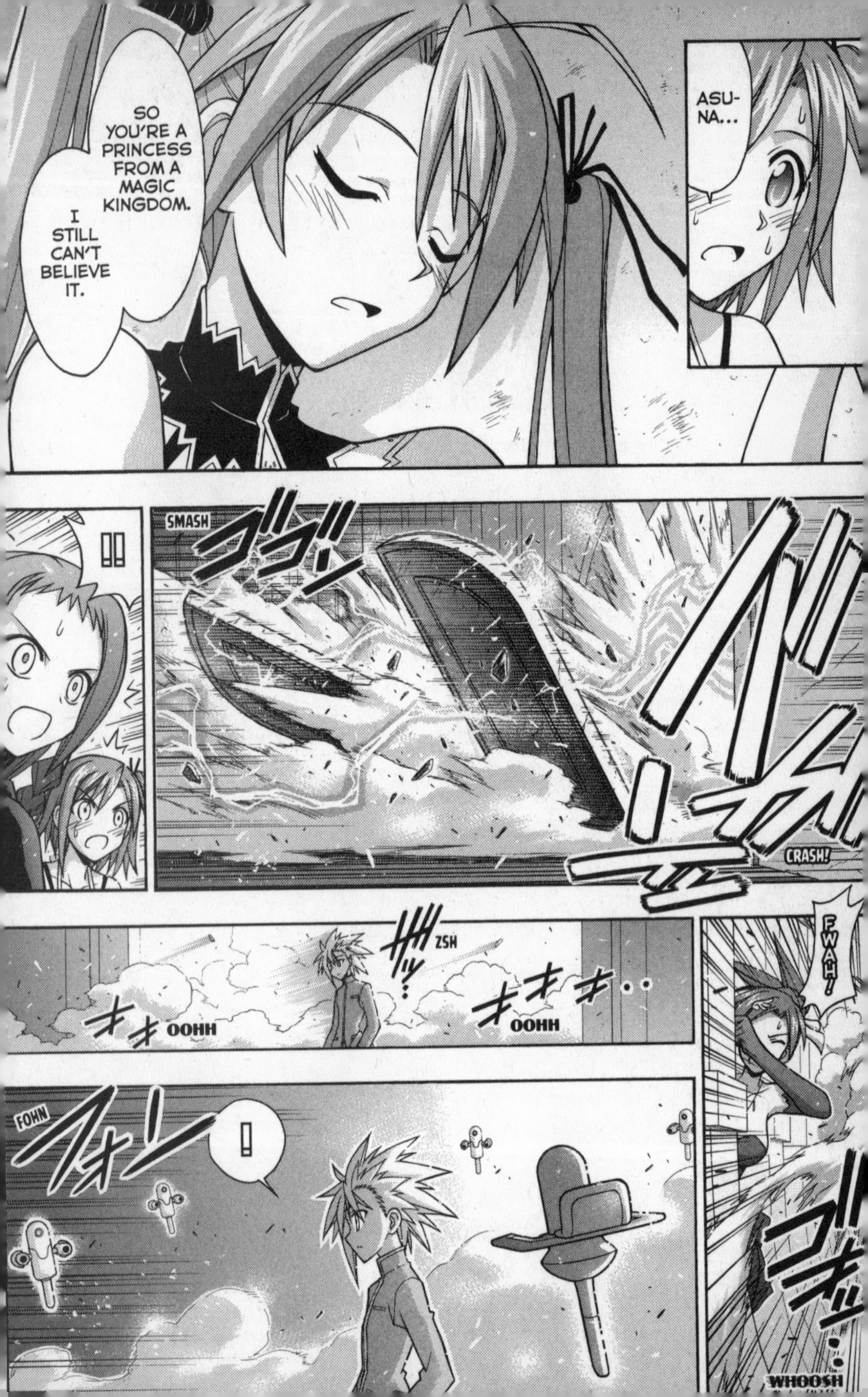
ASU-NA...
SO YOU'RE A PRINCESS FROM A MAGIC KINGDOM.
I STILL CAN'T BELIEVE IT.
SMASH
CRASH!
!!
FWAH!
ZSH
OOHH
OOHH
FOHN
!
WHOOSH

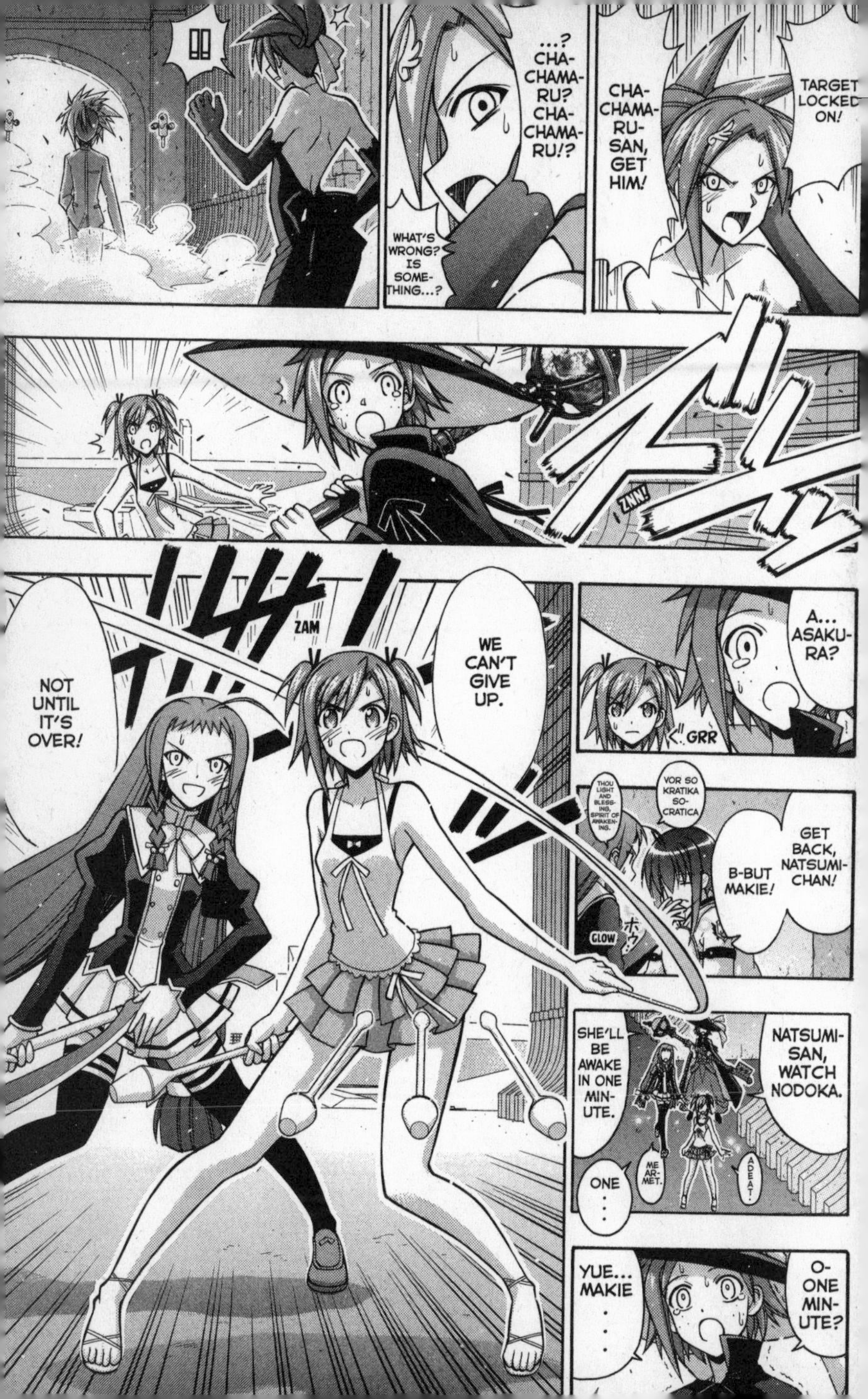
TARGET LOCKED ON!
CHA-CHAMA-RU-SAN, GET HIM!
...? CHA-CHAMA-RU? CHA-CHAMA-RU!?
WHAT'S WRONG? IS SOME-THING...?
!!
ZNN!
A... ASAKURA?
GRR
GET BACK, NATSUMI-CHAN!
B-BUT MAKIE!
VOR SO KRATIKA SO-CRATICA
THOU LIGHT AND BLESS-ING, SPIRIT OF AWAKEN-ING.
GLOW
NATSUMI-SAN, WATCH NODOKA.
SHE'LL BE AWAKE IN ONE MIN-UTE.
ADEAT.
ME AR-MET.
ONE...
O-ONE MIN-UTE?
YUE... MAKIE...
WE CAN'T GIVE UP.
ZAM
NOT UNTIL IT'S OVER!

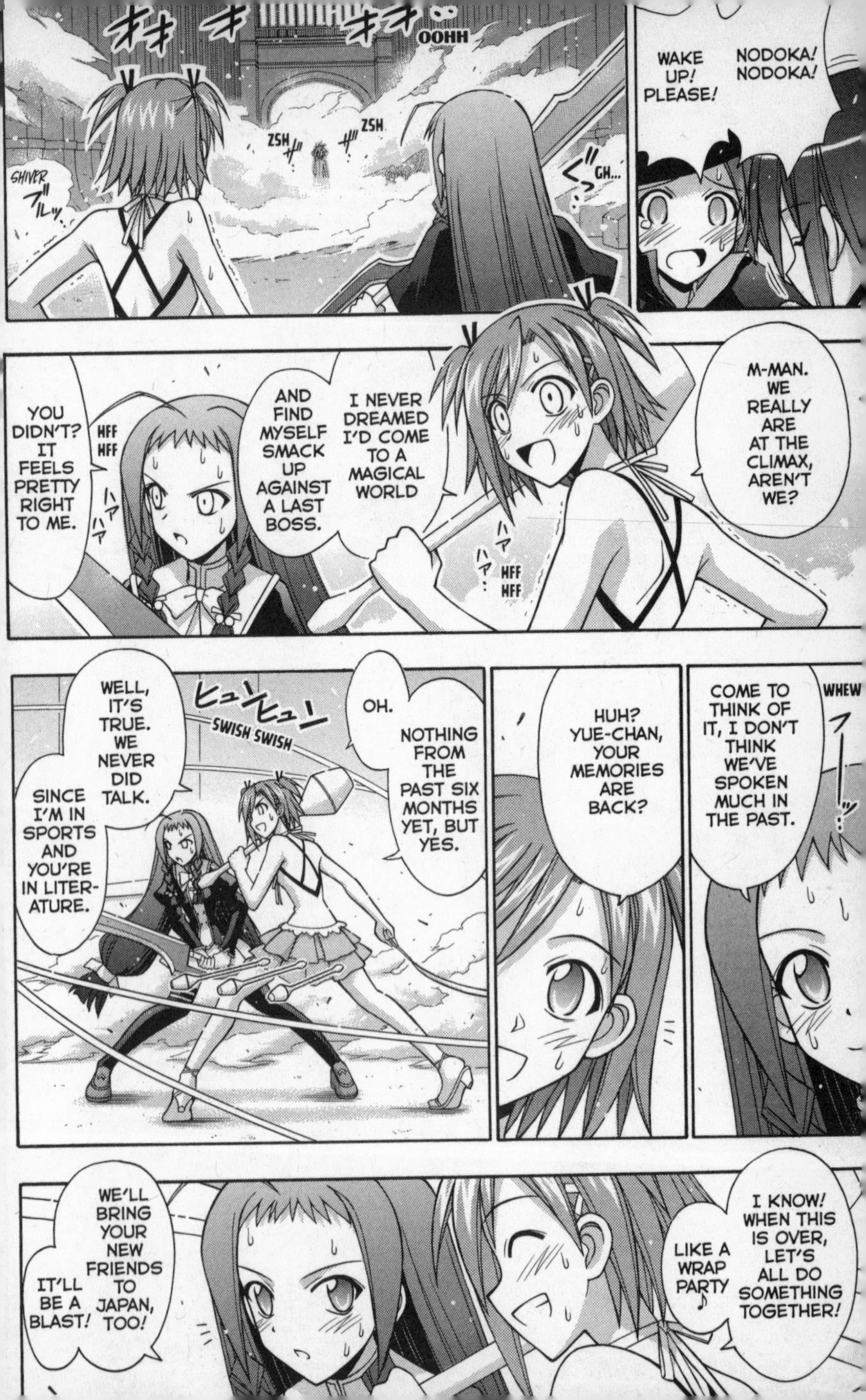
NODOKA! NODOKA!
WAKE UP! PLEASE!
GH...
OOHH
ZSH
ZSH
SHIVER
M-MAN. WE REALLY ARE AT THE CLIMAX, AREN'T WE?
I NEVER DREAMED I'D COME TO A MAGICAL WORLD
AND FIND MYSELF SMACK UP AGAINST A LAST BOSS.
HFF HFF
YOU DIDN'T? IT FEELS PRETTY RIGHT TO ME.
HFF HFF
WHEW
COME TO THINK OF IT, I DON'T THINK WE'VE SPOKEN MUCH IN THE PAST.
HUH? YUE-CHAN, YOUR MEMORIES ARE BACK?
OH.
NOTHING FROM THE PAST SIX MONTHS YET, BUT YES.
SWISH SWISH
WELL, IT'S TRUE. WE NEVER DID TALK.
SINCE I'M IN SPORTS AND YOU'RE IN LITER-ATURE.
I KNOW! WHEN THIS IS OVER, LET'S ALL DO SOMETHING TOGETHER!
LIKE A WRAP PARTY ♪
WE'LL BRING YOUR NEW FRIENDS TO JAPAN, TOO!
IT'LL BE A BLAST!

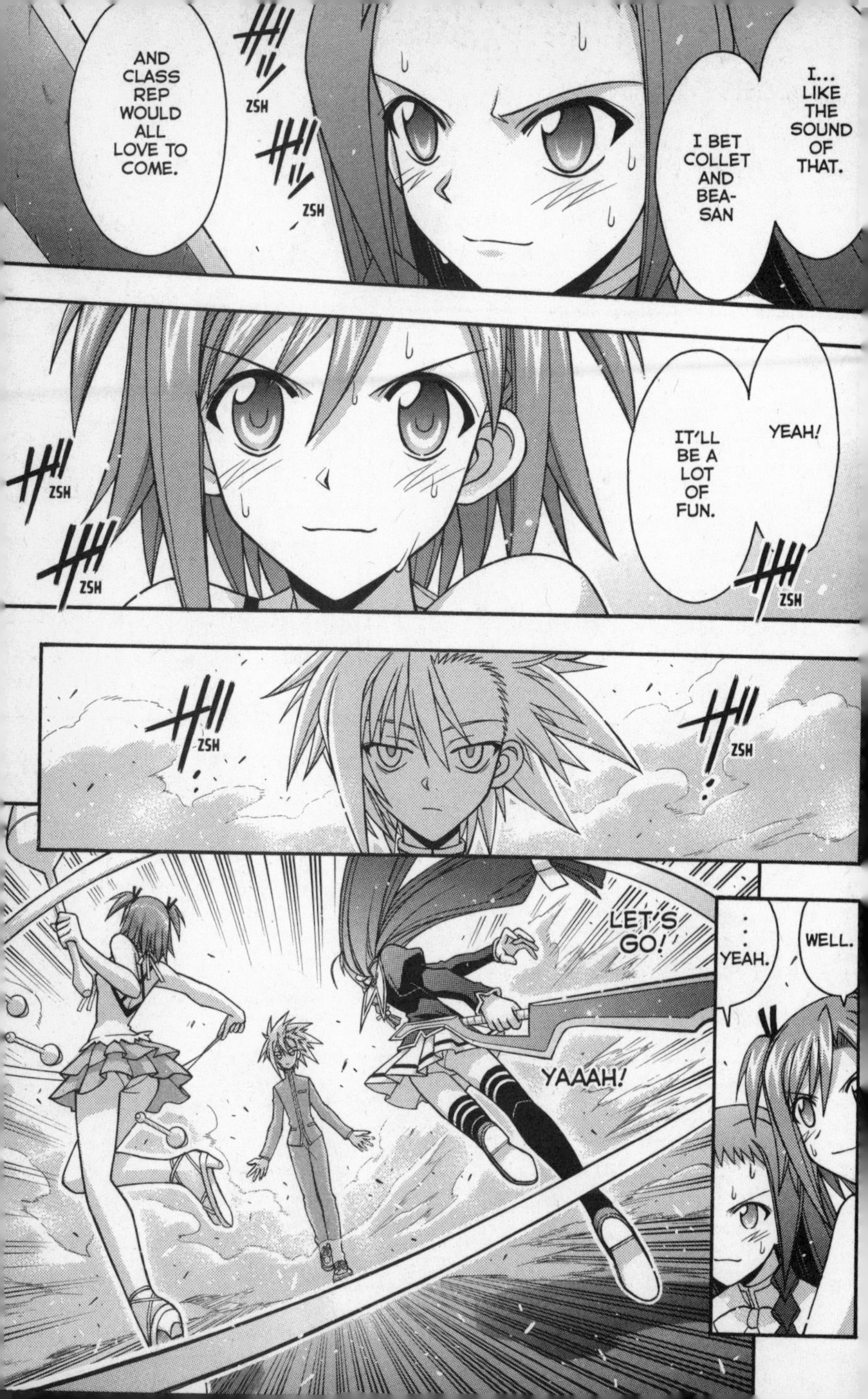
I... LIKE THE SOUND OF THAT.
I BET COLLET AND BEA-SAN
AND CLASS REP WOULD ALL LOVE TO COME.
ZSH
ZSH
YEAH!
IT'LL BE A LOT OF FUN.
ZSH
ZSH
ZSH
ZSH
ZSH
WELL.
...YEAH.
LET'S GO!
YAAAH!

BLAM!

THUD
THUD

ZSH..!
ZSH...

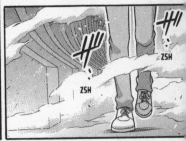

ZSH

ZSH

ZSH

NGH!

CHATTER
カタ
CHATTER
カタ

OOHH
カタ

OOHH

CHATTER CHATTER
カタ カタ

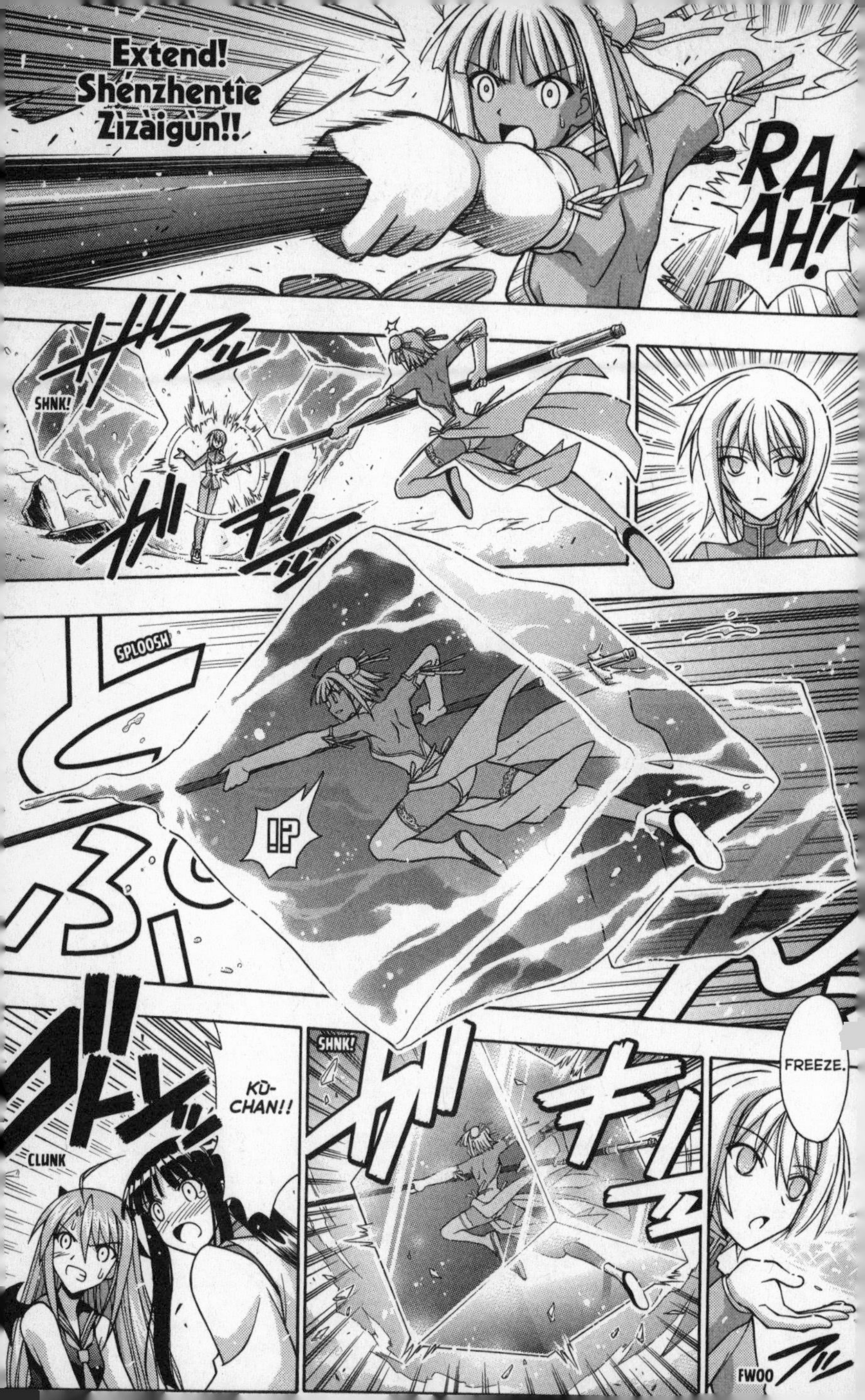
RAAAH!
Extend! Shénzhentie Zìzàigùn!!
SHNK!
SPLOOSH
!?
FREEZE.
FWOO
SHNK!
KŪ-CHAN!!
CLUNK

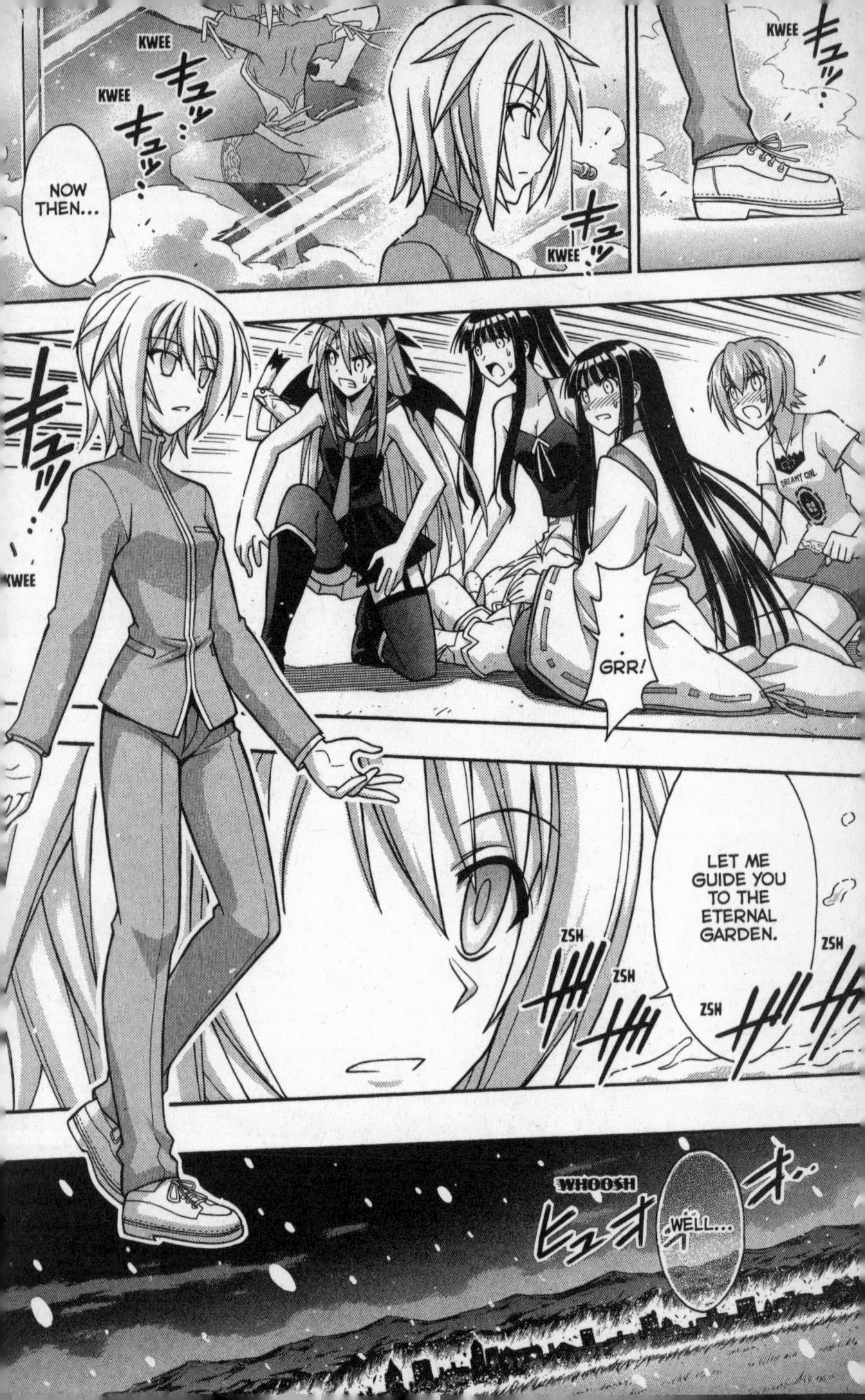
KWEE
キュッ…
KWEE
キュッ
KWEE
キュッ…
KWEE
キュッ…
NOW THEN...
KWEE
キュッ…
GRR!
LET ME GUIDE YOU TO THE ETERNAL GARDEN.
ZSH
ZSH
ZSH
ZSH
WHOOSH
ヒュオオ…
WELL...

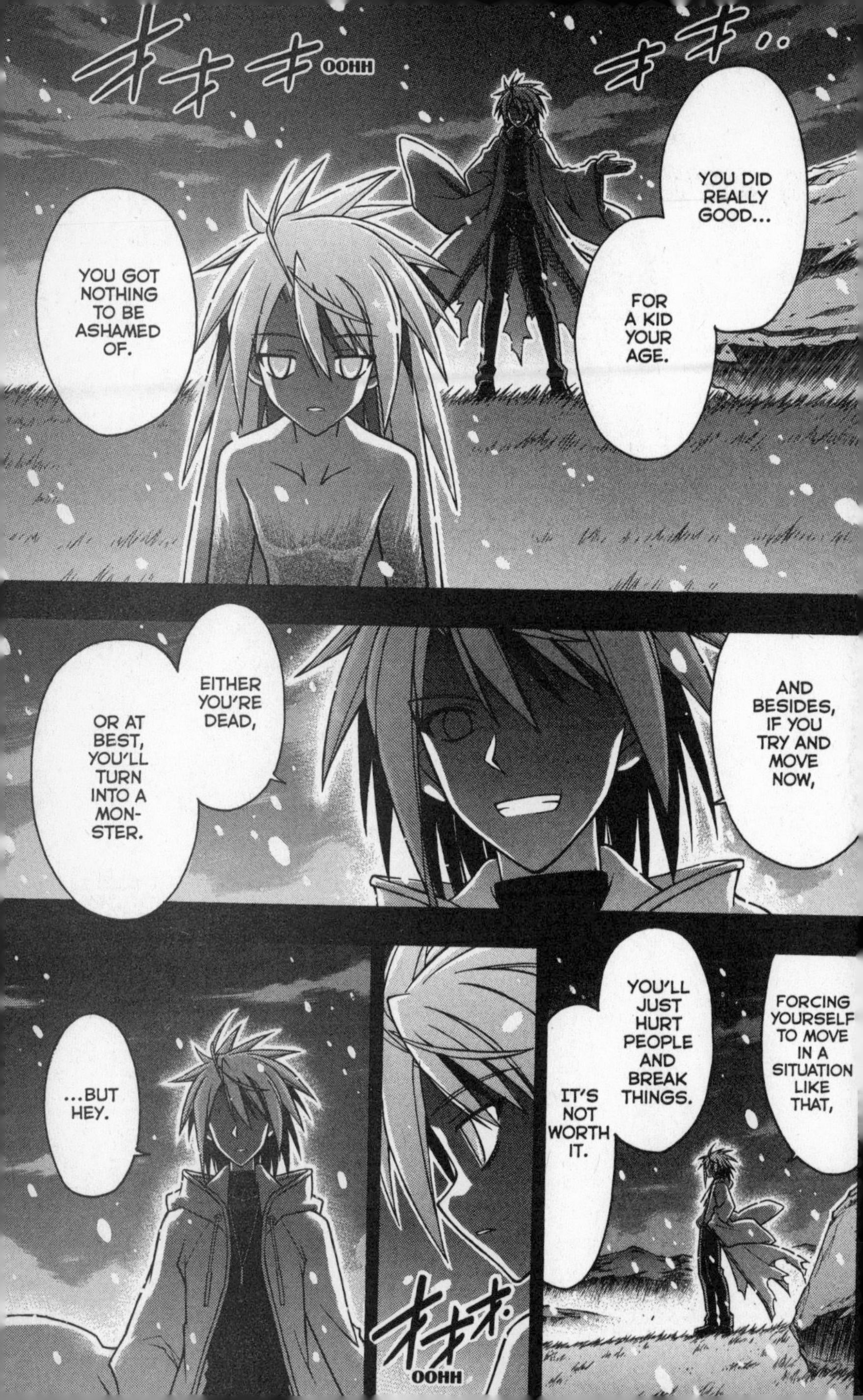
OOHH
YOU DID REALLY GOOD...
FOR A KID YOUR AGE.
YOU GOT NOTHING TO BE ASHAMED OF.
AND BESIDES, IF YOU TRY AND MOVE NOW,
EITHER YOU'RE DEAD,
OR AT BEST, YOU'LL TURN INTO A MON-STER.
FORCING YOURSELF TO MOVE IN A SITUATION LIKE THAT,
YOU'LL JUST HURT PEOPLE AND BREAK THINGS.
IT'S NOT WORTH IT.
OOHH
...BUT HEY.

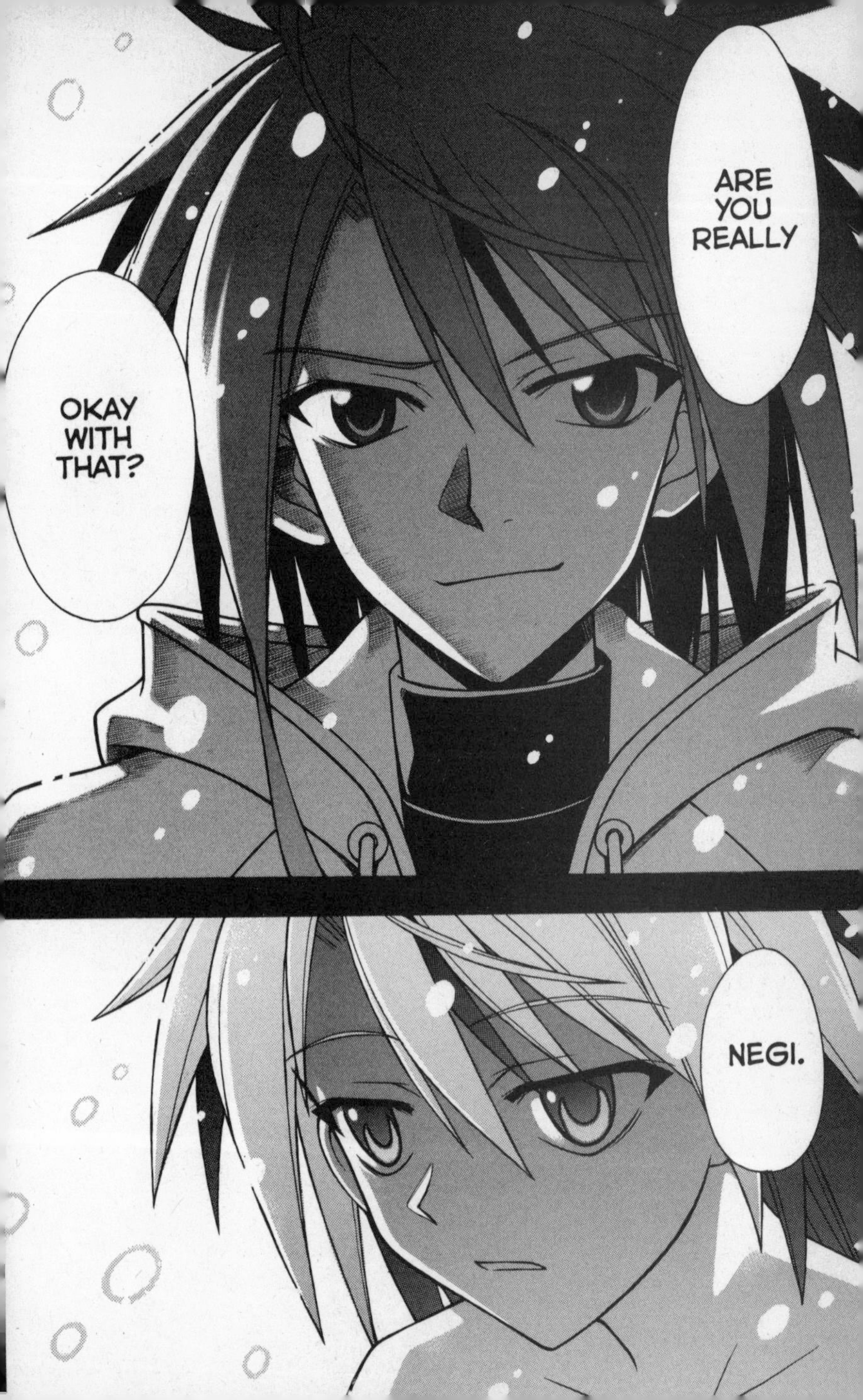
ARE YOU REALLY
OKAY WITH THAT?
NEGI.

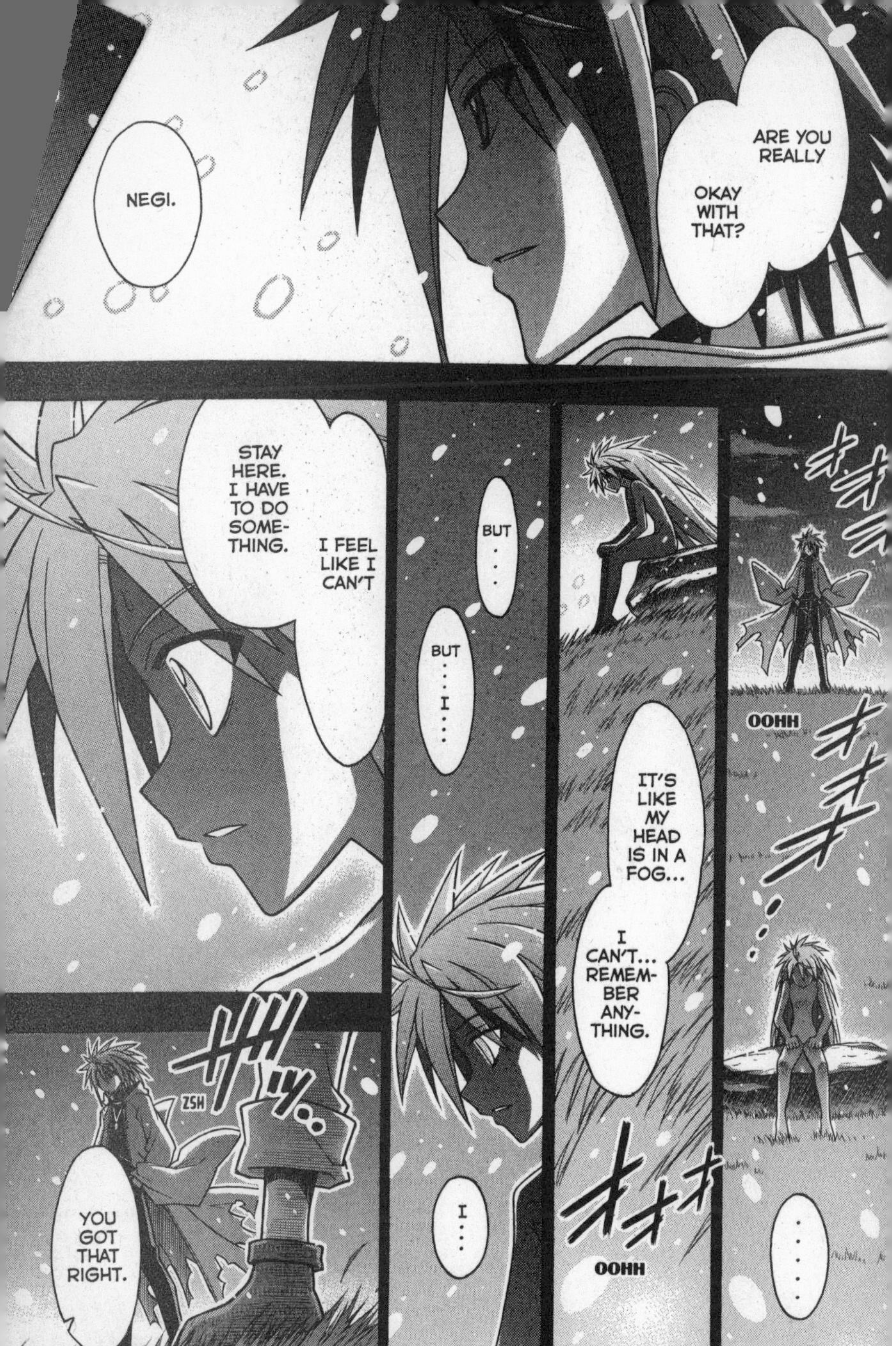
ARE YOU REALLY OKAY WITH THAT?
NEGI.
OOHH
. . . . . .
IT'S LIKE MY HEAD IS IN A FOG...
I CAN'T... REMEMBER ANYTHING.
OOHH
BUT . . .
BUT . . . I . . .
I . . .
I FEEL LIKE I CAN'T
STAY HERE. I HAVE TO DO SOME-THING.
ZSH
YOU GOT THAT RIGHT.

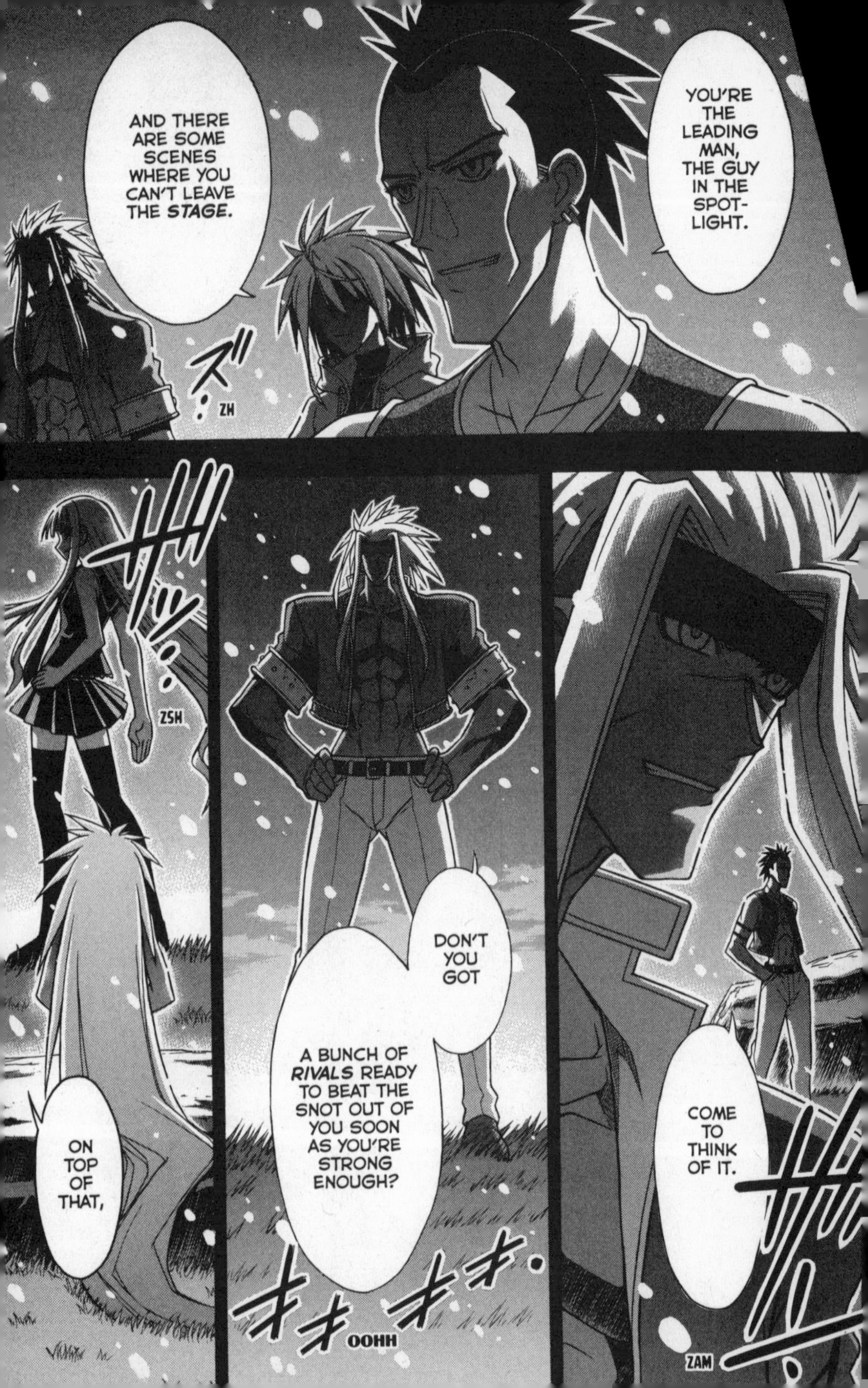
YOU'RE THE LEADING MAN, THE GUY IN THE SPOT-LIGHT.
AND THERE ARE SOME SCENES WHERE YOU CAN'T LEAVE THE *STAGE*.
ZH
COME TO THINK OF IT.
ZAM
DON'T YOU GOT
A BUNCH OF *RIVALS* READY TO BEAT THE SNOT OUT OF YOU SOON AS YOU'RE STRONG ENOUGH?
OOHH
ZSH
ON TOP OF THAT,

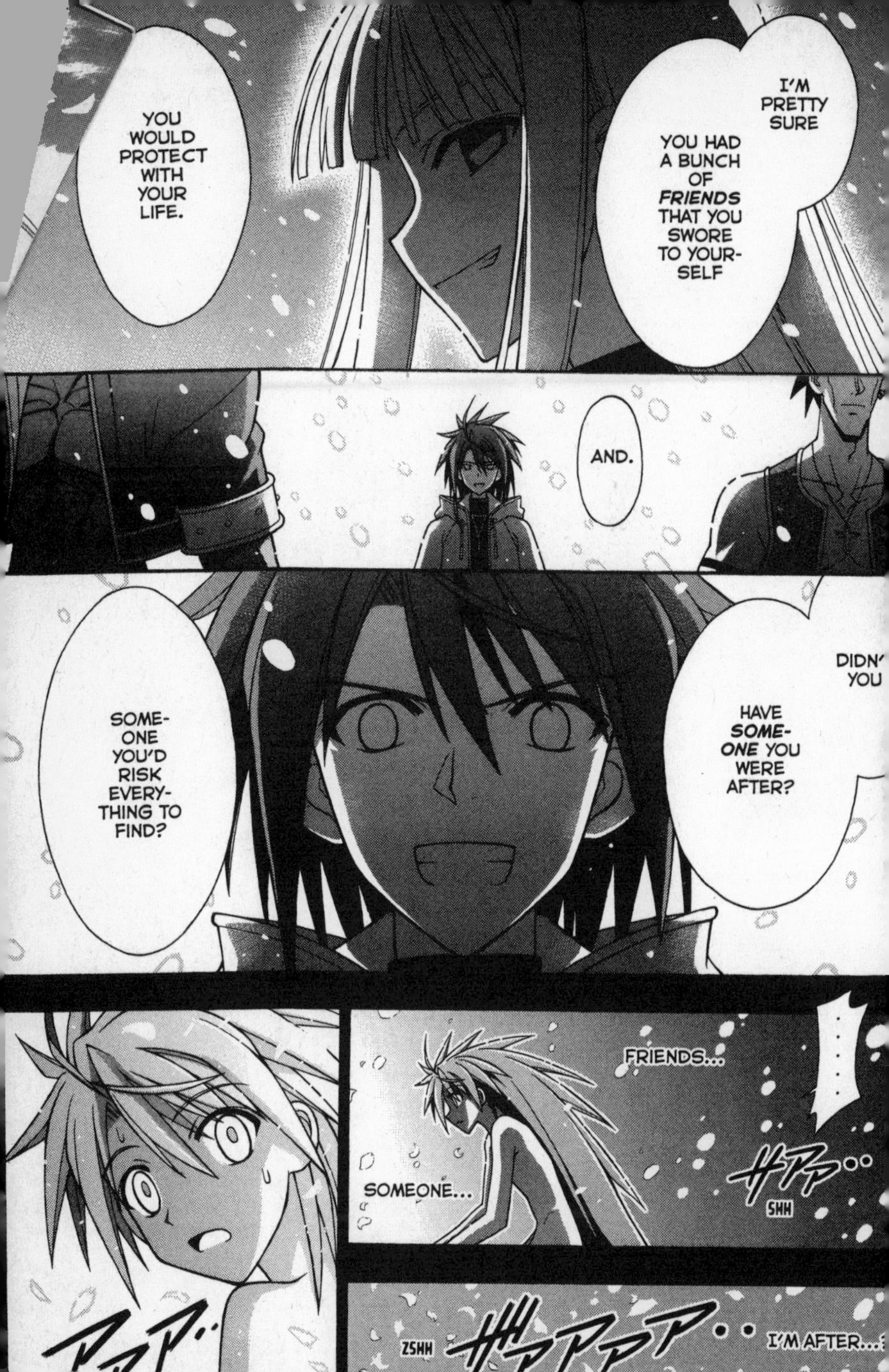
I'M PRETTY SURE
YOU HAD A BUNCH OF *FRIENDS* THAT YOU SWORE TO YOURSELF
YOU WOULD PROTECT WITH YOUR LIFE.
AND.
DIDN'T YOU
HAVE *SOMEONE* YOU WERE AFTER?
SOMEONE YOU'D RISK EVERYTHING TO FIND?
......!
FRIENDS...
SHH
SOMEONE...
ZSHH
I'M AFTER...!

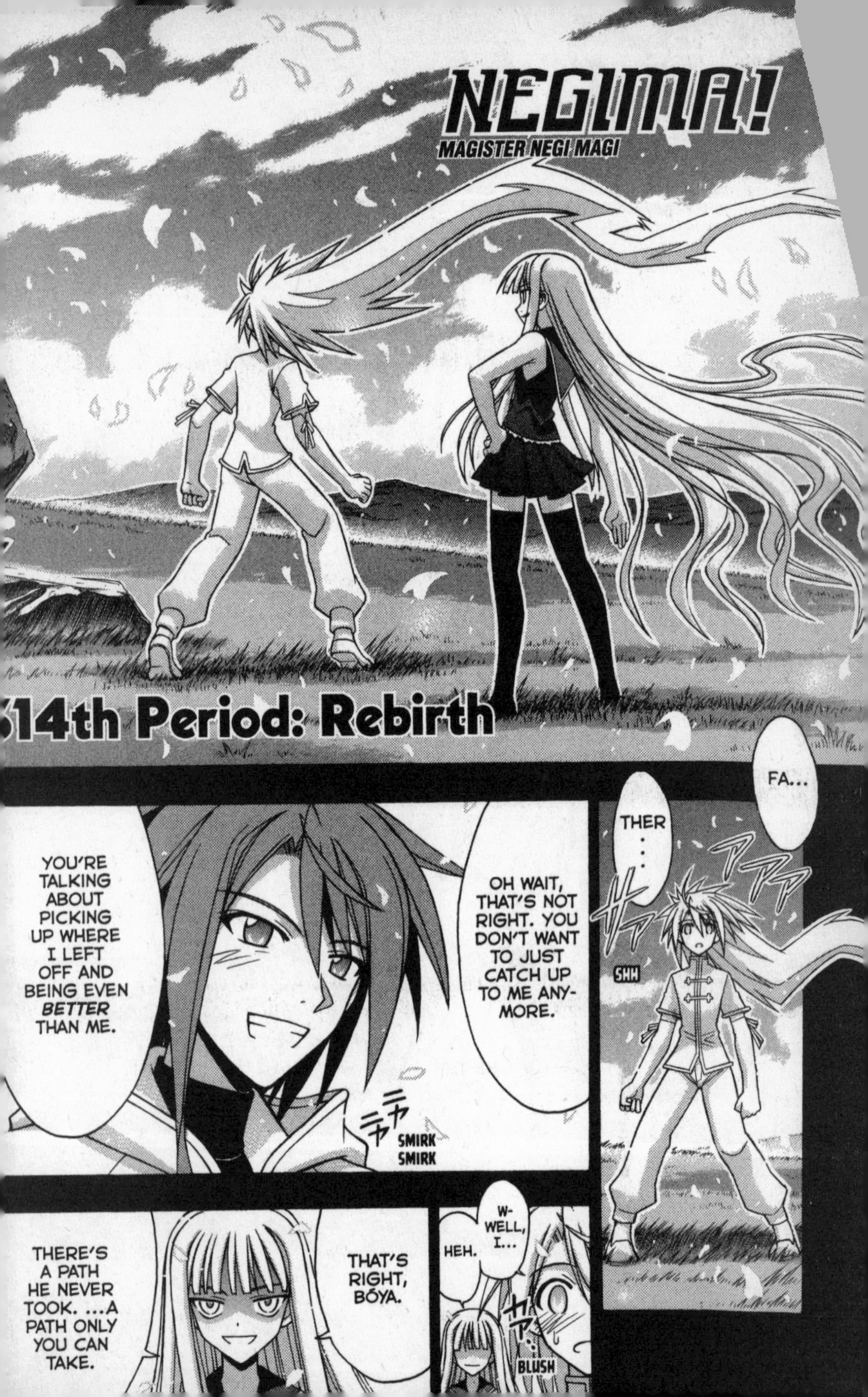

NEGIMA!
MAGISTER NEGI MAGI
14th Period: Rebirth
FA...
THER...
SHH
OH WAIT, THAT'S NOT RIGHT. YOU DON'T WANT TO JUST CATCH UP TO ME ANY-MORE.
YOU'RE TALKING ABOUT PICKING UP WHERE I LEFT OFF AND BEING EVEN *BETTER* THAN ME.
SMIRK SMIRK
W-WELL, I...
HEH.
BLUSH
THAT'S RIGHT, BÔYA.
THERE'S A PATH HE NEVER TOOK. ...A PATH ONLY YOU CAN TAKE.

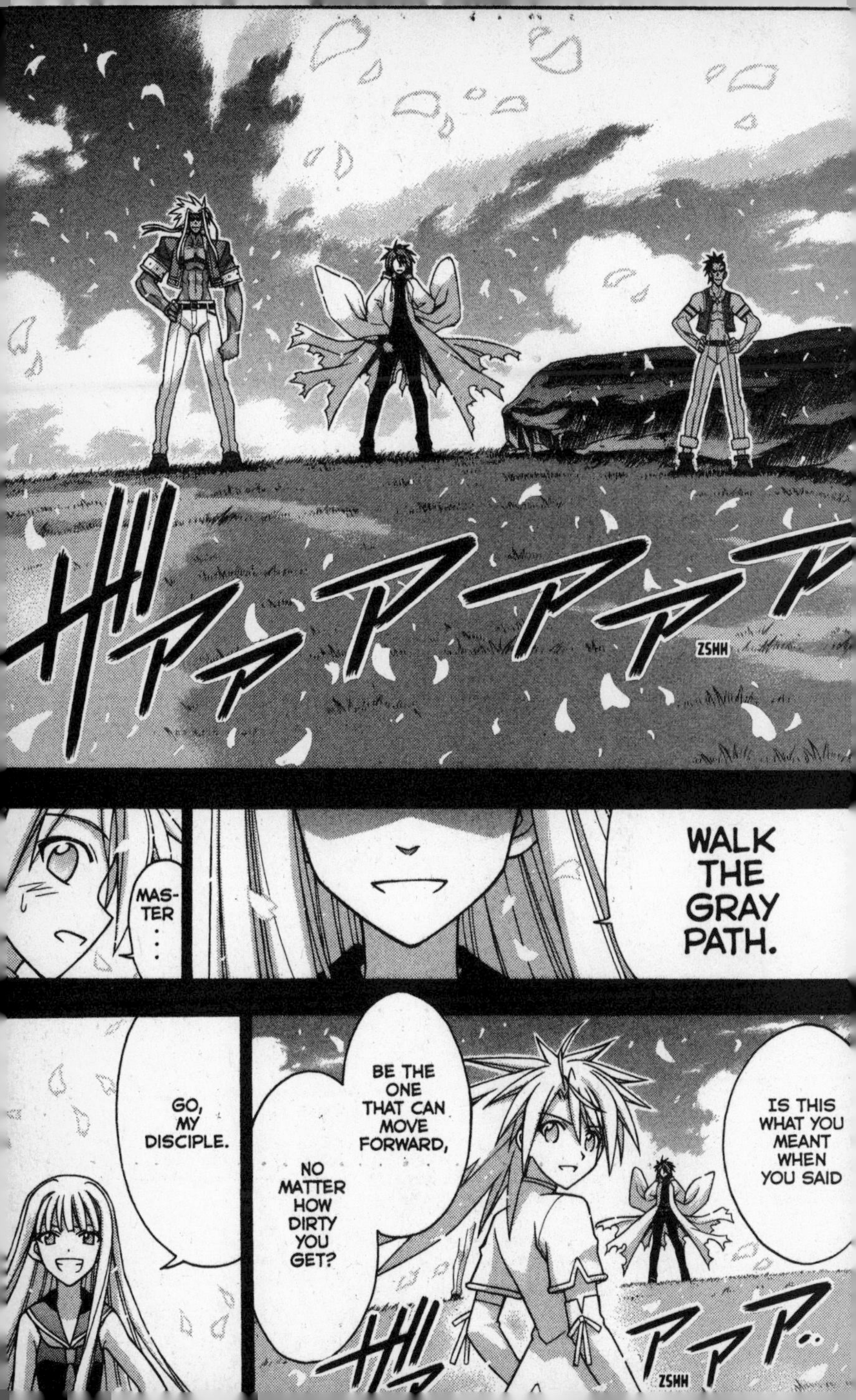
ZSHH
WALK THE GRAY PATH.
MAS-TER . . .
IS THIS WHAT YOU MEANT WHEN YOU SAID
BE THE ONE THAT CAN MOVE FORWARD,
NO MATTER HOW DIRTY YOU GET?
ZSHH
GO, MY DISCIPLE.

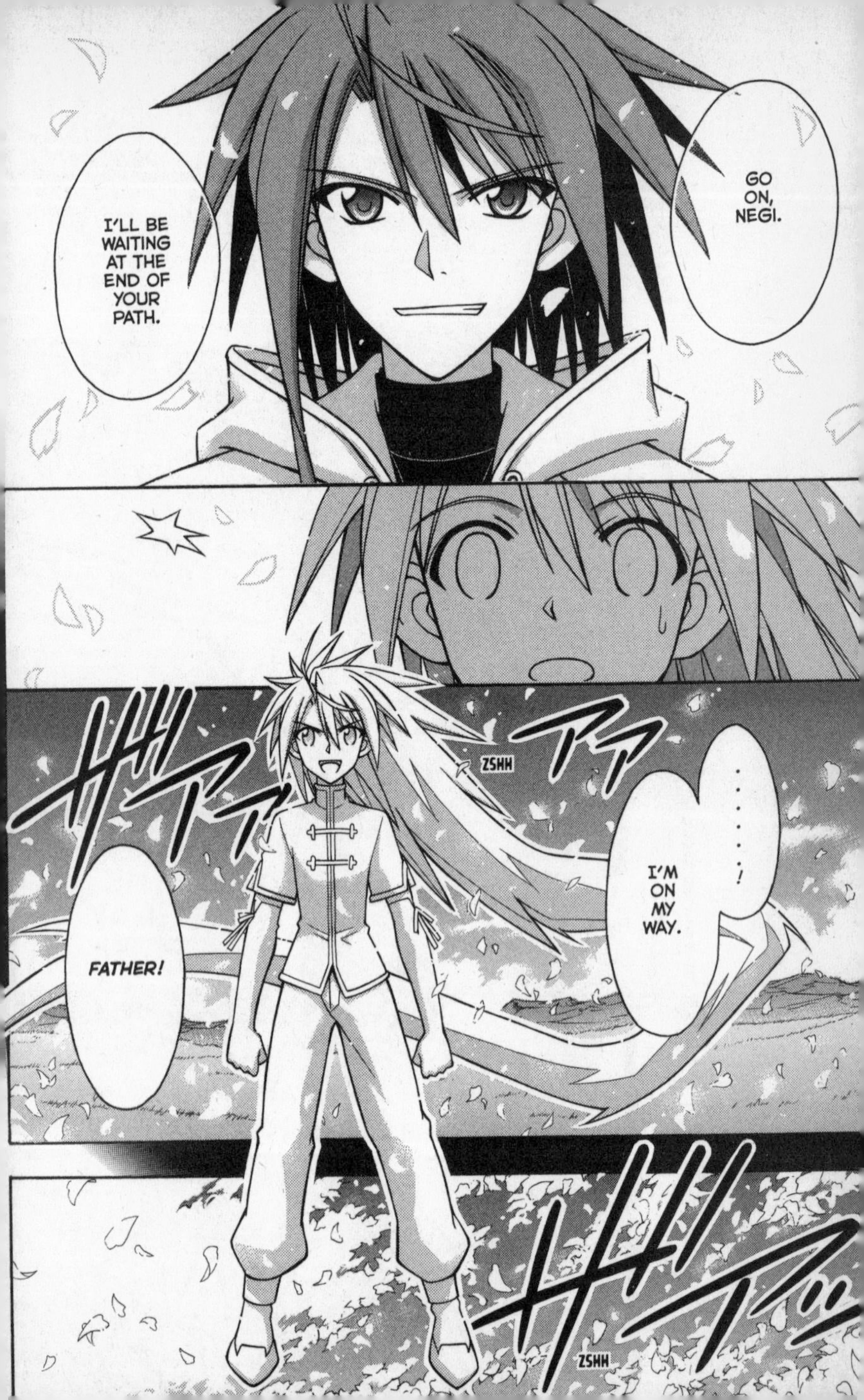

GO ON, NEGI.
I'LL BE WAITING AT THE END OF YOUR PATH.
ZSHH
......!
I'M ON MY WAY.
FATHER!
ZSHH

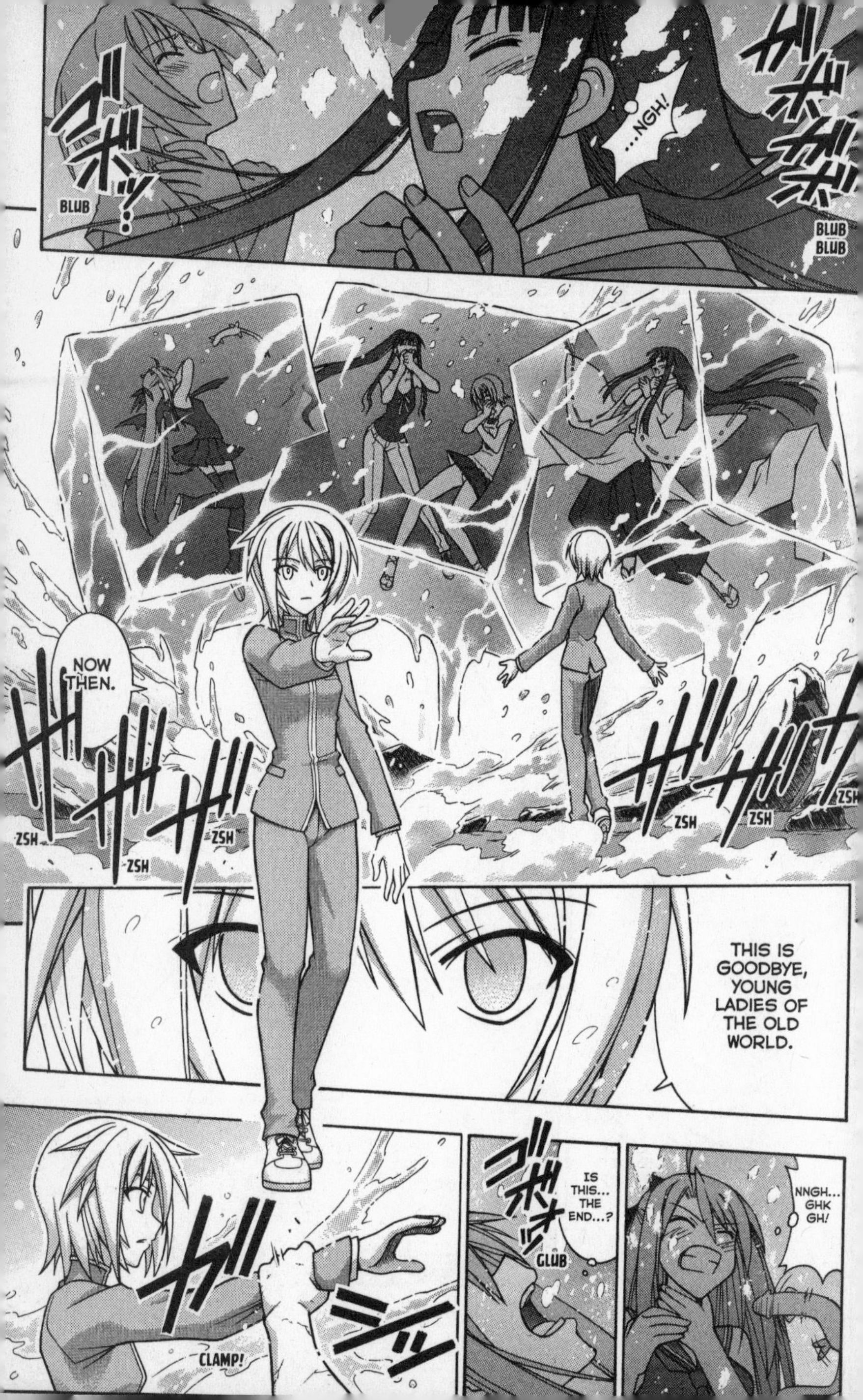
...NGH!
BLUB BLUB
BLUB
NOW THEN.
ZSH
ZSH
ZSH
ZSH
ZSH
ZSH
THIS IS GOODBYE, YOUNG LADIES OF THE OLD WORLD.
NNGH... GHK GH!
IS THIS... THE END...?
GLUB
CLAMP!

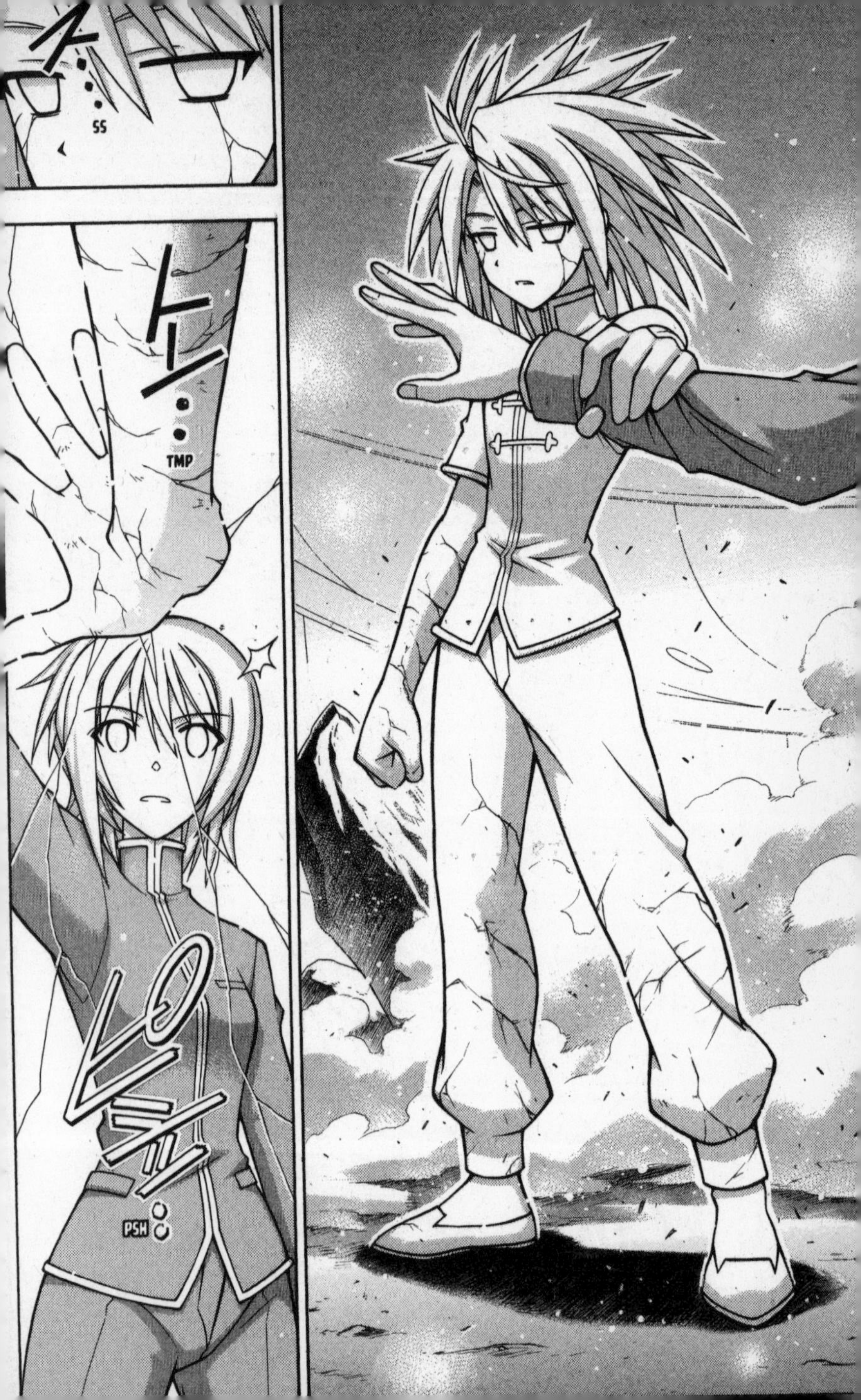
SS
TMP
PSH

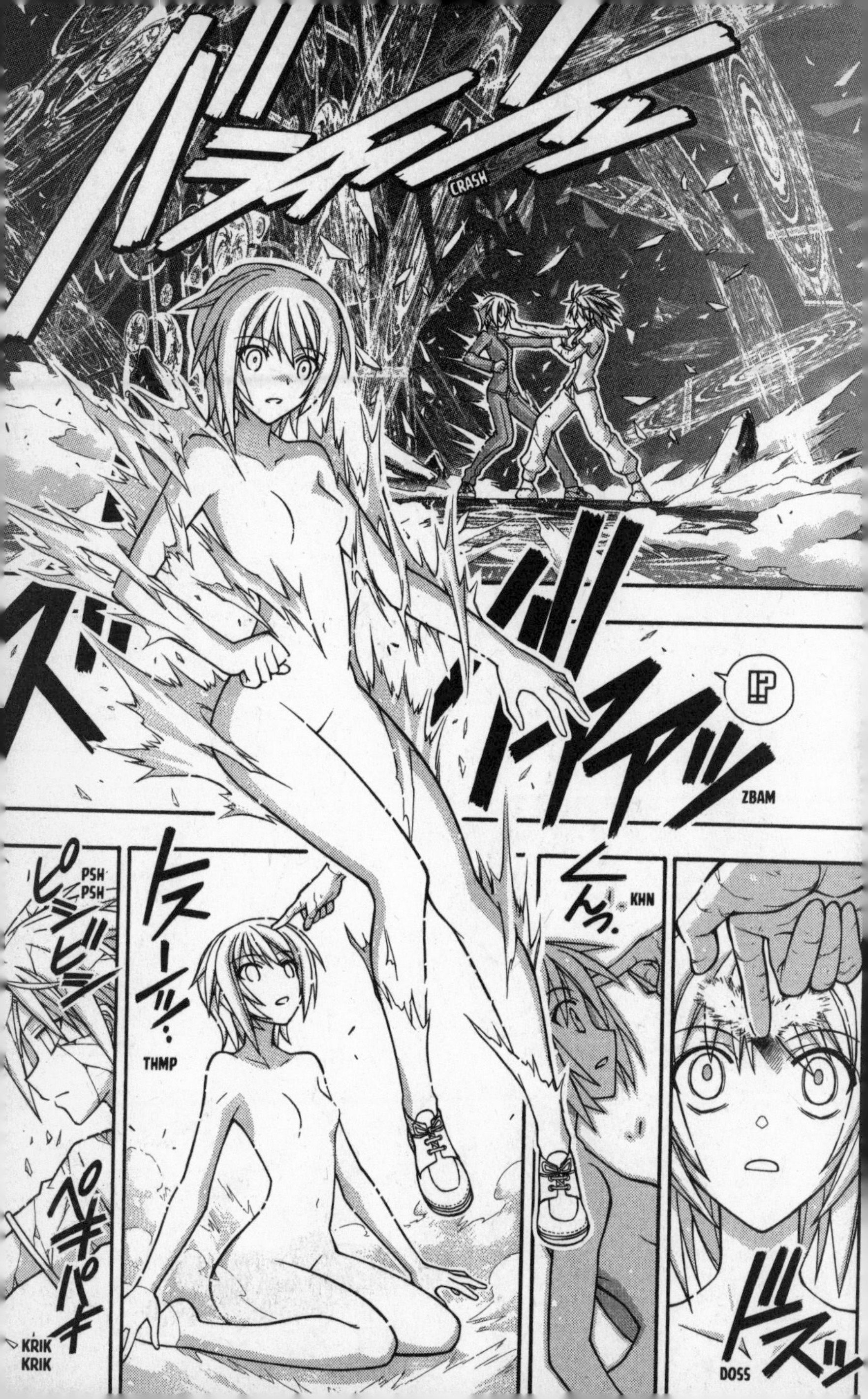
CRASH
!?
ZBAM
DOSS
KHN
THMP
PSH PSH
KRIK KRIK

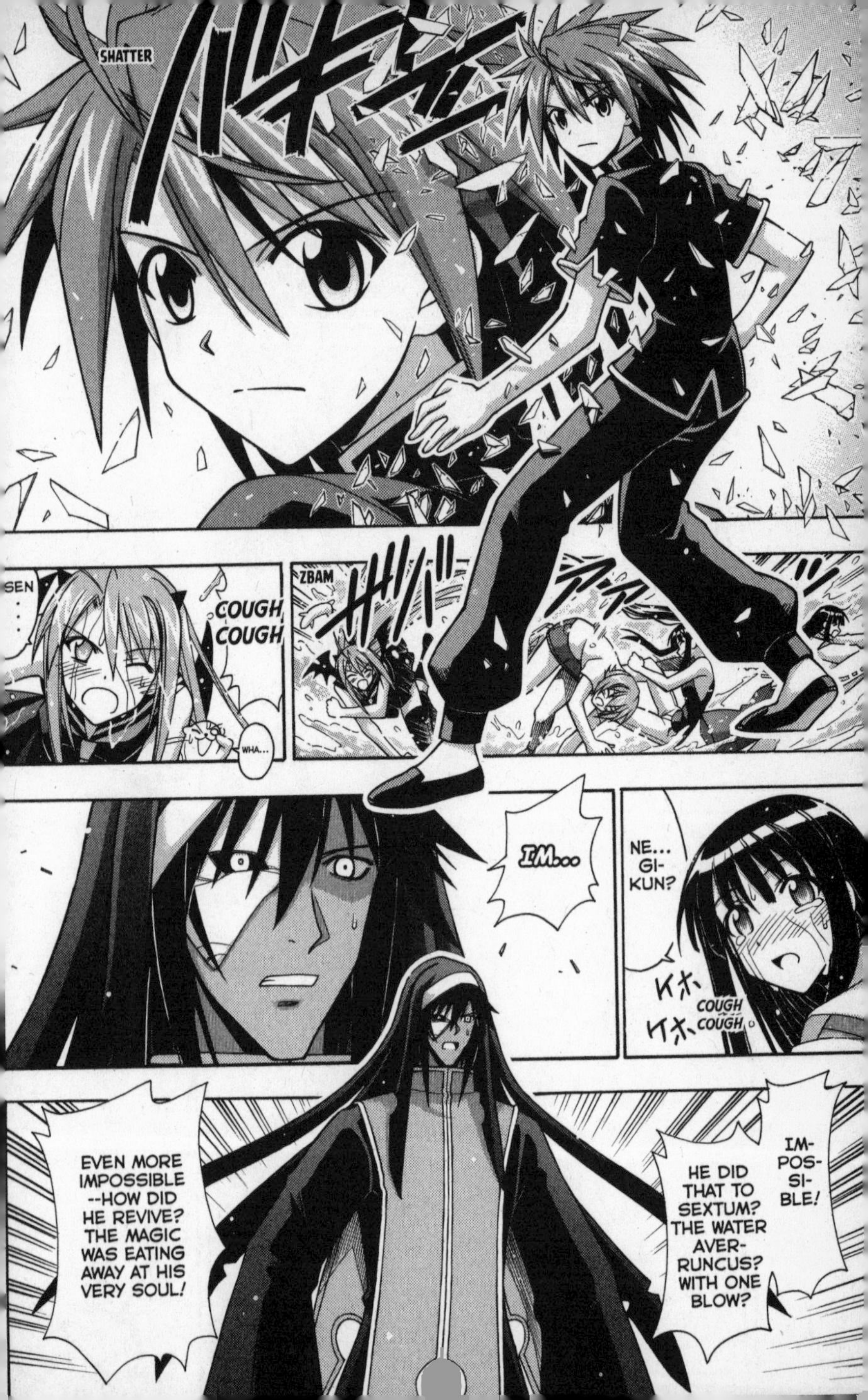
SHATTER
ZBAM
SEN...
COUGH COUGH
WHA...
NE... GI-KUN?
ケホ ケホ
COUGH COUGH
I'M...
IM-POS-SI-BLE!
HE DID THAT TO SEXTUM? THE WATER AVER-RUNCUS? WITH ONE BLOW?
EVEN MORE IMPOSSIBLE --HOW DID HE REVIVE? THE MAGIC WAS EATING AWAY AT HIS VERY SOUL!

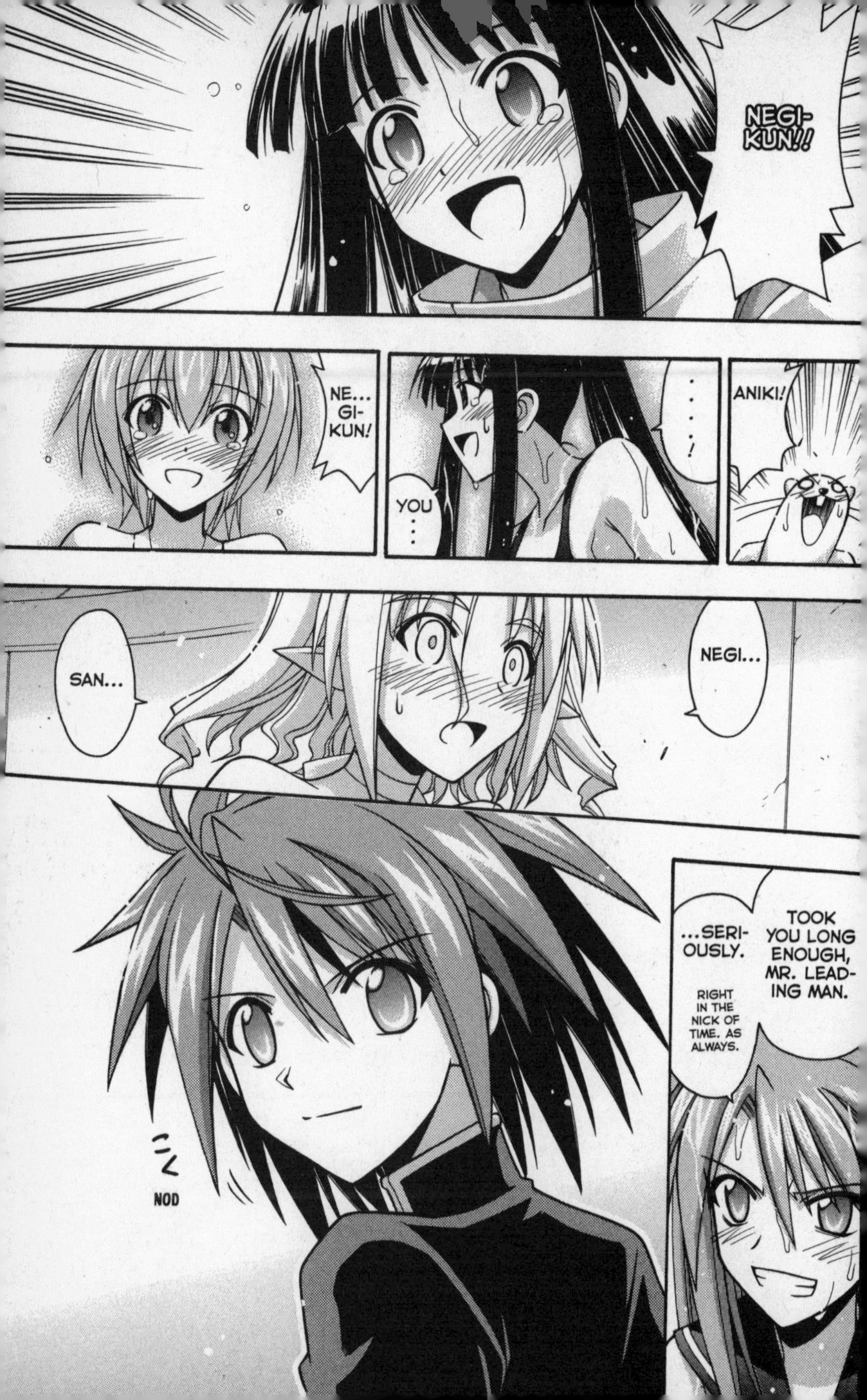
NEGI-KUN!!
ANIKI!
.....!
YOU...
NE... GI-KUN!
NEGI...
SAN...
TOOK YOU LONG ENOUGH, MR. LEADING MAN.
...SERIOUSLY.
RIGHT IN THE NICK OF TIME. AS ALWAYS.
NOD

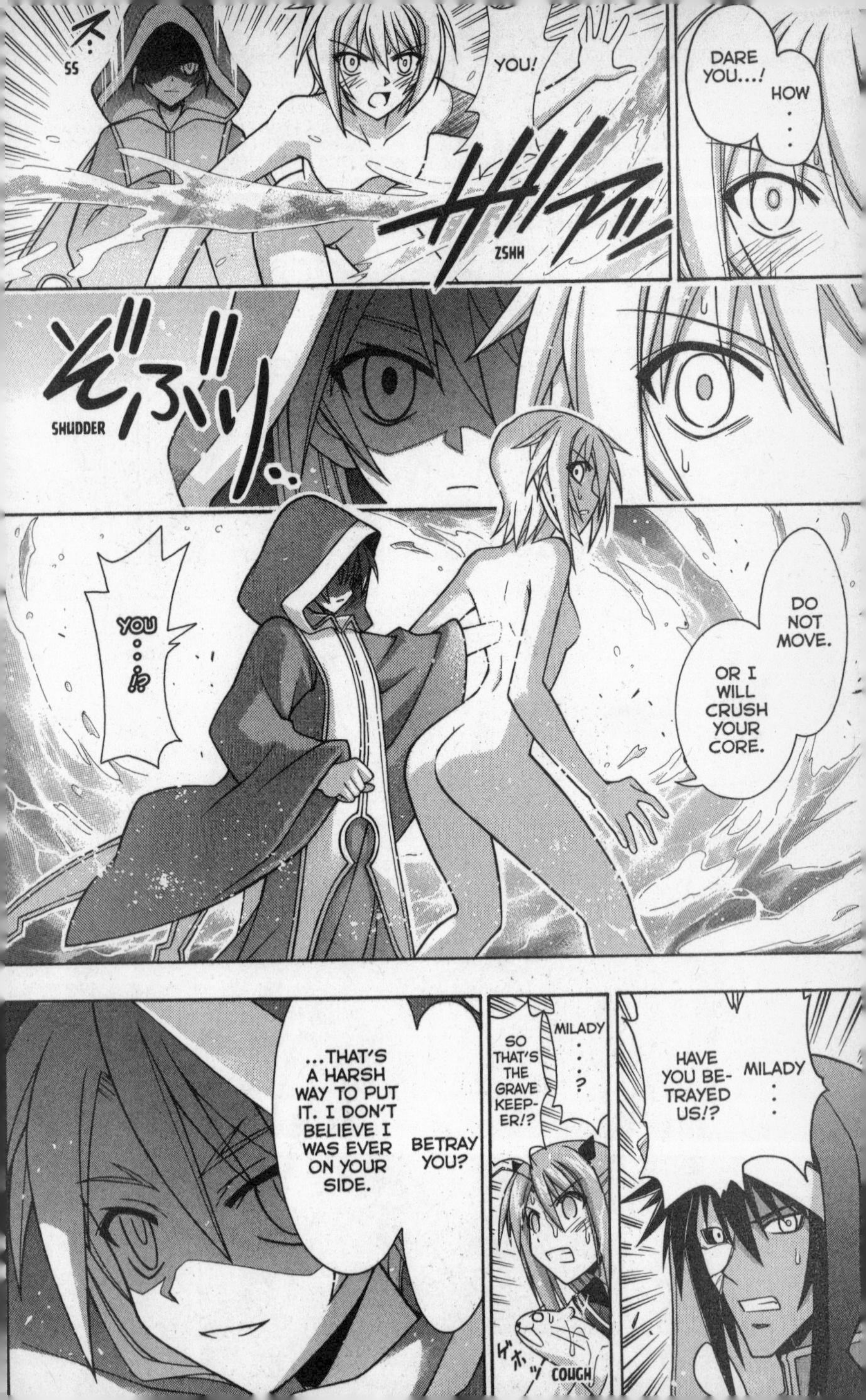
HOW . . . DARE YOU...!
YOU!
ス
SS
ザバァッ
ZSHH
ぞぶっ
SHUDDER
DO NOT MOVE.
OR I WILL CRUSH YOUR CORE.
YOU . . . !?
MILADY . . .
HAVE YOU BE-TRAYED US!?
MILADY . . . ?
SO THAT'S THE GRAVE KEEP-ER!?
ゲホッ
COUGH
BETRAY YOU?
...THAT'S A HARSH WAY TO PUT IT. I DON'T BELIEVE I WAS EVER ON YOUR SIDE.

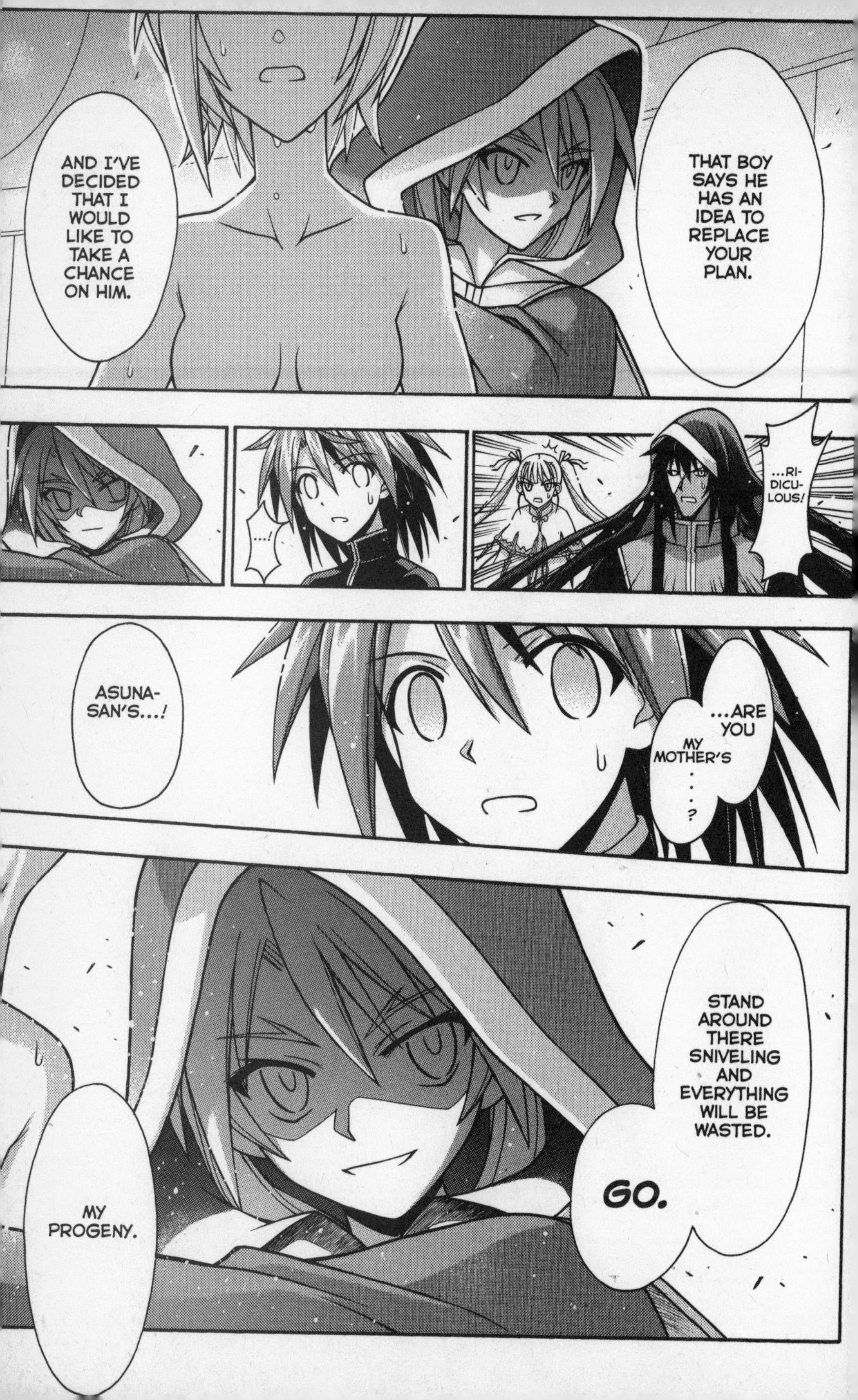
THAT BOY SAYS HE HAS AN IDEA TO REPLACE YOUR PLAN.
AND I'VE DECIDED THAT I WOULD LIKE TO TAKE A CHANCE ON HIM.
...RI-DICU-LOUS!
...!
...ARE YOU MY MOTHER'S ....?
ASUNA-SAN'S...!
STAND AROUND THERE SNIVELING AND EVERYTHING WILL BE WASTED.
GO.
MY PROGENY.

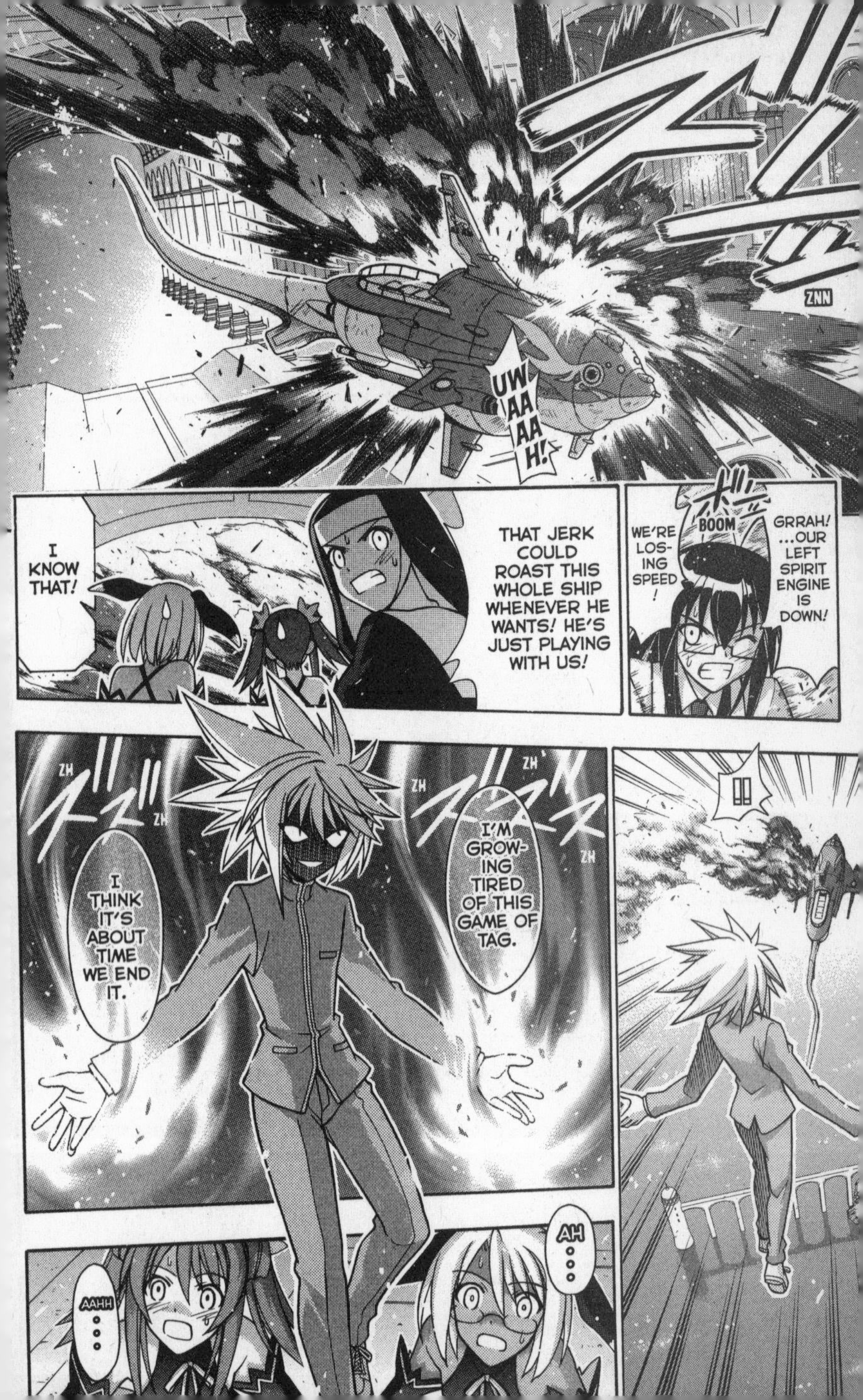
ZNN
UWAAAAH!
BOOM
GRRAH! ...OUR LEFT SPIRIT ENGINE IS DOWN!
WE'RE LOSING SPEED!
THAT JERK COULD ROAST THIS WHOLE SHIP WHENEVER HE WANTS! HE'S JUST PLAYING WITH US!
I KNOW THAT!
!!
ZH ZH ZH
I'M GROWING TIRED OF THIS GAME OF TAG.
ZH ZH
I THINK IT'S ABOUT TIME WE END IT.
AH...
AAHH...

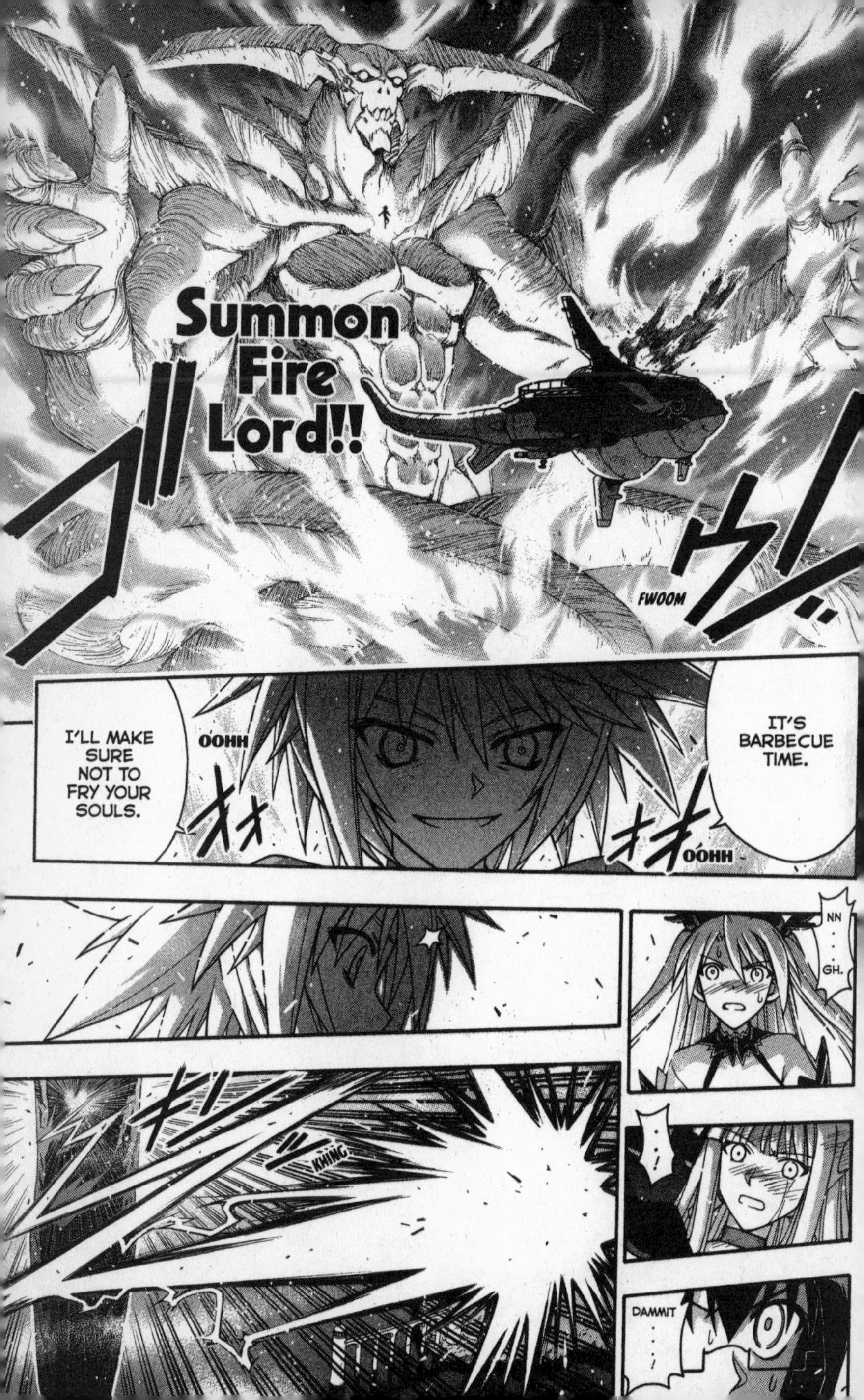
Summon Fire Lord!!
FWOOM
IT'S BARBECUE TIME.
OOHH
I'LL MAKE SURE NOT TO FRY YOUR SOULS.
OOHH
NN... GH.
KHING
DAMMIT...

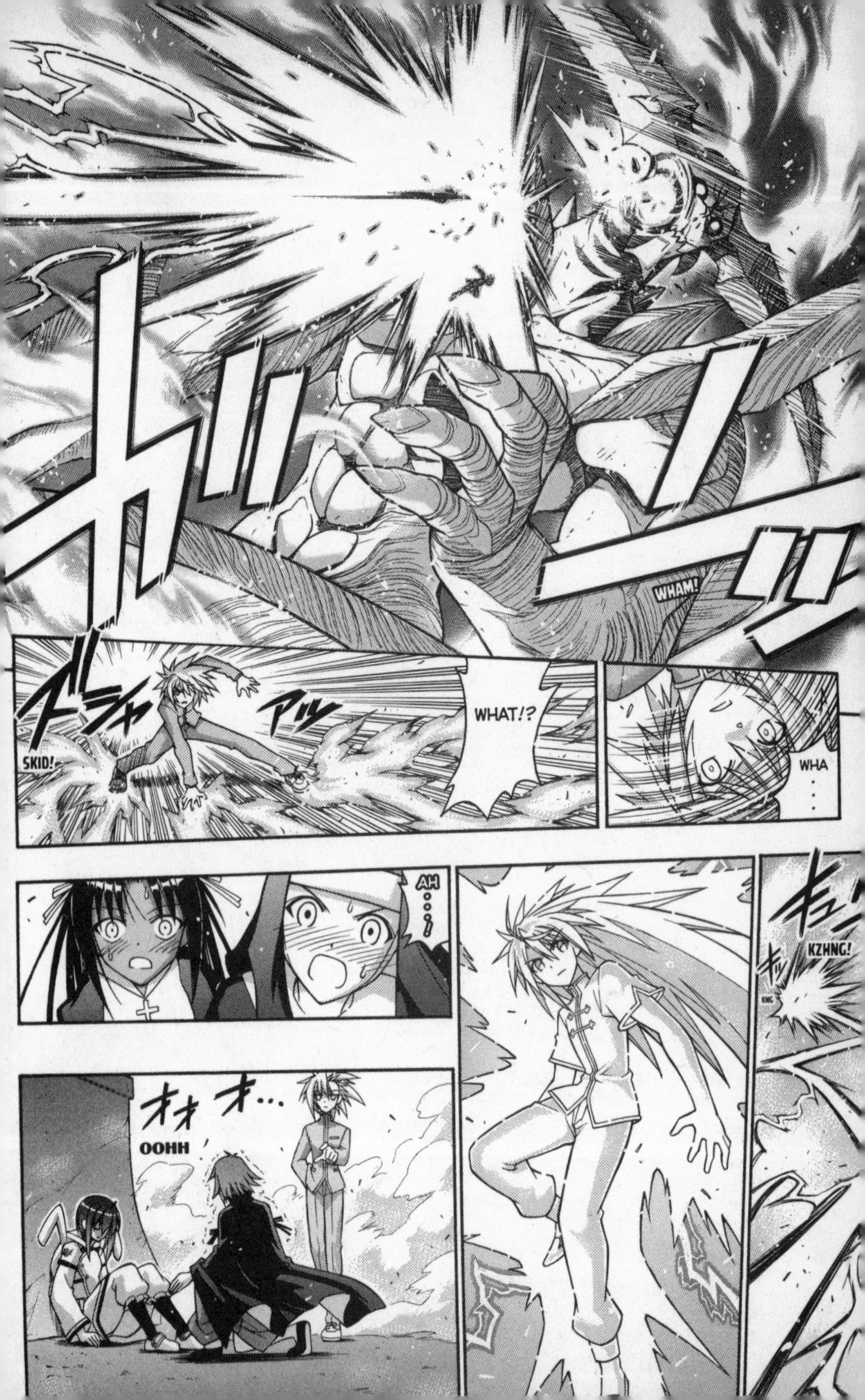

WHAM!
WHA . . .
WHAT!?
SKID!
KZHNG!
KNG
AH . . . !
OOHH

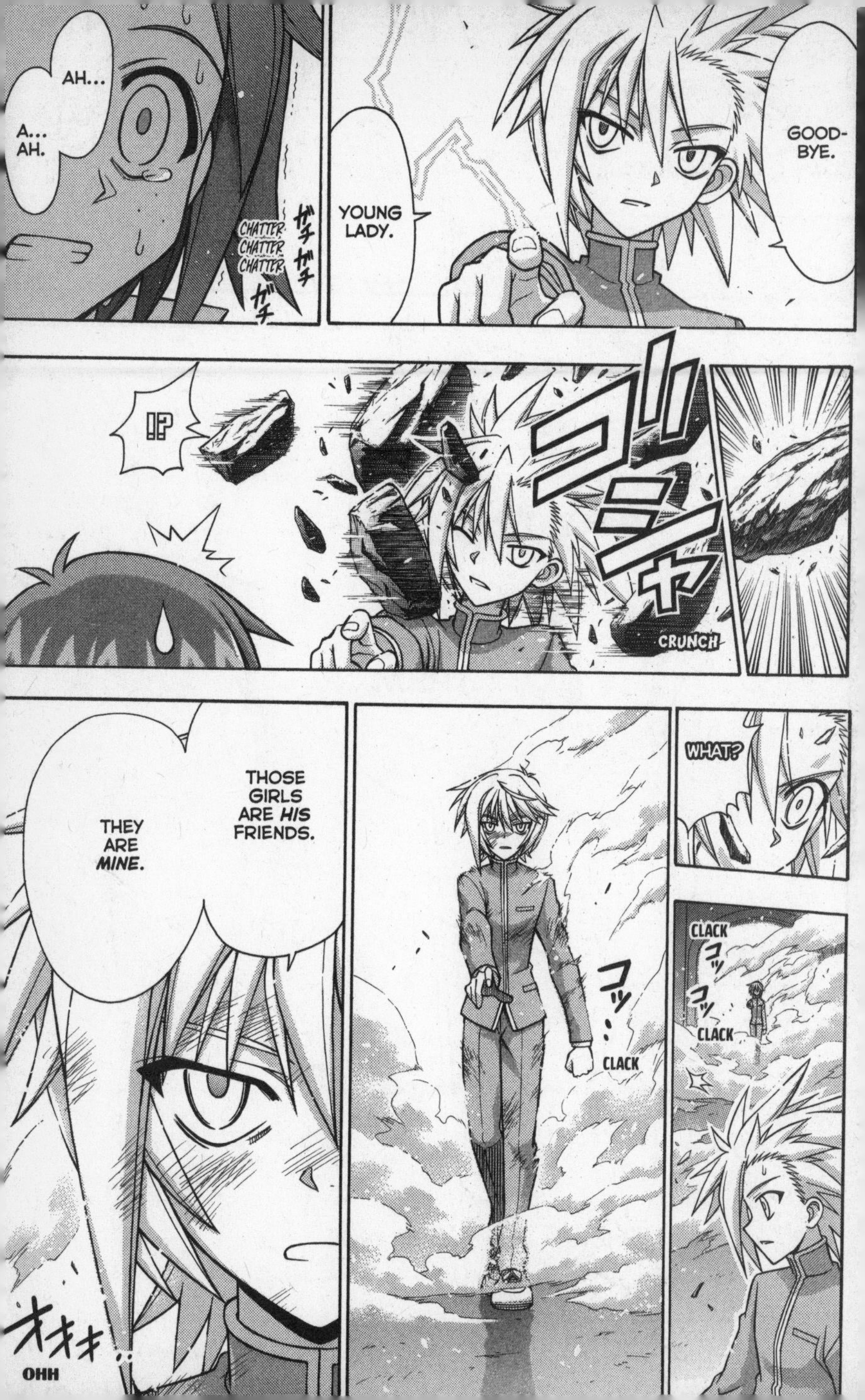
GOOD-BYE.
YOUNG LADY.
AH...
A... AH.
ガチガチ
CHATTER CHATTER CHATTER
ガチ
CRUNCH
!?
WHAT?
CLACK
コッ
コッ
CLACK
コッ...
CLACK
THOSE GIRLS ARE *HIS* FRIENDS.
THEY ARE *MINE*.
OHH

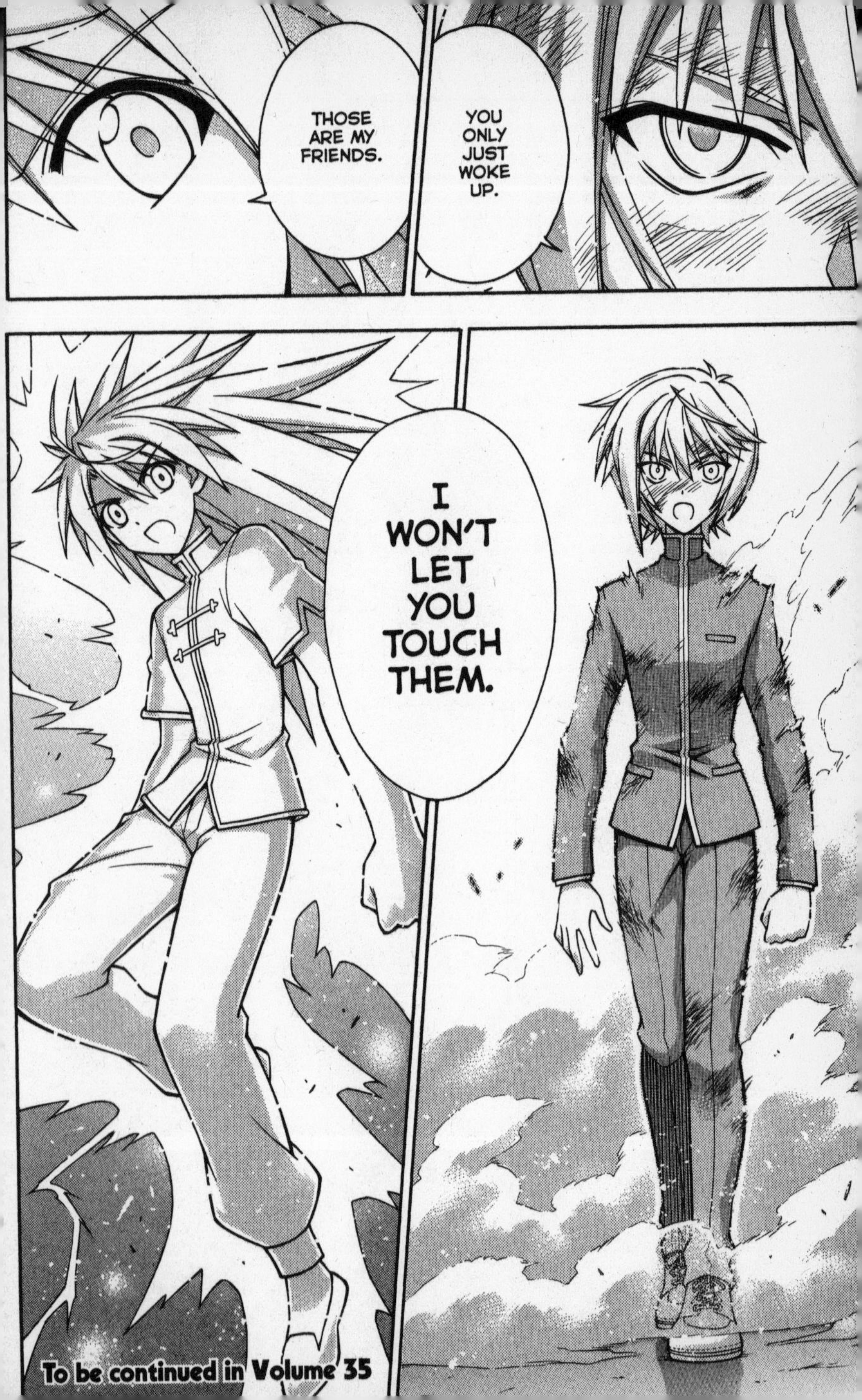
YOU ONLY JUST WOKE UP.
THOSE ARE MY FRIENDS.
I WON'T LET YOU TOUCH THEM.
To be continued in Volume 35

-STAFF-

Ken Akamatsu
Takashi Takemoto
Kenichi Nakamura
Keiichi Yamashita
Tohru Mitsuhashi
Yuichi Yoshida
Susumu Kuwabara

Thanks to
Ran Ayanaga

Pactio with Negi♡

14 Girls!! Plus 1

Compiled by: Shonen Magazine Editorial Department

Negi continues the fight to save the world! And to help him out, the classmates of 3-A have formed probationary contracts with him. Now he has an astounding 14 pactios!! He's formed contracts with almost half of his class. Let's take a look at what order he made these pactios in, and under what circumstances♪

1 Asuna Kagurazaka (*Negima!* vol.3, 23rd-24th Period)

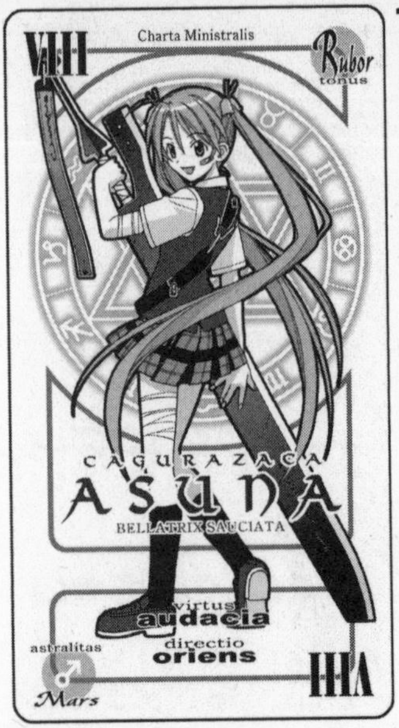
VIII
Charta Ministralis
Rubor
tonus
CAGURAZACA
ASUNA
BELLATRIX SAUCIATA
virtus
audacia
directio
oriens
astralitas
♂
Mars
IIIA

Where: The academy city bridge
Why: To help Negi in his fight against Evangeline.
Artifact: Evil Destroying Sword

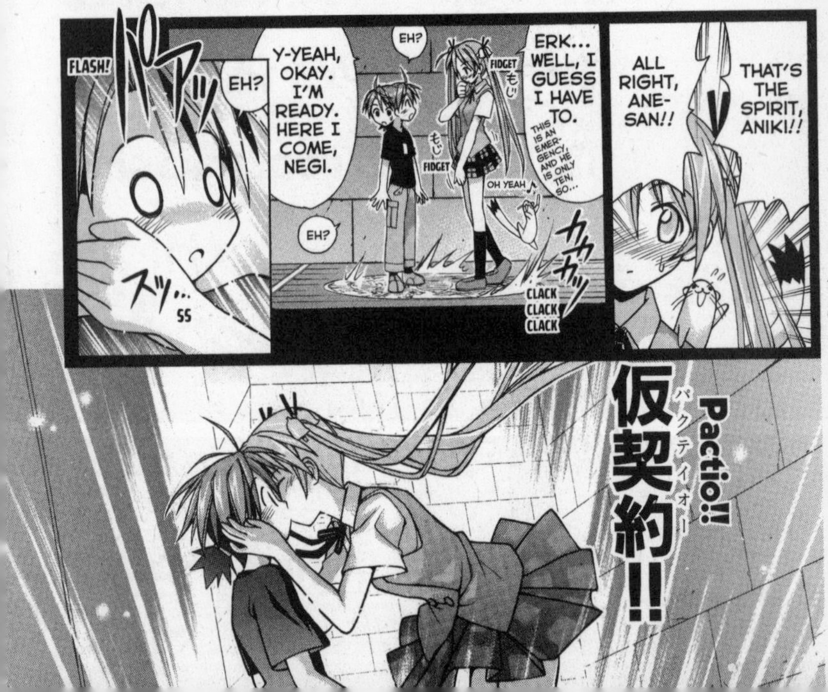
THAT'S THE SPIRIT, ANIKI!!
ALL RIGHT, ANE-SAN!!
ERK... WELL, I GUESS I HAVE TO.
THIS IS AN EMERGENCY, AND HE IS ONLY TEN, SO...
FIDGET もじ
EH?
Y-YEAH, OKAY. I'M READY. HERE I COME, NEGI.
FIDGET もじ
OH YEAH♪
EH?
カカカッ
CLACK CLACK CLACK
EH?
パァッ
FLASH!
ズッ…
SS
仮契約!!
パクティオー
Pactio!!

(*Negima!* vol.3, 23rd-24th Period)

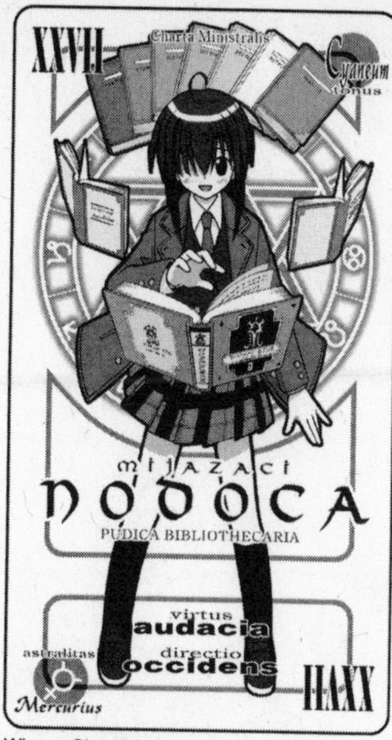

XXVII
Charta Ministralis
Cyaneum tonus
MIIAZACI
NODOCA
PUDICA BIBLIOTHECARIA
virtus
audacia
astralitas
directio
occidens
Mercurius
IIAXX

2 Nodoka Miyazaki (*Negima!* vol.5, 37th Period)

Where: Class trip hotel
Why: Yue tripped her; it was an accident.
Artifact: Id's Picture Diary

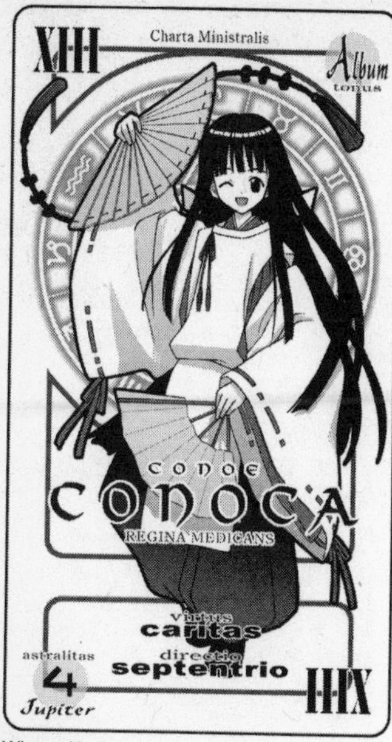

XIII
Charta Ministralis
Album tonus
CONOE
CONOCA
REGINA MEDICANS
virtus
caritas
astralitas
directio
septentrio
4
Jupiter
IIIX

4 Konoka Konoe (*Negima!* vol.6, 52nd Period)

Where: Kyoto
Why: To save Negi from petrification
Artifact: Hae no Suehiro, Kochi no Hiōgi

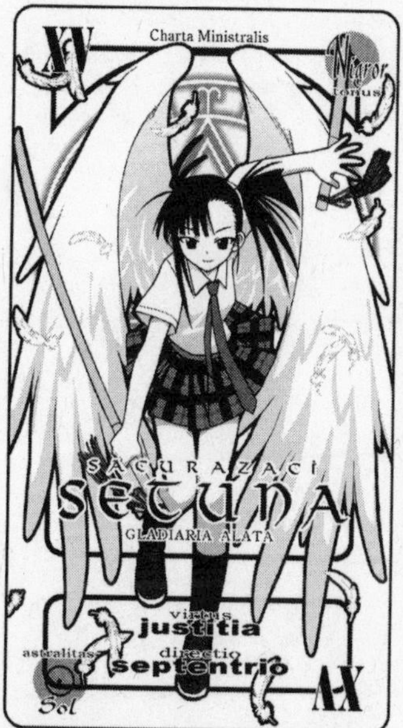

XV
Charta Ministralis
Nigror tonus
SACURAZACI
SETUNA
GLADIARIA ALATA
virtus
justitia
astralitas
directio
septentrio
Sol
AX

3 Setsuna Sakurazaki (*Negima!* vol.6, 47th Period)

Where: Kyoto
Why: To rescue the kidnapped Konoka
Artifact: Sica Shishikushiro

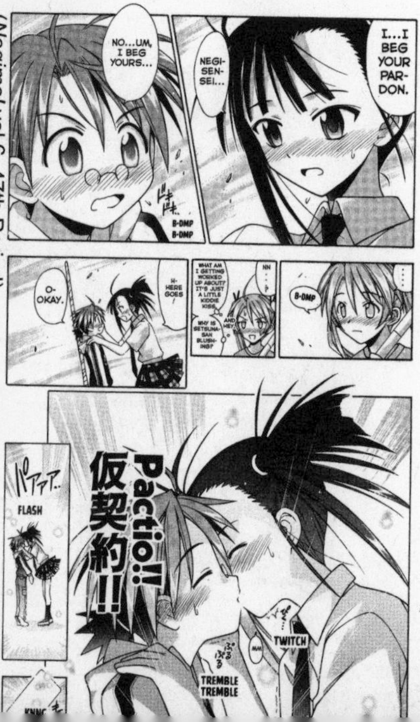

I...I BEG YOUR PARDON.
NEGI-SEN-SEI...
NO...UM, I BEG YOURS...
B-DMP
B-DMP
...
B-DMP
NN...
WHAT AM I GETTING WORKED UP ABOUT!? IT'S JUST A LITTLE KIDDIE KISS.
AND HEY!
WHY IS SETSUNA-SAN BLUSHING?
H-HERE GOES
O-OKAY.
Pactio!!
仮契約!!
TWITCH
TREMBLE TREMBLE
パァァ..
FLASH

(*Negima!* vol.6, 47th Period)

Pactio with Negi♡

Negima! vol.14, 128th Period)

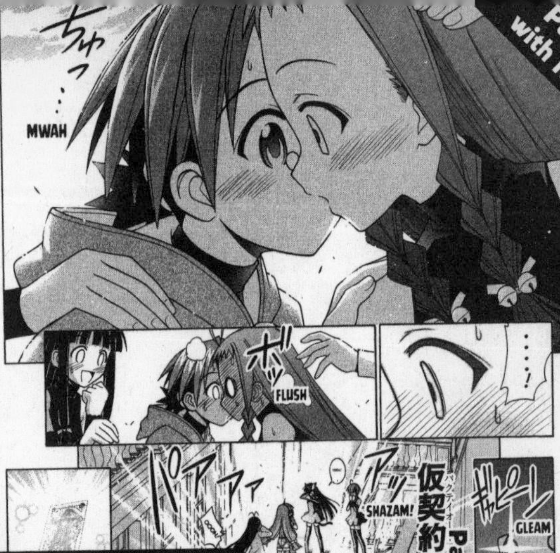

ちゅっ…
MWAH
ボッ
FLUSH
…!
パァァアッ
仮契約!!
Pactio!!
SHAZAM!
ギュピーン
GLEAM

egima! vol.15, 136th Period)

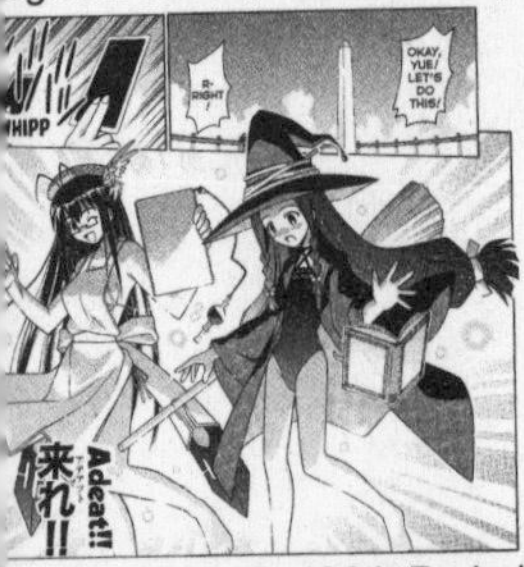

OKAY, YUE! LET'S DO THIS!
R-RIGHT!
WHIPP
Adeat!!
来れ!!

Negima! vol.15, 136th Period)

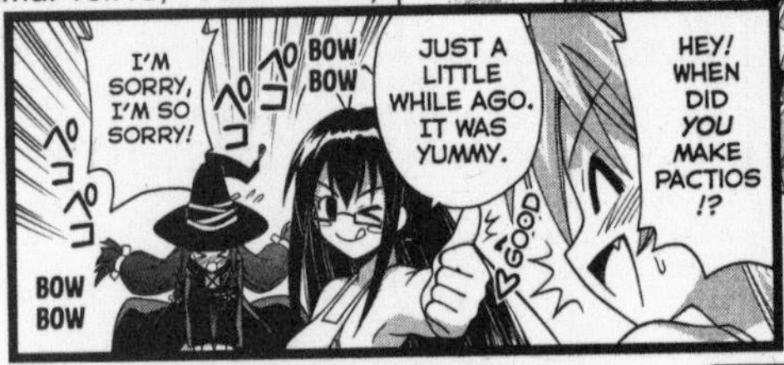

HEY! WHEN DID YOU MAKE PACTIOS!?
JUST A LITTLE WHILE AGO. IT WAS YUMMY.
GOOD ♥
BOW BOW
I'M SORRY, I'M SO SORRY!
BOW BOW

5 Yue Ayase (*Negima!* vol.14, 128th Period)

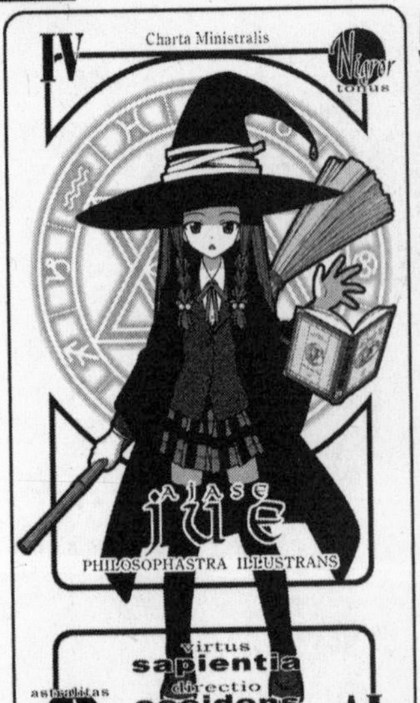

Charta Ministralis
F-V
Nigror tonus
AYASE YUE
PHILOSOPHASTRA ILLUSTRANS
virtus
sapientia
directio
occidens
astralitas
Mercurius
A-I

Where: Library Island
Why: Paru pushed her.
Artifact: Visible World in Pictures

6 Haruna Saotome (*Negima!* vol.14, 128th Period)

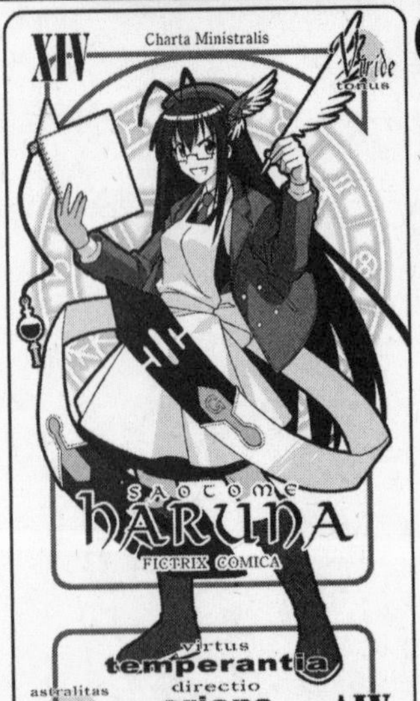

Charta Ministralis
XIV
Viride tonus
SAOTOME HARUNA
FICTRIX COMICA
virtus
temperantia
directio
oriens
astralitas
Neptunus
A-IX

Where: Library Island
Why: Because she wanted an artifact?
Artifact: Scribble Empire

7 Chisame Hasegawa (*Negima!* vol.16, 149th Period)

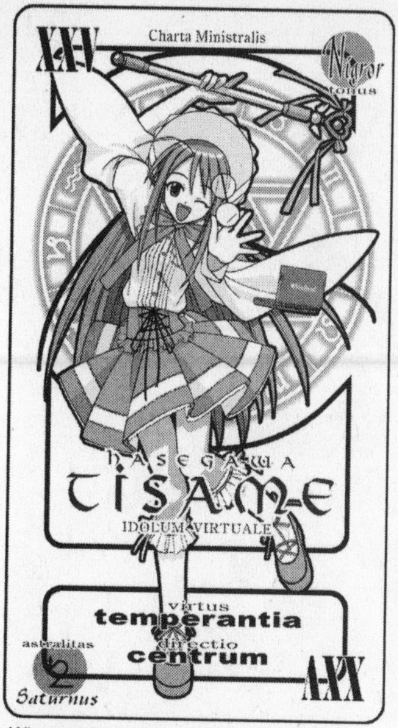
Charta Ministralis
XXV
Nigror tonus
HASEGAWA
TISAME
IDOLUM VIRTUALE
virtus
temperantia
directio
centrum
astralitas
Saturnus
XXV

Where: A library room in the academy
Why: To win the battle against Chao
Artifact: Virtual Sceptre

8 Kazumi Asakura (*Negima!* vol.22, 201st Period)

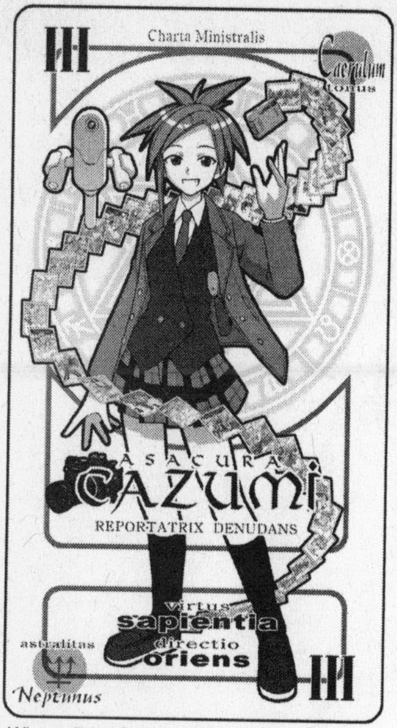
Charta Ministralis
III
Caerulum tonus
ASACURA
CAZUMI
REPORTATRIX DENUDANS
virtus
sapientia
directio
oriens
astralitas
Neptunus
III

Where: The Magical World
Why: To find their friends who had been scattered across the world.
Artifact: Crow's Eye

9 Kaede Nagase (*Negima!* vol.26, 234th Period)

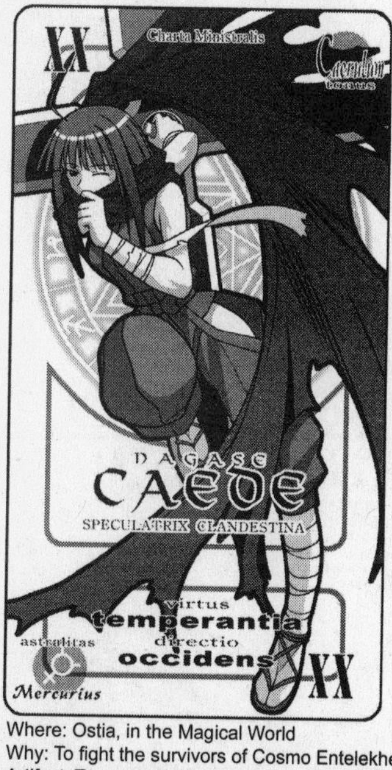
Charta Ministralis
XX
Caerulum tonus
NAGASE
CAEDE
SPECULATRIX CLANDESTINA
virtus
temperantia
directio
occidens
astralitas
Mercurius
XX

Where: Ostia, in the Magical World
Why: To fight the survivors of Cosmo Entelekheia
Artifact: Tengu no Kakuremino

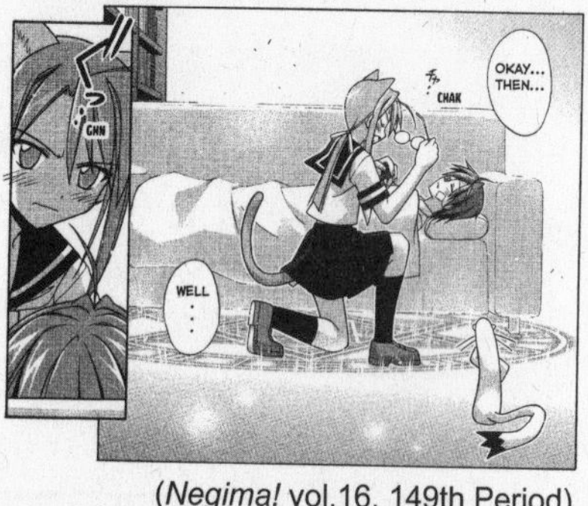
OKAY... THEN...
CHAK
GHN
WELL ...

(*Negima!* vol.16, 149th Period)

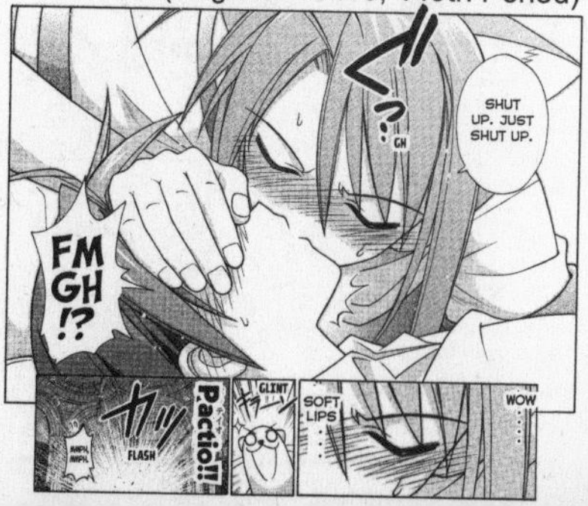
SHUT UP. JUST SHUT UP.
GH
FMGH!?
WOW
SOFT LIPS
GLINT
Pactio!!
FLASH

10

Kū Fei (*Negima!* vol.29, 261st Period)

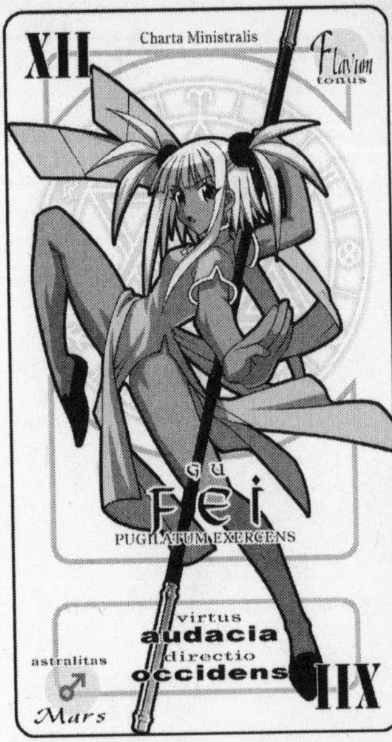
XII
Charta Ministralis
Flavum tonus
GU
FEI
PUGILATUM EXERCENS
virtus
audacia
directio
occidens
astralitas
♂
Mars
IIX

Where: Government-General ballroom in the Magical World
Why: She lost a contest with Negi and had to resign herself to it
Artifact: Shénzhentîe Zìzàigùn

11

Chachamaru Karakuri (*Negima!* vol.29, 263rd Period)

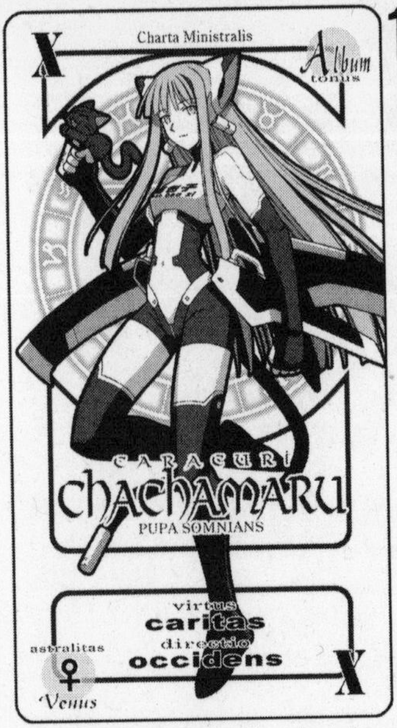
X
Charta Ministralis
Album tonus
CARACURI
chachamaru
PUPA SOMNIANS
virtus
caritas
directio
occidens
astralitas
♀
Venus
X

Where: Government-General garden in the Magical World
Why: To help Negi, although she was worried about whether or not she had a soul
Artifact: Flying Cat

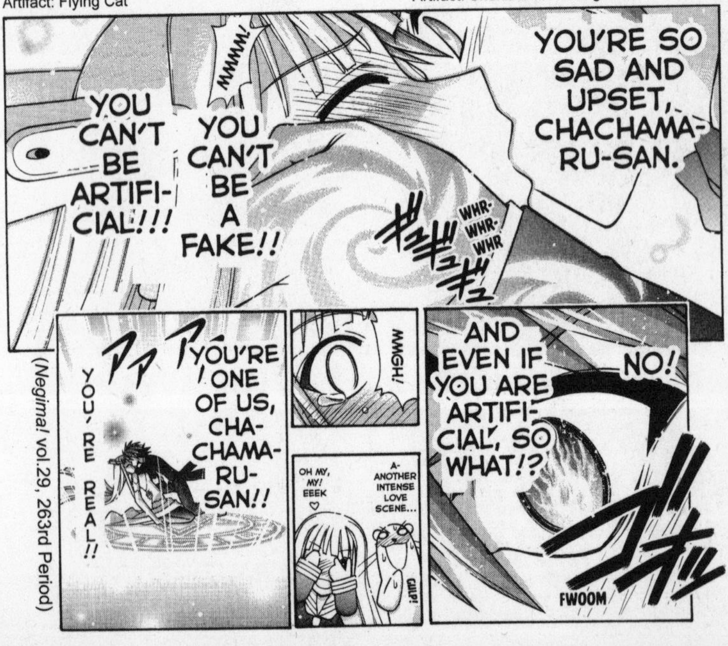
YOU'RE SO SAD AND UPSET, CHACHAMA-RU-SAN.
MMMM!
YOU CAN'T BE A FAKE!!
YOU CAN'T BE ARTIFI-CIAL!!!
WHR-WHR-WHR
NO!
AND EVEN IF YOU ARE ARTIFI-CIAL, SO WHAT!?
FWOOM
MMGH!
A-ANOTHER INTENSE LOVE SCENE...
OH MY, MY! EEEK ♡
GULP!
YOU'RE ONE OF US, CHA-CHAMA-RU-SAN!!
YOU'RE REAL!!

(*Negima!* vol.29, 263rd Period)

12 **Ako Izumi** (*Negima!* vol.32, 289th Period)

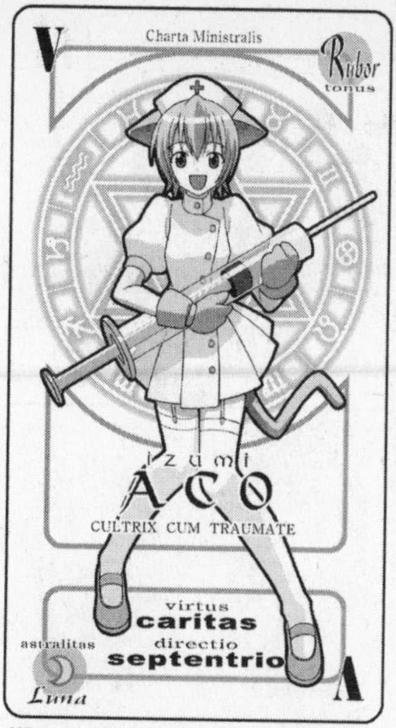
V
Charta Ministralis
Rubor
tonus
IZUMI
ACO
CULTRIX CUM TRAUMATE
virtus
caritas
astralitas
directio
septentrio
Luna
V

Where: Inside the diorama sphere
Why: To get all their Magical World friends back
Artifact: Mysterious Syringe

13 **Yuna Akashi** (*Negima!* vol.32, 289th Period)

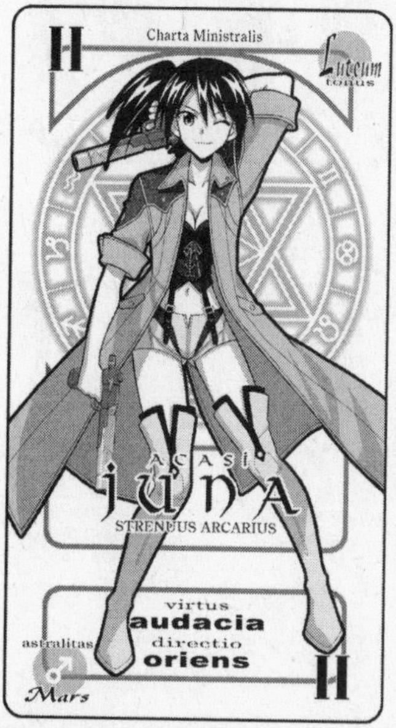
II
Charta Ministralis
Luteum
tonus
ACASI
JUNA
STRENUUS ARCARIUS
virtus
audacia
astralitas
directio
oriens
Mars
II

Where: Inside the diorama sphere
Why: To help Negi
Artifact: Rainbow Guns

14 **Makie Sasaki** (*Negima!* vol.32, 289th Period)

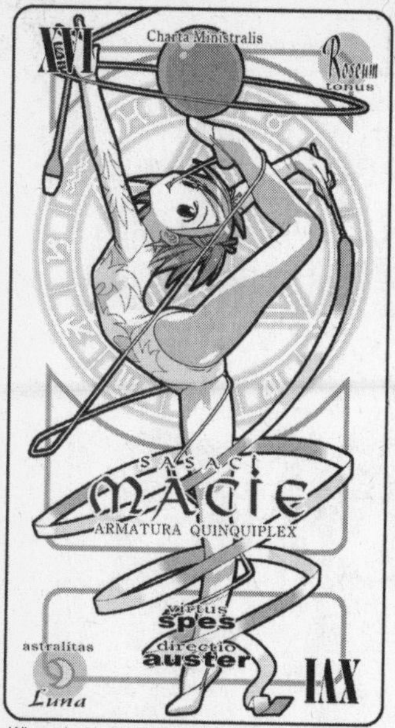
XVI
Charta Ministralis
Roseum
tonus
SASACI
MACIE
ARMATURA QUINQUIPLEX
virtus
spes
astralitas
directio
auster
Luna
XVI

Where: Inside the diorama sphere
Why: Because she is in love with Negi, and wants to help him
Artifacts: Free Ribbon, Slicing Hoop, Explosive Ball, Binding Rope, Crushing Batons

Bonus **15** **Shiori** (*Negima!* vol.31, 283rd Period)

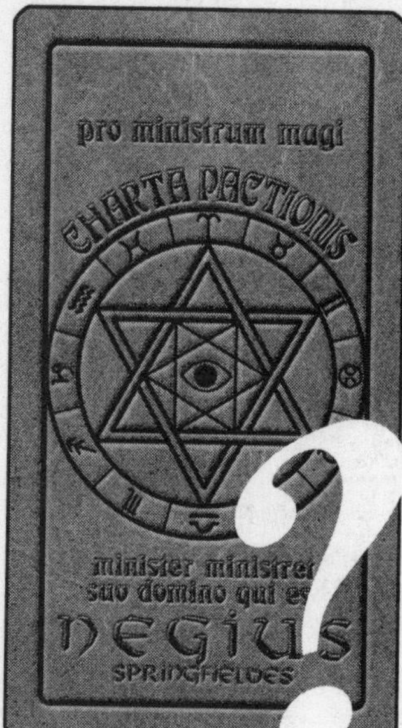
pro ministrum magi
CHARTA PACTIONIS
minister ministret
suo domino qui est
NEGIUS
SPRINGFIELDES
?

Where: Inside the diorama sphere
Why: So Negi and company could find out if she was the real Asuna
Artifact: ?

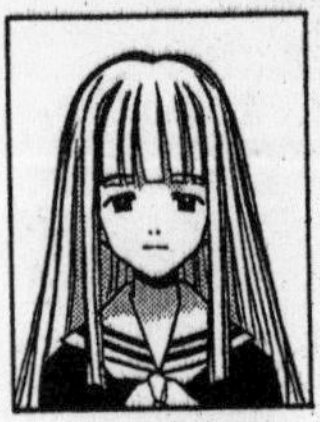

1. SAYO AISAKA

1940 ~

Don't change her seat

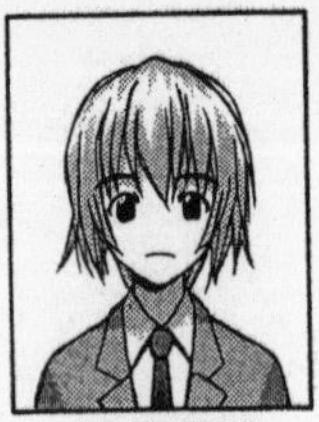

5. AKO IZUMI

Nurse's office aide, soccer team (non-school activity)

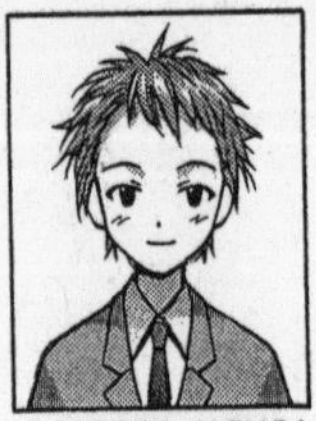

9. MISORA KASUGA

Track & field

Headmaster's granddaughter

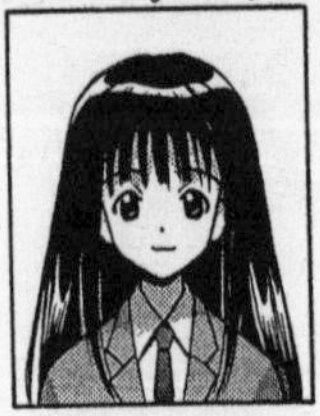

13. KONOKA KONOE

Secretary, fortune-telling club, library exploration club

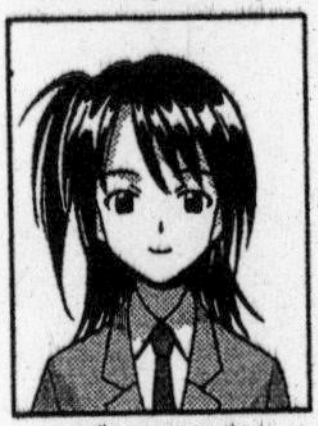

2. YŪNA AKASHI

Basketball team

Professor Akashi's daughter

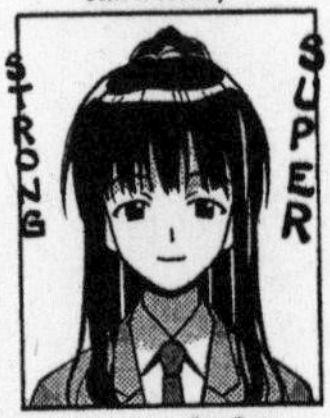
SUPER
STRONG

6. AKIRA ŌKŌCHI

Swim team

VERY KIND

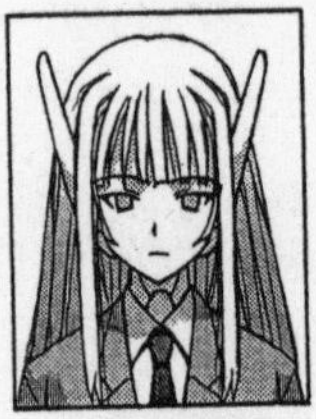

10. CHACHAMARU KARAKURI

Tea ceremony club, go club

In case of emergency, call engineering (ext. A00-7796)

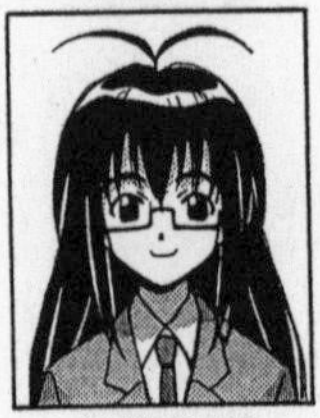

14. HARUNA SAOTOME

Manga club, library exploration club

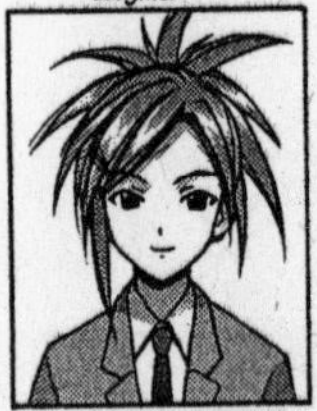

3. KAZUMI ASAKURA

School newspaper

Mahora News (ext.809-3780)

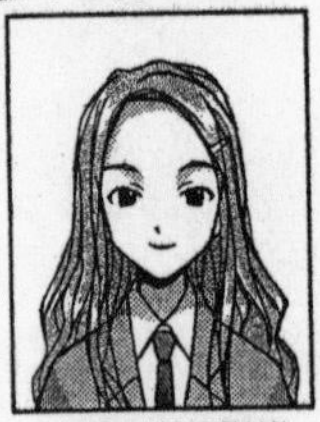

7. MISA KAKIZAKI

Cheerleader, chorus

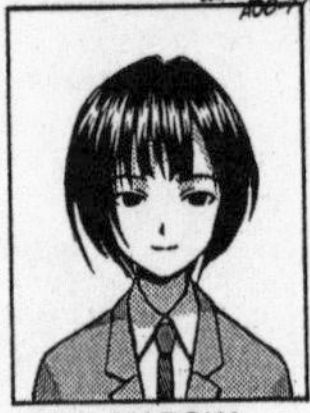

11. MADOKA KUGIMIYA

Cheerleader

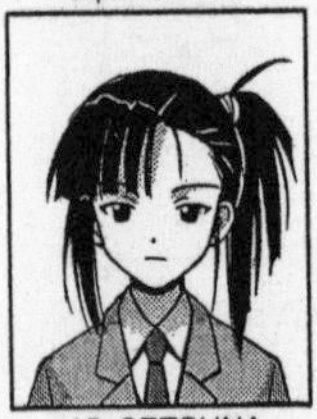

15. SETSUNA SAKURAZAKI

Kendo club

Kyoto Shinmei School

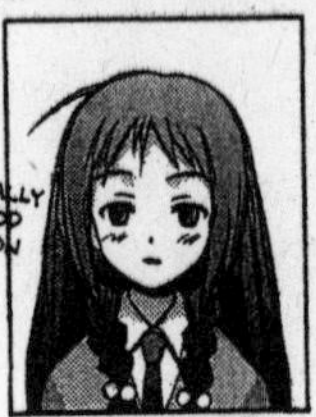

4. YUE AYASE

Kids' lit. club, philosophy club, library exploration club

~~MEANIE~~

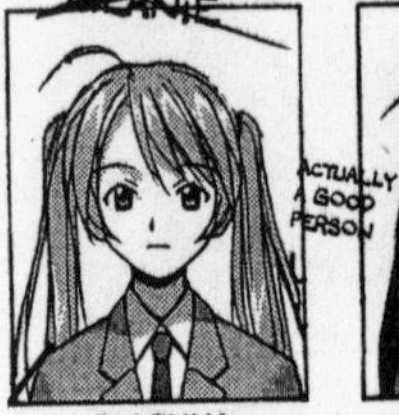
ACTUALLY A GOOD PERSON

8. ASUNA KAGURAZAKA

AMAZING KICK

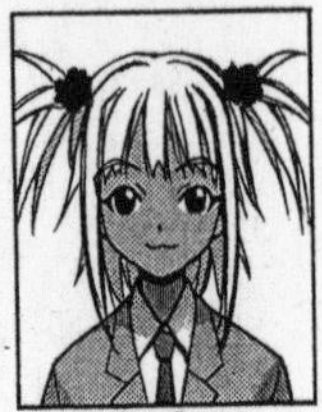

12. KŪ FEI

Chinese martial arts club

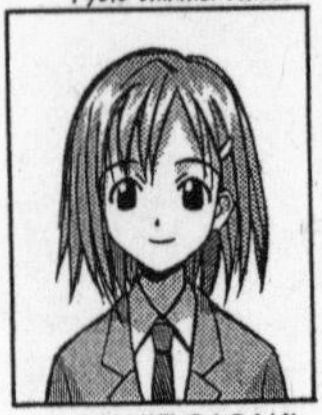

16. MAKIE SASAKI

Gymnastics

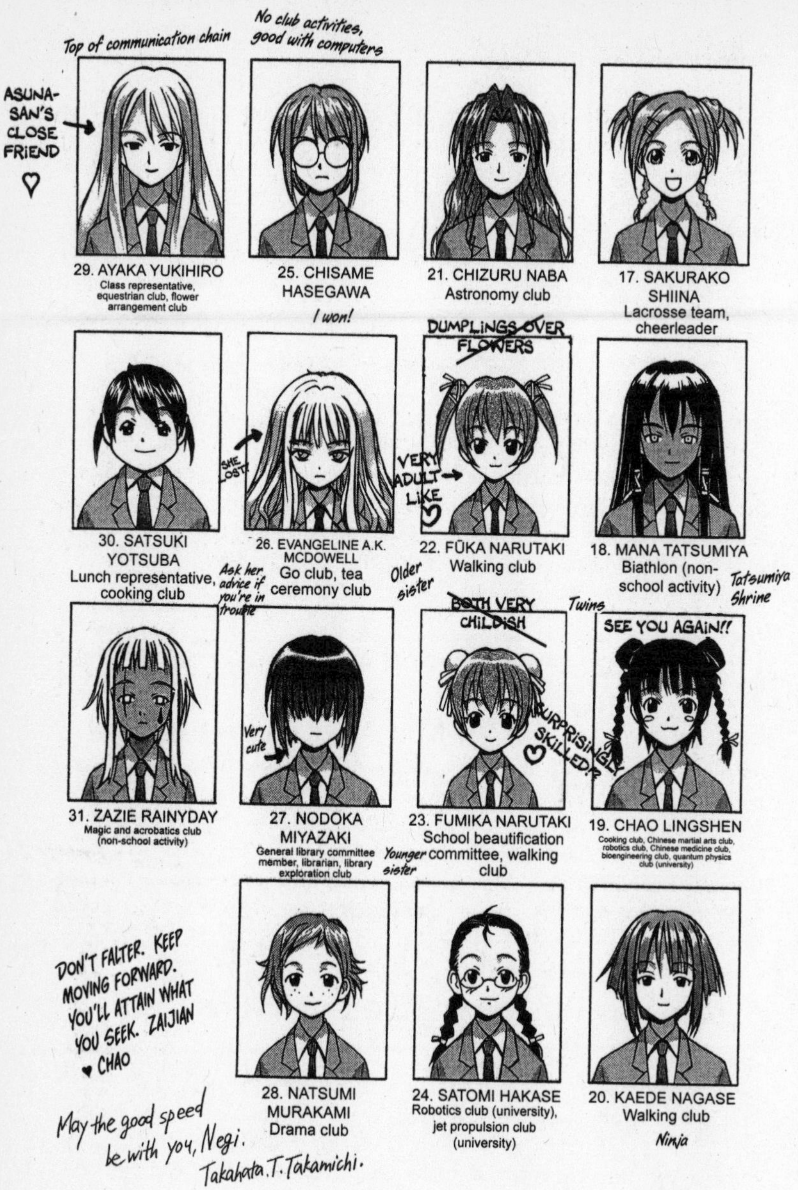

17. SAKURAKO SHIINA
Lacrosse team, cheerleader
21. CHIZURU NABA
Astronomy club
No club activities, good with computers
25. CHISAME HASEGAWA
I won!
Top of communication chain
ASUNA-SAN'S CLOSE FRIEND ♡
29. AYAKA YUKIHIRO
Class representative, equestrian club, flower arrangement club
18. MANA TATSUMIYA
Biathlon (non-school activity)
Tatsumiya Shrine
DUMPLINGS OVER FLOWERS
VERY ADULT LIKE ♡
22. FŪKA NARUTAKI
Walking club
Older sister
SHE LOST!
26. EVANGELINE A.K. MCDOWELL
Go club, tea ceremony club
Ask her advice if you're in trouble
30. SATSUKI YOTSUBA
Lunch representative, cooking club
Twins
SEE YOU AGAIN!!
19. CHAO LINGSHEN
Cooking club, Chinese martial arts club, robotics club, Chinese medicine club, bioengineering club, quantum physics club (university)
BOTH VERY CHILDISH
SURPRISINGLY SKILLED!? ♡
23. FUMIKA NARUTAKI
School beautification committee, walking club
Younger sister
Very cute
27. NODOKA MIYAZAKI
General library committee member, librarian, library exploration club
31. ZAZIE RAINYDAY
Magic and acrobatics club (non-school activity)
20. KAEDE NAGASE
Walking club
Ninja
24. SATOMI HAKASE
Robotics club (university), jet propulsion club (university)
28. NATSUMI MURAKAMI
Drama club
DON'T FALTER. KEEP MOVING FORWARD. YOU'LL ATTAIN WHAT YOU SEEK. ZAIJIAN ♥ CHAO
May the good speed be with you, Negi.
Takahata.T.Takamichi.

Translation Notes

Japanese is a tricky language for most Westerners, and translation is often more art than science. For your edification and reading pleasure, here are notes on some of the places where we could have gone in a different direction with our translation of the work, or where a Japanese cultural reference is used.

Averruncus of Wind, page 121

As we're sure you've noticed, the Averruncus of Wind attacks not with air, but with lightning. While we're sure Ken Akamatsu has a very good reason for this, he doesn't explain it, so we're left to guess. The translators believe it has to do with the bagua trigrams in Taoist cosmology and Wu Xing, also known as the five elements. The trigrams of wind and lightning both correspond to the element of Wood. Furthermore, in Japanese mythology, the wind and lightning gods, Fūjin and Raijin, frequently travel together. Add to all that the Western theory of Aether (meaning air, an element finer than wind) and how it can create light, and there are several reasons that the Averruncus of Wind would be using lightning magic.

Honor your contract and obey me, Fire Spirits. Come forth, page 129

The reason this spell is being incanted in English is that Akamatsu-sensei didn't provide the original language. Normally spells that start out this way are incanted in Greek, but we do know that the last part of this spell is in Latin. The format is like a combination of the average Sagitta Magica and one of Nagi's or Evangeline's High Ancient Greek spells. So because the translators aren't confident in their Latin or their Greek, we left it in English. Incidentally, the name of this spell, "Apes Igniferae," means "fire-bearing bee."

Since I'm in sports and you're in literature, page 154

What Makie literally said here is that Makie is on an athletic team and Yue is in "culture clubs," which basically means that Yue's clubs are not athletic. It's sort of like a division between nerds and jocks, but more because the different types of clubs spend their time in different places, rather than because they can't get along or because they look down on each other.

Negima! volume 34 is a work of fiction. Names, characters, places, and incidents are the products of the author's imagination or are used fictitiously. Any resemblance to actual events, locales, or persons, living or dead, is entirely coincidental.

A Kodansha Comics Trade Paperback Original

Published in the United States by Kodansha Comics, an imprint of Kodansha USA Publishing, LLC, New York.

Publication rights arranged through Kodansha Ltd., Tokyo.

First published in Japan in 2011 by Kodansha Ltd., Tokyo, as *Maho sensei Negima!*, volume 34

ISBN 978-1-61262-116-6

Printed in the United States of America

www.kodanshacomics.com

9 8 7 6 5 4 3 2 1

Translator/Adapter: Alethea Nibley and Athena Nibley
Lettering: Scott O. Brown

TOMARE!

[STOP!]

You're going the wrong way!

Manga is a completely different
type of reading experience.

To start at the *beginning,*
go to the end!

That's right! Authentic manga is read the traditional Japanese way—
from right to left. Exactly the *opposite* of how American books are read.
It's easy to follow: Just go to the other end of the book, and read each
page—and each panel—from the right side to the left side, starting at
the top right. Now you're experiencing manga as it was meant to be!